The Bretton Woods-GATT System

THE BRETTON WOODS-GATT SYSTEM

RETROSPECT AND PROSPECT AFTER FIFTY YEARS

I | A
T | P

INSTITUTE
for
AGRICULTURE
and
TRADE POLICY

Orin Kirshner
editor

——————————— CONTRIBUTORS ———————————

Edward M. Bernstein	Richard N. Gardner	Simon Reisman
Sir Alexander Cairncross	Joseph A. Greenwald	Fred H. Sanderson
Roberto Campos	Andrew M. Kamarck	Tran Van-Thinh
Walter A. Chudson	Jacob J. Kaplan	Victor L. Urquidi
Harlan Cleveland	J. H. McCall	Raymond Vernon
William Diebold, Jr.	Raymond F. Mikesell	Barend A. de Vries
Isaiah Frank	Paul H. Nitze	Margaret Garritsen de Vries

M.E. Sharpe
Armonk, New York
London, England

Copyright © 1996 by M. E. Sharpe, Inc.

Library of Congress Cataloging-in-Publication Data

The Bretton Woods–GATT system : retrospect and
prospect after fifty years / Orin Kirshner, editor.
p.   cm.
Includes index.
ISBN 1-56324-629-5 (alk. paper).
ISBN 1-56324-630-9 (pbk. : alk. paper)
1. International finance. 2. Free trade. 3. United Nations
Monetary and Financial Conference (1994 : Bretton Woods, N.H.)
4. General Agreement on Tariffs and Trade (Organization)
5. International Monetary Fund. 6. World Bank.
I. Kirshner, Orin, 1961–
HG205.B74   1995
332′042—dc20   95-9027
CIP

Printed in the United States of America

The paper used in this publication meets the minimum requirements of
American National Standard for Information Sciences—
Permanence of Paper for Printed Library Materials,
ANSI Z 39.48-1984.

BM (c)   10   9   8   7   6   5   4   3   2   1
BM (p)   10   9   8   7   6   5   4   3   2   1

Contents

Preface

On October 15–17, 1994, over thirty founders and early leaders of the International Monetary Fund (IMF), the World Bank, and the General Agreement on Tariffs and Trade (GATT) gathered at Bretton Woods, New Hampshire, to examine critically the creation of these multilateral economic institutions, their adaptations over the last five decades, and their capacity to respond to current and future planetary challenges. The *Bretton Woods–GATT System: Retrospect and Prospect after Fifty Years* brings together over twenty of the most insightful papers produced for the *Bretton Woods Revisited* conference, which was convened by the Institute for Agriculture and Trade Policy.

The purpose of *Bretton Woods Revisited* was to foster a dialogue between the generations concerning the past, present, and future of the IMF, the World Bank, and the GATT. Our interest in these multilateral economic institutions is twofold: we believe that the best way to address global problems is through multilateral bodies, and we are concerned that a growing number of economic, environmental, and social problems are beyond the ability of the IMF, the World Bank, and the GATT to manage. We convened the *Bretton Woods Revisited* conference to educate ourselves and others about the history of these institutions and their capacity to respond to current and future challenges. Education about the IMF, the World Bank, and the GATT is the first step in determining how these institutions can be made more responsive to a new generation of global problems, or if they should be abandoned in favor of creating new multilateral bodies.

Few people are in a better position to analyze the IMF, the World Bank, and the GATT than the founders and early leaders of the Bretton Woods–GATT system. Not only do these individuals possess a wealth of firsthand knowledge about the history of these institutions, but also because of their five decades of experience they are in a unique position to analyze the capacity of the Bretton Woods–GATT system to meet today's challenges. As we look toward the future, we are extraordinarily lucky to have their insights to draw upon.

This book would not have been possible without the help, encouragement, and support of a number of individuals. Ray Vernon and William Diebold encouraged me to edit the book and, each in his own way, suggested the book's framework. Susan Aaronson promoted the book to Richard Bartel at M.E. Sharpe, Inc., who saw its historical and analytical worth. And Lessa Scherrer, Jean Carruthers, Steve Suppan, and Michelle Thom helped with the book's production here at the Institute.

I would also like to thank the five members of the *Bretton Woods Revisited* conference agenda committee for their hard and inspired work: in addition to Ray Vernon and William Diebold, Margaret Garritsen de Vries, Ray Mikesell, and Jacob Kaplan. Jamilia Suzanne is owed special thanks for her extraordinary effort coordinating conference logistics. Kate Hoff, Gigi DiGiacomo, Neil Ritchie, and Kristin Dawkins helped run the conference—on site and from Minneapolis. Rachel Breen helped raise money for the project. And Mark Ritchie, president of the Institute, had the idea to convene a conference featuring founders and early leaders of the Bretton Woods–GATT system. I would also like to thank the more than thirty founders and early leaders who participated in *Bretton Woods Revisited* for sharing their wisdom and experience with a new generation of globally oriented public interest leaders. It is a very great honor to have worked with them.

Finally, the Institute would like to thank the Ford, MacArthur, and C.S. Mott foundations, and the Foundation for the Progress of Humanity, for their generous support for *Bretton Woods Revisited*.

To all of you, thank you!

Orin Kirshner
Minneapolis, May 1995

Introduction

The fiftieth anniversary of the Bretton Woods–GATT system was marked more by criticism than by celebration. Of course, criticism of the Bretton Woods–GATT system is not new, but it reached a new level of intensity in 1994. During that year, the system was attacked by the right, left, and center; by government officials, academics, policy experts, and the media; by business, labor, and agricultural organizations; and by environmental, community, and consumer groups. Individuals as diverse as economist Milton Friedman, consumer advocate Ralph Nader, and former U.S. Secretary of State George P. Shultz criticized the system. Even the leaders of the International Monetary Fund (IMF), the International Bank for Reconstruction and Development (World Bank), and the General Agreement on Tariffs and Trade (GATT)—the institutions at the core of the Bretton Woods–GATT system—admitted that reforms were needed. So too did the heads of state of the world's seven most industrialized countries, who announced that they would devote their 1995 annual Group of Seven (G–7) summit meeting to the question of reform. Not surprisingly, the concerns and reform proposals emanating from these individuals and groups were enormously varied. But most shared a common perception: that the IMF, the World Bank, and the GATT arc not equipped to address a growing array of global problems that threaten the security of people and the planet. Perhaps this perception was best summed up by GATT Director General Peter Sutherland, who declared: "We have a structural deficit in the world economy, in terms both of the making of policies and of their execution."[1]

When a consensus this broad and deep develops, there is usually something to it and with respect to the Bretton Woods–GATT system at the end of the twentieth century, *there is*.

Put simply, the IMF, the World Bank, and the GATT were created to address the global problems of the 1920s and 1930s, not the problems we face today. More specifically, these institutions were launched at the end of World War II to prevent the recurrence of four interrelated problems: the restrictive trade and exchange policies that followed in the wake of World War I; the worldwide economic depression of the 1930s, which was exacerbated by these policies; the rise of virulent forms of economic nationalism (including fascism), which emerged during the depression; and the consequent outbreak of World War II.

The founders of the Bretton Woods–GATT system sought to avoid these problems by creating international institutions that would promote the development of an open world economy. The primary goal of this economy was to encourage growth and international economic cooperation by allowing goods and capital to flow around the globe as freely as possible. The idea that an open world economy would lead to global growth and international cooperation was rooted in the founders' faith in classical liberal economics—a theory that holds that open global markets promote international prosperity and peace, the former by rationalizing the international division of labor and thereby increasing global production, the latter by generating a common worldwide interest in growth.[2] This faith in classical liberal economic theory was reinforced by the experience of the relatively open world economy of the nineteenth century, an economy that contributed to levels of global economic growth that were unprecedented up to that time, and to a century of relative peace among the world's Great Powers.[3] Finally, the notion that an open world economy would help overcome the problems of the 1920s and 1930s was strengthened by the emergence of the "welfare state" in the leading Allied countries: the conventional political wisdom at the end of World War II was that nation states, at least in the advanced capitalist countries, would use their power to mitigate the negative domestic consequences of open global markets, mainly through the pursuit of robust employment and social policies.[4]

The idea that an open world economy would be the best form of global economic organization for the post–World War II world found its practical expression in the three institutions at the core of the Bretton Woods–GATT system: the International Monetary Fund (IMF), the International Bank for Reconstruction and Development (World Bank), and the General Agreement on Tariffs and Trade (GATT). The IMF was designed to promote an open world economy by encouraging monetary cooperation, currency convertibility, international liquidity, and the elimination of exchange restrictions, all of which are vital to the expansion of foreign trade and investment. The World Bank was established to encourage foreign investment directly by providing guarantees to private investors, participating in private loans, and, when private capital is not available on reasonable terms, investing its own capital. The GATT was designed to promote an open world economy by providing a set of rules for international trade liberalization on a multilateral basis.

In sum, the overriding goals of the IMF, the World Bank, and the GATT were to prevent a recurrence of the nightmare of the interwar period—a period that has been called "The Age of Catastrophe."[5] They were designed to do so by promoting global economic growth and international economic cooperation through the creation of an open world economy, no more and no less. And while major changes have occurred in these institutions since World War II (including the reorientation of the World Bank from Western Europe to developing countries in the early postwar period; the collapse of the IMF's fixed exchange rate system in the early 1970s; and the recent transformation of the GATT into the World Trade Organization [WTO]), but these changes have done relatively little to alter the basic goals of the Bretton Woods–GATT system.

Given these goals, it is safe to say that five decades after its creation, the Bretton Woods–GATT system has achieved its primary objectives. As the twentieth century draws to a close, open global markets have emerged as the central organizing principle of the world economy. Furthermore, while global economic growth has slowed somewhat since the early 1970s, taken as a whole, the post–World War II period has recorded the highest rates of growth in history. Moreover, no major wars have erupted among the principal countries at the center of the system. And while economic nationalism has gathered some steam over the last two decades (particularly in the field of foreign trade), it bears little resemblance to the virulent strains of the 1930s. Thus, judged in terms of overcoming the problems of the interwar period, the Bretton Woods–GATT system must be deemed a success.

Yet as we look at the first fifty years of the Bretton Woods–GATT system, it is difficult not to be struck by the extent to which the institutions at its core have been unable to deal with a new generation of global problems, some of which have emerged from the successful operation of the IMF, the World Bank, and the GATT themselves. Among the most significant of these problems are:

- the gradual loss of governmental control over a wide range of domestic policies due to international economic integration and the concomitant intensification of global competitive pressures on national economies;
- the explosive growth of multinational corporations, which now account for a larger share of global production than ever before but remain unregulated at the international level;
- the growing environmental crisis, including pollution, global warming, ozone depletion, deforestation, desertification, and a decline in biodiversity;
- the increasing gap between rich and poor within and among countries; and,
- the globalization of currency and private capital markets, which are increasingly beyond the control of governments and central bankers.

While some of these problems are the natural outcomes of the successful operation of the Bretton Woods–GATT system, none were foreseen by the founders of the IMF, the World Bank, and the GATT. Nor were these institutions in any way designed to respond to these problems. Given this, it should come as no surprise to find the IMF, the World Bank, and the GATT the targets of broad-based attacks for their inability to cope with the problems of the post–cold war era.

While it was the task of the founders of the Bretton Woods–GATT system to figure out how to resolve the problems of the interwar period, it is the responsibility of their grandchildren to figure out how to meet the global challenges of today. Whether or not the heirs of the Bretton Woods–GATT system meet these challenges—and by what means—will profoundly shape the world of *their* children and grandchildren.

The essays in this volume, by founders and early leaders of the Bretton Woods–GATT system, make a major contribution to the work of the "next generation." They do so by examining the origins of the IMF, the World Bank, and the GATT; their adaptations over the last fifty years; and how these institutions have responded to contemporary challenges. Attention to these historical and institutional matters is fundamental to any attempt to figure out where we go from here.

This book is organized into three sections. Section I examines the history surrounding the creation of the Bretton Woods–GATT system. Section II examines the adaptations of the system over the last fifty years. And Section III explores the capacity of the IMF, the World Bank, and the GATT to respond to a new generation of global problems. Each section contains essays examining the institutions at the core of the Bretton Woods–GATT system, as well as essays exploring critical issues and developments that have affected the system's creation and evolution.

Notes

1. Cited in *Financial Times*, January 30, 1995, p. 4.
2. David Ricardo, one of the founders of classical economics, explains it this way:

> Under a system of perfectly free commerce, each country naturally devotes its capital and labour to such employments as are most beneficial to each. This pursuit of individual advantage is admirably connected with the universal good of the whole. By stimulating industry, by rewarding ingenuity, and by using most efficaciously the peculiar powers bestowed by nature, it distributes labour most effectively and most economically: while, by increasing the general mass of productions, it diffuses general benefit, and binds together, by one common tie of interest and intercourse, the universal society of nations, throughout the ... world.

This brief statement of the classical theory of "comparative costs" (more commonly known as "comparative advantage") may be found in David Ricardo, *The Principles of Political Economy and Taxation* (New York: Dutton, 1965), p. 77.

3. As Karl Polanyi demonstrates in his classic study of the nineteenth-century world economy, the material interests of the Great Powers in the maintenance of an open world economy led to a century of relative peace among them. While wars were fought on the

periphery of the system, major wars among the Great Powers did not occur. See Karl Polanyi, *The Great Transformation* (Boston: Beacon Press, 1944; rpt., 1957).

4. A small but growing literature exists exploring the connection between the creation of the Bretton Woods–GATT system and the welfare state. See for example, G. John Ikenberry, "Creating Yesterday's New World Order: Keynesian 'New Thinking' and the Anglo-American Postwar Settlement," in Judith Goldstein and Robert O. Keohane, eds., *Ideas and Foreign Policy* (Ithaca: Cornell University Press, 1993); John G. Ruggie, "International Regimes, Transactions, and Change: Embedded Liberalism in the Postwar Economic Order," in Stephen D. Krasner, ed., *International Regimes* (Ithaca: Cornell University Press, 1983; rpt. 1989); and E. F. Penrose, *Economic Planning for the Peace* (Princeton: Princeton University Press, 1953).

5. Eric Hobsbawm, *The Age of Extremes: A History of the World, 1914–1991* (New York: Pantheon Books, 1994). The first part of this book, "The Age of Catastrophe," examines the two world wars and the Great Depression.

Section I

History

1

The Bretton Woods Conference and the Birth of the International Monetary Fund

Margaret Garritsen de Vries

Planning for Bretton Woods

Bretton Woods was probably the most successful economic conference ever held.[1] One of the main reasons for its success was the years of planning that went into it. By January 1944, three years of intensive drafting and redrafting by U.S. and U.K. officials had taken place and these officials had met often to exchange ideas and drafts and to negotiate their positions.

The drafts of the officials both of the United States and of the United Kingdom reflected their familiarity with the history of exchange rates and of international monetary cooperation going back to the early nineteenth century. They were, for example, conversant with the advantages of stable exchange rates that the automatic classical gold standard had provided while it lasted, from 1876 to 1914. They were also familiar with the efforts of officials to restore the gold standard after World War I and how that gold standard could no longer be so automatic.

To avoid the scramble of countries to obtain gold, officials held an international conference in Genoa, Italy, in 1922, out of which came a recommendation that central banks cooperate in "managing" the operations of the exchange rate mechanism and make wider use of gold with currencies such as the pound sterling that were convertible into gold. That conference foreshadowed ideas—the need for international cooperation and for a "gold exchange standard"—that were later incorporated into the plans for Bretton Woods.

3

In any event, the "managed" gold standard collapsed in the 1930s, and attempts to secure international cooperation failed, notably at the world economic and monetary conference in London in 1933. However, to give international sanction to the devaluation of the French franc in 1936, France, the United Kingdom, and the United States issued a Tripartite Declaration that recognized international responsibility for exchange rates. The governments of these three countries agreed to hold consultations on exchange rate action and take stabilizing action. Belgium, the Netherlands, and Switzerland announced their adherence to the Tripartite Declaration. In this way, the Tripartite Declaration can be viewed as a precedent for a more comprehensive and inclusive monetary agreement.

Thus it was in the 1930s that U.S. Treasury officials began thinking about an institution for international monetary cooperation with regard to exchange rates. About that time, Henry Morgenthau Jr., secretary of the U.S. Treasury, appointed a group of international economists, including Jacob Viner and Harry Dexter White, who had been studying the balance of payments of a number of countries, to work on exchange-rate stabilization. Both Viner and White had been students of Frank W. Taussig of Harvard University, well known as an international economist, free trade advocate, and teacher. In fact, it was this group in the U.S. Treasury that helped put together the Tripartite Declaration.

Further momentum toward international monetary arrangements took place in February 1940. An Inter-American Committee, assisted by a group of experts, including White, recommended the establishment of the Inter-American Bank. In June 1940, Edward M. Bernstein, who likewise had been a student of Professor Taussig and then a professor himself at the University of North Carolina at Chapel Hill and the author of his own textbook (*Money and the Economic System*), also joined the economists at the U.S. Treasury as director of monetary research.

The intensive planning that eventually led to Bretton Woods, however, really began in the early part of 1941, when White and his associates in the U.S. Treasury started thinking in earnest about a comprehensive international monetary agreement. They had in mind two possible organizations, one to stabilize exchange rates and another to help to provide the long-term capital that would be needed for reconstruction once World War II was over.

At the same time, officials in the U.S. State Department under Cordell Hull, convinced that economics had been the missing ingredient in the failed League of Nations' efforts to secure world peace, were thinking in terms of a liberal international trade regime after the war. The regime they envisaged was one that would be free of all restrictions, especially discriminatory ones. In line with that thinking, when John Maynard Keynes of the British Treasury came to Washington in July 1941 to discuss with U.S. authorities conditions for U.S. wartime financial aid to Britain, the State Department gave him a draft agreement for defense aid that would include a provision for postwar arrangements in which there would be no discrimination by the United States or the United Kingdom against imports from any other country.

This provision upset Keynes. It would abolish the British imperial preference system that had been negotiated in Ottawa with the members of the Commonwealth in 1932. Keynes, who had been working and writing on monetary and exchange rate problems since World War I and who had come to prominence after the war with his criticisms of the reparations provisions of the Treaty of Versailles, was inclined, however, to look with favor on stabilizing exchange rates. He returned to London induced to think further about various proposals that he had been devising for postwar currency stabilization. He had long regarded the gold standard as an unsatisfactory basis for the monetary system, and the prolonged deflation of the 1930s had reinforced his view that the gold standard was a "barbaric relic." Hence, like the officials of the United States, he, too, believed that it was possible and desirable to have a high degree of exchange-rate stability without the rigidity of the gold standard. Thus the U.S. and U.K. officials had a common starting point. Keynes, however, worried that the United States might return to the deflationary policies of the 1930s, and so favored a plan that would give the U.K. authorities freedom to pursue domestic full employment policies without their having to be concerned about the impact on the U.K. balance of payments.

The Plans Emerge

By mid-1941, the time was ripe for serious thinking about monetary plans. In August, President Roosevelt and Prime Minister Churchill, meeting in the Atlantic, agreed to the Atlantic Charter, which, among other provisions, emphasized British commitment to postwar international cooperation, including help in forming a United Nations. (Six months later, in February 1942, under the Mutual Aid Agreement [Lend-Lease], the British were also to agree to a postwar multilateral payments system in exchange for a U.S. commitment to maintain full employment and to help Britain financially after the war.)

It was against this background that on Sunday, December 14, 1941, at 2:00 A.M.—the day of the week and the hour of the day were just one week after Pearl Harbor—Morgenthau asked White to prepare a stabilization plan that would include all the Allies. Edward M. Bernstein began to carry out the bulk of the technical work. The State Department's ideas about a trade agreement, which had drawn negative responses from the British, were thus, in effect, to be superseded by a monetary agreement to be worked out by the Treasury.

Meanwhile, work was proceeding in London. Keynes, working with Lionel Robbins, James Meade, and others, had gone through several drafts of a currency plan, and on February 11, 1942, circulated his *Proposals for an International Currency (or Clearing) Union*. This union was to keep accounts for central banks in the same way as central banks in each country keep accounts for commercial banks. The accounts were to be denominated in a new international currency to be known as *bancor*. Exchange rates were to be fixed in terms of *bancor* and could not be changed without permission of a governing board. Within limits, member countries could run up debit balances with the union. The union would charge interest on both debit and credit balances, a provision that was interpreted by creditors (that is, by the U.S. planners) to mean that both creditor countries and debtor countries would share the burden of balance-of-payments adjustment.

Two months later, in April 1942, the White plan, entitled *Preliminary Draft Proposal for a United Nations Stabilization Fund and a Bank for Reconstruction and Development of the United and Associated Nations*, was circulated. The plan thus covered not only what eventually became the International Monetary Fund but the World Bank as well. The task of the U.S. Treasury and the U.K. Treasury was to reconcile the British plan for the Clearing Union with the U.S. plan for the Stabilization Fund. The exchange-rate provisions would be easy to reconcile, as Keynes held the same view as White. But the financial provisions of the Clearing Union were not acceptable to the United States. The U.S. plan put more emphasis on exchange-rate stability and less on the generous provision for international liquidity than did its British counterpart, although the Fund, under the White plan to be made up of a pool of national currencies and gold, was to total at least $5 billion. All members of the United Nations were eligible to join, provided they were committed both to eliminating controls over foreign exchange transactions and to establishing fixed exchange rates, to be altered only with the consent of the Fund.

Eager to move ahead as fast as possible, a few weeks later in mid-May Morgenthau sent to President Roosevelt the preamble of the White plan with a proposal for an international conference to consider the plan. He also suggested that an interdepartmental committee be set up to coordinate action within the U.S. government, a suggestion that Roosevelt agreed to on the same day. Within nine days, representatives of the Treasury Department, the State Department, the Export-Import Bank, and others had begun to meet as such a committee, and by the end of May a technical subcommittee, chaired by White, was also holding frequent meetings. To broaden the input from economists in other sectors of the government and to help gain support for an international monetary organization, economists of the Federal Reserve Board, the Department of Commerce, and other government agencies were eventually added to the group.

Reshaping the Plans

Now that preliminary versions of both the Keynes and the White plan had been circulated, it was time for reshaping. This started in August 1942 and consumed most of the next eight months, until April 1943. A fifth draft of the Keynes plan was given to the U.S. Treasury, and its differences from and similarities to the

White plan were intently studied by the Treasury and the interdepartmental committee. While, as noted above, the two plans had many features in common, vital differences existed. One crucial difference was that the Stabilization Fund was to be based on a mixed bag of national currencies, while the Clearing Union was to operate with a new international currency (*bancor*). The union also had less strict rules than did the Fund for its use by countries with balance-of-payments deficits.

The U.S. committee was concerned about the potential financial liability of the United States and about the rights of creditor countries, that is, countries with balance-of-payments surpluses. Hence, the committee had serious reservations about the Keynes plan, which had generous liquidity provisions and easy access to liquidity for countries in deficit. In addition, the White plan contemplated the abolition of exchange controls, an important feature for the United States, whereas the union did not put much emphasis on the abolition of exchange controls and even advocated the use of capital controls.

In an effort to get the two plans closer together, White went to London in the autumn of 1942 for discussions with Keynes and other British Treasury officials. The British officials, in an effort to engage in a dialogue with other members of the British Commonwealth, held discussions with representatives of Australia, Canada, India, New Zealand, and South Africa. These discussions resulted in some minor changes to the British plan, and Keynes sent the revised draft to White. The U.S. Treasury, on its part wanting to come up with a version of a plan that might be broadly acceptable, began considerable redrafting of the Stabilization Fund proposals, going through six drafts in November and December of 1942.

White and Keynes and other officials of both governments were keenly aware that any monetary agreement would have to have the support of their legislatures. Various versions of the White plan, for example, had been sent regularly to members of the U.S. Congress. To help gain the support of the U.S. Congress and of the British Parliament, it was necessary also to have wide public support.

Criticism had begun to surface in both countries. In the United States, many congressmen, especially those who had long preferred that the United States play an isolationist rather than an internationalist role, were concerned about binding international commitments. Some economists and many businessmen objected to government institutions that would regulate, or at least interfere with, the free operation of exchange markets. Some bankers feared a government-sponsored and subsidized competitive institution that would be lending money to governments at below commercial rates. In the United Kingdom, in addition to fears that the United States would again experience serious deflation as in the 1930s, there were fears that new international commitments would jeopardize the traditional close ties within the Commonwealth. Hence, by early 1943, the technical experts undertook to familiarize more of the public with the plans. White, for example, delivered a paper to the American Economic Association in January 1943. Within a few months, the two plans were being noted in most professional journals in the English-speaking world and in a host of speeches and pamphlets.

Meanwhile, the experts on both sides of the Atlantic continued to work on their plans. By February–March 1943, White had sent a revised version of his plan to Keynes, who had come to realize that the major objectives of the Clearing Union could equally be achieved under the Stabilization Fund and that the eventual draft would have to be based on the Stabilization Fund. In April, both plans were published and the public debate became vigorous in both countries. All of Bernstein's (Edward M. Bernstein, director of monetary research, U.S. Treasury) time was now being devoted to preparing for the Bretton Woods Conference.

It was time to get the support of other countries. White sent his revised version to thirty-seven countries, with an invitation to an informal conference to discuss the plan. In the summer of 1943, the representatives of forty-six countries in Washington were invited to discuss the U.S. plan, and the U.S. authorities began bilateral talks with a number of countries; for example, Canada, France, Australia, China, Brazil, Mexico, and Chile.

Reconciling Differences

By the fall of 1943, it was imperative for the United States and the United Kingdom to reconcile their differences in order to come up with an agreed-upon plan. Accordingly, from September 15 to October 9, Anglo-American negotiations began. Nine meetings on the two plans were held in Washington, with discussions centering on fourteen points of difference. These meetings resulted in a joint statement, but it included alternative versions on a number of points. Then in November and December some eight drafts and redrafts of the Joint Statement of Experts were exchanged by White and Keynes across the Atlantic. In January–February 1944 the experts got together again in Washington and redrafted their joint statement another three times, having reached agreement on another six points of difference.

A consensus was now emerging. The major remaining difference concerned the nature and use of a proposed international currency: whether the *bancor*, as under the Keynes plan, would be a currency to be issued by the Fund, or whether the *unitas*, as then discussed in the White plan, would be used, but only as an accounting unit. On April 4, 1944 the U.S. and British negotiators finally reached agreement on a Joint Statement of Experts. Among other features of the agreement, the capital of the Fund was to be $8 billion.

All was now ready for an international conference of all the Allied governments. On May 25, 1944, the U.S. secretary of state invited forty-four governments to send representatives to a conference at Bretton Woods, New Hampshire, beginning July 1, 1944, "for the purpose of formulating definite proposals for an International Monetary Fund and possibly a Bank for Reconstruction and Development."

The Bretton Woods Conference

Selecting the Site

Bretton Woods was selected as the site for this conference for a number of reasons. The U.S. Treasury was in charge of the arrangements, and Secretary Henry Morgenthau Jr. wanted a location isolated from the wartime busyness and frenzy of Washington so that the participants could focus their sole attention on the plans for the postwar era. He favored a resort hotel. The Mount Washington Hotel in the remote town of Bretton Woods, New Hampshire, was in the East and it was large and had adequate conference facilities.

In addition, 1944 was an election year and Senator Charles Tobey of New Hampshire, the ranking Republican on the Banking and Currency Committee, was facing a bitter primary election in his state. Senator Tobey, like many other Republican senators of the time, was isolationist-minded and strongly opposed to the United States' "surrendering authority to international organizations." President Roosevelt and Morgenthau, conscious that Woodrow Wilson had ignored Congress and had thereby damaged his prospects of winning approval of the League of Nations, were eager to gain the support of Republicans, if at all possible. Hence, when Senator Tobey urged the New Hampshire location, which was to give him high visibility in his home state, the U.S. planners agreed.

Climate also favored New Hampshire. The British in particular found Washington's tropical heat in July onerous, and Keynes, who had a heart condition, preferred a cool place. An additional reason, which seems incredible now, was that most resort hotels at the time were anti-Semitic, and Secretary Morgenthau could not even make a reservation at most hotels. The Mount Washington Hotel was not anti-Semitic, possibly because a long-standing Hasidic (Orthodox) Jewish community was located nearby.

Fears of Failure

The U.S. planners were by no means confident that the Bretton Woods Conference would be successful, or whether it would in fact take place. And even if the invitees did respond and send delegates, it was still possible that the conference would be a failure.

First, there was no time to lose. The U.S. Treasury planners, like those Americans who were then shaping the United Nations, were concerned that World War II might end before they had put in place an institutional framework for a new world order. By the end of May 1944, when the invitations to Bretton Woods went out, early victory in Europe appeared quite possible. In fact, D-Day was to occur less than two weeks later, on June 6. The Bretton Woods planners were convinced that they had to take advantage of the wartime collaboration of the Allied nations. Willingness to collaborate might suddenly end once the war was over, and there could be a resurgence of the intense economic nationalism that had prevailed before the war. The basic long-term problems of global political and economic organization had to be resolved beforehand.

Second, the U.S. Treasury sensed that the British were not as enthusiastic about postwar monetary relations as the United States had hoped. British cabinet officials were increasingly divided on postwar issues. Some of them anticipated a revival of the American isolationism that had long characterized U.S. policy. They worried that the Americans, especially Congress, might reject international commitments and oppose macroeconomic measures to ensure full employment, the most important point on Keynes's agenda. A bitter debate in the House of Commons in early May had also revealed that many members of Parliament were concerned that the proposed Fund and the lifting of exchange restrictions would bring an end to Britain's special relations with its sterling area partners. At the same time, the new Fund would not adequately shelter Britain from the economic depression that they considered very probable in the United States.

British officials had reason to worry, and so did the Democrats who then held office in the Roosevelt administration. It was an election year in the United States, which included a presidential election. The Democratic and Republican nominating conventions, in fact, would also be taking place in July. The Republicans were optimistic that they could sweep the elections in November, which could spell bad news for those who wanted new international arrangements. Many leading Republicans, especially in the Senate, such as Robert A. Taft of Ohio, were openly outspoken against "international financial panaceas" designed to place "American dollars in foreign hands." Charles S. Dewey, a congressman from Illinois (and a distant cousin of Thomas E. Dewey, who was to be the Republican presidential candidate), had an alternative, more limited plan. In these circumstances, Keynes desired to expedite the negotiations for the International Monetary Fund, and the U.S. planners were even more eager to get the Articles of Agreement for the Fund drawn up in final form before the autumn elections.

Early in April 1944, to help speed up the process of arranging the conference, Morgenthau asked the president to approve an accelerated timetable. As a result, invitations were sent out on May 25 and the conference was scheduled for July 1. Moreover, although throughout the preparations White and his technicians had taken the initiative, generated proposals, and handled bilateral consultations with the United Kingdom, now Morgenthau himself began to take an active part in completing the final arrangements. The Bretton Woods Conference was the first of the major international conferences to be convened for the purpose of establishing an international organization (the United Nations conference, at Dumbarton Oaks and San Francisco, did not take place until 1945 and the conference, resulting in the Food and Agriculture Organization, in 1943 was relatively small), and Morgenthau regarded success at Bretton Woods as essential to President Roosevelt's political fortunes.

To this end, once the United States and the United Kingdom had agreed on a joint statement, Morgenthau undertook to involve the Russians. It was, he believed, essential that both the United Kingdom and the USSR participate, as a test of their willingness to cooperate with the United States in getting these new postwar organizations operating and fully functional after the war. The Russians, however, while wanting to appear to be associated with the plans for the Fund and the Bank so that they could be seen as important players in the world, revealed little enthusiasm for monetary cooperation. They agreed to send a delegation to the Bretton Woods conference but it would not include the commissar of finance. Britain, too, said it would not send cabinet-level officials to the conference. And both the British and the Russians asserted that participation in the conference in no way foreclosed their option to reject eventual membership in the Fund.

The U.S. Delegation

Assured that at least there would be a conference, Morgenthau, with President Roosevelt's involvement, then carefully selected the U.S. delegates. To gain public support for the proposed Fund and Bank, they chose delegates of high rank who represented diverse executive, legislative, and public constituencies. Morgenthau himself was to lead the seven-person delegation, with Fred Vinson (the head of the Office of Economic Stabilization and later secretary of the treasury and chief justice of the Supreme Court) as his deputy and, among others, Dean Acheson (of the State Department) and Marriner Eccles (chairman of the Federal Reserve Board) plus Harry White, Senator Tobey (mentioned above), and Senator Robert F. Wagner, chairman of the Senate Committee on Banking and Currency. Senator Tobey was the only Senate Republican on the delegation: some Democrats objected to his selection and even the president was unsure of his choice. (As events turned out, Senator Tobey became an enthusiastic supporter of international cooperation, and administration aides gave him maximum publicity in his home state during the conference.)

In all there were forty-five U.S. delegates, technical advisers, legal advisers, assistants to the chairman, and technical secretaries. Several of these participants were later board or staff members of the Fund. White was, of course, the first U.S. executive director (undoubtedly missing the chance to be managing director: even at that time, rumors were beginning to surface alleging that he was a Communist and even a Russian spy). Among those who were part of the U.S. contingent and who later joined the Fund were Walter Gardner (deputy director of the Research Department), Richard Brenner (Legal Department), and George F. Luthringer (alternate executive director and later director of the Far East,

Middle East, and Latin America Department). There was also one woman appointed by President Roosevelt as a delegate, Mabel Newcomer, a professor at Vassar College, and three women served as legal adviser, assistants, or technical secretaries. The secretariat for the conference also included a few familiar names of persons who subsequently came to the Fund—Frank Coe (the first secretary of the Fund) and Alice Bourneuf (Research Department)—and of people who later returned to academic life, such as Raymond Mikesell and Arthur Smithies. Orvis Schmidt joined the World Bank. Eleanor Lansing Dulles, sister of John Foster Dulles, also served on the secretariat.

Briefing the Delegates

Preparing the U.S. negotiations presented more than the usual difficulties. A number of the delegates—including the congressional representatives—were no more familiar with the Fund and Bank proposals than was the average citizen. Fortunately, the delegation had been carefully selected and did not include any prominent opponents of the proposals. Moreover, President Roosevelt had carefully circumscribed the delegation's authority, and he reminded them that they had the responsibility for demonstrating to the world that international postwar cooperation was possible. Nevertheless, the U.S. Treasury experts prepared extensive background memoranda on such potentially controversial topics as the allocation of quotas in the Fund, gold contributions, access to the Fund's resources, voting structure, and management. To help inform both the delegation and the general public, the Treasury experts also prepared a detailed commentary called *Questions and Answers on the International Monetary Fund*, which was issued as a public document on June 10, 1944. This document posed thirty-five questions that delegates and the general public might ask about the new Fund and then provided detailed answers.

Atlantic City

By June it appeared that only technical issues stood in the way of a successful conference. To help resolve these issues, Treasury experts arranged another preliminary drafting session at Atlantic City in the second half of June. Morgenthau had doubts about this procedure, for it seemed to shift actual decision making from political officials to technical experts. Nonetheless, representatives from twelve countries joined the four principals (the United States, the United Kingdom, the USSR, and China). Their deliberations, however, did not prove as successful as White had hoped, because security arrangements for the invasion of Europe interrupted Atlantic shipping and delayed until June 23 the arrival of the *Queen Mary*, which was carrying the British officials and the officials of the European governments-in-exile. Five working days did not permit the deadline-conscious experts to resolve many of their disputes and many issues still required top-level political decisions. Nor were these experts able to complete a draft of the Articles of Agreement for the Bank. These delegates boarded a special train from Atlantic City on Friday, June 30, for the all-night trip to Bretton Woods. Others left on a special train from Washington. Even as the train wound its way through New Jersey and New England, two lawyers from the U.S. delegation undertook to transform the documents resulting from the Atlantic City meeting (where some seventy amendments to the joint statement had been proposed) into the basic material for the next stage. Obviously there was still much work left to do at Bretton Woods.

Convening the Conference

The Bretton Woods Conference opened on July 1, 1944, and although it was initially scheduled to end on Wednesday, July 19, it was extended until July 21. The Food and Agricultural Organization (FAO) conference at Hot Springs had lasted ten days, and it had been thought that twice this length of time would suffice for Bretton Woods. Also, the Democratic convention, with the likelihood of President Roosevelt's renomination there and the desire of some of the U.S. high-level delegates to attend, was scheduled to start on July 20.

The Mount Washington Hotel, named for the nearby mountain peak, proved adequate but was not without some inconveniences. It had been closed for two years and was just being prepared for reopening when it was taken over for the conference; and the renovations were not wholly completed by the time the delegates began to arrive. Insufficient office space, inadequate accommodations, rusty plumbing, and an inexperienced staff were supplemented by Boy Scout messengers and military personnel. The rooms were remarkably small and the old-fashioned heating system did not work satisfactorily. (At the time of the fortieth anniversary of the Bretton Woods Conference, the rooms were marked with brass labels indicating which delegations has stayed in those rooms.) But the scenery was magnificent, the recreational facilities were excellent, and the hotel was separated from the road by a river crossed by a single bridge—a feature that readily permitted the proceedings to be secured against intrusion.

Not all the delegates could be housed at the hotel and some had to go into other hotels, up to five miles away.

Present at the Creation

Some 730 persons attended the conference, a number about three times as large as had originally been expected. They represented forty-four countries, most of the Allies of World War II. These countries were now being referred to, at least by U.S. organizers, as the United Nations. Thus, in addition to the United States, the United Kingdom, the USSR, and Canada (which had also suggested a monetary plan), the countries represented included: other countries associated with the

United Kingdom (Australia, New Zealand, South Africa, and India, although India was not yet politically independent), the European governments-in-exile (Belgium, Czechoslovakia, Denmark, Greece, Luxembourg, the Netherlands, Norway, Poland, and Yugoslavia), a French delegation under Pierre Mendés-France, the Allies in Asia (China and the Philippines, although the Philippines was not yet independent) and in the Middle East and Africa (Egypt, Ethiopia, Iran, Iraq, and Liberia), and nineteen Latin American republics (Bolivia, Brazil, Chile, Colombia, Costa Rica, Cuba, Dominican Republic, Ecuador, El Salvador, Guatemala, Haiti, Honduras, Mexico, Nicaragua, Panama, Paraguay, Peru, Uruguay, and Venezuela).

It is of some interest now, fifty years later, to note how many countries were not Allies (or were even enemies) or were not politically independent (they were called territories) or were not politically or financially independent in their own right or did not even exist at that time and hence were not at Bretton Woods. Such a list includes, of course, Germany, Japan, and Italy, as well as several in Europe (Austria, Bulgaria, Finland, Hungary, Portugal, Romania, Spain, Sweden, and Turkey), in the Middle East (Afghanistan, Jordan, Lebanon, Syria, Saudi Arabia, and, of course, Israel, created in 1948), and in Asia (Burma, Ceylon, Indonesia, and Thailand). Other than Liberia and South Africa, Ethiopia was the only sub-Saharan country present and, among the Latin Americans, Argentina was not present.

Many persons who attended, either as delegates or as technical advisers, were to come to the Fund in its early days, just as did many from the U.S. team listed earlier. Camille Gutt, on the Belgian delegation to Bretton Woods, was to become the first managing director. Several others were to serve on the earliest executive boards and several joined the Fund staff. These people, not listed in any particular order, included for example, Louis Rasminsky (Canada), Leslie Melville (Australia), Jan Mdlacek, Ernest Sturc, and Ervin Hexner (Czechoslovakia), Jean de Largentaye (France), A. B. Ebtohaj (Iran), J. W. Beyen, D. Crena de Iongh, and J. J. Polak (Netherlands), Allan G. B. Fisher (New Zealand), Felipe Pazos (Cuba), Y. C. Koo, Y. C. Wang, and T. C. Liu (China), B. K. Madan (India), Ernest de Selliers (Belgium), Rodrigo Gómez (Mexico), G. L. F. Bolton (United Kingdom), and George Blowers (then governor of the Bank of Ethiopia). Still others were to join the World Bank, including Antonin Basch (Czechoslovakia), Aaron Broches (Netherlands), K. Varvaressos (Greece), and Luís Machado (Cuba).

Keynes himself was chairman of the United Kingdom's seven-person delegation, accompanied by, among others, noted academics Dennis Robertson and Lionel Robbins, as well as by several advisers. While some countries had fairly large numbers of representatives (for example, Brazil, China, Cuba, the Netherlands, Peru, the USSR, the United States), other countries had very few participants, especially some of the Latin American republics, and Ethiopia. Andreas Papandreou, recently re-elected prime minister of Greece, was also on the Greek delegation.

Hard Work Brings Success

These delegates worked incredibly hard. They were determined to be successful. Commission I on the Fund was headed by Harry White, since the White plan was to be the basis of the Fund's articles, and Keynes, concerned that the postwar world might be without adequate mechanisms for international investment and reconstruction assistance, agreed to head Commission II on the Bank. Plenary sessions went on all day to draft the Articles of Agreement for both institutions. Since work for the Bank was much less advanced beforehand than work on the Fund, the Fund's articles were used as a model for those of the Bank, especially the provision with regard to the organization and structure of the executive board. So, in many respects, the Bank became the mirror image of the Fund. Many controversies over provisions of the articles were dealt with in informal negotiations, within drafting committees, and through bilateral negotiations, especially between the United States and the United Kingdom.

Harry White impressed foreign delegates with his fairness, inexhaustible energy, and leadership and is reported to have functioned effectively on no more than five hours sleep. Keynes drove himself and the other delegates mercilessly. But, according to reports of many who attended the conference and of entries in Morgenthau's own personal diaries and those of non-Fund historians, the driving intellect of the Bretton Woods conference was Edward Bernstein. For example, one of those who participated in the original Bretton Woods Conference, Felipe Pazos, specified at the fortieth anniversary in 1984 that day after day Bernstein answered question after question from delegates who were unfamiliar with, or confused about, the many provisions of the Fund's articles or how the proposed Fund would work—thereby, of course, helping to gain their support. A professor of history at Ohio State University, Alfred E. Eckes Jr., has written:

> As a technician Bernstein had no equal, and he repeatedly impressed delegates and reporters with his encyclopedic knowledge of the provisions. As another American expert said praisingly, Bernstein was "really an amazing thinking and talking machine. You could push a button and the stuff would pour out with perfect clarity. He worked twenty-seven or twenty-eight hours a day without showing signs of strain."[2]

The Bretton Woods Conference was an incredible success. Fifty years later, it stands out as the most productive economic conference in modern history. And the name Bretton Woods has entered the language of international economics as a shorthand reference to the entire complex of the international monetary system established after World War II.

Obtaining Approval of the U.S. Congress

Once the Bretton Woods Conference was over, it was necessary for the United States to have congressional approval for U.S. participation in the two new organizations being planned, the International Monetary Fund (IMF) and the International Bank for Reconstruction and Development (IBRD, later referred to as the World Bank). The IMF (the Fund) was the more controversial of the two organizations. In fact, it had been to help gain congressional approval that the Treasury aides, as well as Secretary Morgenthau, had been informing members of Congress for some time about the plans for the Fund and why President Roosevelt had appointed two senators and two congressmen as four of the seven-member U.S. delegation to Bretton Woods (two congressmen were also technical advisers). Since U.S. participation was essential if the Fund was to become a reality, after the Bretton Woods conference had ended other countries waited to take additional steps until the U.S. Congress took action.

Congressional approval was by no means assured. After all, the League of Nations had failed to win congressional approval, and prior to World War II the United States had been strongly isolationist. But there were even more specific worries for those who hoped to obtain congressional approval for the new IMF. There were many opponents of the proposed Fund. As an illustration, on July 1, 1944, as the Bretton Woods Conference opened, the *New York Times*, the *Wall Street Journal*, and the *Chicago Tribune* all ran editorials that condemned government management of exchange rates. As another example, Robert Taft, senator from Ohio, frightened delegates from other countries when he asserted that the Congress would not approve any plan that placed "American money in a fund to be dispensed by an international board in which we have only a minority voice."

In September 1944, Winthrop Aldrich, influential chairman of Chase National Bank, delivered a searing indictment of the Bretton Woods accords. The IMF, he said, would become a mechanism for instability rather than stability since it would encourage exchange-rate alterations. Like Aldrich, most bankers—including Allan Sproul and John H. Williams, president and vice president of the New York Federal Reserve Bank—favored a much more limited "key-currency" approach instead of the universal Fund, and they were determined to push such an approach. They called for the Bank, not the Fund, to take responsibility for exchange-stabilization lending and advocated that the Bank come into being and that the Fund be postponed.

In this situation, the U.S. planners decided to take their case directly to the U.S. public and devised one of the most elaborate and sophisticated campaigns ever conducted, at least up to that time. Morgenthau himself went out to give speeches to industrialists; and during the winter of 1945 Edward Bernstein and Treasury lawyer Ansel Luxford turned salesmen and spoke frequently to banking and trade groups, to reporters, and to columnists. They also prepared radio scripts, pamphlets, and articles, and even subsidized short moving pictures. They avoided intricate details about par values or balance-of-payments adjustment and instead stressed the more comprehensible need for world security and expanding trade. They enlisted the aid of academics, such as Seymour Harris of Harvard and Jacob Viner. Viner, in fact, labeled the proposal for the Fund the "magnificent blueprint." As Treasury officials and economists became caught up in selling that blueprint, they relied heavily on two main arguments: the Monetary Fund was essential for U.S. domestic prosperity and high employment; and the United States had to show its willingness to be a world leader in international cooperation in the postwar world. (It may be noted that these are the same arguments that President Clinton used nearly fifty years later to gain support for the North American Free Trade Agreement [NAFTA] and the Uruguay Round of the General Agreement on Tariffs and Trade [GATT] agreement.)

It was to take nearly a year before Congress voted. But when the crucial vote came in the House of Representatives on June 7, 1945, only eighteen Republicans voted negatively. Then came the battle in the Senate, where again Senator Taft, a very skillful debater, led the opposition, but shortly thereafter the Senate also agreed to the necessary legislation, and the U.S. Bretton Woods Agreement Act was passed. On July 31, 1945, President Harry S. Truman, having succeeded to the presidency after the death of President Roosevelt in April, signed the Bretton Woods Act.

Conclusion

With U.S. participation in the IMF and the International Bank for Reconstruction and Development (World Bank) now assured, it was necessary to encourage participation by other nations. The IMF could come into being only if nations that had 65 percent of the quotas agreed to at Bretton Woods were to ratify the Articles of Agreement by December 31, 1945. As of mid-November 1945, only six weeks before the deadline, only South Africa and Venezuela were ready to ratify. But further progress came quickly and by December 18 eleven countries had completed the necessary legislation and eight more were expected to do so shortly. These nineteen countries were enough to bring the IMF into existence. The U.S. planners arranged a formal ceremony at the State Department, and on December 27, 1945, twenty-nine countries signed the Articles of Agreement. By December 31 another six had also signed, so that thirty-five countries, with quotas representing more than 80 percent of the total, had given life to the IMF eighteen months after Bretton Woods.

Notes

1. This chapter is reproduced from "Caravan," the newsletter of the International Monetary Fund's Retirees Association. For additional information on the founding of the IMF and its early years, see Margaret Garritsen de Vries, *The IMF in a Changing World, 1945–1985* (Washington, D.C.: International Monetary Fund, 1986); Alfred E. Eckes Jr., *A Search for Solvency: Bretton Woods and the International Monetary System, 1941–1971* (Austin and London: University of Texas Press, 1975); and J. Keith Horsefield, *The International Monetary Fund, 1945–1965: Twenty Years of International Monetary Co-operation* (Washington, D.C.: International Monetary Fund, 1967).

2. Eckes, *A Search for Solvency*, p. 139.

Some Issues in the Bretton Woods Debates

Raymond F. Mikesell

Introduction

When I joined the Treasury Department's Division of Monetary Research in September 1942, Edward Bernstein gave me a copy of Harry White's *Preliminary Draft Proposal for a United Nations Stabilization Fund and a Bank for Reconstruction and Development of the United and Associated Nations*, dated 1942.[1] I was asked to study the document and to make comments and suggestions. The subject occupied most of my time in the division during the next five years. White's 150-page plan for a Fund and a Bank was a far cry from the dull, legalistic Articles of Agreement for the two institutions that emerged from Bretton Woods. It was a rambling personal statement that combined certain basic policies of the United States, such as exchange-rate stability and nondiscrimination in trade and payments, with a number of White's own ideas on the functions of an International Stabilization Fund (ISF) and a world bank. The proposed ISF was a multilateralized model of the operations of the U.S. Exchange Stabilization Fund (ESF) and the 1936 Tripartite Agreement with France and Britain.

Following a series of meetings by members of the U.S. Interdepartmental Committee and informal discussions with foreign representatives, the ISF plan was greatly simplified and the July 10, 1943, edition[2] became the basis for the Joint Statement by Experts of United and Associated Nations on the Establishment of an International Stabilization Fund negotiated in September–October 1943 by the British and American delegations. The joint statement became the agenda on the Fund at the Bretton Woods Conference and most of its provisions were accepted. White's Bank plan received relatively little consideration during the pre–Bretton Woods discussions and took its present form during the course of negotiations at the Atlantic City conference in June 1944, prior to Bretton Woods. The issues discussed in this paper are limited to those relating to the Fund.

During the deliberations on the White plan with the British and other foreign representatives in the spring and summer of 1943, the principal rival to the ISF was John Maynard Keynes's International Clearing Union (ICU) plan, which was formulated in 1941. Neither Keynes nor White was aware of the other's plan until early 1942. Both plans provided for a par value system and for the elimination of discriminatory exchange arrangements; both provided for international liquidity to assist members in dealing with balance-of-payments deficits. However, the arrangements for providing international liquidity under the two plans were quite different. Under the ISF plan, members would contribute their own currencies and gold to the Fund. Members needing assistance would draw currencies from the Fund to meet deficits with the members whose currencies were drawn. Under the ICU, central banks or treasuries would report their bilateral positions with other members to the Clearing Union and receive credits or debits on the books of the ICU. These credits were denominated in *bancor* and were transferable among the members for settlement of debts. *Bancor* was defined in grains of gold, while par values under the ISF were defined in dollars or grains of gold equivalent to the gold content of the dollar as of July 1944.

After considerable discussion of both plans at meetings in Washington, the U.S. delegation made it clear to Keynes that the ICU concept was unacceptable to the U.S. government, in part because the concept was unfamiliar to the American public and Congress, and in part because the U.S. obligation to accept *bancor* depended upon the aggregate amount of deficits in the Clearing Union. Under the ISF plan the obligation of the U.S. government to subscribe dollars and gold was fixed by the U.S. quota. Also, the ICU plan provided for periodic adjustments in the total quotas on the basis of the volume of world trade. Thereafter, the agenda for the negotiation of the joint statement was reconciling the differences between American and British interests over the provisions found in the ISF.

The remainder of this paper is devoted to the following issues that were intensely debated during the preconference meetings, as well as at Bretton Woods and at the inaugural meeting of the IMF and World Bank in Savannah, Georgia, in March 1946:

1) establishment of an international currency and multilateral clearing;
2) the right to draw from the Fund;
3) the par value system;
4) the transition period;
5) the governance of the Fund.

The first four issues appeared to be settled by the joint statement completed in April 1944, but the issue on the governance of the Fund was unilaterally determined by the United States at the inaugural meeting in Savannah. There were ambiguities and technical flaws in the joint statement that carried over into the Articles of Agreement of the IMF. Some of these flaws reflected efforts to resolve conflicting positions of the American and British governments, and some reflected a conflict between the way the Fund was designed to function and the realities of the postwar world.

International Currency and Multilateral Clearing

A major difference between Keynes's ICU proposal and White's ISF plan was that the Clearing Union provided for both an international currency (other than the dollar) and a mechanism for multilateral clearing, while the White plan provided neither. The July 1943 edition of the White plan stated that the Fund could make available to a member the currency of another member, provided that "the foreign exchange demanded from the Fund is required to meet an adverse balance of payments predominantly on current account with any member."[3] Since members were permitted to maintain controls on capital movements and most members were expected to do so for an indefinite period after the war, most currencies purchased from the Fund could not be sold on free exchange markets for another currency. Also, members of the Fund had no obligation to convert balances of their currencies held by another country into third currencies. In effect, this meant that a member could only draw a currency from the Fund to settle a bilateral deficit on current account with the member whose currency was drawn. Thus, if a member had a bilateral deficit with a country whose currency was not available from the Fund, it would need to acquire a currency that was freely convertible (e.g., dollars) into the currency required. The absence of general currency convertibility also meant that, if one member had a current account *deficit* with another member, it might need to purchase from the Fund the currency of that member (even though it had an overall current account surplus). Under a regime of capital controls, foreign exchange transactions were expected to take place between private entities and officially designated banks, or between central banks, rather than in a free market. The multilateral clearing problem could have been dealt with if members had been required to convert balances of their own currencies acquired in current transactions into gold or a fully convertible currency such as the dollar, but this obligation was not specified in the July 1943 draft of the ISF.

The absence of a multilateral clearing mechanism in the ISF plan greatly disturbed Keynes, and he sought to correct this defect during the negotiations on the joint statement. The July 1943 ISF plan provided for an international unit of account called *unitas*, with a gold value equivalent to the gold content of ten U.S. dollars. The accounts in the Fund and the value of each member's currency were to be expressed in *unitas*, which was transferable and redeemable in gold or in the currency of any member country. However, *unitas* was not a true international currency. The Fund did not provide credits to members in *unitas* nor were members obligated to settle their bilateral deficits with one another in *unitas*. Keynes put forward the idea that *unitas* should become a true international currency to be used by the Fund for making credits available to members, and all members would be obligated to accept *unitas* in settlement of balances. However, White refused to accept this arrangement because it would obligate the United States to accept *unitas* in excess of the U.S. subscription to the Fund, thereby creating additional dollar credits. White regarded Keynes's proposal as a way of realizing the fundamental principle of the Clearing Union, and of obligating the United States to supplying an indefinite amount of dollar credits in exchange for *unitas*.

Keynes was determined to find a way of bringing multilateral clearing into the Fund system. He proposed a clause in the joint statement requiring that a member buy back its own currency from any other member with that member's currency or gold, so long as its own currency was acceptable to the Fund and the other currency was available from the Fund. This obligation would apply regardless of whether the first member's currency was acquired as a consequence of a current transaction with the member. Thus, when a member was asked to buy back its currency with the currency of another member, it could acquire the other member's currency from the Fund. This would have the effect of reducing the Fund's holdings of the other member's currency, thereby increasing the other member's drawing right on the Fund, so that the member could draw any currency it needed. By means of this convoluted series of transactions, a member acquiring the currency of another member could, in effect, convert that currency into a third currency. White objected to this arrangement, but the U.S. delegation did agree to a provision in the joint statement designed to accomplish the same purpose: "Subject to VI below, a member country may not use its control of capital movements to restrict payments for current transactions or to delay unduly the transfer of funds in settlement of commitments."[4] This language was included in the Articles of Agreement of the IMF (Article VI, Section 3), but it is by no means clear whether a member is obligated to allow the transfer of its currency between two other members to settle an imbalance, thus providing for multilateral clearing. Article VIII, Section 4, of the IMF Agreement defines a member's obligation to maintain convertibility as follows:

> Each member shall buy balances of its currency held by another member if the latter, in requesting the purchase, represents (i) that the balances to be bought have been recently acquired as a result of current transactions; or (ii) that their conversion is needed for paying current transactions. The buying member shall have the option of paying either in the currency of the member making the request or in gold.[5]

There appears to be no explicit obligation of a country to redeem its own currency, say, in dollars, or to allow its currency to be traded in a free market for a third currency.

The multilateral clearing problem was discussed at Bretton Woods by other delegations, but nothing was done about it. The British delegation was not anxious to insist on a multilateral clearing system that would have required free exchange markets for sterling. They wanted a system whereby central banks could clear their balances multilaterally, as was the case with the Clearing Union.

Had the ICU plan been adopted instead of the ISF plan, the U.S. goal of eliminating bilateral payments agreements and discriminatory exchange arrangements might have been achieved a decade earlier than it was. A fully multilateral clearing system was delayed until the major European currencies became convertible in the 1960s. Meanwhile, in the early 1950s, the European Payments Union (EPU) was established. The EPU provided for multilateral clearing and liquidity for financing most of the world's non-dollar trade. The EPU was a regional clearing union. However, the Fund refused to play any role in this system, which was managed by the Bank for International Settlements (BIS). Ironically, the Bretton Woods Conference voted to recommend that the BIS be abolished; fortunately, it still exists today.

The U.S. government's rejection of the ICU on grounds that it would create a large potential U.S. obligation to supply credits was presented in terms of a worst-case scenario. Keynes's proposal suggested that the initial quotas might be equal to 75 percent of average annual prewar trade. Total world trade in 1937 and 1938 (exports plus imports) averaged about $50 billion, three-fourths of which would have been $38 billion. Assuming a U.S. quota of $8 billion, this would have meant maximum U.S. *bancor* holdings of $30 billion, assuming all other countries would become members of the ICU and all would accumulate debt positions equal to their quotas. The Keynes plan also provided that quotas be adjusted every five years to reflect growth in trade during the postwar period. A U.S. Treasury economist estimated that the United States would be obligated to provide credits totaling $75 billion or more during the next decade.

During the debates, the arguments against the ICU were criticized as unrealistic for several reasons. First, the United States would not be the only surplus country in the world. Many primary producing countries, such as Canada and the Latin American countries, would experience large surpluses as a result of heavy demand and high prices for their exports. Second, the U.S. government had policy instruments for limiting the U.S. export surplus to control inflation or to limit its external credits. Third, the ICU gave substantial power to the governing board to require members to limit their deficits when their debit balances exceeded one-half of their quotas. Fourth, measures could be taken to prevent the United States from having to acquire a disproportionate share of *bancor* credit balances. The possibility of such measures was suggested by Keynes and explored in conversations between the U.S. and British delegates, but no acceptable formula was found. There was concern that any limitation on the obligation of a creditor to accept balances in *bancor* would begin to impair confidence in *bancor* when a large creditor approached the point at which the limitation would take effect.[6] (It may be noted that the same problem arose in 1969 when the IMF was authorized to distribute special drawing rights [SDRs]. The problem was solved through a process of designating specific allocations of SDRs among creditor countries and by limiting a member's obligation to provide currency against SDRs at twice the level of its net cumulative SDR allocation. A similar arrangement for limiting the obligation of the United States to accept *bancor* could have been worked out, had the U.S. government been willing to seriously consider adopting the ICU proposal.)

The Scarce Currency Clause

One consequence of a fund whose assets consist largely of generally inconvertible currencies is that the supply of gold and dollars would be smaller than the potential demand. In the event that each member drew dollars up to the amount of its quota, the total demand for dollars could be as much as three times the U.S. subscription. To deal with this problem, White introduced the scarce currency clause into the December 1942 draft of the ISF. When the Fund's supply of a particular currency was in danger of being exhausted, the clause stated, the executive board should propose a method for equitably distributing the Fund's holdings of that currency. If rationing the member's currency became necessary, other members would be permitted to discriminate in their trade against that member to the degree necessary to restrict the demand for that member's currency. The scarce currency clause was embarrassing to the U.S. administration since a major argument for U.S. ratification of the Bretton Woods Agreements Act was to avoid discrimination against U.S. exports. During the congressional hearings on the Bretton Woods agreements in 1945, White testified that the dollar would never be declared scarce. What he meant in effect was that the United States would use its power to limit drawings so that the demand for dollars would never exceed the Fund's supply (subscribed dollars plus gold). The U.S. concern that the dollar might be declared scarce may have influenced the Fund to limit the use of its resources during the early postwar period. Had Keynes won his argument for the Fund to provide credits in an international currency, the scarce currency clause would not have been necessary. On the other hand, as Alexander Cairncross points out in his essay in this volume, Keynes regarded the scarce currency clause as protection against a general scarcity of dollars. But this was not what White had in mind.

The Right to Draw

The dispute over conditions for drawing currencies from the Fund reflected a fundamental difference between Keynes and White regarding the operation of the Fund. White's April 1942 proposal gave the Fund broad powers over the foreign exchange and trade policies of members. Drawings were conditioned on Fund approval of the efforts of the borrower to restore balance-of-payments equilibrium. Some of these intrusive powers were eliminated in the July 1943 edition, but drawings continued to be conditioned on the judgment of the Fund that satisfactory measures were being taken by the member to correct its balance-of-payments deficit.

It was Keynes's position that the Fund should provide a fixed amount of liquidity unconditionally so that members could count on a supplement to their official reserves. He was also concerned that the Fund might try to interfere with domestic policies such as those dealing with unemployment. Under the Keynes Clearing Union, members could run deficits up to half their quota without conditions; additional deficits were subject to conditions, such as currency devaluation or other measures to restore equilibrium. The U.S. delegation, on the other hand, was of the opinion that the U.S. Congress would not ratify the Bretton Woods agreements unless the Fund (and ultimately the U.S. administration) could prevent the use of Fund resources by members that refused to adopt sound financial policies. In the long debates over this issue during the negotiation of the joint statement, Keynes was able to liberalize the conditions for drawings, but in both the joint statement and the Final Act of the Bretton Woods Conference, the Fund retains the right to deny a member the use of its resources if it is believed they are being used in a manner contrary to the purposes of the Fund.

Keynes never really accepted the position that members would not have the right to draw unconditionally substantial amounts from the Fund, and this became the basis for his strong belief that the day-to-day operations of the Fund should be in the hands of the Fund staff rather than under the control of its executive directors. Had Keynes known that the Fund would become a development assistance agency rather than an organization mainly concerned with supplementing the foreign exchange reserves of the developed world, he might have felt differently about conditionality. With the emergence of standby agreements and special development assistance programs, intervention by the Fund in the domestic affairs of developing countries (and now of the former Soviet countries) has gone well beyond anything even White envisaged.

Keynes saw no reason for the executive directors to be in continuous session at the Fund headquarters, and asked what twelve highly paid executive directors and twelve alternates could possibly do to keep from being bored, let alone earn their salaries. Keynes and White fought bitterly over the salaries proposed by the salary committee at Savannah. In a private meeting which I attended, Keynes accused White, who was expected to be designated U.S. executive director, of pursuing selfish personal interest by promoting a salary considerably higher than any British minister earned. This was perhaps a cheap shot. Keynes should have known that after the U.S. Congress and the British Parliament had ratified Bretton Woods, the U.S. government would make the rules.

The Par Value System

A system of international oversight for changes in par values was the centerpiece of the White ISF plan. Competitive exchange depreciation and discriminatory exchange rates were regarded as major barriers to U.S. exports during the 1930s, and the Fund was designed to abolish them. White's initial draft gave the ISF power to set the rate at which it would exchange one member's currency for another at the time operations began, and provided that a member could change its par value only with the approval of three-fourths of the members.[7] Because the United States expected to have more than one-quarter of the total votes, it would have the power to determine every member's initial exchange rate and bar any change thereafter. This was not only unacceptable to foreign delegates, it was even questioned by members of the American Technical Committee that carried on the negotiations with foreign representatives. Subsequent drafts of the ISF proposal limited Fund control over changes in par values. The joint statement provided that members could change the initial par value of their currencies up to 10 percent without the approval of the Fund. However, members were not to propose changes in their par value "except to correct a fundamental disequilibrium," a concept that has never been defined in fewer than ten pages! The reasoning behind the concept is that normally balance-of-payments disequilibrium should be corrected by monetary and fiscal measures. However, if structural changes in trade patterns or in relative price levels were to occur, resulting in disequilibrium that could not be corrected without a substantial decline in economic activity and employment, an appropriate adjustment in the par value could be made. This limited the use of exchange rate changes as a policy instrument.

Keynes and other foreign delegations accepted the idea of a par value system but wanted much greater flexibility, and looked upon alterations in exchange rates as an instrument for dealing with recession and unemployment. *Bancor* was defined in terms of gold, but its gold content could be changed by majority vote of the members of the Clearing Union. I have often wondered why Keynes tied *bancor* to gold since he was not a devotee of the gold standard, which was generally unpopular in England. In supporting the Bretton Woods agreements before Parliament, Keynes argued that the Fund's par value system was just the opposite of the gold standard, while White told Congress that it was the gold standard. Perhaps Keynes thought that, unless *bancor* were tied to gold, the Clearing Union would never be acceptable to the U.S. government, and he was probably right. It would have been possible under the ICU to change the value of the dollar in terms of *bancor*, but this would have required a change in the gold content of the dollar, which could not have been made without congressional approval. The fundamental flaw in the IMF par value system was that it was virtually impossible to change the value of the standard in terms of all the other currencies. Ideally, the standard should have been a basket of currencies, such as the SDR, but the SDR was not invented until 1969.

By providing more authority for countries to change their par values and even requiring devaluations by countries running substantial debits as a condition for additional credits in the ICU, Keynes anticipated that the major problem of the early postwar period would not be competitive exchange depreciation but the unwillingness of countries to devalue. The Bretton Woods par value system was predicated on a more or less permanently strong U.S. balance of payments and the expectation that the dollar would never be devalued. In view of the fact that the dollar had been devalued a decade before, the economic pundits at Bretton Woods should have realized that one day the dollar would become overvalued. It is just as conceivable that, had a mechanism for changing the value of the standard been formulated in the IMF agreement, the par value system could have been preserved.

The Transition Period

White believed that, with the assistance of the Fund and the Bank, the world could launch into a multilateral foreign exchange and trading system with stable exchange rates almost immediately after the war. Keynes thought otherwise and argued strongly for a transition period during which members would be permitted to maintain restrictions on payments for current transactions. White gave in and agreed to a transition period, which was included in the joint statement and later as Article XIV in the final agreement. Article XIV provides that after five years members still retaining restrictions on current transactions must justify them to the Fund and be subject to expulsion if they denied the Fund's request to terminate the restrictions. There was an understanding between the American and British delegations that the Fund would limit drawings by those members retaining restrictions on current account transactions during the transition period. The transition period actually lasted about fifteen years before major currencies became convertible, and the Fund was largely inoperative during this period. Instead of using its resources and technical advice to assist members in restoring trade on a multilateral basis, the Fund simply shut down.

Keynes believed the Fund should be governed on a day-to-day basis by an international staff that was independent of the member governments, and that its executive directors would only meet occasionally, say, two or three times a year, to formulate general policies. Keynes maintained this position at both Bretton Woods and the inaugural meeting at Savannah in March 1946. This was consistent with his view that drawings from the Fund up to a fixed limit would not be conditioned on judgments regarding the correctness of the drawing members' economic policies. White's position was that the executive directors should operate full-time at the principal office of the Fund, should exercise their judgment on requests for drawings, and should maintain oversight on how members were living up to their obligations. It is difficult to believe that Keynes was not aware of the position of the U.S. government on this issue. It was true, of course, that the language of the Fund agreement is obscure on the matter of conditionality of drawings, but it should have been clear that implementation of the Fund agreement did not lend itself to a set of rules that could readily be applied by international civil servants. The implementation called for judgments in which important political interests of member governments were involved. The United States, at least, was unwilling to leave these judgments to civil servants. In this context, only representatives of governments working under instructions from their finance ministers should reach them.

The Bretton Woods Debates in Retrospect

How important were the issues I have discussed for the future of the IMF and of the international monetary system? Would a different outcome have mattered? In the longer run, I do not believe it would have made much difference since the principal functions of the Fund bear little resemblance to what was conceived at Bretton Woods. Western countries would very likely have abandoned exchange controls as incompatible with a world economy dominated by transnational corporations; the par value system would probably not have survived under either the White or the Keynes plan; the transition period was a transition to another universe; and the change in function from providing reserves for exchange rate stability to development assistance rendered the debate over conditionality irrelevant. Had Keynes won the argument for an international currency, multilateral world trade might have been established earlier and world recovery hastened. At least we might have heard less about the dollar shortage, a concept that economists helped to perpetuate.

In celebrating the fiftieth anniversary of Bretton Woods, how should we evaluate the products of what was probably the greatest assemblage of economic talent the world has ever seen? The charters of both institutions were technically flawed, were utterly unsuited for the immediate postwar problems, and were not designed for dealing with the major financial problems of the second half of this century. As Alexander Cairncross and Ray Vernon show in their papers in this volume, the charters reflected political objectives and constraints that took precedence over rational planning. Issues were often settled on the basis of what would be approved by the U.S. Congress or accepted by the British Parliament. There was an attempt to create institutions that would both serve the immediate postwar problems and provide a framework for long-term international monetary and financial policies—and the two objectives were in conflict. There was a lack of foresight regarding the nature of both the immediate postwar problems and the long-term economic and political environment. In view of these conditions, the longevity and expansion of the Fund and the Bank have been remarkable. I see two reasons for this. First, the reconciliation of the conflicts among participants resulted in sufficient ambiguity and flexibility to enable the institutions to adapt, however slowly, to the realities of emerging world conditions. Second, they had too much money to fail. They have continued to increase their assets and staffs throughout the postwar period. Their successful aggrandizement has been due in large measure to the fact that increases in financial resources do not require their members to make budgetary outlays. In the Fund, larger subscriptions are matched by larger reserves of the contributors. In the Bank, most of the increase in subscriptions is not paid in, but subject to call only if the Bank is unable to meet its debts. Because both institutions are now mainly sources of financing for developing countries, industrial countries can provide large amounts of multi-lateral aid with little economic or political pain. Ultimately, the value of the institutions lies in whether the world economy has been made better than it would have been without them. I can't answer this question. I *can* say that had the IMF and World Bank not been created in 1944 at Bretton Woods, it is highly unlikely they would have been established at all.

Notes

1. The material in this chapter is taken largely from Raymond F. Mikesell, "The Bretton Woods Debates: A Memoir," *Essays in International Finance*, no. 192 (Princeton: Princeton University International Finance Section, 1994).

2. Reproduced in *International Monetary Fund, 1945–1965*, vol. III (Washington, D.C.: International Monetary Fund, 1969), pp. 83–96.

3. Ibid.

4. *International Monetary Fund, 1945–1965*, vol. III, p. 134.

5. Ibid.

6. *International Monetary Fund, 1945–1965*, vol. I (Washington, D.C.: International Monetary Fund, 1969), p. 49.

7. *International Monetary Fund, 1945–1965*, vol. III, p. 60.

3

Reconstruction vs. Development: The IMF and the World Bank

Victor L. Urquidi

Early Notions

Looking back some fifty-odd years, it amazes me to realize how little we knew, in Mexico, of what was going on in international trade and finance, even before World War II. The Mexican economy during the 1920s had depended heavily on exports of crude oil and nonferrous minerals, and a few farm products, mostly to the United States. Petroleum exports had declined steadily after 1921, partly as a result of nationalistic policies deriving from the 1917 Constitution inspired by the Mexican Revolution. Zinc, lead, and copper concentrates hardly offset the loss of oil exports. External debt negotiations on Mexico's decades-long defaults were a prime contentious issue throughout the 1920s, to which was added the need to negotiate compensation for nationalized farmlands and, in 1938, the foreign-owned oil industry. As in many other developing nations, the steep fall in world commodity prices in the 1930s had deprived Mexico of much needed foreign exchange. Only exports of silver, mostly a byproduct of lead and zinc output, could be counted on to some extent, depending upon price support from the U.S. silver purchase legislation. The external financial institutions were hostile to Mexico, and no help was in sight from general world trade conditions.

Some alleviation, however, began to appear on the scene after the start of World War II, especially upon the passing of Lend-Lease legislation in the United States in 1941 and from the moment that President Roosevelt's administration openly supported the United Kingdom's war effort. Mexico's payments position began to improve noticeably in 1941 as prices of some basic products began to rise; it was also helped by an inflow of European refugee capital and a first, relatively small, loan from the U.S. Export-Import Bank. The central bank authorities, fearing shortages, encouraged an expansion in indispensable commodity imports. A modest increase in foreign exchange reserves took place in 1942–43, which in turn raised the specter of too much liquidity and severely tested the limited functions of the central bank.

This new situation was in sharp contrast to that which Mexico had experienced during the revolutionary period, particularly since 1913. During the civil war years, hyperinflation, capital flight, foreign exchange stringency, budget disorder, de facto depreciation, formal devaluations, and generalized uncertainty had prevailed. After 1921, when a semblance of order was established, mounting accrued interest on the defaulted nineteenth-century borrowings urgently required settlement with foreign creditors. Between 1942 and 1946, the bulk of the external debt, including interest overdue, was settled for ten cents on the dollar, and annual payments were accordingly resumed.[1] The agrarian and petroleum debts were also settled amicably, which cleared the way for expected new inflows of external capital.

As a young, recently graduated economist, I was far from being able to understand the inner and finer workings of the Mexican monetary and financial system. Essential data were fairly primitive and inadequate. However, I delved into whatever came my way or I could find in libraries, including accounts of Mexico's trade and finances before and after the 1910 Revolution. I also interviewed people with considerable local experience. Had we really been the first country to go off the gold standard in 1930? Had we not been through a steady de facto depreciation during the 1920s, which was merely recognized in 1930, and then practiced a "floating rate" for a while? Did Kemmerer's teachings make any sense for a country like Mexico? How were we specifically linked to the U.S. trade cycle? I did not find ready answers.

On the other hand, my modest training in money and banking and international trade issues, and my reading of the *World Economic Surveys* and other reports of the League of Nations, as well as books and articles on exchange restrictions and trade policies in Europe, provided me with a background that facilitated my taking a broader view. Quite early I joined and helped organize working groups in Mexico on the postwar outlook and on the prospects for the Latin American economies, and had access to books, studies, and reports that were beginning to appear in the United States and Great Britain. I also followed the U.S. financial press and read leading economic weeklies and academic journals, even some from the Far East. Colin Clark's *Conditions of Economic Progress* was a steady reference on development processes.

The prewar monetary stabilization agreement between the United States, Britain, and France had particularly attracted my attention, even as a student. I was also sensitive to the problem of commodity prices and agreements and to international economic relations in general. I could not help following international political events as well; my closeness to the Spanish Civil War and its implications had alerted me.

First Intimations

In June 1942, shortly after Mexico declared war on the Axis, the director of the Bank of Mexico, Eduardo Villaseñor, included me in the Mexican delegation that he was heading to an Inter-American Conference on Financial Cooperation and Control of Enemy Assets convened by the U.S. Treasury in Washington. This was to be my first international conference, and it was an eye-opener in more ways than that represented by the specific topic. In those days we had hardly any contact with Latin American central banks or universities. I was eager to meet colleagues from other countries in the region, for no other reason than as a child having lived for several years in Colombia, El Salvador, and Uruguay, when my father was the diplomatic representative of Mexico in those countries. In fact, I did meet many Latin American central bank officials and economists at the Washington conference, among them Felipe Pazos and some Venezuelans and others. I was thus able to learn directly of our shared concerns about possible postwar developments.

However, the outstanding event in my memory concerning 1942 is that at the closing dinner at the Mayflower Hotel I happened to sit next to Dr. Harry White. I was familiar with some of his academic writings, and I engaged readily in a lively conversation with him on postwar international monetary, banking, and trade matters. Dr. White invited me to visit him at his office in the Treasury Department the next day. After our conversation, I departed holding a mimeographed copy of his April 1942 *Preliminary Draft Proposal for a United Nations Stabilization Fund and a Bank for Reconstruction and Development of the United and Associated Nations*, marked "Strictly Confidential." He asked me to read it carefully, with the recommendation that I should not fail to relay its contents to the central bank and Ministry of Finance authorities I was in contact with in Mexico. I was unaware of the earlier ideas and preparations, which have recently been so charmingly related by Professor Raymond F. Mikesell.[2] I studiously read Dr. White's proposals for a Stabilization Fund and a Bank for Reconstruction and Development, which also included proposals to "organize and finance an international essential raw material development corporation" and an International Commodity Stabilization Corporation.

I had known already, by the way, of earlier proposals, made in 1890, 1901, and 1933 at the Pan-American conferences, to create a Pan-American (later "Inter-American") bank. At the 1933 conference held in Montevideo, Uruguay, Mexico had been especially active in promoting the idea. The recommendation adopted in 1933 was reaffirmed at the Buenos Aires Pan-American Conference of 1936, at the Lima conference of 1938, and at a meeting of foreign relations ministers in Panama in 1939, which decided to convene a meeting of ministers of finance in Guatemala to discuss the proposal. At this meeting, the Mexican delegation, headed by the undersecretary, Eduardo Villaseñor, resubmitted the proposal. As a result, the Pan-American Union was entrusted with arranging to have a basic agreement and statutes drawn up, which were signed in May 1940 by nine Latin American countries and the United States, but never ratified.[3]

The next step, which again ended in frustration, was taken at the Inter-American Conference at Bogotá in 1948, which transformed the Pan-American Union into the Organization of American States. At this conference, Mexico once more tried to obtain approval of the Inter-American bank proposal. This time, the disruption of the conference by the riots that followed the assassination of a Colombian political leader, and an outrageous competing proposal made with great bombast by Argentina, prevented any agreement from being reached, and even interfered with the discussion. Moreover, the U.S. delegation argued that the International Bank for Reconstruction and Development (World Bank) could fill the need and that the U.S. Congress was expected to approve a new allocation of funds to the Export-Import Bank for loans to Latin America. The U.S. delegation, indeed, also maintained a preference for creating a climate that would be favorable to foreign direct investment, which had been the position taken since 1945, and reiterated by the secretary of state, General George Marshall, in his opening speech.[4]

Six years later, in 1954, the notion was again revived, mainly by Chile, with help from the ECLA (Economic Commission for Latin America) secretariat, at the Inter-American Conference of Ministers of Finance held at Quitandinha, Brazil. A recommendation that an Inter-American bank be established was voted on by all countries present except the United States and Peru, whose chief delegates once more turned the idea down. Nevertheless, with the change in policy during the Eisenhower administration, the IDB (Inter-American Development Bank) at last came into existence in 1959!

Mexico's Study of the White and Keynes Plans

In the following months of 1942, at the Bank of Mexico we began to hear considerably more about postwar monetary plans. I thought it might be useful to publicize the U.S. Treasury's proposals, and wrote to ask Dr. White's permission; his reply came at once, making it clear, very politely, that the document was still confidential and that, in any event, new proposals would be advanced before long.

In fact, in January 1943 we heard of a second "preliminary draft," which apparently was communicated to governments in March and made public in April 1943, at the same time as the British white paper proposing the creation of an International Clearing Union, widely attributed to Lord Keynes. Mexico was officially asked to consider the White plan (the Keynes plan had not reached Mexico officially), and the Bank of Mexico and the National Development Bank (Nacional Financiera) duly undertook the study of the new draft.[5]

The director of the central bank soon asked the head of the Economic Research Department, Daniel Cosío-Villegas,[6] to make a thorough study of the White plan for presentation to the minister of finance, Eduardo Suárez. (We also considered the Keynes plan, as well as French and Canadian proposals that had come to our attention.) Cosío-Villegas requested that he be given the opportunity to spend a month at a comfortable hotel in Acapulco to carry out this study in isolation—that is, far from daily pressures—and that I be his direct assistant. What we produced—with appropriate breaks for a daily swim in the ocean and some good lobster meals—was a report dated June 15, 1943, entitled "El Proyecto Norteamericano de Estabilización Monetaria Internacional," marked "Strictly Confidential." The report started out by outlining the general international context and by pointing to the rather "immature" nature of the proposal, and then went on to a general analysis of the White plan and, finally, a series of detailed comments, clause by clause. Throughout our report we considered in particular Mexico's position with regard to the proposal. We added a full translation into Spanish, made by us, of the U.S. Treasury preliminary draft of April 1943.

On presentation of our report, a process of discussion followed involving a number of central-bank, Mexican Treasury, and other financial officials, which required, in addition, a careful consideration of legal and even political aspects. A Bank of Mexico official, Rodrigo Gómez—who attended Bretton Woods and in 1947 became the first Mexican executive director of the IMF—was soon involved in frequent consultations in Washington, and later attended the meetings leading up to the joint statement of 1944, the Atlantic City meeting, and finally Bretton Woods.

By then articles began to appear in the daily press and the weekly journals in Mexico, seminars were held, and, among other things, we benefited from visits of economists in the U.S. Treasury, the Federal Reserve Board, and the New York Fed, and occasionally from some of the Latin American central banks. An outstanding occasion was the visit, for several weeks in 1944, of Dr. Raúl Prebisch, the former general manager of the central bank of Argentina, whom we had first met in 1943 (we were already aware of this bank's excellent annual reports, and the deputy manager, Edmundo Gagneux, had been present at the Washington conference on enemy assets in 1942).

My own reward came when the minister of finance invited me to join the Mexican delegation to Bretton Woods as technical secretary. Cosío-Villegas and I traveled on a commercial airliner to New York—a twenty-one-hour trip in those days—and in Washington, D.C., we joined the rest of the delegation, among whom were Espinosa de los Monteros and Rodrigo Gómez.[7] I had regularly held long conversations with Gómez from the start, and his insight and practical experience turned out to be most valuable at all times and especially at the conference, where he was the main representative of the Bank of Mexico.

At several meetings with the minister of finance in Mexico City, the main positions to be taken by the delegation were discussed, and we were each allocated a committee or committees to attend at the conference. To my surprise, I learned that Mexico should strive to have silver recognized as a monetary metal and accepted by the IMF as part of authorized monetary reserves. I had at one point made a study of bimetallism and the role of silver, and was very doubtful about the proposal. Perhaps out of deference to Mexico and its interest in silver, the head of our delegation, Eduardo Suárez, was nominated as chairman of Commission III, and was asked moreover to make the speech nominating Henry Morgenthau as permanent president of the conference at the first plenary session.

We had also studied at the Bank of Mexico the proposals for the IBRD, or World Bank, and prepared comments and briefs for the minister of finance and the directors of the bank and of Nacional Financiera, and we reviewed the relevant literature, taking account of the earlier Inter-American bank initiative.

The Conference

This chapter is concerned with "Reconstruction vs. Development," but I must briefly mention one of Mexico's contributions to the IMF discussions, for they were relevant to Mexico's future trade position and, indirectly, to "development." Mexico argued at Commission III that, like gold, silver should be accepted as an international reserve, given its long history of being used as a monetary metal and as a regular form of savings ("hoarding" was the term used by the delegation). The outcome in Commission III was that the delegations politely rejected the notion that this was of any consequence to the postwar international monetary order, with a recommendation that the Final Act state: "Due to the shortage of time, the magnitude of the other problems on the agenda, and other limiting considerations, it was impossible to give sufficient attention to this problem at this time in order to make definite recommendations. However, it was the sense of Commission III that the subject should merit further study by the interested nations."[8]

It should be noted that trade matters, though mentioned in the opening speeches of the conference and discussed in committee, were not dealt with either, except for a general recommendation to governments that:

> . . . they seek, with a view to creating in the field of international economic relations conditions necessary for the attainment of the purposes of the Fund and of the broader primary objectives of economic policy, to reach agreement as soon as possible on ways and means whereby they may best: (1) reduce obstacles to international trade and in other ways promote mutually advantageous international commercial relations; (2) bring about the orderly marketing of staple commodities at prices fair to the producer and consumer alike; (3) deal with the special problems of international concern which will arise from the cessation of production for war purposes; and (4) facilitate by cooperative

effort the harmonization of national policies of Member States designed to promote and maintain high levels of employment and progressively rising standards of living.[9]

In quoting this recommendation, I am reminded that, in the early proposals by White and Keynes, much had been said about the need to encourage world trade and stabilize prices of basic products. Also, I remember sitting on a small committee at Bretton Woods until late in the night, arguing with other delegates about the importance of coordinating short-term policies among the main trading nations as a condition for achieving monetary stabilization—they must have realized I was still "wet behind the ears." However, in July 1994 I heard it said in Washington, on presentation of the Report of the Bretton Woods Commission, *Looking to the Future*,[10] that this was still an "impossible task" and certainly one that the IMF did not wish to be involved in.

I also recall that at the Drafting Committee of Commission II, of which I was a member, one of our colleagues (possibly Dean Acheson) suggested that in Article I, Paragraph 3, of the World Bank's charter there was *no* need to keep the additional phrase, "thereby assisting in raising productivity, the standard of living and conditions of labor in member countries" at the end of one of the stated purposes of the World Bank, which read, "[t]o promote the long-range balanced growth of international trade and the maintenance of equilibrium in balances of payments by encouraging international investment for the development of the productive resources of member countries *thereby assisting in raising productivity, the standard of living, and conditions of labor in member countries*"[11]—even though this phrase had already been accepted in Committee I in connection with the IMF. His argument was, first, that it was obvious, and second, that a similar purpose had already been assigned to the Fund (it was not identical—see below). However, Lionel Robbins of the United Kingdom, a former professor of mine at the London School of Economics, strongly insisted that the additional phrase be kept, "because my minister, Mr. Bevin, would be very unhappy if it were left out," and the Drafting Committee as a whole had to concur. Incidentally, somewhere along the way to the Final Act, apparently on July 19, the expression "conditions of labor in member countries" became "conditions of labor in their territories."[12]

In any event, in both the Fund and the Bank, the notion that they should contribute to the expansion of world trade was quite clear. In the case of the Fund, however, one of its approved purposes also referred to employment: "To facilitate the expansion and balanced growth of international trade, and to contribute thereby to the promotion and maintenance *of high levels of employment and real income* [italics added] and to the development of productive resources of all members as primary objectives of economic policy." In this respect, both the White and the Keynes plans had contained similar concepts.

Thus the notion of what some years back we named "development" was vaguely present at the creation, even though it is now fashionable in the IMF and other quarters to speak only of "growth," with post-Rio "sustained development" barely beginning to be accepted as a new objective. Over the years, and especially since the early 1980s, the IMF, however, seems to have forgotten what development is all about, and it no longer seems to be concerned with either "development" or "employment," or even "trade," but only with severe adjustment policies and "zero inflation," which seems to fascinate central bankers as an aim.

Returning to the question of silver, Mexico did achieve at least a passing mention of this metal in the IMF charter, as possible collateral security in cases where the Fund was entitled, at its discretion, to waive any of the conditions prescribed in Article V, Section 3 (a) relating to the use of the Fund's resources. Specifically, the Fund ". . . shall also take into consideration a member's willingness to pledge as collateral security gold, *silver* [italics added], securities, or other acceptable assets."[13] The Mexican delegation, through Antonio Espinosa de los Monteros, had argued that "silver-hoarding" countries, particularly those issuing coinage with a high silver content, should enjoy additional credit facilities from the Fund, "in an amount not exceeding 80 percent of the gold value of that country's silver hoardings, which will be assigned to the Fund as collateral guaranty."[14] Some delegations supported the idea, but the majority rejected it, with the result as noted. It was obviously not possible for Mexico to make special pleading for its silver bullion reserves and its silver coinage in circulation.

In the past, Mexico's money supply, made up very largely of silver coins, had suffered undue fluctuations when the price of silver on the world market, largely determined in the 1930s by U.S. policy, went up beyond the melting point. In later years, after Bretton Woods, Mexico ended up with a very large surplus of silver in its monetary reserves and found great difficulty in disposing of it because of wartime official ceiling prices and the large holdings of the U.S. Treasury, as well as the inability of European countries to return after the war to full silver coinage (for which some, like the Netherlands, had obtained Lend-Lease silver bullion and were pledged to return it). Most countries were shifting to alloys of a low silver content and other metals. In India and the Far East, currency restrictions prevented legal importation of precious metals, but did not stop a flourishing black market which had its source in the Middle East and perhaps among the London bullion brokers. The domestic market price of silver in India in 1947 was about 2.5 times the U.S. ceiling price. The Reserve Bank of India, which I visited that year, had already opted for alloyed coins. Later that year, as a result of contacts I had been instructed to start in Shanghai and Nanking, China nevertheless made a purchase of Mexican silver bullion for minting in Philadelphia, paid for by the U.S. government, for shipment to China—supposedly to help bring down galloping inflation. (We all should have known better!) A year or two later, Mexico made a modest deal with Saudi Arabia to coin rials in the Mexican mint. And that was the extent of Mexico's special trade in silver, until very recently. It was also, evidently, a trade issue and not merely a monetary one.

The Mexican delegation also submitted various amendments to the articles of the proposed Fund agreement regarding voting, the country quotas, and other points which need not be mentioned here.

Reconstruction vs. Development

It is evident that the proposal for creating the World Bank had as its major purpose the provision of a financial mechanism that would channel funding to Europe for reconstruction purposes. This appears in the early drafts; for example, the April 1942 proposal of Dr. White, where at some point the Bank was to be merely a "Bank for Reconstruction [*sic*] (title of Part III) to "provide capital for the economic reconstruction of the United Nations; facilitate a rapid and smooth transition from a war-time economy to a peace-time economy in the United Nations; supply short-term capital for the financing of trade among the United Nations—where such capital is not available at reasonable rates from private sources; and help strengthen the monetary and credit structures of the United and Associated Nations by redistributing the world gold supply."[15]

The above hardly strikes me as assuming that the Bank was to play an important role in development, however defined—quite apart from the strong hint of overlap with the proposed International Stabilization Fund. The text went on to mention among the purposes to "reduce the likelihood, intensity and duration of world-wide economic depressions," but also to "raise the productivity and hence the standard of living of the peoples of the United Nations" (not quite "development"), and even to "promote a greater degree of economic cooperation . . . [and] make easier the solution of many of the economic *and political* [italics added] problems that will confront the 'peace conference.'" Moreover, the Bank was to

> enhance the opportunity throughout the world for a healthy development of democratic institutions . . . help assure a distribution at fair prices of important scarce raw-materials . . . promote stability in prices of important commodities . . . [and] finally, . . . provide for the financing and distribution of foodstuffs, clothing, and other essential commodities that will be needed in large quantities for the relief of populations devastated by war conditions.

A few lines later, the text continued:

> . . . factories and public works will have to be rebuilt; hundreds of thousands of homes and farms will have to be rehabilitated; public utilities [and] transportation systems . . . will have to be reconstructed and improved. Millions of farmers will need to be supplied with seed, fertilizer, livestock, and new equipment.[16]

How was this to be achieved? "To supply this capital at rates of interest low enough with period of repayment long enough to give the borrowing country reasonable hope of being able to repay the loan, is the *prime task and justification* [italics added] for a Bank of the character described in this report."[17] And since "it must be recognized that private capital will not perform this function . . . only an international governmental organization can make such loans under the kind of conditions that would help promote and sustain prosperity rather than sow the seeds for future trouble." Combined operations of the Fund and the Bank were conceived to restore confidence in free exchanges and free withdrawal of profits, and thus pave the way for "foreign investments [that] will take the form more likely of branch plants, complete ownership of mines, factories, and plantations," and at a later stage "for loans to governments, to municipalities, and finally to foreign corporations."[18]

Whatever the merits of these ideas, it is quite apparent that "development" of the less developed nations was not to be one of the primary purposes of the Bank as outlined by White, though some recognition was given to the role of private direct investment. In any event, none of what followed in the White proposals of 1942 had anything to do with development, and there was much extraneous material for instance on note issues by the Bank in a "new international currency," on examples of trade between "Massachusetts and Mexico," on the foreign-exchange transactions of an American tourist going to Mexico. Incidentally, White opposed the idea that a new international unit could be used as a supplement to local currency to facilitate international trade and finance.[19] (The IMF still refuses to make special supplementary issues of special drawing rights [SDRs] to developing countries.) The Bank also was seen by White as a clearinghouse, and was even "to perform virtually the same services for the participating governments that a central bank performs for the banks within a country," plus organizing international corporations to "promote the exploitation of natural resources in distant areas" (meaning the colonies of European nations), and establishing an International Commodity Stabilization Corporation.[20] A tall order indeed! As Robert Oliver has said, there is "no doubt that White was thinking in terms of a world central bank."[21] And, one might add, many other things as well.

The Keynes plan for an International Clearing Union included similar notions, with emphasis on reconstruction of war-torn territories, although among its purposes mention was also made, for instance, of "investment aid, both medium and long-term, for countries whose *economic development* [italics added] needs assistance from outside," and a creditor country was to be encouraged, among other things, to make "international development loans."[22] However, it is not evident that this last provision referred to the less developed countries, and in any event the Clearing Union was thought of mainly as a mechanism to provide an international currency, regulate exchange rates, and help reestablish short-term balance-of-payments equilibrium.

No specific proposals were made by Keynes for the creation of an international bank such as the early White report had advanced. However, the union might also be made responsible, it was suggested, for other functions, including financing of postwar relief, rehabilitation, and reconstruction; the preservation of peace and the maintenance of international order; some kind of technical support for a Board of International Investment; financing of stocks of commodities held by an international body; and influencing policies to "combat the evils of the Trade Cycle." Moreover, the union "might become the pivot of the future economic government of the world."[23]

No wonder a modest delegation such as that of Mexico was not too sure what the Bank proposals were all about. They seemed rather unstructured and in parts obscure. No one could deny the importance of dealing somehow with European reconstruction once the war was over, but the main long-range concern of a then-developing or less developed nation was obviously with the financing of development rather than of reconstruction, although European postwar recovery would be essential also, on many grounds.

The Mexican delegation thus arrived at Bretton Woods ready to inject some interest in economic development issues into the debate. The IBRD proposals as finally submitted by the U.S. Treasury in late 1943 seemed more readily understandable, and were more akin to the kind of institution in which a country like Mexico could participate and also gain access to long-term loans and, at some eventual stage, to capital markets. Mexico also foresaw a difficult transition to a peacetime economy, and, in addition to looking to the IMF for short-term support in that transition, was interested in pursuing at least the expansion of its development infrastructure.

It should be recalled that no one, certainly not the Mexican delegation, could imagine during 1942–44 that a specific Marshall Plan would arise in 1947–48 to deal with the "reconstruction problem." Thus at Bretton Woods it was a delicate matter to try to clarify the "development interest" of an Allied nation which was making a contribution, albeit small, to the war effort, but was looking essentially to the postwar development of its own territory and for its own people, assuming that the major Allied nations would deal out of their own resources with the reconstruction issues. Mexico had its mind on foreign loans for highways, electricity, irrigation, and possibly other aspects of infrastructure and general financial support for industrial and agricultural expansion.[24]

The Mexican delegation, from the outset, thought that Article III of the proposed IBRD charter needed clarification on the subject of development. Article III, Section 1, on Use of Resources Restricted (*sic*) stated: "The resources and the facilities of the Bank shall be used exclusively for the benefit of members." On July 10, our delegation submitted Alternative B, which added to the above sentence a second paragraph as follows: "The Bank shall give equal consideration to projects for development and to projects for reconstruction, and its resources and facilities shall always be made available to the same extent for either kind of project."[25]

Lord Keynes, in his opening speech on July 3 at the first meeting of Commission II, which he had been nominated to chair, had at least made some remarks that encouraged us to be so bold. True, he started out by referring to "loans to the countries of the world which have suffered from the devastation of the war, to enable them to restore their shattered economies and replace the instruments of production which have been lost or destroyed." However, he continued:

> It is likely . . . that the field of reconstruction from the consequences of the war will mainly occupy the proposed Bank in its early years. But as soon as possible, and with increasing emphasis as time goes on, there is a second primary duty laid upon it, namely, to develop the resources and productive capacity of the world, with special attention to the less developed countries, to raise the standard of life and the conditions of labour everywhere, to make the resources of the world more fully available to all mankind, and so to order its operations as to promote and maintain equilibrium in the international balances of payments of all member countries.[26]

The head of the Mexican delegation, Minister of Finance Eduardo Suárez, approved our proposed amendment and asked Cosío-Villegas and me to draft a statement to be read at the corresponding session. As transcribed in a press release, it read in part:

> It is very far from our purpose to place obstacles in the way of reconstruction. . . . We are fully aware of the damage that the war has done to the productive capacity of our Allies in Europe and Asia. We are no less aware of the direct sacrifices undergone by all these nations. . . . Our reasons for asking you to provide that "reconstruction" and "development" be put on the same footing are threefold:
>
> First, we believe the agreement we are to reach here is to be embodied in a permanent, and not in a provisional international instrument. . . . In the long run, Mr. Chairman—before we are all too dead, if I may say so—development must prevail if we are to sustain and increase real income everywhere. . . .
>
> Secondly, we believe that we and other nations not actually in need of funds for reconstruction can greatly assist in the reconstruction of those who necessitate it, provided our economies be developed more fully at the same time as the rehabilitation of the war-torn nations takes place. . . . If we tackle [our domestic problems]—and for that we require sums of capital we do not dispose of at home—we will undoubtedly benefit not only ourselves but the world as a whole, and particularly the industrial nations, in that we shall provide better markets for them and better customers. . . .
>
> Third and last, . . . it is our considered opinion that in contributing part of [our unprecedented holdings of gold and foreign exchange] . . . to the Bank, for the benefit of all nations constituting it, we should desire at least an assurance that our requests for capital for development purposes shall . . . be given equal consideration as is given to reconstruction projects, and, further, the assurance that the resources and facilities of the Bank shall always be made available to the same extent for either kind of project. . . .

> We do wish to make it perfectly clear, however, Mr. Chairman, that we do not desire to impose on the Bank a rigid fifty-fifty rule. . . . we do not contemplate a rigid interpretation of the phrase "to the same extent."[27]

Because my English was better than Cosío-Villegas's, though far from entirely correct (English, by the way, was the only official working language and no simultaneous interpretation was available), I had drafted this statement myself, and read it out. My recollection is that two delegations immediately supported us, Peru and Norway, but there followed a silence. Keynes at one point shoved his eyeglasses to the tip of his nose, shuffled some papers and other proposed amendments in front of him, and said something like this: "With regard to the amendment submitted by Mexico, I should think it can be made shorter and can be adopted substituting equitable consideration for equal consideration." Thus it was approved to read: "The resources and the facilities of the Bank shall be used exclusively for the benefit of members with equitable consideration to projects for development and projects for reconstruction alike."[28]

At a fifty-year distance, this may seem rather too subtle or perhaps unnecessary, since obviously Europe's reconstruction was not to take twenty-five or even fifteen years to achieve. However, the immediate effect of Keynes's elegant solution to the problem seemed important, for as I have tried to show, development did not seem to be clearly in the minds of the early authors of the proposal for the IBRD or of the delegations of most of the industrialized countries. Nor did the message from President Roosevelt mention development, though it referred to the need for "a dynamic and soundly expanding world economy" and for living standards to be "advanced."[29]

Morgenthau's address on being elected president of the conference also emphasized the "creation of a dynamic world economy" and, toward the end, stated: "For long-range reconstruction purposes, international loans on a broad scale will be imperative . . . [as well as] . . . loans to provide capital for economic reconstruction . . . [and] . . . an International Bank for Postwar Reconstruction [*sic*]."[30] Nothing was said about "development."

In his closing address on July 22 at the last plenary session, after a reference to "long-term financial aid" for reconstruction, Morgenthau added: "Long-term funds must be made available also to promote sound industry and increase agricultural and industrial production in nations whose economic potentialities have not yet been developed. . . . They must be enabled to produce and sell if they are to be able to purchase and consume. The Bank for International Reconstruction and Development [*sic*, Development now included] is designed to meet this need." Moreover, in an attempt to clarify that the Bank would not "restrict the investment sphere in which bankers could engage," he went on to say that "the chief purpose of the Bank . . . is to guarantee private loans made through the usual investment channels. It would make loans only when these could not be floated through the normal channels at reasonable rates. The effect would be to provide capital for those who need it at lower interest rates than in the past and to drive away the usurious money lenders from the temple of international finance"(!)[31]

Keynes, who had chaired Commission II on the Bank and had hinted at some interest in the "less developed countries," did not refer to development in his final words at the plenary. The record shows, however, that the term, as an isolated word, did creep into the closing speeches of the delegation heads of the Soviet Union, France, and Cuba (but not Brazil or Norway).

A Rapid Transition from Reconstruction to Development

Apart from the rhetoric in the statements quoted, what is evident is that the concept of *development* was practically absent. The concerns of Mexico, and I am sure of many others among the less developed nations represented at the conference, seemed justified.

On my way back from a brief post–Bretton Woods visit to Canada to study the exchange control system (in case we should have to establish exchange restrictions in Mexico at the end of the war), I had been invited to give a talk at a graduate student seminar at the Littauer School at Harvard University. I had not reread my improvised text until quite recently. I began by reminding the audience that, according to Colin Clark's calculations, Latin America (except for Argentina and Uruguay) was well within the lowest category but one of income per head in the world, productivity was low, and we showed every feature of underdevelopment. We needed to raise farm productivity and widen our domestic markets as a basis for industrialization, for which we required "investment for development purposes, better technique, and more education." I saw all this as an argument for obtaining foreign assistance, since "it is not in the interest of capital exporting countries that we curl up in our shell and shut ourselves off from the rest of the world . . . nor in our own interests." I did not see private investment alone as doing the job, given the need for social reforms. Dependency was high on foreign markets for primary products and on "full employment levels" of activity in the industrialized countries; however, external market prices fluctuated considerably and there was uncertainty about the prospects. I saw Latin American development as long overdue, and I was skeptical about relying on U.S. trade policy and uncertain about "the U.S. balance-of-payments–full-employment situation." I feared that, unfortunately, the Bank for Reconstruction and Development (I actually said that "one almost forgets to add this word") would place "too little emphasis on development" and that its operations "would be mostly to supplement private investors . . . instead of lending its own money," whereas we were "by no means sure of being able to resort to private capital on reasonable terms"; among other things, "investors . . . will be after profits, or lower corporation taxes, but [would not be] interested in our organic development or industrialization as a whole." I was also disappointed in "some of the Bank's features: reconstruction vs. development, limitations on loans, approval of lending country." The Bank agreement "was undoubtedly useful and valuable to the world, but as an international investment institution it [did] not come to grips with the real problems."

I thought in addition that development and long-term investment should not take place in a haphazard manner, but should be planned with a view to "best utilization of natural resources; best utilization of manpower and better distribution of population; better distribution of income; equalization of living standards; strengthening of balance-of-payments positions," and that "plans for investment must include compensatory spending in times of loss of export markets and be coordinated with them." Finally, I argued for "inter-American coordination: . . . no unnecessary duplication of industries; tariff unions or preferential treatment, regional or continental; study of price effects of Latin American industrial production on imports of products from other countries in the region." I also asked: What was the scope of government planning; did private enterprise really exist in Latin America; was it not government-aided, monopolistic, etc.; should foreign trade be planned, at any rate regulated?

I recall that the Latin American graduate students present seemed to share some of my views, but also that Professor Gottfried Haberler was analytically critical, of course, in a most friendly way.

These were our fears and concerns in 1944. By 1948, with congressional approval of the Marshall Plan—which the president of the World Bank, John J. McCloy, supported in testimony to the U.S. Congress but called "a tight fit"—it became clear that the IBRD, nevertheless, was to start emphasizing the "D" in its name. But in April 1948, at the Bogotá Inter-American conference of the OAS, General Marshall stated in no uncertain terms—as William Clayton before him in early 1945 at the Inter-American Conference on Problems of War and Peace (the Chapultepec Conference)—that there would be no public funds for Latin American development, and that free trade and foreign private investment should do the job. Ambiguity and confusion were the hallmarks of development policy, then as now.[32]

First Loans to Latin America

The IBRD had already made, in 1947, three loans for "Reconstruction" (thus specified), notably to Denmark ($40 million), France ($250 million), and the Netherlands ($91 million), and a loan to Australia that probably had some similar purpose. Quite independently, in 1947–48, four Latin American countries, Brazil, Chile, El Salvador, and Mexico, submitted loan requests to the Bank for electric power development. The loan to Chile was approved in March 1948, in the amount of $13.5 million to the state-owned electric power company, at 4.5 percent interest.

Brazil's loan application came, oddly enough, from a Canadian transnational corporation which owned power plants, waterworks, the telephone service, and the streetcars in Rio de Janeiro and São Paulo. Bank officials, mostly seconded from U.S. and European commercial and investment banks, and from the Bank of England, thought very highly of the possibility of supporting the private sector; however, a failure to negotiate with the Brazilian government on the assumption that a local lawyer could readily obtain the necessary official guarantee gave rise to considerable delays and difficult revisions, until a $75 million loan, at 4.5 percent interest, was finally approved in January 1949, cosigned by the government of Brazil.

Mexico in turn had submitted a long-range electric power development plan, for which a loan was requested for a hydroelectric system being constructed by a public agency, the Federal Electricity Commission; almost simultaneously a U.S. electricity corporation with investments in Mexico, headed at the time by a former U.S. ambassador to Mexico, presented a separate request for improvement and expansion of its own facilities. The outcome of Mexico's two loan applications was approval by the Bank of both requests: that of the FEC in January 1949 for $24.1 million, and that of the Mexlight Company in April 1950 for $26 million, both at 4.5 percent, for a total of some $50 million. However, there was a condition: the loan to the U.S. company be channeled through the Mexican governmental agency, since Mexico planned to develop a national power grid, and, moreover, electricity rates, a touchy subject also in Brazil, were controlled by the government. This threw some doubt on the capacity of the private company to service the loan, but in any event the Mexican government gave its guarantee. (In 1960, by the way, Mexico nationalized all privately owned electric power companies.)

A loan for electric power development was also approved for a state-owned enterprise in El Salvador, in December 1949, for $12.5 million at 4¼ percent interest. (Was El Salvador a better risk?)[33]

"Development" in the Bank's Context

At that first stage, during October 1947 to May 1949, I was a staff member of the Bank, first in the Loan Department, where I was in charge of economic research in the so-called Eastern Latin American Division, and later in the Economic Department. We had little contact with the "Western" Latin American Division, and moreover, as a Mexican, I was not supposed to know what was going on in the negotiations with Mexico. During that period I was able to sense the reluctance of the Bank to get involved in discussions at the United Nations on general development issues and on UN proposals for the financing of development which had been brought up at the UN Economic and Social Council. And, within my "geographical" sphere, I also met a refusal among the policy-making staff of the Bank to even entertain inquiries from Colombia as to the possible financing of the expansion of a government-owned steel plant.

In 1948, there was much hesitation in the Bank about an approach that Venezuela had made regarding possible loans for a long-term development plan that would ultimately make Venezuela less dependent upon oil. The Bank staff's argument was that Venezuela, being a major exporter of crude oil and having "no balance-of-payments problem," did not require such long-term loans. In any case, it was decided to respond by sending a loan officer to obtain direct information from the Venezuelan government. Quite by accident—for I was no longer in the Loan Department—I was asked at the last minute to join the loan officer in Caracas to gather data and assist him in his contacts. I eventually drafted a report for the Economic Department reviewing Venezuela's development experience and outlining why that country might require long-term loans for infrastructure as well as for industrial and agricultural development in spite of its petroleum assets and its oil exports. As I remember, only Paul Rosenstein-Rodan in the Economic Department, Antonin Basch, who was then my immediate boss, and Vittorio Marrama and Sven Andersen, my colleagues, showed much interest in this report. A little later, shortly after it was approved by the director of the Economic Department, a military coup d'état took place in Venezuela. The report apparently was never presented to the new government, but I recall that copies circulated among some of the deposed cabinet members in exile for future reference.

My next encounter with development and the IBRD occurred after I had decided to resign from the Bank staff—after going through two internal reorganizations and feeling I had better return to Mexico to work on Mexican issues rather than carry out inconsequential studies, such as one on the trade position of the British colonies. In August 1949, I joined the Mexican Ministry of Finance to help start a meaningful classification of public expenditures as an element in the preparation of the national accounts which had been undertaken by the Bank of Mexico. One evening in Mexico in 1950, I suggested to Fred Consolo, of the World Bank's Loan Department, on one of his periodic visits, that a new approach to Mexico might be to engage in a fairly comprehensive study of development issues and the need for foreign capital to supplement local financing, and that rather than have a bank mission carry out the study, a combined bank and Mexican government commission might be set up to do the evaluation. He proposed this idea to the director of the Development Bank (Nacional Financiera), Antonio Carrillo Flores, who accepted it, and once it was cleared both at the bank and in the Mexican government, a combined working party was established in April 1951, composed of Raúl Ortiz Mena and myself on the Mexican side, and Albert Waterston and Jonas Haralz on the bank side. We jointly drew up a detailed agenda and set to work. This led to an exhaustive review and elaboration of data in Mexico, interviews, and endless discussion and drafting, until a report was submitted to both the director of Nafin, and through him to the minister of finance as well as to the World Bank.

This report was published in English two years later as *The Economic Development of Mexico*,[34] but draft copies were available in English and in Spanish by late 1951, which were useful in Mexico in outlining a strategy for external borrowing in the next administration (1952–58). The only specific recommendation made in the report was that an autonomous technical group be set up by the Mexican government to follow up the work of the combined working party, with a view to taking measures to formulate an economic development program, including the coordination of public investment and its financing under presidential approval. We thought the study had enough information and guidance in it to help the government adopt an overall development program. For a number of years this worked fairly well, and subsequently led to a more formal agency in charge of programming and the budget. The report also involved compiling the first statistical tables, 1939–51, on public-sector investments, including the main parastatal enterprises and their sources of domestic and external financing, and included objective reviews of Mexico's principal development issues, sector by sector, and the policies being pursued in agriculture, petroleum and mining, electric power, transportation, industry, education and health, and public finance. Each sector came under close scrutiny, with implications for improvement clearly stated.

From around 1950 through the 1970s, the World Bank became much more intellectually involved in development issues as its operations expanded, and gave substantial support to development programs and plans in a number of countries in Asia, Latin America, and Africa. The bank also established the International Development Association (IDA) and the International Finance Corporation (IFC), and the Development Institute for training purposes, and engaged in vast research on issues from industrial structure to agriculture, population, urban growth, education, and health, and most recently the questions of poverty and environment. It is not the purpose of this chapter to cover that period, nor to judge it.

The IMF in Relation to Trade and Development

As to the IMF, which was given to me as part of the title of this paper, and which, quite rightly, from the start was linked in the early proposals to both international trade and international investment, I have pointed above, in the discussion on silver, to the indirect support that trade in a given staple commodity could give to the payments position of a country and to the fulfillment of the Fund's objectives with respect to exchange rate stability, elimination of restrictions, orderly adjustment of parities, and so on.

Both White and Keynes had a broad view of world trade, its problems and its potentials, and of the need to have a dynamic, expanding world economy—in strong contrast to the experience of the 1930s depression and to the phase of intricate trade and payments restrictions of the late 1930s. On the other hand, they did not seem to have a clear idea of the usually quite different structural problems of the less developed countries vis-à-vis the then-industrialized countries, and thought of the former mostly as providers of raw materials and holders of abundant natural resources. The phrase "prosperity is indivisible," found in many of the Bretton Woods pronouncements, was not much more than a platitude applied at a high degree of aggregation, for development not only implied catching up in terms of what the industrialized countries had achieved over decades in productive capacity, use of technology, and provision of rising living standards; it also meant, for many economists and other social scientists in developing countries, a series of structural changes that could help to break down or weaken the historical, institutional, social, and political resistances to change that stood in the way of those apparently smoother processes that had operated in the past in the more advanced countries.

The IMF proposal, useful as it could undoubtedly be in helping to achieve an expanding volume of world trade and employment, could not have been meant to contribute directly to development. Nevertheless, it could be counted on to assist indirectly, for instance, by reducing risks to new domestic and international investment, by giving more certainty to ordinary business transactions, by restoring confidence in the "key" currencies, as Professor John Williams called them, and by improving generally the international financial atmosphere. One should not forget that the IMF was seen by many as a super-central bank, and central banks have never been known to be concerned with much more than the short-term monetary, financial, and trade outlook. During the IMF discussions, so far as I can recall, specific references to development were not made.

Nor indeed was much said specifically about the role of the IMF in reconstruction—though this question was uppermost in the minds of all delegates to Bretton Woods, who thought IMF intervention to be essential in the immediate postwar situation in order to realign currencies, help hold down inflation, eliminate distortions such as those caused by inconvertible sterling and other currency balances, and remove the accompanying exchange controls and quantitative restrictions, the rationing of domestic investment funds, and a host of wartime economic regulations. The aim was to return to free exchange markets, free trade, and unhampered capital movements, with a substitute, slightly watered-down gold-exchange standard as the pivot of a new international monetary system. Reconstruction was seen as a necessarily costly financial support for the war-devastated countries which would require long-term funds—hence the Bank—but which also had to be shored up with short-term support of the currencies. Once reconstruction was achieved, the IMF, various degrees of transition notwithstanding, could concentrate on its basic functions. (The IMF soon had to accept the role of European institutions in settling among themselves the currency-stability and exchange-rate issues.)

Conclusion

In the early years, there seemed to be very little consultation or even communication between the Fund and the Bank; on the contrary, a certain jealousy prevailed. Although some of us participated in Bank-Fund car pools in Washington, during which interesting conversations took place—for instance, on events in a number of Latin American countries—my recollection is that, on a more formal basis, contact and coordination between Bank and IMF staff was not particularly encouraged. In evaluating the electric power project in Brazil, we tried in the Bank to size up the financial, monetary, and fiscal situation and prospects in that country, but we could not go very far on our own and we did not get much help from the Fund. The Bank's "bottom line" in judging a project was the "times earned column" on a spreadsheet, that is, the factor by which the income expected to be earned on the new investment project in the borrowing country would cover year by year the amortization and interest payments on the loan. Considerations about general development issues—the role of, say, electric power development in triggering other domestic or foreign investments and raising productivity, employment, and real wages—were not seen by the prevailing "bankers' mentality" as particularly interesting. And exchange rates and the like were a matter best left to the IMF staff to write about.

Again, within the scope of this chapter, I am not looking back beyond the initial stages of the Bretton Woods institutions, but I cannot help ending on a note of cautious optimism: What would have happened had they not been brought into existence? But I also end on a feeling that much more could have been done. A historic opportunity was missed even at the beginning (and especially after the fleeting "reconstruction period" of the Bank gave way to gradual immersion in world development), which would have required much more interinstitutional coordination and a closer relationship with many more of the UN specialized agencies. What was needed, above all, was as clear a vision for the future of *developing countries* as, for instance, John McCloy held of *European* reconstruction when he left the Bank to become U.S. high commissioner for Germany.

Notes

1. During the 1920s, attempts to negotiate a settlement and resume payments had twice failed under pressure from the Committee of Bankers and because of the deteriorating trade and fiscal outlook.

2. Raymond F. Mikesell, "The Bretton Woods Debates: A Memoir," *Essays in International Finance*, no. 192 (Princeton: Princeton International Finance Section, 1994).

3. See, for example, Eduardo Villaseñor, "The Inter-American Bank: Prospects and Dangers," *Foreign Affairs* 20, no. 1 (October 1941): pp. 165–174; and "El Banco Interamericano" in *Ensayos Interamericanos*, Ediciones Cuadernos Americanos 8 (1944).

Mention of the Guatemala proposal is made in Robert W. Oliver, "Early Plans for a World Bank," *Princeton Studies in International Finance*, no. 29 (Princeton: Princeton International Finance Section, 1971), p. 24, n. 34, where, however, the authorship seems to be attributed to Dr. Harry White and others, whereas it clearly came from the Mexican delegation at Guatemala. White and his colleagues, however, undoubtedly contributed by participating in the Pan-American Union meeting to draw up the statutes in 1940.

4. An account of what happened at the Bogotá conference can be found in Eduardo

Villaseñor, *Memorias—Testimonios* (Mexico: Fondo de Cultura Económica, 1974), pp. 127–138, and particularly in the report by the author, who attended the conference as a Mexican delegate, entitled "El Banco Interamericano en la Conferencia de Bogotá," reproduced on pp. 323–338 of his memoirs.

5. The director of Nacional Financiera, Antonio Espinosa de los Monteros, had been a classmate of White at Harvard. At Bretton Woods, White referred to him as "Tony."

6. Cosío-Villegas had spent some time doing postgraduate work in agricultural economics at Harvard University, and had also been to the University of Michigan. He had also carried out research on trade policy in the Ministry of Finance, been on the Mexican delegation to the Montevideo conference of the Pan-American Union, attended League of Nations economic committees, and been financial attaché of the Mexican Embassy in Washington.

7. The full list of delegates can be seen in *United Nations Monetary and Financial Conference. Provisional List of Delegates and the Officers of the Conference, Bretton Woods, New Hampshire, July 1944* (Washington, D.C.: Department of State, 1945); and in *Proceedings and Documents of the United Nations Monetary and Financial Conference, Bretton Woods, New Hampshire, July 1–22, 1944,* vols. I–III (Washington, D.C.: Department of State, 1945); also of interest, "Representation of Delegations on Commissions and Committees 403–421" (Doc. 247) in *Proceedings,* pp. 403–321.

8. *Proceedings,* vol. I, Final Act (Doc. 492), Resolution IV, p. 939.

9. *Proceedings,* vol. I, Final Act, Resolution VII, p. 941.

10. Bretton Woods Commission, *Bretton Woods: Looking to the Future* (Washington, DC: Bretton Woods Commission, 1994).

11. *Proceedings,* vol. I, Art. I, para. 3, p. 568 (Doc. 340), July 12, 1944.

12. *Proceedings,* vol. I, Art. I, para. (3), p. 838 (Doc. 468), July 19, 1944, which became para. (iii), p. 1050 (Doc. 505), July 21, 1944.

13. *Proceedings,* vol. I, Final Act, Article V, Section 4, p. 949 (Doc. 492).

14. *Proceedings,* vol. II, "Statement by the Delegation of Mexico," p. 1157 (Doc. 135).

15. H. D. White, assistant to the secretary, U.S. Treasury Department, "Preliminary Draft Proposal," April 1942, mimeographed, p. III–1.

16. Ibid., pp. III–2 and III–3.

17. Ibid., p. III–3.

18. Ibid., pp. III–3 and 4.

19. Ibid., pp. III–14 to 27.

20. Ibid., pp. III–29 to 36.

21. Robert Oliver, "Early Plans for a World Bank," p. 47.

22. *Proceedings,* vol. II, International Clearing Union, pp. 1549 and 1556.

23. *Proceedings,* vol. II, pp. 1569 and 1570.

24. The failure of attempts to establish an Inter-American bank made it all the more important that the IBRD should not concentrate on reconstruction loan operations only (see above, section 1).

25. *Proceedings,* vol. I, pp. 373–374.

26. *Proceedings,* vol. I, pp. 36–38.

27. *Proceedings,* vol. II, pp. 1175–1177 (Doc. 306).

28. *Proceedings,* vol. I, Article III, Section 1 (a), p. 1053.

29. *Proceedings,* vol. I, p. 71.

30. *Proceedings,* vol. I, pp. 80, 82–83.

31. *Proceedings,* vol. I, pp. 1118–1119.

32. See also the treatment of the Inter-American bank proposal, mentioned above in Section 2.

33. Data on the amounts of the loans and dates of approval taken from World Bank,

Seventeenth Annual Report, 1961–1962, Appendix K, "Statement of Loans," June 30, 1962 (Washington, D.C.: World Bank, 1962).

34. Combined Working Party of the Mexican government and the World Bank, *The Economic Development of Mexico* (Baltimore: Johns Hopkins University Press, 1953). The Spanish language edition was Raúl Ortiz Mena, Víctor L. Urquidi, Albert Waterston y Jonas H. Haralz, *El desarrollo económico de México y su capacidad para absorber capital del exterior* (Mexico: Nacional Financiera, 1953).

4

The U.S. Government at Bretton Woods and After

Raymond Vernon

Introduction

Since the development of the Bretton Woods institutions during World War II, the United States has played a distinctive role in international economic affairs. Two characteristics of that role have been especially evident. First, the officials who direct the executive branch of the U.S. government, exercising a power of initiative that is uncommon in national governments, have been among the richest generators of proposed projects for intergovernmental economic cooperation. Second, despite the source of these initiatives, the final position of the United States after negotiations over such proposals has typically been much more constrained, especially avoiding provisions that seemed significantly to narrow U.S. policy choices in the future. That pattern, visible in the development of the Bretton Woods institutions, could be seen again and again in the negotiations that filled later decades. The typical role of the U.S. government in international economic issues during this period, therefore, can fairly be described in these terms: often creative, usually benign, sometimes magnanimous, but not prepared in the end substantially to constrain its policy options as part of any scheme for international economic cooperation.

The pattern, as I have suggested, has not been fortuitous. It stems from the exceptional structure of the U.S. government. This is a structure that gives ambitious and creative officials plenty of leeway in the development and early promotion of creative ideas, often permitting them to introduce their ideas for discussion in international forums. But, in the end, these ideas are obliged to run the gauntlet created by an elaborate system of checks and balances inside the U.S. political structure; and in the process, any measures that would seem to tie the hands of the Congress or the courts have usually been cut back or abandoned.[1]

The diffusion of power inside the U.S. government runs very deep, and it was as evident half a century ago as it is today. That characteristic was easily apparent in the decade of the 1930s leading up to the outbreak of World War II, a decade whose events set the stage for the Bretton Woods negotiations.

Prelude to Bretton Woods

In the decade before the creation of the Bretton Woods institutions, the United States faced a series of grave crises, including the Great Depression and the beginning of World War II. Yet, in spite of the unusual nature of the period, some endemic characteristics of U.S. policy making continued to shine through. Throughout the various administrations of Franklin D. Roosevelt, one had a continuous sense of creativity coupled with inconsistency, and leading to outcomes that avoided any impairment of the autonomous powers of the United States.

Numerous scholars, friends, and critics have examined microscopically President Roosevelt's values, tactics, and strategies.[2] There is wide agreement on a number of critical points that help to explain his complex and confusing role in the 1930s. There is not much doubt of Roosevelt's liberal international outlook, reinforced by his earlier association with the Wilson administration and with the northeast liberal wing of the Democratic party.[3] But it is also clear that he and his immediate advisers in the early stages of the New Deal saw the root causes of the Great Depression in the United States as primarily domestic, not international.[4]

In the first few years of the New Deal, Roosevelt was operating in a national environment that was largely turned inward. Workers were preoccupied with the high levels of unemployment, the lack of social security, and the lack of protection for the rights of organized labor. In the conviction that the heart of his problems lay in the domestic economy, Roosevelt refused to let his liberal international outlook divert him from what he perceived as his main task. Accordingly, the U.S. delegation to the London Economic Conference, meeting in the summer of 1933 to discuss joint efforts at battling the world depression, was kept under a tight rein from Washington; and in the end Roosevelt, in a personal message to the assembled conferees, destroyed any hope of cooperative international action.[5]

Roosevelt's seeming inconsistencies arose in part from his determination to do something drastic about the high levels of unemployment. But that determination was not attached to any overriding ideology such as was common for political parties in the European democracies. "The country needs," he said, "and, unless I mistake its temper, the country demands, bold persistent experimentation."[6] If Roosevelt had been driven by an explicit ideology, the range of innovative proposals that sprang unbidden out of the sprawling executive branch might have been narrower and less heterogeneous. But without obvious preferences for the means by which to achieve economic recovery, the innovations that were proposed by Roosevelt's team of officials were enormously diverse.[7]

Roosevelt's administration experimented with national planning through a National Recovery Administration, which fostered a series of dirigiste industry codes, replete with price-fixing and production-sharing; and for a year or more, any ideas inside the administration for economic cooperation with other countries were brushed aside.[8] But soon, some elements in organized labor were worrying that the NRA structure had been captured by big business, while many businessmen were convinced that the structure was under the control of labor.[9] Besides, the approach offended the general sense of many Americans, visible in their antitrust tradition, that too much power rested in too few hands. So the Supreme Court's decision in 1935 that the program was unconstitutional generated only a few regrets, most of these coming from labor leaders.[10] With surprisingly little difficulty, the program was quietly liquidated.

Meanwhile, another part of the piebald New Deal coalition, the Democratic leaders from the agricultural South, had a very different set of concerns from those of labor; for them, the highest priorities were to increase agricultural prices and to find foreign markets for their apples, cotton, tobacco, and peanuts. Roosevelt himself had firsthand exposure to their problems from his long sojourns in Warm Springs, Georgia, during the 1920s, where he had convalesced from his bout with crippling polio. For the South's Democratic interests, therefore, the Roosevelt administration offered a series of agricultural programs that entailed subsidies, import protection, and governmental purchases of surplus crops. Although this approach was as dirigiste as the NRA programs, the political reactions were quite different. Providing direct benefits to the southern interests that were so well positioned in the Democratic party and the Congress, these programs survived and thrived, drawing support from Democrats as long as the party retained its dominant position in the South.[11]

The Reciprocal Trade Agreements Act of 1934 may have seemed a strange bedfellow alongside the National Recovery Administration and the Agricultural Adjustment Administration, given its objective of reducing tariffs and other trade barriers. But, apart from the fact that the 1934 trade act offered an outlet for the liberal international orientation that Roosevelt had felt obliged to curb, it also coincided with the remnants of the Wilsonian tradition in the Democratic party and—if appropriately administered—with southern interests as well. So far as those interests were concerned, the powers afforded the president to reduce import barriers under the act were best administered by demanding the opening of agricultural markets abroad while reducing the U.S. tariffs on industrial goods. The persuasiveness of that position was enhanced by the fact that Cordell Hull, Roosevelt's secretary of state, had been a longtime leader of the southern Democrats and a longtime political ally of Roosevelt.[12] The combination was sufficient to carry this legislation over the top and to ensure its periodic renewal, so long as the administration used its power to reduce tariffs judiciously and with appropriate restraint.

Exchange-rate policy in the United States, in sharp contrast to that of trade, had typically been managed, to the extent that it was managed at all, with some insulation from day-to-day political processes; and so it was in the 1930s. The reasons for that insulation are familiar. The transactions of the United States with other countries, though often of considerable importance to those countries, appeared inconsequential in the huge U.S. economy.[13] Besides, unlike the pound and the franc, the U.S. dollar had not suffered after World War I; the principal exchange-rate problem, as far as the United States was concerned, was the competitive devaluations of other countries. So, apart from some export interests, few organized groups in the United States saw much reason to struggle over exchange-rate policy.

Nevertheless, two events relating to the dollar's exchange rate in the 1930s decade merit some attention.[14] One was the decision of the president, shortly after taking office in 1933, to reduce the gold content of the U.S. dollar; by February 1934, when the United States stabilized its gold price at thirty-five dollars an ounce, the gold content of the dollar had been reduced nearly 40 percent. Another was the U.S. participation in the so-called Tripartite Declaration of 1936, an action by France, Great Britain, and the United States, declaring in parallel statements their intention of consulting with one another over future exchange-rate changes. The first measure was a unilateral act undertaken by the United States without any international consultation. The second, though providing for consultation, had no substantive effect on subsequent U.S. behavior.[15] In the years following the declaration, the U.S. dollar played the role of King Log in the frog pond, exhibiting its dominance by inaction.[16] Where exchange-rate policy was concerned, that reaction presaged the role that the United States would eventually define for itself in the Bretton Woods agreements.

With the United States' entry into the war in December 1941, the international position of the United States was forever altered. After more than two centuries of faithful adherence to Washington's advice against entangling alliances, the United States assumed the leadership role in the formation of a new world order. Gone were the declarations of the Neutrality Act, and the one-vote margin in the House of Representatives that had made the military draft a possibility.[17] The extensive efforts to support the Allied side in forms such as Lend-Lease, which had proceeded throughout the two prior years, could now come out into the open. So too could planning inside the U.S. bureaucracy for a braver, newer postwar world.

The events of the next decade would confirm that the policy makers in the executive branch were remarkably free to formulate, propose, and publicly argue for new arrangements in the global interest; but it would demonstrate, too, that there were strict limits to the distance that the U.S. political establishment as a whole was prepared to go in its role as leader of a new international order. The situation, it was apparent, called for substantial financial support of the country's allies and of the institutions that were to form a part of the new order. It called for a tolerance of measures undertaken by other countries that discriminated against U.S. short-term interests, such as restrictions on the importation of dollar goods. But in the end the U.S. government drew a line in the sand against any provision that imposed significant restraints on its freedom to follow any economic policy it wished to pursue in the future; where provisions of this sort were contemplated in the early stages of any negotiation, they eventually melted away in the movement toward closure.

The Fund and the Bank

The early proposals that eventually matured into the Bretton Woods institutions provided a striking manifestation of the leeway of the U.S. bureaucracy in developing and proposing major innovations.[18] Any discussion of the U.S. role in the formation of the Bank and the Fund soon turns to the central role of two people: Henry Morgenthau Jr., the secretary of the treasury, and Harry Dexter White, his principal assistant in Bretton Woods matters. In terms of the U.S. policy-making process, each was a familiar prototype.[19]

From the descriptions of various contemporaries, Harry Dexter White emerges as an intense, driving civil servant, with strong views regarding the direction the United States ought to take in shaping a postwar economic world. In the parlance of political economists who study the U.S. executive branch, White was the prototypical policy entrepreneur, determined to push his point of view through a tortuous policy-making maze as far as he could make it go. In the decades following World War II, most such operators in the executive branch would come from the pool of political appointees brought in by each successive administration to head the principal executive agencies; but occasionally, as in White's case, an extraordinary career civil servant could rise to perform that role.

That White was able to make as much headway as he did in promoting the Bretton Woods institutions depended, of course, on much more than his own personal abilities. He was, for instance, buttressed by an extraordinary staff that included Edward Bernstein and by a network of distinguished economists that included Jacob Viner, Lauchlin Currie, and Alvin Hansen.[20]

But their collective abilities probably would have carried little influence if White had not had a direct line to Secretary Morgenthau. Even then, White's ideas would probably not have advanced very far if Morgenthau had not possessed the most valuable asset of all in most U.S. administrations, an inside track to the Oval Office. That inside track, in turn, cannot be attributed altogether to the simple fact that Morgenthau was the secretary of the treasury; officials in that position, under the U.S. system, cannot always count on the weight of their office to secure the president's ear. The fact that Morgenthau and Roosevelt were close neighbors in their growing-up years in New York's Dutchess County is often mentioned as a reason for Morgenthau's inside track.[21]

The importance of direct access to the president varies, of course, with the style of each presidential administration and with the nature of the problem to be addressed. But even when elaborate coordinating mechanisms exist on paper, most administrations find it difficult to develop a real consensus inside the executive branch on economic issues that have strong domestic ramifications. And where consensus among the ranks is difficult, access to the president's ear becomes especially critical as a prelude to action.

The problem of achieving a genuine consensus inside the executive branch appears to have been particularly acute in the Roosevelt administration. For one thing, the problem usually seems greater in Democratic than in Republican administrations, largely because the Democratic party represents a more heterogeneous coalition of economic and ideological interests and because it is usually more disposed to an activist role for the federal government. And it seems greater in periods in which a new wave of policy makers is being absorbed in the federal machinery, as in the early stages of the New Deal and of the wartime economy.

In any event, one knowledgeable Canadian official who negotiated extensively with Washington on economic matters during the Roosevelt era concluded that each federal agency was being allowed to come up with its own formulation of a foreign economic policy.[22] And Keynes's plaintive outburst on a visit to Washington in 1940, "But you don't have a government in the ordinary sense of the word," was a reaction to the same sense of confusion and disorder.[23]

In the early stages of the negotiations over the Bretton Woods institutions, there was scarcely a pretense of consensus-building inside the executive branch, let alone in the larger forums of the U.S. government and the U.S. body politic. As is so commonly the case in U.S. negotiations, the early representations of the "U.S. position" in discussions with the British were largely positions developed by a small coterie of Treasury officials, with some side discussions among a few carefully selected friends and allies in the State Department and in academia.[24] In the two-level chess-game metaphor of political scientists, the domestic game had not yet really begun before the international game was launched.

These early positions of the U.S. team proposed to constrain the behavior of national governments and to concede autonomous powers to international institutions to a far greater degree than was to appear in the final agreements. The original concepts, for instance, laid substantial obligations on creditor countries (for which read the United States and possibly Switzerland) to institute national policies that would reduce the balance-of-payments strain on debtors (of which Great Britain was the most notable). But as the chess game advanced and as the U.S. team gradually engaged the Congress and the U.S. public in the domestic level of the game, these obligations melted away.[25] Responsibility for the general policies of the Bank and Fund was entrusted to a group of full-time directors representing national governments. And, as added assurance that the United States would be in control of its own national policies, voting power was distributed among the member countries according to their contributions to the resources of the institutions, thereby giving the United States unassailable dominance. Finally, at U.S. insistence, the headquarters for the two institutions were placed in Washington, where U.S. oversight could be close.

Of symbolic importance in this process was the change during the negotiations in the contemplated role of the U.S. dollar. In the last stages of the negotiations, bolstering the distinctive role of the U.S. dollar, that currency was accorded the official status of the key currency in the Bretton Woods system, the currency to be used as the medium of intervention and the unit of account.

Of course, what the United States achieved through its economic and political muscle at the time was probably not very different from what policy makers in Britain or other countries would like to have achieved if they could. And the dominant position accorded the dollar reflected the pervasive assumption among the negotiators that most countries would be struggling with a chronic dollar scarcity. With the United States holding more than half the world's monetary gold, accounting for nearly half the world's industrial output, and dominating the world's export markets, any other view of the future seemed implausible. As long as other countries were in need of dollars, the one authority capable of producing dollars from thin air, the United States, could if it chose assume a totally passive role in its exchange-rate policies. King Log, it seemed, had returned to the pond.

With the conclusion of the Bretton Woods negotiations in 1944, a number of points regarding the role of the United States seemed clear. The United States was prepared to assume the role of leader in the world's postwar economic arrangements. By any historical standard, it was prepared to be generous in the disposition of material aid. But, apart from tolerating the possibility that other countries would be allowed to discriminate against dollar goods with impunity, it was not prepared to constrain its options regarding future monetary, trade, or investment policy.

The ITO and GATT

In the traditions of the United States as they stood in 1940, international trade had been a subject apart from other aspects of international economic relations. A provision of the U.S. Constitution explicitly identified trade policy as a special preserve of the Congress. And the tariff had been the subject of a succession of bloody struggles between opposing political parties, with Democratic populists and southern farmers usually attempting to reduce tariff rates over the opposition of Republican industrialists. It was not a difficult decision for Roosevelt, therefore, to allow Cordell Hull in 1934 to try to persuade a Democratic Congress to delegate some of its tariff-reducing power to the president.

That campaign produced the Reciprocal Trade Agreements Act, which authorized the president, in connection with the negotiation of trade agreements with other countries, to reduce by as much as one-half the statutory tariff rates embodied in the Smoot-Hawley Tariff Act of 1930. And it produced the string of initiatives that culminated in the negotiation of the Charter for an International Trade Organization, completed in 1948.[26]

Because tariff policy had for so long been the cause of pitched political battles in the United States, there was little chance that it could be totally captured for long by any one government agency. And, in practice, although the State Department managed to retain leadership over the trade agreement program for almost three decades after its inception, the consultations of the department with other executive agencies, with members of Congress, and with the public were a good deal more extensive than those practiced by the U.S. monetary authorities in the case of exchange-rate policy.

Yet, in spite of this critical difference between the two areas of policy, both the process and the outcome of the negotiations of the 1940s in these two areas bore striking similarities. In trade policy as in exchange-rate policy, the entrepreneurial drive of a group of bureaucrats seemed critical to the outcome. Once again, privileged access to the president seemed an indispensable element in the mix; in this case, it was Hull rather than Morgenthau who provided the critical link. Again, the U.S. government was prepared to give other countries more in the short run than it demanded for itself, at least as measured by the yardsticks used in trade agreement negotiations.[27] But, in the end, the United States refused to accept international commitments, such as general rules governing the conduct of its trade, that would effectively inhibit its choice of policies in the future.

Despite the factors that limited the possibilities of dominance by any one agency in the formulation of trade policy in the United States, the State Department under Hull's leadership managed to hold the lead in the early negotiations with Britain over a postwar trade regime. Driving the department's policies were not only the interests of the South and the Wilsonian traditions of the Democratic party but also the strong neoclassical bent of economists strategically located in the federal establishment; some of these, established in high positions in the Tariff Commission, the Commerce Department, and the State Department, had fought a decade earlier against the enactment of the Smoot-Hawley tariff.[28]

The State Department's prime objectives in these early negotiations were to secure a firm British commitment to support the creation of an open global trading regime in the postwar era, accompanied by the liquidation of the trade preferences that went with the imperial preference system and the sterling area. An article of the Mutual Aid Agreement, consummated in February 1942 and accepted by the British with great misgivings, foresaw just such developments.[29]

Six years later, after extensive negotiation, the provisions of a Charter for an International Trade Organization were unveiled, adopted by fifty-seven countries at Havana.[30] Its nine chapters and 106 articles were more ambitious than any economic agreement negotiated up to that time, covering rules with respect to labor standards, economic development and international investment, foreign trade practices, restrictive business practices, and intergovernmental commodity agreements.

Yet, despite the breadth of the agreement and the copious negotiations leading to its final formulation, the bulk of the ITO charter was the product of a relatively small group of technocrats from a very few countries, notably the United States, Great Britain, and Canada.[31] Though the document contained many concessions to the demands of the developing world, even those conciliating provisions were largely the product of a small group of specialists from those three countries. Overshadowed by the prosecution of the war, by the crises of postwar recovery, and by the emergence of a cold peace, the deliberations of this little group had generated very little public discussion. Suddenly, having completed the international phase of creating a new international trade regime, the U.S. negotiators were faced with completing the domestic processes required for adoption.

In the U.S. case, the domestic phase meant persuading Congress to accept an agreement that made major concessions to the views of other countries and that could be construed as tying the hands of Congress in some areas of policy in which it had traditionally claimed primacy.[32] Adopting the charter would, for example, hold the Congress to a definition of dumping and to a policy with respect to trade preferences that might not suit its future preferences.

In 1948, the ITO charter entered the maze of congressional ratification, a process from which it never emerged. While other countries marked time, U.S. interests dissected the agreement clause by clause. Meanwhile, the world itself was moving on. In 1948, the National Security Council secretly adopted a decision, known as NSC 68, acknowledging the existence of the cold war and proposing major shifts in U.S. policy; in that year, the Marshall Plan moved into high gear; and in 1950, the Korean War engaged the full attention of the highest levels of the U.S. government. In December 1950, the Truman administration abandoned its efforts to secure congressional approval of the ITO charter, and the international project died. Many who observed the process at the time could still hear echoes of the demise of the London Economic Conference.

All that survived the ITO debacle was the orphaned General Agreement on Tariffs and Trade (GATT), a little-known and little-publicized agreement salvaged out of the text of the ITO charter. Even without the adoption of the charter, the U.S. president already had the power to enter into trade agreements, a power that he derived in part from the existing trade legislation authorizing the continuation of the reciprocal trade agreements program and in part from his general authority as the country's executive. One chapter of the ITO charter, dealing with foreign trade, had been carefully tailored so that with a few critical adaptations it could be adopted and implemented by the U.S. president under his existing powers. A protocol was added to the text of that chapter relieving its signatories of any obligations to modify any conflicting national legislation already on the books; and, with that critical change, twenty-three countries promptly launched a General Agreement on Tariffs and Trade.

The ITO affair reaffirmed what the Bretton Woods agreements had strongly suggested. The U.S. polity was prepared for the country to accept a leadership role in the formation of international regimes. As part of the price for creating such regimes, U.S. negotiators were even prepared to accept what seemed like lopsided exchanges favoring other countries; in the GATT negotiations, for instance, the U.S. negotiators readily agreed to sharp reductions in U.S. tariff levels while most other countries were expected to continue their various restrictive licensing schemes in order to hold the importation of dollar goods in check. But the United States continued to draw the line on agreements that seemed to tie its hands significantly in the choice of future policies.

The ITO negotiations, therefore, led to a set of outcomes that were similar in many respects to those embodied in the Bretton Woods agreement, albeit reached by a different route. In the Bretton Woods case, the retreat of the ambitious U.S. innovators from their original positions took place while the international side of the negotiations was still in play; in the ITO case, the retreat followed the close of the international negotiations. One can speculate on why the U.S. negotiators in the ITO case were slower to recognize the congressional hurdles they would eventually have to face. Perhaps it was a difference in the times; the ITO affair, after all, evolved later, at the end of a victorious war and in the full flush of self-assurance on the part of the foreign policy community. Whatever the reason, the demise of the ITO emphasized the fact that major international agreements on economic matters had to be consonant with some widely held if amorphous views in the American polity that could still hear the echoes of Washington's farewell address. Alliances with foreign governments, it appeared, could not be so entangling that they greatly constrained the United States in the adoption of future economic policies.

The European Recovery Program

The various postwar programs for the recovery of Europe generated even more evidence of the limits of U.S. commitments in the creation of postwar regimes. For a year or two after the end of hostilities, the United States preferred to look on the postwar problems of Britain and France as if they were temporary balance-of-payment crises, to be dealt with by dollar loans. As a telling indication of U.S. thinking regarding the role of the IMF at the time, that institution was not assigned the primary responsibility for dealing with those crises. Instead, by making major dollar loans directly to the United Kingdom and to France, the U.S. government addressed the problem through the more traditional route of intergovernmental agreements.

Soon thereafter, the U.S. government had to face up to the fact that the problems of reconstruction were larger and deeper than a balance-of-payments approach could encompass. The reconstruction of Europe was now the issue. With that reformulation of the problem, one might have expected that the Bank, formally the International Bank for Reconstruction and Development, would be invited to play a significant role. True, the resources then at the disposal of the Bank would not have been sufficient to take on the task, but more money would have to be appropriated in any case.

From the viewpoint of the United States, the challenges presented by Europe's reconstruction differed in one fundamental respect from those encountered in the formulation of the IMF and the ITO. The role of the United States in Europe's reconstruction was primarily to provide the inspiration and the resources, and thereafter to exhort the Europeans to greater political effort and greater economic sacrifice. Apart from the appropriation of funds, therefore, the domestic policies of the United States were not directly involved. That difference would play a major role in the style with which the United States approached the issue of European reconstruction.

Not that the U.S. establishment was wholly agreed on the purpose and structure of the Marshall Plan as it evolved in 1947 and 1948. One group in the foreign policy community, centering on the geopoliticians in the State Department, saw the Marshall Plan primarily as a counter to the Soviet threat in Western Europe. Another, heavily represented in the economic side of the State Department, emphasized reconstruction as a necessary condition for the creation of a functioning global economy, requiring among other things the consolidation of the protectionist European states in a more efficient economic unit. Still a third element in the foreign policy establishment, dominated by the formidable General Lucius D. Clay, U.S. high commissioner to Germany, saw the Marshall Plan not only as a counter to Soviet aggression but also as an umbrella for the reintegration of West Germany into the European structure. Throughout the four years of the Marshall Plan's operations, the tensions among these groups in the U.S. establishment were palpable. But U.S. domestic policies did not figure very importantly in their quarrels, leaving the executive branch much less inhibited in the exercise of its penchant for innovation and action.[33]

Curiously, in the early discussions of how the Marshall Plan should be shaped, this disparate group of policy makers found themselves able to agree on one critical issue: not to exclude the Soviet Union from the invitation to join in the reconstruction program. Some economists entertained the wistful hope that Soviet participation might loosen its hold on the economic life of Eastern Europe; and the geopoliticians were determined that the onus for separating Western from Eastern Europe should not fall on U.S. shoulders, especially as the Soviet Union could be expected in the end to reject the invitation. In any case, inasmuch as the Soviet bloc countries had elected not to join the Bretton Woods institutions, one more reason existed for denying those institutions a significant role in the plan.

Even apart from the fact that the Bank's membership did not include the Soviet bloc members, the prospect that it might be assigned a major role in the European reconstruction project seemed dim for other reasons. Support for such a proposal was unlikely to come from the State Department; oversight of the Bretton Woods institutions, after all, lay in the domain of the Treasury Department. Besides, from the viewpoint of Congress, which would have to appropriate the money, a bilateral relationship with the Europeans betokened far greater influence and control on the part of the United States. Accordingly, it soon became evident that the structure through which the United States would offer its support to Europe, as in the case of the British and French loans, would be outside the Bretton Woods framework.[34] The Europeans were invited to formulate a structure for the development of reconstruction plans, which eventually led to the creation of an intergovernmental Organization for European Economic Cooperation. And the U.S. government undertook to enter into bilateral agreements with each of the European participants, creating a basis for foreign aid.

The most vexing organizational questions in the execution of the Marshall Plan, as it turned out, focused on what the implementing institutions of the U.S. government should be, and, more particularly, on whether the State Department should have a substantial hand in the execution of the program.[35] In characteristic American fashion, the principal question before the Congress was not how to achieve coordination among the federal agencies concerned but how to ensure the "independence" of the executing agency from the rest of the bureaucracy, especially the State Department, and how to guarantee a "businesslike" approach. In the end, after bitter squabbling among the federal agencies and heavy pressure from influential members of Congress, it was decided to support the creation of an independent Economic Cooperation Administration as the implementing agency, and to endow that agency with the right to be represented in the National Advisory Council.

Having established a rich mix of institutions and agreements to deal with a new world order, the bureaucracy of the U.S. government turned to the task of providing guidance for the various projects that it had helped create. In that challenging task, as noted earlier, the U.S. executive was freed of one major inhibition that had restrained it in other major postwar initiatives. Apart from appropriating money for the venture, the policies of the United States itself were not at issue; so the power and prerogatives of Congress were not directly involved.

In the end, the legislation authorizing and appropriating the necessary funds was loaded down with the aspirations, conditions, and directives that reflected the predilections of the lawmakers. But those provisions, as it turned out, had only marginal effect on the style with which the bureaucracy carried out its mandates. The bureaucracy proved once again its endemic capacities for creative initiatives, proposing one project after another for the consideration of the Europeans. At the same time, the policy-making establishment demonstrated its usual untidy tendencies toward the diffusion of power and the avoidance of tight internal coordination. To the extent that the Fund and the Bank continued to be relevant, the Treasury Department, staffing and dominating a National Advisory Council, could be expected to call the shots. In matters of international trade policy, except for the subject of security export controls, the economic side of the State Department would continue to lead the U.S. government. And the Economic Cooperation Administration, armed with generous funds appropriated by the Congress for the recovery of Europe, would eventually overcome the dominance of the established agencies to emerge as a freewheeling actor in the drive for Europe's recovery.

This is not the place to review in any detail the policies adopted under the aegis of the European Recovery Program. It is worth noting, however, that the dominance of the ECA in the program took a little time to emerge and was constantly under challenge. Members of Congress ran true to form, championing their pet policies and their district interests. And policy entrepreneurs from all parts of the U.S. government, including those from Agriculture and Interior, were constantly attempting to use the existence of the European Recovery Program as an outlet for their innovation and energy. For instance, an extraordinary policy entrepreneur from the Treasury Department, William M. Tomlinson, used his position as Treasury attaché in Paris to forge a tight partnership with Jean Monnet, then head of France's Commissariat du Plan; between them, they dominated the allocations of aid to France over several critical years.

In other ways, the continued diffuseness of power in the federal establishment in this period was repeatedly affirmed. While the Treasury staff continued to push for a world free of discriminatory financial arrangements through the IMF, the ECA supported and financed discriminatory payments systems inside Europe. And while State continued to push for the reduction of trade preferences in GATT, the ECA helped the Europeans devise a collective system of discrimination against dollar goods. Indeed, at one point, the Belgian government protested to the State Department that it was the recipient of two conflicting sets of messages from the U.S. government. One came from the ECA, demanding in the name of European unity that Belgium tighten its restrictions on the importation of dollar goods so that its imports from the rest of Europe could be increased; the other, coming from Treasury, demanded that Belgium suspend its discrimination against dollar goods in view of its ample dollar reserves.[36] Inside the U.S. establishment, no one was surprised.

Yet one consistent feature of the U.S. role in the Marshall Plan managed to shine through: a propensity to play down the use of governmental controls, such as rationing and other regulatory devices, in favor of measures that favored trade liberalization and market mechanisms. In part, that bent in U.S. policy reflected the dominant outlook of the U.S. leadership, a value to be pursued as long as they were not quarreling about the distribution of costs and benefits inside the U.S. economy. As long as Europe was the target for U.S. advice, it was relatively easy for the Congress, the administration, and the special-interest groups to push in the direction of trade liberalization and market mechanisms.

The tendency in that direction was strengthened by the fact that, following congressional preferences, ECA had recruited much of its leadership from U.S. industry, including such luminaries as Paul Hoffman and Clarence Randall. These proved natural allies for those in the State Department who saw the key European problem as one of technological backwardness and low productivity, to be dealt with by open markets and increased competition.[37] In the end, this bent may have been the most enduring part of the U.S. contribution to Europe's recovery.

Hints of the Future

Other essays in this volume are devoted to addressing the lessons offered by the experiences of the Bretton Woods institutions and the prospects for the future. But it would be misleading to leave an account of the 1940s decade without a few added words on what those experiences foreshadowed for the future behavior of the United States.

One lesson to be drawn in appraising the behavior of the United States is the importance of history's shadow, a lesson repeatedly reaffirmed in the study of national policies. The historical stability of the U.S. political system has allowed precedent to play a particularly important role in shaping its current behavior. Despite the extreme stresses of the Great Depression and World War II, some basic institutions and some cherished values continued to manifest their influence in the immediate postwar period.

For instance, even as Americans demanded efficiency and responsiveness from their government in Washington to meet these emergencies, they supported the institutions and the values that ensured dissent and that inhibited coordination. The relative role of political appointees in the federal bureaucracy was significantly enlarged in the postwar period, and the deliberations of federal agencies were opened up further to the day-to-day scrutiny of those outside the bureaucracy. As a result, even as Americans acknowledged a fundamental change in the international position of the United States, they took added steps to ensure that the country would retain its historical freedom of action in the shaping of its international economic relations.

Yet none of the U.S. institutions and values that have supported these tendencies has been altogether impervious to change. In the decades following the Bretton Woods negotiations, as the U.S. dollar weakened and the U.S. trading position grew vulnerable, the United States found itself obliged to shed its King Log role and to enter into earnest discussions with other countries regarding monetary policies and exchange-rate changes. An early manifestation of this basic change was the round of discussions initiated in the mid-1960s by the Johnson administration, aimed at reducing the role of gold in international settlements and at creating special drawing rights in the Fund, instruments that might one day come to take over some of the functions of the U.S. dollar as the world's key currency and guarantor of international liquidity. A more dramatic illustration was the extended round of international negotiations following the close of the U.S. gold window, an event generally regarded as marking the demise of the Bretton Woods system.

The U.S. abandonment of the remnants of the gold standard, however, can also be described as the abandonment of its role as King Log in exchange-rate and monetary policies. In place of that role, U.S. negotiators have found themselves obliged by circumstances to engage in continuous negotiations with other countries on those critical issues, leading to unprecedented agreements among key countries, such as the Plaza and Louvre accords, and occasionally producing coordinated interventions in foreign exchange markets. If Bretton Woods died with the abandonment of fixed exchange rates, something a good deal more interactive and vital emerged to fill the policy vacuum.

Something like the same thing could be said for the field of trade policy. As the U.S. trade position became more vulnerable in the 1960s, the studied disregard that members of Congress exercised toward the provisions of GATT eventually gave way to a grudging recognition of the opinions of its contracting parties, leading to occasional actions that took those opinions into account. For instance, when in the 1960s GATT's members exhibited their acute displeasure over an anachronistic protectionist device by which U.S. tariffs were set for organic chemicals, the Congress finally undertook to modify the offending practice.[38]

In later decades, as U.S. interests in foreign markets grew increasingly important for the U.S. economy, Congress ended its make-believe that GATT did not exist. In the 1970s, it faced up to the responsibility for placing its imprimatur on agreements negotiated in the GATT. And policy entrepreneurs in the U.S. government launched an unending succession of projects, culminating in the Tokyo round of 1979 and the Uruguay round of 1993. Each of these agreements introduced new departures, widening the range of subjects covered, providing firmer ground for the commitments undertaken, and adding another strand to the restraining of Gulliver. The free trade agreement with Canada established in 1987 and the three-way NAFTA agreement in 1993 added further curbs on the United States in the trade field. In all these cases, an increased sense of vulnerability in the United States pushed its leaders to entertain international commitments that the country would have rejected in earlier years.

One characteristic of U.S. behavior, however, remains essentially unchanged. This is the value that the U.S. polity places on maintaining an open, penetrable political system, one whose decisions are rarely final and irrevocable in the face of a determined onslaught by domestic forces that feel their interests slighted.

In the trade field, the struggle is particularly marked. It accounts in part for the very considerable gap between the initial proposals floated by the policy entrepreneurs in exercises such as the Uruguay round and the final positions taken by the U.S. negotiators in those rounds. In the beginning, it was the U.S. team that led the drive in the Uruguay round for a wholesale freeing up of trade in services; but in the end, it was the U.S. negotiators who led the move for a drastic cutback in the scope of the agreement.

More often than not, the starting initiatives of the policy entrepreneurs in the executive branch point in the direction of increased cooperation with the country's trading partners. More often than observers expect, the U.S. Congress acquiesces, albeit reluctantly, in further international agreements to promote the growth of international trade. Eventually, however, the U.S. negotiators are obliged to parallel the actions of Harry Dexter White in the 1940s, and to pull back from any measures of cooperation that would unambiguously tie U.S. hands for the future. Moreover, even as the Congress allows itself to be dragged a little way toward the cooperative positions promoted by the executive branch, it simultaneously tries to increase the pressure on the executive to exert unilaterally the full economic force of the United States in its dealings with other countries. The current debate in the Congress over the ratification of the World Trade Organization exhibits all these tendencies, with no certainty as to the outcome.

How to preserve the extraordinary openness of the U.S. policy-making process while permitting the country to engage responsibly in joint economic undertakings with other countries remains a challenge of monumental proportions. With economic interactions between national economies growing at a breathtaking pace, it is apparent that increasing cooperation among national governments will be essential in a wide range of activities, from controlling the environment to maintaining the probity of securities markets. There is a race between constructing the international regimes that can master some of the consequences of the dizzying growth in international linkages, and coming to terms with interests within the United States that have the power to thwart any constructive response. It is far from clear at this stage how the race will come out. But in the end, the propensity of Americans to engage in serious international negotiation will depend strongly on how vulnerable they feel in the international economic environment.

Notes

1. The literature on this subject is voluminous. See for instance Louis Hartz, *The Liberal Tradition in America* (New York: Harcourt Brace, 1955); Stephen O. Cohen, *The Making of United States Economic Policy* (New York: Praeger, 1988); and Raymond Vernon, Deborah L. Spar, and Glenn Tobin, *Iron Triangles and Revolving Doors* (New York: Praeger, 1991).

2. Illustrative are Samuel I. Rosenman, *Working with Roosevelt* (New York: Da Capo Press, 1972); Rexford G. Tugwell, *In Search of Roosevelt* (Cambridge: Harvard University Press, 1972); Daniel S. Fusfeld, *The Economic Thought of Franklin Delano Roosevelt and the Origins of the New Deal* (New York: Columbia University Press, 1956); Raymond Moley, *After Seven Years* (New York: Harper, 1939); the numerous works of Frank Freidel, including notably *FDR: Launching the New Deal* (Boston: Little, Brown, 1973); and Robert A. Divine, *Roosevelt and World War II* (Baltimore: Johns Hopkins University Press, 1969); and various works by Arthur M. Schlesinger Jr., including notably his three-volume work, *The Age of Roosevelt* (Boston: Houghton-Mifflin, 1960 and 1961).

3. The idea of reducing tariffs to increase imports appears in passing in a 1932 campaign speech. See Samuel I. Rosenman, *Working with Roosevelt*, p. 62.

4. See, for instance, the observations of "brain trust" member Raymond Moley, *After Seven Years* (New York: Harper, 1939), pp. 23–24: ". . . we proceeded on the assumption that the causes of our ills were domestic, internal, and that the remedies would have to be internal, too. . . ." See also Robert W. Oliver, *Bretton Woods: A Retrospective Essay*, discussion paper 105, California Seminar on International Security and Foreign Policy (Santa Monica, Calif.: June 1985), p. 16.

5. Arthur M. Schlesinger Jr., *The Age of Roosevelt: The Coming of the New Deal* (Boston: Houghton-Mifflin, 1960), pp. 213–232.

6. Quoted in Fusfeld, *The Economic Thought of Franklin Delano Roosevelt*, from *Public Papers and Addresses* (New York: Random House, 1938), pp. 641–646.

7. Arthur M. Schlesinger Jr., *The Age of Roosevelt: The Politics of Indecision* (Boston: Houghton-Mifflin, 1961), pp. 211–241.

8. Frank Freidel, *FDR: Launching the New Deal*, pp. 454–505.

9. Rexford G. Tugwell, *In Search of Roosevelt*, p. 302.

10. Arthur M. Schlesinger, *The Age of Roosevelt*, p. 283.

11. Frank Freidel, *F.D.R. and the South* (Baton Rouge, La.: Louisiana State University Press, 1965), pp. 37–56.

12. Ibid., p. 24.

13. Robert W. Oliver, *Bretton Woods: A Retrospective Essay*, p. 16.

14. Barry Eichengreen, *Elusive Stability* (New York: Cambridge University Press, 1990), pp. 145–150.

15. See, for instance, Robert Oliver, *Bretton Woods: A Retrospective Essay*, pp. 16–17, 31; and Barry Eichengreen, *Elusive Stability*, pp. 144–151.

16. Aesop tells of a decision by the frogs to elect Log their king, attracted temporarily by the knowledge that Log will sit quietly by rather than engage in some active policy as ruler. Joseph Jacobs, ed., *The Fables of Æsop* (London: Macmillan and Co., 1894), pp. 31–32. That expectation suited the preferences of the United States during the 1930s and 1940s, and it suited Britain and France as well so long as the policy was accompanied by ample dollar support.

17. For an account of Roosevelt's difficulties with isolationist sentiments in the United States prior to Pearl Harbor, see Samuel I. Rosenman, *Working with Roosevelt*, pp. 260–271; and Robert A. Divine, *Roosevelt and World War II*, pp. 24–47.

18. For an elaboration of this point, see Raymond Vernon and Debora L. Spar, *Beyond Globalism: Remaking American Foreign Economic Policy* (New York: Free Press, 1989), pp. 15–34.

19. For materials on the negotiations over the Bretton Woods, see for instance, Richard N. Gardner, *Sterling-Dollar Diplomacy in Current Perspective* (New York: Columbia University Press, 1980); Michael D. Bordo and Barry Eichengreen, *A Retrospective on the Bretton Woods System* (Chicago: University of Chicago Press, 1993); A. L. K. Acheson, J. F. Chant, and M. F. J. Prachowy, eds., *Bretton Woods Revisited* (Toronto: University of Toronto Press, 1972); R. F. Harrod, *The Life of John Maynard Keynes* (New York: Augustus M. Kelley, 1969); Robert W. Oliver, *Bretton Woods: A Retrospective Essay*; and Fred L. Block, *The Origins of International Economic Disorder* (Berkeley: University of California Press, 1977)

20. G. John Ikenberry, "The Political Origins of Bretton Woods," in Bordo and Eichengreen, *A Retrospective on the Bretton Woods System*, p. 164.

21. See Richard N. Gardner, *Sterling-Dollar Diplomacy*, p. 72, among several who emphasize this point.

22. Comments of A. F. W. Plumptre in A. L. K. Acheson, J. F. Chant, and M. F. J. Prachowy, *Bretton Woods Revisited*, pp. 41–43.

23. Quoted in Walter Salant, "The Collected Writings of John Maynard Keynes," *Journal of Economic Literature* 18, no. 3 (September 1980): pp. 1056–1062.

24. For some of the early positions of the U.S. side in the negotiations see A. L. K. Acheson, J. F. Chant, and M. F. J. Prachowy, *Bretton Woods Revisited*, p. 28; Richard N. Gardner, *Sterling-Dollar Diplomacy*, pp.75–81; Fred L. Block, *The Origins of International Economic Disorder*, pp. 42–60; and Robert W. Oliver, "Early Plans for a World Bank," *Essays in International Finance* (Princeton: Princeton University International Finance Section, 1971).

25. Richard N. Gardner, *Sterling-Dollar Diplomacy*, pp. 77, 91; A. L. K. Acheson, J. F. Chant, and M. F. J. Prachowy, *Bretton Woods Revisited*, pp. 28, 36. The final positions of the United States, ceding much less power to the institutions, was probably much more in accord with Roosevelt's own views; see Robert A. Divine, *Roosevelt and World War II*, pp. 50–71.

26. The leadership position of the State Department in this period is widely noted by commentators. See for instance Acheson, Chant, and Prachowy, *Bretton Woods Revisited*, pp. 23, 34–37, 43; Richard N. Gardner, *Sterling-Dollar Diplomacy*, pp. 6–20; G. John Ikenberry, "The Political Origins of Bretton Woods," pp. 157, 170; R. F. Harrod, *The Life of John Maynard Keynes*, pp. 510–515.

27. The yardsticks employed at the time were based on the principle that every tariff reduction or tariff binding was a "concession," and the negotiators sought to achieve "concessions" among the negotiating parties that were equal in the amounts of imports covered.

28. Raymond Vernon and Debora L. Spar, *Beyond Globalism*, p. 42.

29. Despite the misgivings, British contributions thereafter were important. Indeed, the economic adviser to the wartime U.S. ambassador in London attributes to British sources, including notably James Meade, the principal ideas and principal initiatives leading to the GATT. See E. F. Penrose, *Economic Planning for the Peace* (Princeton: Princeton University Press, 1953), pp. 91–115.

30. For an account of the negotiations and their relation to the GATT, see John H. Jackson, *The World Trading System* (Cambridge: MIT Press, 1989), pp. 27–58.

31. For an exploration of the role of the U.S. executive branch in the process, see Susan A. Aaronson, "How Cordell Hull and the Postwar Planners Designed a New Trade Policy," *Business and Economic History*, second series, vol. 20 (1991): pp. 171–179.

32. A definitive analysis appears in William Diebold Jr., "The End of the ITO," *Essays in International Finance* no. 16 (Princeton: Princeton University International Finance Section, 1952).

33. For a detailed account of these internal struggles, see Michael J. Hogan, *The Marshall Plan: America, Britain, and the Reconstruction of Western Europe, 1947–1952* (Cambridge: Cambridge University Press, 1987), p. 26; and Charles L. Mee Jr., *The Marshall Plan* (New York: Simon and Schuster, 1984). See also George Kennan, *Memoirs, 1925–50* (Boston: Little, Brown and Co., 1967), p. 336; Joseph H. Jones, *The Fifteen Weeks* (New York: Viking Press, 1955), pp. 252–253. The German issue is especially elaborated in John Gimbel, *The Origins of the Marshall Plan* (Stanford: Stanford University Press, 1976).

34. For a detailed account, see Hadley Arkes, *Bureaucracy, the Marshall Plan, and the National Interest* (Princeton: Princeton University Press, 1972), pp. 43–58.

35. Ibid., pp. 59–84.

36. Compare the conclusions in Hadley Arkes, *Bureaucracy, the Marshall Plan, and the National Interest*, p. 175 et seq.

37. Michael Hogan, *The Marshall Plan*, is particularly perceptive on this point. See especially pp. 427–445.

38. The story is elaborated in Ernest H. Preeg, *Traders and Diplomats* (Washington, D.C.: The Brookings Institution, 1970), p. 135.

5

A British Perspective
on Bretton Woods

Sir Alexander Cairncross

At the time of Bretton Woods the economic outlook in Britain differed some-what from that in the United States and made very different policies seem appro-priate in the years ahead.

From early in the war the British government had become well aware of the tremendous difficulties it was likely to face once the war was over in meeting the cost of necessary imports. Early estimates of the postwar balance of payments showed a large deficit even with imports severely reduced. The country was using up its capital and incurring debts abroad on an unprecedented scale, losing in the six years of war a quarter of its wealth. From being the richest country in the world in 1914, it was to find itself in 1945 with no more capital than thirty years earlier. Instead of being the world's largest creditor country with overseas assets comparable in value with the stock of fixed domestic assets other than dwellings, Britain would end the war as the largest debtor the world had ever known, its net overseas assets now a negative quantity.

The outlook for the balance of payments in the immediate postwar years was particularly alarming. Apart from the loss of invisible income from over-seas assets and the great reduction in size and earnings of the merchant navy, exports had been deliberately allowed to fall to 30 percent of the prewar level so as to make it possible to mobilize all available man-power for the conduct of the war. Further, deficits were inevitable in the postwar years. Preliminary estimates in 1945 showed an external deficit stretching out over several years before balance was restored, and likely to reach a cumulative total of at least $5 billion. In the first year alone, the deficit might amount to $3 billion or more. But who would lend so large a sum to a country already in financial difficulties?

These estimates assumed a strict limitation of imports to about 70 percent of the prewar level. They paid no regard to possible drawings on the sterling balances accumulated in the war by India, Egypt, and other countries, which had mounted to a total of some $14 billion by the autumn of 1945 compared with perhaps $4 billion required as working balances on the basis of prewar experience. Against these liquid liabilities, the gold and dollar reserves amounted only to $2.5 billion. Before the war the reserves had exceeded sterling balances at that time by a handsome margin; now they were about one-sixth.

Two further problems lay ahead. One was a sharp deterioration in the terms of trade which in 1947–49, and still more in later years, raised the price of imports in terms of exports by 17 percent above the 1938 level. Some deterioration had been foreseen but this was far beyond expectations. A second difficulty was the dollar problem. Almost every country except the United States was in deficit. For much of the world's commerce, the United States was virtually the only source of supply. As a result, there was pressure to settle international accounts in dollars and great difficulty in earning dollars by trade with third countries. Long after British trade had returned to balance, a large dollar deficit remained, causing a continual outpouring of gold and dollars from the reserves. Before 1939, British exports to the United States were roughly a quarter of imports from the United States so that direct dollar earnings paid for little more than imports of film and tobacco.

The prospects for the balance of payments inevitably colored British thinking on postwar trade and payments arrangements. They might recognize the virtue of free trade and nondiscrimination, having supported both for the better part of a century, and agree with the Americans that competitive devaluation, discriminatory practices, and trade restrictions sharpened national antagonisms and could have led to war. But in the 1930s they had been driven to take account of the qualifications necessary to free trade doctrine in a lopsided world of unbalanced trade and mass unemployment, and looked back to the Ottawa agreements as a means of sustaining trade when an American depression was draining other countries of their gold. The United States, on the other hand, was determined to free international trade from restrictions that bedeviled international relations and looked on imperial preference and the sterling area as prime examples of efforts to exclude America (and other countries) from markets they were anxious to supply.

This difference of view emerged early. Keynes was one of the first to give thought to Britain's postwar difficulties, and he went through a period in which he favored a Schachtian solution. In December 1940 he declared that "the underlying idea [of the Schachtian system] is sound and good. In the last six months the Treasury and the Bank of England have been building up a system which has borrowed from the German experience all that was good in it. If we are to meet our obligations and avoid chaos in international trade after the war, we shall have to retain this system. . . ." This appeared in the prologue to a memorandum by Keynes intended for a major ministerial statement of policy, but the memorandum itself was more general and spoke only of international trade returning "to what it should always have been, namely a means for trading goods against goods."[1]

Keynes also drew attention to the system of trade controls being built up. Although Keynes soon modified his ideas, the Bank of England continued to espouse them, arguing for continued exchange control backed by quantitative restriction of imports and discrimination, and hoping to build on the wartime system of monetary and payments agreements that they had established. Negotiations over trading relations with the United States had already begun as part of a British export drive and had raised the issue of some "consideration" for any opening of the American market to British imports. The same issue arose over the Lend-Lease: the "consideration" that America sought, in the first draft of Article VII of the Mutual Aid Agreement, was an undertaking by Britain that would have banned all forms of trade discrimination, including imperial preference, import controls, and exchange controls. Debate on Article VII stretched over many months and ended with a rephrasing in December 1941 that was followed by prolonged negotiations over its significance. The revised version called for "agreed action" directed toward "the elimination of all forms of discriminatory treatment in international commerce, and to the reduction of tariffs and other trade barriers." This could be (and was) interpreted differently by different parties and led to lasting disagreements over the commitment implied for imperial preference. For some in Britain it appeared to barter imperial preference and the freedom to frame one's own economic policy after the war for Lend-Lease assistance during the war. For others it had a symbolic significance as an undertaking calculated to weaken the links holding the Commonwealth together.

Although taken aback in the summer of 1941 by the restrictionist and discriminatory American proposals for a new international wheat agreement, Keynes soon backed away from what he came to see as "the horrid complications and complicated horrors" of bilateralism[2] and developed proposals toward the end of 1941 for an International Clearing Union. In the transition to such a system, however, it would still be necessary to engage in bilateral agreements on a goods-for-goods basis, make bulk purchase arrangements, develop the wartime system of payments agreements, and strengthen capital controls. The transition would last three to five years from the adoption of these proposals. Keynes's proposals also contained the germ of an eventual international bank to deal with relief and reconstruction in the early postwar years and a scheme for buffer stocks and commodity controls to help in moderating price fluctuations.

Neither Keynes nor the Treasury at that stage hoped for much in the way of American help at the end of the war or of tariff reductions and restraints on American agricultural exports. They were also doubtful about America's ability to maintain a sustained high level of employment, which by itself would be a major contribution to the removal of trade restrictions. Keynes's proposals, embodied in a much longer Treasury document, were approved by the Cabinet in May 1942 and looked forward to Anglo-American talks after consultation with officials of the Dominion and Indian governments.

There was then, as Presnell remarks, "a succession of delays, disappointments and seeming prevarications over these proposed conversations."[3] Instead, consultation and cooperation took place in a more fragmentary way over specific elements in postwar policy that had been separately devised. After the preparation of Keynes's plan for an International Credit Union and Harry White's plan for a Stabilization Fund, the Anglo-American monetary discussions that followed over the year from the middle of 1942 to the middle of 1943 prepared the way for the conference at Bretton Woods in 1944.

From the British point of view, the major issues outstanding in September 1943 were four in number.[4]

First, there was disagreement over the size of the proposed Fund, tempered by proposals to assist in dealing with Britain's sterling balances. American disagreement was hardly surprising since Keynes wanted the Clearing Union to have overdraft facilities of at least $26 billion to which America might be called upon to contribute $23 billion. The United States insisted on basing any international monetary authority on the contributory principle and limiting the American contribution to $2 billion or $3 billion. Keynes's plans for large overdraft facilities had therefore to be abandoned. In return, the Americans agreed to some enlargement of their contribution. At Bretton Woods they agreed to contribute $3.175 billion to fund resources totaling $8.8 billion. Britain succeeded, however, in gaining acceptance of the scarce currency clause (discussed below), to which it attached great importance.[5]

Second, Britain pressed for automatic access to the resources of the Fund all the more strongly because of the reduced limit to its account. Since the American plan provided not for a new international unit like *unitas*, but for a mixed bag of currencies subscribed by members, the liquidity of the Fund's resources would be diminished. This too made it more necessary that the resources of the Fund be available on request by individual members. The Americans, however, argued that "discretion on the part of the Fund was essential if the Fund's resources were to be conserved for the purposes for which the Fund was established and if the Fund were to be influential in promoting what it considered to be appropriate financial policies."[6]

Third, how free should countries be to change their initial rate of exchange? Britain had abandoned the fixed rates assumed in the International Clearing Union and was now asking for greater freedom to make unilateral adjustments, while the Americans wanted not only to limit the extent of any changes but also to make them virtually dependent on the unanimous agreement of other members.

Finally there were differences over the length of the transition period. The White plan had originally envisaged a period of one year but this had subsequently been extended to three years. Britain wanted this to be further extended to five years, but Keynes himself, hopeful of post-war aid, shared some of the American fear that if restrictionist policies were continued through a lengthy transition period, they might become implanted too firmly.

A fifth problem, also to be discussed at Bretton Woods, was that of the enormous wartime sterling balances. On these the British remained largely silent and had no agreed policy, partly because it was difficult to say anything in public, partly because there were wide differences within the British government. The Americans did not shrink from drastic solutions, including a proposal in a draft of the White plan for selling the balances to the Fund. But nothing came of their proposals nor of any eventual proposals by the British except to block wartime balances as far as possible.

The first four of these issues were pursued in the Washington talks in September–October 1943 but remained unsettled. A Joint Statement of Experts was issued in April 1944, and the Bretton Woods discussions followed in July after a preliminary conference in Atlantic City.

In the months surrounding the Bretton Woods Conference, the views expressed in the British press and in Parliament were highly critical of the proposals. On the Left was a school of thought seeking freedom to plan for full employment without regard to the impact on the balance of payments. Its proponents envisaged a bloc of planned economies in Europe and the Commonwealth bound together by bilateral clearing and bulk purchase agreements and insulated from the economic fluctuations in the United States that were confidently predicted. On the Right was the Bank of England, mistrustful of the vision of free, multilateral trade and fearful of the displacement of sterling by the dollar in financial settlements. In between were organs of opinion like the *Manchester Guardian*, the *Times*, and the *Economist*, which wanted shelter against American instability and contemplated a system of planned discrimination against imports from America with qualitative import controls, state trading, and bulk purchase agreements. The economists who might have spoken up for the government's plans were mostly in government service and forced to keep silent.

When the proposals were debated in Parliament in May 1944,

> all the participants were cautious or critical over one or more aspects of the monetary plan. They complained that it could tie sterling too closely to gold; that it made inadequate provision for adjustments by creditor countries; that it would prejudice the maintenance of wartime controls in the sterling area; and that it precluded resort to devices of commercial policy such as Imperial Preference, quantitative restrictions and bulk purchase. There was no effective defense of the plan from any quarter. Even the members who spoke on its behalf were quick to recite its deficiencies.[7]

As happened over the Bretton Woods agreement, the only wholehearted support of the plan came from Keynes: "To suppose that a system of bilateral and barter agreements, with no one who owns sterling knowing just what he can do with it . . . is the best way of encouraging the Dominions to center their financial systems on London, seems to me near frenzy."[8]

But Keynes also went further to reassure opinion than was justified. He made it appear that the plan conceded the automatic access to the Fund's resources for which he had argued. He cited the scarce currency clause as "protection against a recurrence of the main cause of deflation during the inter-war years, namely the drawing of the reserves out of the rest of the world to pay a country which was borrowing and exporting on a scale immensely greater than it was importing and lending. . . . The creditor country will always have to find a way to square the account on imperative grounds of its own self-interest."[9]

Here, too, Keynes went too far. A scarce currency was scarce *in the Fund*, and the United States took care to make sure that situation did not arise in the postwar years when dollars were again being "drained . . . out of the rest of the world."

These and other assurances—especially assurances on commercial policy— laid all the emphasis on what the plan allowed, made little mention of positive undertakings, and were silent as to obligations assumed under Article VII. The *Manchester Guardian*'s comment was typical: "We are free to maintain exchange control, free to do away with gold except as an accounting device, free to vary our exchange rate, and free to discriminate against the goods of any country which is declared an under-importer."

British opinion in 1944 was predominantly agnostic. The monetary proposals were part of a larger package that could only be assessed once Congress had made it clear how far it was prepared to go. It was to be over eighteen months before Parliament again debated the Bretton Woods proposals, and by then it had to pronounce not only on the Bretton Woods agreement but also on the Anglo-American financial agreement and the proposals for an International Trade Organization (ITO). The Bretton Woods agreement, as Robert Boothby complained, never came before Parliament by itself for separate debate.[10]

At the Bretton Woods Conference itself, the British delegation cleared up two points in dispute. The first related to a country's freedom to vary the exchange rate and had been pressed by Lord Catto, the governor of the Bank of England: Could the country not be allowed to alter the parity subject to the Fund's right to suspend the member from continued use of the Fund's facilities if the Fund were in disagreement with the proposal? In essence this was agreed and embodied in the Fund agreement.

A second point related to the use of controls during the transition period. After a proposal that seemed likely to limit controls, the British delegation secured an agreement to the exclusion of a specific obligation to remove restrictions during the transition. The Fund was asked simply to report on restrictions after three years and members were to consult the Fund about them annually after the fifth year.

A third matter that suddenly acquired more prominence was the International Bank. The United Kingdom had shown little interest in the American proposals but now offered strong support. It had feared that the Bank might seek to raise funds that the United Kingdom could ill afford to supply, but had begun to appreciate how the Bank might not only promote international development of benefit to all but might also provide a channel through which dollars could flow abroad with advantage to British exporters. Keynes found himself in the chair of the commission dealing with the Bank and this added to the interest he developed.

There was also much discussion of sterling balances, with the Indian delegation seeking to widen the scope of the Fund to "promote and facilitate" its settlement. After much debate, it was pointed out that the Fund was concerned only with current transactions, not with repayments of capital balances, and the proposal was blocked. There remained a difficult issue over the convertibility of balances used as resources, since the agreement failed to introduce as joint conditions that: (1) the balances had been "recently acquired as a result of current transactions," and (2) "their conversion is needed for making payments for current transactions." These appeared instead as alternative conditions, to the alarm of the authorities in London who feared that the optional conditions would open the door to the free use of balances and to drains on the reserves.[11] Much confusion resulted and much disagreement within the British delegation, which I forbear to elaborate.[12]

Apart from this issue, which troubled the British authorities for a couple of years, there remained several issues not settled at Bretton Woods. One was the location of the two new international institutions. The United Kingdom accepted that the international bank should be located in the United States, although it would have preferred New York. But it opposed the siting of the Fund in America and suggested London or Amsterdam. The British, as happened again with the European Payments Union, wanted to make the Fund as nonpolitical as possible and to provide for a mixed secretariat that would develop an ethos and standards of their own. The subsequent disagreement at Savannah over the salaries of the executive directors was a further illustration of the same difference over how international institutions should take shape.

Publication of the Bretton Woods agreement did little to change the views expressed by the British media. The *Economist*, for example, thought that the changes to which the British delegation had subscribed were concessions and for the worse. The key issue was whether any system of the kind proposed could be expected to be appropriate to the conditions of the postwar world: the Fund might not represent a return to the gold standard but the two payments systems were "different species of the same genus."[13] Would such a system have survived the Great Depression or was it to be assumed that the world of the future would be free of Great Depressions? Would the system "work more successfully than a less ambitious alternative such as might well consist, for example, partly of groupings of currencies on the analogy of the sterling bloc (within which concerted policies of full employment and balanced payments could be pursued) and partly of relations between the key currencies based upon the postwar Tripartite Agreement"?[14] The only possible course for the government to take was for as long as possible neither to accept nor to reject the agreement.

The *Economist* put little faith in the scarce currency clause and was doubtful whether capital controls could be effective without control over export proceeds. It wanted a long transition period, recalling that it had taken six and a half years after the First World War to restore the gold standard and insisting that "the mistake of 1925 must not be made again." As for the banning of discrimination, did that rule out restrictions on investment outside the sterling area so long as investment inside the area was uncontrolled? For that matter, did the United States itself abstain from discrimination? Did it not discriminate openly in its loan policy in making use of tied loans, in its shipping laws, and in its immigration legislation? Why then should Britain refrain from discrimination in making use of its large import market as a bargaining lever in securing entry to export markets? The catechism ended with the usual pronouncement that it was impossible to count on the United States' pursuing an effective employment policy or greatly increasing its imports to bring international payments into balance.[15]

Nowhere is there any insistence on the importance to Britain of freeing international trade as far as possible or any recognition of Britain's dependence in postwar years on American aid. The argument implies that the more Britain seeks to get along without America, the better, and that the British standard of living can be maintained by a series of deals with other countries in which, in practice, neither partner would be able to supply what the other needed.

When at last the Bretton Woods bill was brought before the House of Commons on December 12, 1945, a few days after the signing of the loan agreement, it was a kind of annex to an omnibus resolution seeking approval for the Bretton Woods agreement and the loan agreements and welcoming the American commercial policy proposals. The debate lasted two days, each about six hours, and no amendments were allowed. Inevitably attention was concentrated on the financial agreement, which had to be ratified by the end of the year so that there was no time for delay. The debate in the Commons was followed by a further two days of debate in the Lords on the same resolution. It was, in fact, the Lords debate that was critical, since whereas the Labour government had a substantial majority in the Commons, it could not count on the support or acquiescence of the mass of Conservative peers. Only the small number of Liberal peers were free to offer unqualified support.

In the Commons, the resolution was carried by 345 to 98 and the second reading of the Bretton Woods bill by 314 to 50 after a rather perfunctory discussion. Churchill announced that his party would abstain, but large numbers voted against, and so, too, did several members of the Labour party, including James

Callaghan, Michael Foot, Barbara Castle, and Jenny Lee (the wife of Aneurin Bevan, minister of health). Callaghan, however, voted for the second reading of the Bretton Woods agreement bill.

Most of the doubts expressed in the parliamentary debates related to the terms of the loan agreement rather than the Bretton Woods agreement. In both houses there were speakers who predicted default, some of them quoting Hubert Henderson's letter to the *Times* on the morning of the debate in the Commons: "The financial agreement with the U.S. is for a loan upon conditions which are calculated to ensure default."[16] The chancellor of the Exchequer, had he felt free to speak his mind, might have said the same. He noted in his diary after the debate in the Lords: "My cynical and secret reflection . . . is that . . . it is quite certain that the conditions will have to be 'revised' long before AD 2001 and that even in the next year or two it may well be that this will require a considerable variation which might even be 'unilateral.' "[17]

Several speakers expressed their support for Bretton Woods at the same time as they opposed the loan agreement. Others claimed that opposition to Bretton Woods was "well nigh universal." The main lines of attack were on the shortening of the transition period, the conditions governing convertibility, and above all, "the weakening of the bonds of Empire."[18] Even on these points it was what was in the loan agreement or the Mutual Aid agreement, not Bretton Woods, that caused most disquiet. Much of what was said about imperial preference in the Lords came from old enthusiasts for empire free trade such as Lord Beaverbrook and Lord Croft, who had failed to convert their party before the war and were still feeding on illusions.

The Lords debate on December 17–18 began on the day after Keynes's return from America. Not only did he take part, but also his speech is generally thought to have played an important part in the approval given by Parliament to the arrangements proposed. According to Lionel Robbins, for example, "before Keynes spoke there were strong rumors of some sort of adverse resolution. . . . After Keynes' speech, which I heard, the atmosphere had completely changed."[19] Of ninety-eight votes cast in the Lords, only eight were against the motion; but there were many abstentions. Of those who spoke, more were against than for the arrangements, but two-thirds of those who spoke against abstained from voting.

Keynes did his best to convey the American point of view. "Our American friends," he pointed out, "were interested not in our wounds, though incurred in the common cause, but in our convalescence. . . . What the United States needs and desires is a strong Britain endowed with strength and facing the world on the equal or more than equal terms than we were wont to do." What, he asked, was the alternative to what was now proposed? It was, he said, "to build up a separate economic bloc which excludes Canada and consists of countries to which we already owe more than we can pay, on the basis of their agreeing to lend us money they have not got and buy only from us and one another goods we are unable to supply."[20]

In his peroration, Keynes almost for the first time in the debate drove home the British interest in the revival of multilateral trade. "These policies," he said,

> . . . seem to me to be in the prime interest of our country, little though we may like some parts of them. They are calculated to help us regain a full measure of prosperity and prestige in the world's commerce. They aim, above all, at the restoration of multilateral trade which is a system upon which British commerce essentially depends. . . . This determination to make trade truly "international" and to avoid the establishment of economic blocs which limit and restrict commercial intercourse outside them is plainly a condition of the world's best hope, an Anglo-American understanding, which brings us and others together in international institutions which may be in the long run the first step towards something more comprehensive. . . . I beg those of you who look askance at these plans to ponder deeply and responsibly where it is they think they want to go.[21]

It was Keynes's last speech in Parliament and it had the desired effect. The resolution was passed by a large majority when its rejection was a real possibility and would have changed everything. The whole set of resolutions might have been defeated. The financial agreement would have been nullified and it would have been necessary to reintroduce the Bretton Woods agreement bill with no certainty that it would pass. What would have followed is hard to say and would have depended very much on American reactions. There was certainly some danger of a breakdown in Anglo-American relations, an earlier end to American assistance in Europe, and a repetition of the long deflationary struggles of the interwar years.

Leaving aside that speculation, there can be no doubt that it took much longer to restore external balance everywhere than had been assumed. In the British case the domestic economy was quickly adapted to peacetime conditions; and in most European countries industrial production was soon back to the prewar level or above it. What took time was the balance of payments—not least because domestic production recovered so late—and within the balance of payments it took much longer to achieve a balance of hard currency. Even with a vastly greater amount of American aid than the $3.75 billion of the American loan, Western Europe was far from establishing convertibility five years after the war and did not establish it for over thirteen years. Between 1945 and 1952, the United Kingdom alone had to find not just the $5 billion of the U.S. and Canadian loans but an additional $5 billion to meet all outgoings, and this in spite of running a current account deficit totaling no more than $2 billion over the entire period.

Perhaps the most important single factor prolonging disequilibrium between North America and the rest of the world was the slowness of recovery in the dollar-earning countries outside Europe. It was not just Europe that had been ravaged by war. Ravaged too were large parts of the world to which Europe exported to earn the dollars needed to pay for American imports. If there was to be a recovery of multilateral trade, there had to be a recovery of the countries giving rise to it. Before the war the United Kingdom had exported relatively little to the United States and had earned a large part of the dollars with which to pay for imports from America through her trade with primary producing countries like Malaysia. But the flow of dollars from multilateral settlements more or less disappeared in the war, and its recovery was delayed in postwar years by the disruption created by the war and postwar disturbances. In addition, the large surplus that Britain ran with the sterling area in postwar years was largely offset by a flow of capital in the other direction: the amount lent, repaid, or invested abroad that went to the sterling area in the years 1945–52 was nearly as much as the American loan.

It has been argued that convertibility could have been readily achieved and the Bretton Woods agreement implemented without additional American help. All that was necessary, it has been suggested, was a balanced budget and a devalued currency. Failure to follow this prescription is put down to profligacy and excessive social expenditure. In Britain, however, the budget was balanced from the end of 1947 and the pound devalued in 1949. In the early postwar years, devaluation was calculated to increase the external deficit because of the large excess of imports even when severely limited. So far as the budget was concerned, it was military more than social expenditure that put an excessive strain on the economy in 1945–46. In 1948–50 the budget was in surplus even with the inclusion of heavy capital expenditure. It was only in 1947 that financial control was ineffective. In 1951 the dollar shortage was worse than ever in spite of devaluation and fiscal correctness.

On the long road to convertibility, things fell out more as the critics of Bretton Woods predicted than as the agreement required. The Bank of England set about rebuilding its monetary agreements, trade was governed by quotas and bilateral deals, and the IMF was almost completely quiescent. It was necessary to be content for the time being with semiconvertibility in the European Payments Union if recovery was to continue. Rates of exchange remained distorted all over the world and it was a long time before they were adjusted. Not until the late 1950s did the IMF come into its own. The Bank, on the other hand, was an early success and a valuable and thriving institute from the start.

Notes

1. Quoted in L. S. Presnell, *External Economic Policy since the War* (London: H.M.S.O., 1986), pp. 18–19.
2. Ibid., p. 71.
3. Ibid., p. 79.
4. Ibid., pp. 93–94.
5. Richard N. Gardner, *Sterling-Dollar Diplomacy: Anglo-American Collaboration in the Reconstruction of Multilateral Trade* (London: Oxford University Press, 1956), pp. 112–113.

6. Ibid., p. 113.
7. Ibid., p. 124.
8. Ibid., p. 125.
9. Ibid., p. 126.
10. At the third reading of the Bretton Woods Bill, Boothby insisted on "putting on record the astonishing and melancholy fact that this Bill . . . should have been passed through this House without any discussion of the principles underlying the Bretton Woods agreement as such."
11. L. S. Presnell, *External Economic Policy*, pp. 167–168, 170.
12. Ibid., pp. 70–79.
13. *Economist*, August 12, 1944, pp. 207–208.
14. *Economist*, October 10, 1944, p. 502.
15. *Economist*, August 12 and October 10, 1944.
16. *Times*, December 12, 1945.
17. Dallons diary, entry for December 19, 1945.
18. House of Lords, vol. 138, December 18, 1945, pp. 793–794.
19. L. S. Presnell, *External Economic Policy*, p. 341, n. 26.
20. House of Lords, vol. 138, December 18, 1945, p. 790.
21. House of Lords, vol. 138, December 18, 1945, pp. 793–794.

6

The Birth of a World Trading System: ITO and GATT

Simon Reisman

World War II was in full rage—and the outcome far from certain—when the story begins. As early as 1941, a few brave and dedicated officials in the U.S. government and several professors expert in international trade and finance began to plan for a liberal world system of trade and payments to replace the beggar-thy-neighbor autarkic policies of the 1930s. A few like-minded zealots from Britain and Canada were involved in this work from the very beginning.

What drove these people? The strongest driving force was fear. Memory of the devastating interwar years was still fresh in people's minds. The Great Depression of the 1930s, and the widespread trauma in its wake, were attributed to the restrictive trade and exchange policies of that era. Economic warfare led to the outbreak of military hostilities and the tragedy of World War II. There was widespread fear that failure to pursue economic cooperation after the war would lead to a repetition of the shattering interwar experience.

These early leaders also had faith. They were inspired by classical economic theory; an open, liberal, competitive, multilateral trading system would contribute to the growth and prosperity of nations as well as to their peace and security.

It was clear from the beginning that, to be whole, the postwar economic order would require progress on three broad fronts: exchange policy, trade policy, and investment.

The early work toward a liberal world trade and payments system was given formal impetus in three major intergovernmental arrangements in which the United States played a leading role. The Atlantic Charter of 1941 included a broad undertaking among the signatories to work for postwar economic cooperation. Similar undertakings of a rather more specific nature were included in the Lend-Lease agreements with the United Kingdom and other countries. A fuller commitment relating mainly to a more liberal, nondiscriminatory trading system was contained in the Anglo-American loan agreement of 1945.

The Bretton Woods Conference of July 1944 produced the Articles of Agreement for an International Monetary Fund (IMF) as well as agreement to create the International Bank for Reconstruction and Development (the World Bank). It took several more years to reach agreement on international trade. Why this dichotomy?

People are prepared to leave the complexities of international finance to experts. This is not true for international trade, which touches the lives of people in very direct and visible ways. Perhaps more important was the simple matter of money. The willingness of the United States to make available substantial sums to get the two Bretton Woods institutions started inspired a willingness to reconcile the very real differences in perceptions of national self-interest and broad economic philosophy held by the two principal protagonists on these issues. There was no such cement to bind together the conflicting views about national interests and fundamental differences in economic philosophy that divided the United States and the United Kingdom on international trade issues.

I will say no more about the Fund and the Bank. My subject deals essentially with trade: the International Trade Organization (ITO) and the General Agreement on Tariffs and Trade (GATT).

Reference was made earlier to discussions mainly between the United States, the United Kingdom, and Canada during the war to elaborate the major elements of a new international trading system. This collaboration was continued after the peace. In the fall of 1945, only a few months after the surrender of Germany and later Japan, the U.S. Department of State issued a document entitled, "Proposals for Consideration by an International Conference on Trade and Employment." These proposals called for the convening of a United Nations conference for the purpose of negotiating an international trade charter and for the establishment of an International Trade Organization.

In February 1946, the United Nations Economic and Social Council (ECOSOC) at its very first session established a preparatory committee of eighteen countries to prepare the groundwork for a United Nations Conference on Trade and Employment. These eighteen countries were broadly representative of the various regions of the world. Germany, Japan, and Italy had not yet won their way into the comity of nations, and Czechoslovakia was the only state-trading country in the group.

Over the next several months the United States in consultation with the United Kingdom and Canada elaborated the summary December 1945 proposals into a detailed draft trade charter. This "suggested charter" was adopted as a basis for discussion by the preparatory committee and constituted the agenda for its first session held in Church House, London, during October and November of 1946.

An intense debate—you might call it a negotiation—ensued on virtually every provision. Good headway was made, although there remained many difficult issues that would require further work. This, of course, was to be expected. There were fundamental differences in the political and economic philosophies of the various participants as well as marked differences in their economic strength and stage of economic development. The raw expression of intense rivalry between the dominant United States and the declining world power of the United Kingdom emerged from time to time to mar the proceedings and was never far below the surface.

The debates concerned such fundamental issues as how to reconcile freedom of trade and open competition with the objectives of full employment and economic growth: how much sovereignty would countries be prepared to delegate to an international institution and an international charter; what sanctions would be available to ensure conformity with the rules; what departures from the rule of nondiscrimination could be tolerated to accommodate regional groupings or other political associations such as the British Commonwealth and the emerging European grouping?

A second session of the preparatory committee was convened in Geneva at the splendid Palais de Nations, the home of the old League of Nations, and now the European headquarters of the United Nations. The preparatory committee now developed into many subcommittees and working parties, and labored long and hard and sometimes bitterly from April 1 to October 30, 1947.

There were two major tasks to be carried out at the second session. First was the completion of a draft trade charter for submission to the United Nations Conference on Trade and Employment scheduled for November 1947 in Havana. Work on the draft charter was completed in July. Second, and no less arduous, was a series of detailed negotiations among the principal countries of the preparatory committee to eliminate or reduce tariffs and tariff preferences.

A highly innovative system was designed to facilitate these tariff negotiations. Pairs of countries would deal bilaterally on products where the negotiating countries were each other's principal supplier. Under the most-favored-nation rule—a central provision of the trade charter—all the concessions made in the course of the bilateral negotiations were to be extended to all participating countries. The tariff negotiations between many pairs of countries were completed by October and provided for major reductions in tariffs and preferences and other trade restrictions. The results took the form of a tariff schedule for each participating country. These tariff schedules together with those articles of the draft charter that were required to protect the integrity of the trade concessions were combined in an instrument titled the "General Agreement on Tariffs and Trade," or GATT for short. The articles drawn from the charter were the traditional provisions common to most bilateral trade agreements covering such matters as valuation for duty, national treatment on internal taxation and regulation, quantitative restrictions, subsidies, antidumping, countervailing duties, and state trading. The GATT did not include other provisions of the draft charter such as employment, investment, restrictive business practices, commodity agreements, or the organizational provisions that related to the proposed international trade organization.

The Final Act establishing the GATT was signed by all the participants (now twenty-three) of the preparatory committee. It came into effect on January 1, 1948, pursuant to an ingenious instrument entitled the "Protocol of Provisional Application." This protocol was designed to be capable of implementation by the United States pursuant to the powers delegated to the executive branch of government by the Reciprocal Trade Agreements Act. Congressional approval of the GATT would not be required. This protocol constitutes the legal foundation for U.S. participation in GATT to this day.

As its name implies, the Protocol of Provisional Application was intended to be a temporary instrument which would soon be superseded by the Havana World Trade Charter. The charter would of course be more comprehensive, would attach tariff schedules as appendices, and would come into force following ratification by the signatory countries.

The Havana conference was convened in November 1947. It was attended by some fifty-four countries (most of the sixty-one countries that made up the United Nations at the time). It completed its work on March 24, 1948, with signature of the Final Act authenticating the Havana World Trade Charter and providing for the establishment of the International Trade Organization. The draft charter which formed the agenda of the Havana conference had many weaknesses as seen from the vantage point of liberal economic philosophy. The Havana charter had many more exceptions and escape clauses.

Post-Havana rationalization by liberal trade protagonists described the results as far from perfect, but the best that could be achieved at the time. With the benefit of hindsight and as a participant in many trade negotiations since Havana, it strikes me that the Havana charter was confirmation of an elementary negotiating principle: No deal is better than a bad deal!

Approval by the U.S. Congress would be required to authorize the U.S. government to accept the Havana World Trade Charter and to participate in the International Trade Organization. The Havana charter found its way onto the legislative calendar of Congress, but it was never voted upon. After languishing unattended before Congress for nearly two years, the administration withdrew it from the legislative calendar in 1950. Thus, the Havana charter and the ITO faded ignominiously into the dustbin of history.

The story of the demise of the Havana charter has inspired many volumes. For our purposes, it is perhaps sufficient to note that the whole project appealed to very few protagonists on the various sides of the traditional U.S. trade debate. For protectionists, the charter contained too many concessions and commitments. For the supporters of liberal trade, the charter had too many exceptions and loopholes. For the pragmatists, it had little to offer that was concrete and timely.

Congress was increasingly averse to delegating to the administration the trade powers that participation in the ITO would entail.

No less important in explaining the failure to approve the charter was the fact that the problems of reconstruction were now recognized to be deeper and longer lasting than was anticipated in the first blush of postwar optimism. This meant trade and exchange restrictions, currency inconvertibility, and continued discrimination against the United States would persist for a long time. It was unrealistic to expect much enthusiasm in the United States for major unrequited trade and tariff concessions with no certainty as to when payment might be made, if ever. Then, too, other and more pressing matters associated with the Marshall Plan, the formation of the North Atlantic Treaty Organization (NATO), and the retrogression into the cold war took priority in the concerns of both the administration and the Congress. There was no time and no enthusiasm for what had become a rather stale and disappointing enterprise.

Immediately upon the signing of the Havana Final Act, the contracting partners to the GATT held their first session and agreed to amend the relevant GATT articles to reflect the numerous changes that were made to the charter at the Havana conference. What remained then as the only fruit of the noble enterprise to build a multilateral liberal trading system was GATT. Because it was orphaned, with only short-term support and status in the United Nations system, weakly supported by the temporary Protocol of Provisional Application, and with no provisions to establish a continuing organization, few people would have predicted a promising future for GATT. They were, of course, wrong. What we have today, and what we have worked with for the past half century as the principal institution governing international trade relations is GATT. It, of course, provides the foundation for the World Trade Organization (WTO), which passed Congress in December 1994.

It will be for others in this book to evaluate the accomplishments and the failures of GATT. Let me say simply that I am on the side of those who would judge GATT, against all odds, to have been a major success in the story of post–World War II international economic cooperation.

Section II

Adaptations

7

The Making and Remaking of the Bretton Woods Institutions

Edward M. Bernstein

How the Bretton Woods Institutions Were Made

The Bretton Woods Conference was remarkably successful. In three weeks the delegates agreed on the establishment of two permanent institutions for international cooperation on monetary and financial problems. This was possible because of the thorough preparation in the three preceding years. It is particularly noteworthy that these countries agreed on how to deal with the postwar problems they expected, although they did not agree on what the problems would be.

All countries were concerned about a recurrence of the economic devastation that followed the end of World War I—the Great Depression, the sharp contraction of world trade, the disorderly exchange conditions, and the problems associated with reparations, interallied debts, and defaults on government loans. A number of conferences were held in the 1920s and 1930s without achieving agreement on how to deal with these problems. Even at the height of the depression in July 1933, the World Economic and Monetary Conference in London could not agree on such a basic question as the appropriate exchange rate for the dollar. It was not until 1936 that the United States, the United Kingdom, and France agreed in the Tripartite Declaration on a common policy to support orderly exchange arrangements. This experience showed that plans for dealing with postwar economic problems should be made before rather than after the end of World War II.

In the view of the United Kingdom, the Great Depression was mainly due to a chronic inadequacy of demand in the United States. The depression was transmitted to other countries through the U.S. balance-of-payments surplus, which drained other countries of their reserves and compelled them to follow deflationary monetary policies.

To deal with these problems and the exchange and trade disorders they generated, Lord Keynes proposed the establishment of an International Clearing Union. Members would be required to fix a par value for their currencies, which could be changed after consultation with the Clearing Union, and in some cases only with its approval. Surplus countries would share with deficit countries the responsibility for balance-of-payments adjustment. They would have to provide generous credits to the deficit countries through the Clearing Union and they would pay interest on these credits at the same rate as the deficit countries. "The necessity of some such plan as the above," Keynes wrote in a letter in April 1941, "arises from the unbalanced creditor position of the United States."

The United States Treasury had a quite different view of the problems of the 1920s and 1930s. It believed that the Great Depression resulted from the interaction of wartime inflation and the gold standard. The inflation exhausted the free gold reserves of central banks, and reduced gold production after the war and the amount of newly mined gold available for the growth of the money supply. The deflation this caused was aggravated by the restoration of the gold standard in a number of countries at inappropriate parities, particularly an overvalued rate for sterling. The United States did not agree that its balance-of-payments surplus spread the depression to other countries. Actually, the United States' surplus on current account fell considerably in the 1930s. The large overall surplus in 1938–40 was due to European imports for rearmament and the capital outflow from Europe just before World War II. The depression was intensified and spread, however, by competitive devaluations and restrictive trade and exchange practices.

In the opinion of the U.S. Treasury, a similar depression would not occur after World War II because very few countries would attempt to restore the gold standard. The greater danger was that the large outlays necessary for reconstruction would create huge balance-of-payments deficits that might lead to a renewal of competitive devaluations and trade and exchange restrictions. To avoid such disorders, Harry D. White proposed the establishment of an International Stabilization Fund and an International Bank for Reconstruction and Development (IBRD). The Stabilization Fund would have responsibility for maintaining stable exchange rates and orderly exchange arrangements. It would help finance current account deficits to enable members to adjust the balance-of-payments without resorting to measures destructive of national or international prosperity. The International Bank for Reconstruction and Development would provide credits for reconstruction immediately after the war, and later it would assure the availability of long-term loans for development.

Apart from the financial provisions, the differences between the U.S. plan for an International Stabilization Fund and the U.K. plan for an International Clearing Union were not great. Both plans provided for international responsibility on changes in the par value of members' currencies and the elimination of exchange restrictions on current transactions. Both agreed that balance-of-payments adjustment had to be made by surplus as well as deficit countries. The major differences were on the degree of responsibility that surplus countries had for adjustment and on the amount and conditions for financial assistance to deficit countries.

The Keynes plan did not deal with the problem of reconstruction. The White plan called for the establishment of an international bank to help finance postwar reconstruction and the development of the low-income countries. There was little discussion with the United Kingdom of the plan for the World Bank, although the U.S. Treasury provided written answers to the questions submitted by the British economists on the Bank as well as the Fund.

The discussions between the United States and the United Kingdom went on for two years. During that period, the United States also held discussions with the Soviet Union, the free French, China, Canada, and a number of developing countries. The United Kingdom held discussions with the Commonwealth countries and the London-based governments of the occupied countries. France wanted a larger role for gold to give greater assurance of stability of exchange rates. Canada emphasized the importance of convertibility and multilateral settlements. The European governments in exile thought that prompt reconstruction was essential for social and political reasons as well as economic reasons. The Latin American countries stressed the need for stable and remunerative prices for basic commodities and for long-term credits for development.

In April 1944, the United States and the United Kingdom agreed on a Joint Statement of Experts on the Establishment of an International Monetary Fund. The exchange rate provisions were much the same as in the White and Keynes plans. The Fund would have larger resources than proposed in the White plan but much less than proposed in the Keynes plan. Provision was made for the possibility of a large and persistent surplus in the United States balance of payments. If the International Monetary Fund were to find that this had occurred, members would be authorized to impose restrictions on dollar payments. In any case, members could continue wartime restrictions on current transactions during a transition period.

After the joint statement was published, President Roosevelt invited the Allied and associated countries to a United Nations Monetary and Financial Conference at Bretton Woods to establish an International Monetary Fund "and possibly an International Bank for Reconstruction and Development." To prepare for the conference, the U.S. Treasury invited a smaller group of countries to send representatives to a preliminary drafting meeting in Atlantic City in mid-June. About thirty economists from thirteen other countries joined the U.S. economists in Atlantic City. They agreed that the Bretton Woods Conference should establish the World Bank as well as the Monetary Fund. They prepared a working paper for the conference that offered alternative wording for the provisions in draft agreements on the Fund and Bank. In addition, the U.S. Treasury issued a document entitled "Questions and Answers on the International Monetary Fund" and "Questions and Answers on the International Bank for Reconstruction and Development," which explained how these institutions were expected to work.

The conference convened on July 1, 1944, with Henry Morgenthau Jr., the secretary of the Treasury and head of the U.S. delegation, presiding. The conference was organized to deal with the Monetary Fund and the World Bank in two commissions presided over by White on the Fund and Keynes on the Bank. Most provisions were adopted unanimously on the basis of committee reports written by the technical advisers. A few difficult issues on the Monetary Fund were referred to a Committee on Unsettled Questions. An able and imaginative drafting committee, chaired by Louis Rasminsky of Canada, smoothed out remaining differences by a judicious choice of words.

Neither the World Bank nor the Monetary Fund provided much financial assistance to Europe in the early postwar years. The World Bank made a few reconstruction loans immediately after the war. The supplementary resources that Europe needed for reconstruction came mainly from the Marshall Plan. The Monetary Fund engaged in a few transactions with Europe before the Marshall Plan but none while the plan was in effect.

The Postwar Economic Situation

The world economy evolved quite differently after the war from what had been expected. Instead of a deep depression, as was widely feared, there was a remarkable growth of output in the United States, the other industrial countries, and many of the developing countries. Instead of large surpluses, the United States developed a persistent deficit in its overall balance of payments. Ultimately, this made it necessary to amend the Articles of Agreement.

The Fund agreement adopted at Bretton Woods reflected the preference of its members for an exchange-rate system based on par values without the rigidity of the gold standard. It was assumed that, if the United States were to maintain a high level of output with stable prices, other countries would follow policies that would enable them to have an appropriate balance of payments and to keep the dollar exchange rates for their currencies within the 1 percent margin above and below parity prescribed at Bretton Woods.

The Great Depression caused a radical change in the objectives of economic policy. The gold standard endured for nearly a hundred years in the United Kingdom and for more than fifty years in the United States without a change in the par value of the pound and the dollar. That was possible, despite protracted periods of deflation and depression marked by occasional monetary crises, because the maintenance of the gold value of the currency was the primary objective of economic policy. In the 1930s, after years of deflation and depression, every country abandoned the gold parity of its currency. The gold standard came to be regarded as having a deflationary bias.

The members of the International Monetary Fund accepted the obligation to maintain stable exchange rates based on par values, but not as a primary objective of economic policy. Article I (ii) of the Fund Agreement states that one of its purposes is to "facilitate the expansion and balanced growth of international trade, and to contribute thereby to the promotion and maintenance of high levels of employment and real income and to the development of the productive resources of all members as primary objectives of economic policy."

The par value system required all members to give the same importance to price stability and to the level of output and employment, and to follow compatible fiscal, monetary, and wage policies. At times, some members of the Monetary Fund, including the United States, were unable to follow such policies. More recently, even the European countries with similar social and economic objectives were unable to maintain the exchange rates for their currencies within the wider margins from the central rates permitted by the exchange-rate arrangements of the European Monetary Union.

The U.S. balance-of-payments deficit on an official reserve basis fell into deficit in the 1960s because of the large increase in foreign investment. The current account remained in surplus until 1970. The United States tried to restrain the capital outflow by a tax on purchases of foreign securities and by restrictions on the transfer of funds for direct investment in the industrial countries. Investment in the United States by the European surplus countries in the 1960s was relatively small. Instead, they accumulated large reserves, much of which was in dollars and converted into gold.

It was thought that one reason for the persistent U.S. deficit on an official reserve basis was the unavailability of sufficient reserves other than dollars derived from the U.S. balance-of-payments deficit. It was hoped that if adequate reserves were available in another way, the U.S. deficit on an official reserve basis, and the drain on U.S. gold reserves, would be eliminated. The Fund agreement was amended to authorize it to create reserve assets, designated as special drawing rights (SDR), initially equal in value to one gold dollar. The Fund distributed SDRs to members on the basis of their quotas. This increased their reserves, but it did not halt the U.S. deficit or the converting of dollars into gold.

In August 1971, when the payments situation became critical because of a flight from the dollar, the United States notified the Monetary Fund that it would no longer convert foreign official dollar holdings into gold. It also placed a tariff surcharge on most imports. In order to retain the central role of the dollar in the international monetary system and to secure the withdrawal of the tariff surcharge, the industrial countries and the Monetary Fund agreed in December 1971 on a realignment of par values. The dollar was to be devalued and the strong European currencies and the yen were revalued. Moreover, the other industrial countries undertook to support the foreign exchange value of the dollar, although it was no longer convertible.

In spite of the realignment of par values, the U.S. deficit increased and the dollar fell in the exchange market. In February 1973, the dollar was devalued again, but the pressure on the dollar continued. The other industrial countries stopped supporting the dollar because the accumulation of dollars in their reserves was causing inflation. In March 1973, the twice-reduced par value was abandoned and the dollar became a floating currency, convertible into other currencies through the exchange market.

Remaking the Bretton Woods Institutions

The floating of the dollar effectively ended the system of fixed but adjustable par values. The second amendment to the Fund agreement provides a new basis for international responsibility on exchange rates. Members are required to cooperate with the Monetary Fund in maintaining orderly exchange conditions. They are allowed to have any exchange-rate system they want, provided they do not manipulate the exchange rate to obtain an unfair advantage in international trade or to prevent balance-of-payments adjustment. Thus, a member can have a floating rate, or base its exchange rate on another currency, or on the SDR, or on a basket of currencies, but not on gold. A number of European countries decided to link the exchange rates for their currencies within a wider margin around the par value or central rate. The United States and most other members chose to have a floating exchange rate. The SDR has been redefined to consist of a fixed amount of dollars, yen, deutsche marks, French francs, and sterling. It has replaced the dollar as the accounting unit of the Monetary Fund.

The financial operations of the Bretton Woods institutions have been broadened to meet new problems. The World Bank was originally designed to guarantee loans of members made through bond issues and to make loans directly to members out of its capital and funds it raises in the market. The World Bank found that such operations gave too much emphasis to government projects and too little encouragement to private investment. To facilitate the development of the private sector, it established the International Finance Corporation, which invests in private companies in developing countries. And to encourage foreign direct investment in developing countries, the World Bank provided means for arbitrating disputes between foreign direct investors and the host country.

As some members are too poor to finance their development by loans at market rates of interest, the World Bank established the International Development Association (IDA) to make loans to them on concessionary terms. It is able to do this because the funds for the IDA come from contributions of the high-income countries rather than from borrowing in the market. When the IDA needs additional funds, they come from further contributions (replenishment).

The Monetary Fund was originally intended to help finance current account deficits, mainly of a cyclical character, that could be corrected within two or three years. For this purpose, annual drawings of 25 percent of the quota were thought to be adequate. Where adjustment of the balance of payments required a change in the par value of the currency and changes in fiscal and monetary policies, the annual quota drawings would not be sufficient to finance the deficits until the balance of payments was restored. The Monetary Fund devised a method of assuring members of financial assistance in excess of the quota limits through waivers and standby agreements for larger drawings.

Experience showed that a balance-of-payments deficit could arise from causes beyond a member's control. The sharp increase in the cost of oil imports, for example, caused a difficult payments problem for many members. The Monetary Fund created special facilities to provide credits, outside the quota limits, for dealing with such problems. More recently, the Monetary Fund and the World Bank have acquired new members from Central and Eastern Europe, some of them former constituents of the Soviet Union. These members need technical and financial assistance in converting from a state-managed economy to a market-oriented economy. For this purpose, the Monetary Fund has created the systemic transformation facility. The financing of the credit operations of the Monetary Fund comes primarily from the quota subscriptions of its members (capital), now amounting to SDR 145 billion, equivalent to more than $200 billion. The Monetary Fund can also borrow from its members, which it has done on occasion.

As the broadening of the operations of the Monetary Fund and the World Bank indicate, they have been indispensable for dealing with some of the critical financial problems that have arisen in recent years. They can provide financial assistance promptly, without the delay inevitable in parliamentary proceedings for granting aid. And they can offer technical assistance to their members that would be politically unacceptable if it were to seem imposed by other countries.

Further Evolution of the International Monetary System

The inability of the United States to restore its balance of payments after two devaluations of the dollar led to the second amendment to the Fund agreement, which authorized floating exchange rates. One reason for adopting floating rates was the belief that it would result in automatic balance-of-payments adjustment.

The appropriate balance of payments for a country is the same under a system of floating rates as under a system of par values. A high-income country that would normally generate more savings than can be profitably invested at home should have a surplus on current account offset by net foreign investment. The function of the exchange rate is to enable a country to maintain an appropriate balance of payments with policies directed toward stability of prices and a high level of output and employment. Under a system of par values, such an exchange rate is presumed to reflect relative prices and costs—purchasing power parity.

This is expected to result in an appropriate balance on trade in goods and services. Monetary policy should be able to bring about an offsetting balance on capital flows.

With floating exchange rates, the supply of and demand for a currency are equated in the foreign exchange market. That does not assure an appropriate balance of payments. It may merely mean that an inappropriate surplus or deficit on current account is matched by an offsetting, but inappropriate, balance on capital account. And with floating rates, capital flows may be greatly distorted because of inappropriate differences in interest rates and speculation on changes in exchange rates. In fact, with floating exchange rates, capital flows may make it more difficult to achieve an appropriate balance on current account.

That happened in the United States in the 1980s. A huge inflow of foreign capital for direct investment and for the purchase of American securities, augmented by speculative funds, resulted in an enormous increase in the foreign exchange value of the dollar. Between mid-1980 and mid-1985, the dollar rose by over 100 percent against the deutsche mark, even more against most other European currencies, but less against the yen and the Canadian dollar. This was one of the major causes of the large and persistent U.S. deficit on current account. In 1980, the United States had a current account surplus of $7 billion. Since then, the current account has been constantly in deficit, reaching a peak of $167 billion in 1987. Although the dollar has fallen well below its 1980 level, the current account deficit was still $109 billion in 1993 and will probably be much larger this year. The anomalous appreciation of the dollar in the 1980s is not the only reason for the persistence of the U.S. current account deficit, but it created conditions that have made it much more difficult to adjust the U.S. balance of payments.

When the exchange rate for a currency rises and falls considerably in a short period, it must be either overvalued or undervalued, measured by relative prices and costs, at some time during the period. This not only distorts the pattern of international trade but has adverse effects on the economy. An overvalued currency is like a too-tight monetary policy. It restrains the rise of prices, but it also holds down the growth of output and employment. An undervalued currency, on the other hand, is like a too-easy monetary policy. It stimulates the expansion of output and employment, but it also facilitates a rise of prices.

For this reason, the exchange rate is an inherent aspect of monetary policy; and the monetary authorities cannot ignore large changes in the foreign exchange value of the currency. With floating rates, the foreign exchange market needs guidance by the monetary authorities, not only through the usual instruments of monetary policy, but at times also directly through intervention. The problem is what the objective of intervention should be and how it should be integrated with other aspects of monetary policy.

The experience with the Exchange Rate Arrangements (ERA) of the European Monetary Union may be helpful on this. The countries that participated in the ERA undertook to maintain their exchange rates with the currencies of the other participants within 2¼ percent of the central rate, although Italy and Spain were allowed to have a margin of 6 percent above and below the central rate. From the end of June 1979 to the end of June 1989, in the first ten years of these arrangements, the French franc, a key currency in the ERA, fell by 32 percent against the deutsche mark, the standard currency in the ERA, while the British pound fell by 24 percent, although the United Kingdom was not in the ERA in this period. Nevertheless, the franc fluctuated much less than the pound. In this ten-year period, the average change in the rate for the deutsche mark, at six-month intervals, was 2.1 percent for the franc and 5.6 percent for the pound. Apparently the monetary authorities were able to reduce the volatility even when they could not maintain the stability of exchange rates. The objective of intervention, under a system of floating rates, should be to minimize the volatility of exchange rates.

It has been suggested that, with floating rates, the monetary authorities should establish a target zone with a wide band, within which they would maintain the exchange rate. In the ERA of the European Monetary Union, Italy and Spain were allowed a 6 percent margin from the central rate—in effect, a target zone with a 12 percent band. That did not prevent large fluctuations in the exchange rates for the lira and the peseta, and it increased the volatility of the rates for these currencies. If the policy is to intervene only at the top and bottom of the band, the target zone may encourage volatility. When the exchange rate begins to fall, speculators may quickly drive it to the bottom of the target zone, as the monetary authorities are not expected to intervene before then.

A better policy would be for the monetary authorities to intervene at any point in the target zone, whenever there is a large and rapid change in the exchange rate. As intervention in the exchange market affects other countries, it should be undertaken only after consultation with the Monetary Fund and in cooperation with the countries whose currencies are used for intervention. A fall in the foreign exchange rate may be a signal that the exchange market believes that a change in monetary policy is necessary. Therefore, when the monetary authorities intervene in the exchange market, they should consider whether the intervention should be accompanied by a change in policy.

Intervention itself changes the monetary situation as it affects the money supply and the reserves of the banking system. Thus, selling foreign exchange to support the exchange rate has the same effect as selling Treasury bills in order to tighten the monetary situation. In the 1930s, some countries established exchange equalization accounts to insulate the money supply and bank reserves from transactions in gold and foreign exchange reserves. When the monetary authorities intervene in the exchange market, they must consider whether the magnitude of the consequent monetary changes is consistent with the broader objectives of economic policy. The amount of intervention is not a proper measure of the change in the monetary aggregates that is appropriate for the economy. If the intervention causes too large a change in the money supply and bank reserves, the monetary authorities may have to undertake open market operations to offset the excess. The behavior of the exchange rate is only one, and not the most important, indication that a change in monetary policy is necessary. As the U.S. Treasury stated in the "Questions and Answers on the International Monetary Fund" submitted to the Bretton Woods Conference: "It would be a complete inversion of objectives if a high level of business activity were to be sacrificed to maintain any given structure of exchange rates."

8

Fifty Years of Bretton Woods

Roberto Campos

Introduction

In the conference of Bretton Woods, which I attended as a young diplomat, there was a great hope and a great fear. The hope was that we would put an end to the era of confrontation in monetary and foreign exchange matters that characterized the 1930s. The fear was the return of the twin devils that also plagued the 1930s: depression and competitive currency devaluations. This was insofar as the IMF was concerned. The World Bank, on the other side, would address itself to the structural problems of reconstruction and development.

Economists Are Not Good Prophets

As I look back over the years, I become more and more skeptical about the predictive ability of the economic profession. Contrary to the fears of the galaxy of talented economists gathered at Bretton Woods, the real dangers of the post-war period were inflation and currency overvaluation rather than the other way around. Quite a few countries indulged in exchange rate overvaluation, partly to cheapen essential imports and partly as a misguided device to abate inflationary pressures. In Latin America, this behavior was the rule rather than the exception. Those were the types of problems which Keynesianism, then the mainstream economic doctrine, was not particularly well equipped to handle.

In regard to the World Bank, the fear of the underdeveloped countries was that its resources would be almost completely absorbed by the task of reconstruction, with precious little left for development help. This forecast was again wrong. The main burden of financing reconstruction was taken up by the Marshall Plan. But assistance for development was slow to come, partly because of the very conservative lending policies of the Bank, anxious to win the confidence of Wall Street in the solidity of its loan portfolio.

Congenital Imbalances of the International System

Expressing the views of Latin American countries, the Brazilian delegation to Bretton Woods pointed out a critical flaw in the architecture of international cooperation then being erected. This was a lack of a specialized agency to deal with the instability of trade in primary commodities. This was of particular importance to underdeveloped countries, for their balance-of-payment problems were directly affected by erratic swings in commodities prices.[1]

The Brazilian delegation accordingly tabled a resolution proposing the immediate convocation of a UN conference "to promote stability of prices of raw materials and agricultural products and to formulate recommendations for attainment of a more balanced growth of international trade."

Lord Keynes recognized the intellectual validity of the point. In fact, the original proposal of the British Treasury included a scheme to combat the "evils of the economic cycles," traceable in part to the erratic behavior of commodity prices. It was thought, however, that the creation in Bretton Woods of two international agencies was of itself a complicated affair. Trade issues were to be treated separately. For that purpose the United Nations Conference on Trade and Employment was convoked to meet in the fall of 1947. The Havana charter, which provided for the creation of the International Trade Organization (ITO), was not ratified by any of the major countries. The substitute organ that entered into operation shortly afterward was the General Agreement on Tariffs and Trade (GATT), which dealt mainly with tariffs and trade in manufactures. Agricultural protectionism proved then an insurmountable obstacle and continued along the years to be a thorny problem. Only forty-six years later, with the conclusion of the Uruguay Round of the GATT in December 1993, a new trade charter was agreed upon aiming at the creation of the World Trade Organization (WTO). This agency has a broad coverage encompassing not only agriculture but also services, investment rules, and protection of intellectual property.

The Changing Roles of the IMF and World Bank

It would be impossible to review here the role and vicissitudes of the institutions created in Bretton Woods. Even condensing it in a few broad strokes would require too much space and time and would add but a drop into the sea of literature already existing on the matter. Perhaps the most useful contribution I might give is to focus on both institutions from the perspective of Latin American developing countries.

The original role of the IMF in supervising the system of fixed parities was just about exhausted by the early 1970s, as the major industrial countries switched to the system of floating exchange rates. The IMF survived, however, and was to play a role in major events: the petrodollar recycling process of the 1970s and the international debt crisis of the 1980s.

The relations between the IMF and Latin America have a checkered history. During the late 1950s and throughout the 1970s, most of the Latin American countries were afflicted by the disease of the "isms": nationalism, populism, structuralism, protectionism, and statism. This did not create a congenial atmosphere for the operation of the Bretton Woods sister institutions. The IMF in particular became the *bête noire* of the Left, the symbol of the capitalist order. But the ideological position from the Left was not the only significant source of vocal criticism. The governments of developing countries soon showed an unquenchable thirst for spending more than they could manage to collect from taxes and contributions on current income. Foreign counsels on the need for fiscal austerity and budget trimming looked like advice from the devil, a bitter medicine after an indulgent binge.

It might be useful to relate my own experience in dealing with the IMF as minister of planning of Brazil in the early 1960s, when a major reform and stabilization program was carried out in my country.

The IMF was much less flexible than today and we quarreled on three issues. Having in mind the history and experience of war-induced European hyperinflations, the IMF recommended what amounted to shock therapy. We advocated "gradualism," because of the distorted asset structure of the firms which, fearful of inflation, overinvested in fixed assets to the detriment of working capital. The IMF also suffered from what we called "the mechanist syndrome." It insisted on very rigid quantitative targets for monetary expansion and public sector deficits, as if there were a scientifically predictable relation between those aggregates and the rate of inflation. We favored a more qualitative approach, centered on an agreement on the basic strategy and instruments of monetary and fiscal control, more important in our view than quarterly benchmarks. Another of our arguments was that the political system was less amenable to drastic political changes than in the case of countries torn out by the war. Finally, we could not count on massive foreign aid, such as that of the Marshall Plan, to attenuate the stabilization crisis. The differences between the Latin American chronic type of inflation—we argued—and the European hyperinflations was similar to that between an abscess that can be quickly punctured and body poisoning that demands slower purification. Over the course of the years, as several of the main partners of the IMF fell prey to inflation and balance-of-payments difficulties, the Fund's postures mellowed considerably from the rigid orthodoxy of the 1960s.

The Emergence of the "Washington Consensus"

To vilify the IMF as the great capitalist Satan was, of course, for three decades— until the collapse of socialism—the favorite sport of the Latin American Left, with undisguised sympathy of governments anxious to justify their inflationary misdemeanors. There were, however, some valid reservations which I expressed as far back as 1961 in a conference in West Berlin: (1) the technical inconsistency of the IMF in requiring simultaneously currency devaluation and internal stabilization measures; (2) the underestimation of the political resistance to rigid cost-cutting programs; (3) the "fallacy of aggregation" in requiring global cost cuts, without paying much attention to the need to preserve investment in bottleneck sectors; (4) concentration on demand management, with little attention to supply-side measures.

In the late 1980s and the beginning of this decade some basic postures of the IMF became less controversial. The effects of the oil shocks and the debt crisis were largely absorbed with the cooperation of the IMF, as an auditing agency for agreements under the Brady plan. The collapse of socialism and the clear superiority of the Asiatic export-oriented and market-friendly approach, over the Latin American heavily interventionist import-substitution doctrine, contributed to the emergence of a new consensus, inappropriately labeled the "Washington consensus." A much better designation might be a "market friendly" convergence. The disease of the "isms" was gradually healed by the prevalence of the new suffix "ation." Disinflation, privatization, deregulation, trade liberalization, and international integration became the new *mots d'ordre* of reformist governments in Latin America.

A word might be said on structural adjustment as contrasted with monetary and financial problems. Many people insist on an impossible differentiation between the IMF and the World Bank, alleging that the latter should concern itself with long-term structural reforms, while the former only with monetary and exchange problems. The two aspects are, however, inextricably related and specialization should not be overdone. I believe, for instance, that the programs of the IMF should stress, as part and parcel of the macroeconomic adjustment process, some reforms such as privatization and trade liberalization. In the case of my country, Brazil, the fiscal problem arising from the high cost of rolling over the internal public debt would be almost insoluble by tax and expenditure cuts and easily soluble through the sale of government assets for the purpose of canceling the debt. Then the vicious circle created by the crowding out of the private-sector financial markets could be expeditiously converted into a virtuous circle through the decline in interest rates and the transformation of heavily subsidized state-owned enterprises into normal taxpayers.

The World Bank, which never aroused the same degree of antagonism as its sister institution, has experienced a welcome evolution from strict project financing to broader structural adjustment programs, and has veered its lending policy from basic industries and infrastructure to education, health, and poverty-alleviation measures. This is all to the good, as private-risk capital is taking up the role of financing not only industry but also the infrastructure. A full cycle is thus completed. The infrastructure in Latin America was largely built by foreign capital. Starting in the 1950s there was a wave of statism through the nationalization of public utilities and transport facilities. The combination of rising inflationary costs and politically fixed rates expelled private investors from those sectors. More recently the bankruptcy of governments, under the weight of social welfare needs, opened up again, through privatization, the field for private capital investment in the infrastructure. It is necessary for the World Bank to adjust itself to the new trend, by accepting direct financing of privately built infrastructure without governmental intervention or guarantees.

Recent Transformations in the Global Scenario

I would like to mention briefly four recent transformations in the world scenario, two of which impinge on the work of the IMF and the others on the World Bank: (1) the globalization of financial markets; (2) the emergence of alternative coordination mechanisms; (3) the resumption of large-scale international private investment; (4) the new "conditionalities."

The supervisory and coordinating functions of the IMF on monetary and exchange matters have been enormously complicated by the globalization of financial markets. Exchange-rate volatility has been considerably heightened, giving rise to new complex risk-handling devices such as "derivatives," which remain outside the control of central banks.

A possible medium- or long-term solution, as hinted by the Bretton Woods Commission in its recent report, might be the creation of a system of exchange-rate fluctuations within a band, centered on three major currencies—the dollar, the yen, and the deutsche mark (or whatever other European currency might emerge within the European Union). This, of course, would require a closer worldwide coordination of monetary and fiscal policies, a daunting task indeed if one considers the recent problems of the European monetary system.

A second factor is the emergence of the Group of Seven (G–7), which, although having broader political and security tasks, involves itself also in the coordination of monetary and fiscal policies of its members. Given the economic weight of its participants, the G–7 certainly subtracts some clout from the IMF as a surveyor of financial discipline. An indication of the tensions that might arise was the recent clash during the IMF meeting in Madrid over the issuance of additional special drawing rights. The G–7 would agree to expand the supply of SDRs, provided it was targeted to assist the market conversion of ex-communist countries, while the managing director and the majority of the board of governors favor a nondiscriminatory access to the new SDRs.

With regard to the World Bank, the major event of today is the revitalization of the international flow of private-sector investment. One of the traditional functions of the World Bank—the financing of public-sector projects in the infrastructure—is being quickly (and fortunately) superseded by a revival of international private capital flows. This largely is due to the worldwide drive for the privatization of utilities, transportation, and telecommunication systems. The wave of nationalization of infrastructure sectors that began in the postwar period had two components: one was the political manipulation of rates and prices to blur the effects of cost inflation, and the other was the ideological socialist preference for preserving in the hands of the state the control of the "commanding heights of the economy." This cycle has now been reversed. Ideological tenets have been eroded, and the governments, strapped for cash to bear the burden of social welfare expenditures, are only too willing to lure back private finance, the availability of which has increased by the globalization of capital markets.

The World Bank should adjust itself to this new situation either by amending its statute, which now requires government guarantee for any lending operation, or by transferring bigger resources to the International Finance Corporation (IFC), which lends directly to, or subscribes equity in, private-sector projects.

A cautionary word might be said on the question of newly emerging "conditionalities." We are of course familiar with the "traditional conditionality" of the IMF, related to fiscal responsibility and monetary restraint. This conditionality is fortunately now being enforced with somewhat less dogmatism than in earlier times when the Keynesian obsession with macroeconomic aggregates led to an underestimation of the importance of microeconomic adjustments such as deregulation and privatization.

It is in the field of operation of the World Bank that a gray area of conditionalities seems to appear. Those are only indirectly and at times only vaguely connected with the core objectives of development financing. The most explicit new conditionality relates to environment. The rich developed countries have become environmentalists with a vengeance, and are not beyond using this concern as a protectionist device. For the developing countries the issue is less clear and the need for urgent alleviation of poverty may collide with environmental sophistication. What is needed is a careful analysis by the World Bank in its project financing of the cost of antipollution measures versus projects for direct alleviation of poverty.

A few other implicit or "creeping" conditionalities might be mentioned. One that is justifiable in principle takes into account the wastage of armament expenditures as a negative factor in the economic performance of borrowing countries. Another is the withdrawal of assistance to countries deemed to be guilty of gross and systematic violation of basic human rights.

Much more obscure and intricate is the attempt to evaluate countries' performance in relation to the so-called economic and social rights. This involves questions of income distribution and labor standards. The latter issue would be more relevant to the operations of the new WTO, for the reason that demand for higher labor standards in the developing countries, through internationalization or precepts akin to the European "social charter," might become a protectionist device. It would deprive those countries of a comparative advantage—cheaper labor costs—which serves as a temporary offset to their lower productivity.

The Bretton Woods institutions served us in good stead for half a century, but they need some restructuring and considerably better coordination to meet the challenges of the years ahead.

Two major events mark the end of this century that is also the end of a millennium: the collapse of communism and the modernization of Asia. We do not know how the new international order will shape itself in the mist of the future. But we do know that two of its salient features are likely to be the spread of political democracy and increasing adhesion to market mechanism as superior to socialist planning.

This is not the end of history. But it is a magnificent—and I hope enduring—chapter of it.

I am glad to have been, as a young man, present at the creation of the Bretton Woods institutions.

Note

1. There has been a dynamic evolution in developmental semantics. During the Second World War, the expression used to describe the nonindustrialized world was "poor" or "backward" countries, a verbiage that carried a connotation of fatalism. In the immediate postwar period, the jargon was changed to "underdeveloped" or "less developed" countries. A note of optimism was added later through the expression "developing" countries. In the wake of the success of some Latin American countries in the late 1960s and of the rise of Asiatic tigers (South Korea, Taiwan, Hong Kong, Singapore) in the late 1980s, the expressions "emerging countries," "threshold countries," or "newly industrialized countries" (NICs) came into vogue. Reflecting not only economic conditions but also the ideological rift of the cold war, the expressions "First, Second, and Third World" became part of the vocabulary, until the collapse of socialism in the late 1980s and the steady advance of the NICs rendered that verbiage obsolete.

9

The World Bank: Challenges and Creative Responses

Andrew M. Kamarck

Introduction

It is now largely forgotten that, in the first years of its life, there was more than a reasonable doubt that the World Bank would survive or become a useful organization. Six months after it opened its doors in June 1945, the president, Eugene Meyer, resigned without waiting for the election of a successor. Unlike the platoons of vice presidents in the current Bank, the Bank had only one vice president, Harold Smith. When he died a few weeks after Meyer's resignation, the Bank was left leaderless. Several prominent financial people refused to consider taking the job because they thought the Bank was a hopeless cause: the Bank had made no loans, the capital markets were hostile, and no securities had been floated. Moreover, there was an unresolved conflict over the relationship between the executive directors and the management.

The Bank did not begin to function in reality until March 17, 1946, when the governments accepted that the management would actually manage the Bank while the executive directors would restrict their role to general supervision. John J. McCloy became president, Robert L. Garner vice president, and Eugene R. Black the U.S. executive director.

At this new beginning, the Bank, a historically unique organization, had no precedents or experience to draw on. It was further handicapped by the prevalent belief that it was bound to fail or should soon be wound up. Finally, the Bank found that the world was quite different from the one the Bretton Woods founders had tacitly assumed would exist.

Yet by the end of the presidency of George Woods in 1968, roughly around the twenty-fifth anniversary of its conception at Bretton Woods, the World Bank, with very little dissent, was universally regarded as a success.

The Bank has a record of outstanding accomplishments. The Bank staff is still one of the most talented and effective of any international organization and compares well with any institution in the private or public sector of any country. The magnitude of the capital it makes available to its borrowers, the coordination of bilateral aid through its consortia and consultative groups, the training of thousands of less developed country (LDC) officials through its Economic Development Institute, the contribution to tropical agriculture productivity through its organization of financing for the network of tropical research institutes across the world, the help to private-sector industry through the International Finance Corporation (IFC), and its many other contributions altogether make the Bank a most valuable institution.

The Bank's statement on its fiftieth anniversary included a timeline of major Bank events that listed what it considered the Bank's innovative introductions:

- (1951) international competitive bidding on projects;
- (1956) organizing the International Finance Corporation to help developing countries mobilize and encourage private venture capital;
- (1956) setting up the Economic Development Institute to train top Third World officials;
- (1958) organizing an aid consortium for India that became the model for consultative groups for coordinating lending and aid for the less developed countries;
- (1960) establishing the International Development Association (IDA) to provide near-grant aid for countries whose urgent need for capital could not be met on World Bank terms;
- (1962) recognizing the need for investment in human capital and beginning to lend for education projects;
- (1964) financing programs of cooperative work with the Food and Agriculture Organization (FAO) and other United Nations agencies, leading to upgrading the levels of competence in these agencies and multiplying the assistance to LDCs in the preparation of investment projects for financing by the Bank and other capital sources;
- (1968) beginning lending for family-planning projects;
- (1971) organizing the financing of a network of tropical agricultural research centers around the world;
- (1978) beginning the publication of the World Development Reports;
- (1980) beginning structural adjustment lending;
- (1987) establishing an Environment Department; and,
- (1988) formally establishing the Multilateral Investment Guarantee Agency (MIGA).

What is striking about this list is that the majority of the successful, innovative, and creative actions it shows were taken in the first quarter century of the Bank's history. Of the last six, which fall in the second quarter-century, three were essentially begun earlier, and one is a failure, not a success. The World Development Reports evolved out of the economic analysis sections of the Bank's annual report which were initiated in the 1964–65 annual report. During the presidency of Robert S. McNamara, the executive directors called attention to the fact that under the Articles of Agreement the Bank's annual report was their report and not the management's. Since then, the annual report has appeared over their signatures. The Bank staff, in consequence, moved the analysis of economic and financial matters from the annual report into a new series of World Bank Development Reports. Work on MIGA was started earlier. The tropical agricultural research institutes were pioneered by the Rockefeller and Ford Foundations. Their sponsorship by the Bank was spearheaded by Richard Demuth, who was involved in practically every one of the early creative innovations.[1] Finally, structural adjustment lending was a failure.

This leaves only lending for family-planning projects and the establishment of an Environment Department as the innovative introductions of the Bank's second quarter-century. That is, two out of twelve were successful innovations.

Henry Owens, the cochairman of the U.S. Bretton Woods Committee, praised the World Bank's record of accomplishment in a recent article in *Foreign Affairs*. The only specific contribution that he cited, however, was that the World Bank's aid "has been a major factor in making India agriculturally self-sufficient."[2] This again was an accomplishment of the first twenty-five years.

The Bank list omits the International Center for Settlement of Investment Disputes, an arbitration and mediation center for disputes between foreign investors and governments. This was an important innovative initiative of the Bank and of its Bank sponsor, Aaron Broches, the general counsel of the Bank. It also was an accomplishment of the first quarter-century.

It is notable that neither the Bank list nor Owens makes any mention of any contribution made by the Bank to the solution of the international debt crisis of the 1980s. While the Bank did help, the initiative, creativity, and leadership in coping with the crisis came from the U.S. government and the International Monetary Fund, not from the Bank. Similarly, it is the Fund that the international community looks to for leadership in helping Eastern Europe and the former– Soviet Union restructure. Again, the Bank is providing important help but not the policy leadership. In the past, the Bank was usually the innovative leader, with the Fund following suit after some delay. For example, the Fund's training institute, its publication of applied research in occasional papers and books, and its annual world economic survey all followed the Bank's early example.

It is not merely nostalgia that leads one to regret seeing the old melange of Bank buildings, constructed at different times and in different architectural styles, now being replaced by a beautiful, gleaming glass-covered ultramodern office building. Readers of Parkinson will remember that he observed that institutions that are lively and productive flourish in shabby and makeshift surroundings. When an institution builds a headquarters of perfection and beauty and dignity, it is a symptom of decay. While an institution is in its period of creativity and exciting progress, there is no time to plan and to build the perfect headquarters. This comes later when it is in its decline.[3]

Now, at the fiftieth anniversary of Bretton Woods, the Bank is under general attack for its record on the central core of its work, its lending policy. Some forty development, environmental, human rights, and religious organizations have adopted the slogan "Fifty Years Is Enough" and are attacking the Bank for projects and policies "that have drastically increased global poverty and debt and promoted development that is undemocratic, inequitable, and harmful to the environment." And, what's more, "billions have been spent on poorly conceived projects—dams, roads, and power plants—37 percent of which have been colossal failures, even according to the World Bank's own internal documents."[4] The attack from the right also criticizes the Bank as having been positively harmful to the less developed countries because it has tended to reinforce the statist inclination of their leaders as against supporting the private economy.[5] To cap all this, the *Economist* has announced, "The Bank's goal is to work itself out of a job—and faster progress towards that goal is needed."[6]

While Lewis Preston, the current Bank president, does not accept that the Bank is in crisis, he has recognized that a drastic reorientation of Bank policies is necessary.

The First Quarter-Century: Hopelessness to Success

How was the success of the first quarter-century accomplished and what went wrong in the last twenty-five years?

In the beginning the Bank had to overcome a series of initial obstacles that, once mastered, were eliminated forever. First of all, the Bank had to establish an effective working relationship between Bank management and the executive directors and governors who represent the stockholders of the Bank. The initial negotiations that McCloy, Garner, and Black had with the governments before they took their jobs set the general shape of this relationship—giving management substantial autonomy in running the Bank—for many years. It was agreed that the initiative in processing loans was the responsibility of the president and staff, and the board of directors would not approve any loans not recommended by the president. The president was also given power to recruit and manage staff on the basis of effectiveness, not political influence. Jobs were not allocated according to nationality.

Some of the other early problems of the Bank were matters of consequence when the Bank was still finding its way and gaining acceptance.

In order to sell securities in the United States, the Bank had to persuade the legislatures of the then forty-eight states, one by one, to pass legislation to make investment in Bank bonds legal investments for trustees, trust companies, state banks, and savings institutions. This was necessary to establish a market for its bonds. The activity of educating and lobbying state legislatures took a considerable investment of time and effort on the part of management and some of the staff.

A somewhat related problem was that, when the Bank opened its doors, the bulk of its paid-in capital was actually unusable. Of the 20 percent of the value of its shares that a country was required to pay into the Bank, 18 percent was payable in its own currency. This amount could only be loaned with the approval of the member whose currency was involved; and most members felt they were not in a position to give approval. The Bank did not give up. The currencies were available for use for administrative expenditures in the countries concerned. And so a staff member traveling on a mission was given local currency checks or local currency traveler's checks to cover expenses in each country visited. Then the Bank systematically asked governments to release their currencies to pay for any equipment or services being purchased in their territories under Bank loans. These measures freed up a considerable portion of the 18 percent capital and eventually, as the international economy improved by the early 1960s, governments liberalized the remainder.

When the Bank opened its doors, most of Latin America as well as countries in Eastern Europe had defaulted on the international loans that they had received in the 1920s. The creditworthiness of any debtor is clearly questionable if the debtor does not respect debt obligations that it has incurred in the past. Deciding what Bank policy should be on lending vis-à-vis these countries was not an easy problem. The Bank recognized that many of the defaulted loans had been bad loans—used for uneconomic ends, completely wasted, or diverted into the pockets of corrupt, long-departed officials. Also, it was quite clear in a number of cases that the country concerned just could not bear the burden of the debt service required at the time. It would be unconscionable to neglect helping the country to develop its economy until the country had recovered sufficient paying capacity. But the countries had undertaken obligations and they had to be respected.

The Bank finally decided that its rock-bottom condition for lending was that the country must negotiate in good faith with its creditors for a settlement of its debt. It would not impose any conditions on what kind of settlement should eventually be reached. The Bank went further in some instances where it was necessary. In 1953, when President Black informed the Yugoslavs that their pre–World War II defaulted debt was a barrier to Bank lending, the Yugoslavs said they could not afford to resume debt service. Black said that, if they wished, he would send a Bank mission to appraise the situation and advise them and the Bank. They agreed and that was my first mission to Yugoslavia. I concluded, and the Yugoslavs agreed, that they could not resume full debt service, but that the economy was sufficiently recovered to be able to negotiate with the bondholders on some sort of debt settlement. The Bank and Yugoslavia accepted the recommendation, and Yugoslavia reached agreement with the bondholders on a settlement of its prewar debt on quite generous terms for the country.

The World Bank is, of course, the International Bank for Reconstruction and Development (IBRD). The Bretton Woods fathers thought that it would play a major role in the reconstruction of war-devastated Europe. The Bank's first loans were to European countries, but it quickly became plain that the task was far beyond the resources of the Bank and the main burden was assumed by the Marshall Plan. The Bank thus became very quickly an institution engaged in the task of helping in the economic development of poor countries.

During the first decade, the Bank was largely a dollar bank. That is, the money available for lending was almost completely in U.S. and Canadian dollars from the 18 percent tranches and the money raised in the U.S. bond markets. At the end of World War II there was an enormous international dollar shortage. The rest of the world wanted and needed commodities from North America and had little to sell to it. The academic economists were writing books to prove that the dollar shortage was not a temporary phenomenon but a lasting fixture of the international economy. The argument was that there had been a dollar shortage for most of the twentieth century and that there would always be a dollar shortage—the U.S. economy was unique and so productive it would always run a huge export surplus. This was so much the conventional wisdom that anyone who disagreed in academic circles ran the risk of being regarded as, in Professor Barro's term, "not respectable." It is true Keynes had written an article in 1946 that disagreed, but this was regarded as an aberration by an otherwise brilliant economist.

Dependent as the Bank was on the American security markets, it was important for the Bank not only to be prudent in its lending policies but also to *appear* prudent in these early years. Consequently, the economists in the Bank had to emphasize the bilateral "dollar" creditworthiness of borrowers. This emphasis on dollar creditworthiness lasted until the middle of the 1950s. At that time, as the economic adviser on Europe, Africa, and Australasia, it became obvious to me and my colleagues that the currencies of our borrowers were sufficiently convertible into dollars that dollar creditworthiness could be abandoned in favor of general creditworthiness. The recommendation to this effect was made in a memorandum from me to the staff Loan Committee, and accepted.

Picking the Right Measure for Success

Once the early problems of the Bank were solved, they were and are no longer of consequence. With a competent management in place, the ground cleared of legal obstacles, and the relationship with its political masters clarified, the Bank had to make the fundamental decisions that affect everything the Bank is and does. That is, it had to decide what its fundamental purpose or goals were, what its strategies should be to reach these goals, how it should manage its affairs accordingly, and what kind of organization was needed to do its job. It is my thesis that the Bank in the first quarter-century made the right choices on the vital questions of strategies, management, and organization, and that the Bank in the second quarter-century made the wrong choices. And, as we will see, these were decisive.

Under the Articles of Agreement, the first purpose laid down for the Bank is "to assist in the reconstruction and development of the territories of members by facilitating the investment of capital for productive purposes, including . . . the encouragement of the development of productive facilities and resources in less developed countries."[7]

Consistent with the articles, in the first quarter-century the Bank regarded economic development of its member countries as its fundamental purpose. In the second quarter-century, Bank presidents changed the rhetoric. McNamara talked about alleviating poverty and improving the distribution of income. New goals were added: concern about health; rate of population growth; protection of the environment; role of women in development; concern about human rights; quality of governance; and democracy. The overarching goal of the Bank in recent years is officially stated as "poverty reduction."

This goal clearly has some implications that differ from those flowing from the goal of economic development. It seems, for example, to give up on the possibility of achieving development, being satisfied with reducing poverty. The accumulation of the diverse subgoals during the second quarter-century and the addition of dedicated Bank staff and internal organizational units have responded to various outside pressures. However, it has not made the Bank a more effective organization.

The Bank is a nonprofit international financial institution. The usual economic criterion or measure—profits, the bottom line, the verdict of the market—by which success of ordinary corporate organizations can be judged is not applicable. Therefore, the Bank has to have another measure of success/failure. The essential difference between the Bank's first quarter-century and its second is in the measure that the Bank chose in these two periods. From this also flowed the difference in how the Bank was organized and how it operated.

Organizations operate by controlling inputs, process, outputs, and outcomes. The two main criteria that organizations not driven by the profit motive can use to measure their success are *outcome* or *output*. The early Bank was concerned with *outcome*—the results in helping economic development in its member countries. The later Bank was concerned with *output*—the volume of loans made by the Bank. These choices have great consequences.

If *output* is chosen, it can be closely controlled and measured. It fits in with the approved theory of "management by objectives." It can be easily quantified and easily controlled from the top: the subordinate either met his target or he didn't. It lends itself to centralized management. By using *output*—the volume of lending—as the measure of success, Bank presidents were free to announce whatever goals they wished to declare were the Bank's purposes. For example, when McNamara introduced output—the volume of lending—as the Bank's measure of success, from the very beginning it sabotaged his rhetoric on using Bank lending to help the poor in the LDCs. In evaluating McNamara's first five years in office (1968–73), Escott Reid observed that, in spite of the president's statements, there was little evidence of any help to the poor in Bank lending, and that this was because Bank officers were convinced that McNamara's overriding goal was the volume of lending. They did not believe that he would drastically reduce lending to any country that did not tailor its program to helping the poor. Further, when he subjected the officers of the Bank to great pressure to double the volume of lending, they were compelled to abandon the more complex and time-consuming projects that were designed to give priority to providing jobs and a better distribution of income.[8]

In contrast to the present Bank, the early Bank took the economic development *purposes* laid down in the Articles of Agreement for its guide. That is, it took as its criterion of success *outcome* (or results).

Outcomes, unlike outputs, are much more difficult to measure. Progress in promoting the development of a member country depends necessarily on a more cooperative, intimate working relationship with the member country. Progress depends not only on what the Bank does but even more on what the country does. It requires, therefore, that the Bank engage very closely and directly with the government and the member country.

Outcome is also not an easy objective to work with. It calls forth the need to exercise ingenuity and creativity. The Bank management was very aware of the fact that there was no one simple solution, and it was therefore very open to ideas and initiatives, as the record shows.

The founders of the Bank as well as the Bank staff in the early years were highly aware of the need to avoid the mistakes that lenders had made between the wars in lending without any control on how the money was to be used. Consequently, the World Bank charter provided that Bank lending should be for projects. Beginning with the processing of the first loan made to a less developed country, Chile, in 1948, the Bank learned how to flesh out this provision: as explained in the 1949–50 annual report, the Bank interpreted this provision as requiring it to lend only for clearly defined and agreed purposes that would result in an increase in the productive capacity of the borrowing country, and that appropriate institutional arrangements in the recipient country should exist or should be created to ensure that the purposes of the loan would be achieved. The Bank felt that willingness to repay loans was enhanced if people and officials in the borrowing country could identify the contribution that a particular debt had made to the economy of the country. To ensure that the loan would confer its planned benefits, disbursements on a loan were made only in phase with progress on the project.

In its first quarter-century, Bank presidents were very conscious that the Bank could provide only a small marginal addition to the capital resources of a country. To help countries develop, the Bank almost instinctively realized that Bank help had to be used as a way to get improved economic management of resources in the borrowing country. Economic development comes through making more effective use and improving the management of all resources—existing capital as well as new capital, manpower, land, and other natural resources. This does not mean that providing more capital is not important; in fact, it may be that a greater supply of capital is essential to make it possible to take the necessary measures to improve economic performance. The point is that concentration on increasing the *amount* of capital as the central element in the economic development process represents the wrong approach to getting faster growth.

There was also a fundamental issue of philosophy involved. The process of economic development is much too complex to be covered by a single policy prescription. Bearing this in mind, there is a fundamental difference between those people who emphasize the dependence of development in the poor countries on the volume of the transfer of resources from rich to poor, and those who instead emphasize that development depends, first and foremost, on the improvement in the allocation and management of the resources (in the widest sense) at command of the poor country. Both the "transfers" people and the "economic management" people recognize the importance of the other point of view, but the different emphasis results in very different methods of operation.

One corollary of this is that, if you believe that improvement in economic management is key, then the contribution that an amount of capital makes to development depends on the rate of return the investment throws off. A 100 percent grant that finances a white elephant in an LDC makes no, or a negative, contribution. A loan, on the other hand, may make a substantial contribution even at a high interest rate. The British and American 100 percent grants to the Libyan Arab Republic in the early 1950s provided much less help to Libya's economic development than the oil companies' investments, even if the latter resulted in high profits to the oil companies.

A second corollary is that not only is the "grant equivalent" of a loan or credit an inadequate indication of the outcomes' worth of economic aid, so also is the "net flow" concept. Even if a new investment is offset exactly by an equal outflow of amortization and interest payments on older investments, an LDC can get considerable additional help from the new investment if it makes possible a project with a sufficiently higher productive return and also if it contributes to improving the return on other capital from improved economic management.

The Bank used the project technique of lending not only as a way of having a specific purpose identified with the loan but also as a means of securing some progress in a more effective use of resources—both borrowed and domestic—in the recipient country. The improvement in performance sought concerned more than the actual investment being financed—it often extended to an entire sector and to the building or improvement of key institutions. For example, the first loan made in Africa by the Bank was to Ethiopia in 1950 for telecommunications. The loan financed the import of telecommunications equipment. While vital, this was only a small part of the real contribution made by the loan. A new organization—manned and managed by Ethiopians—was created and strengthened over the years with the initial help of a team of foreign experts from Sweden to manage and maintain the new telecommunications system.

When the Bank did make program loans in the 1950s, the first to the Belgian Congo, then to Southern Rhodesia, Australia, the Federation of Rhodesia, and Nyasaland, the program loans were all tied to particular projects. This modus operandi that Raymond Cope, the loan director responsible for these countries, and I, as economic adviser, worked out blended the advantages of both types of lending. The decision to lend and the amount of the loan were related to securing agreement on various macroeconomic policy agreements and the needs of the country's development program. The disbursements were tied to a concrete project or projects. Both the governments and the Bank were satisfied with the implementation of the agreements.

In the 1960s, after the African countries became independent, the Bank largely abandoned as futile any effort to reach similar broad macropolicy agreements with their politically fragile, administratively weak governments. When the Bank, for instance, in making the loan for the major Volta project, secured an agreement on the size and composition of Ghana's investment program and on its financial and investment policies, the government failed to implement it (as W. Arthur Lewis, whom the Bank had persuaded the government to appoint as its economic adviser, testified). Consequently, until the 1980s, Bank economists and loan officers made little explicit attempt to secure overall macroeconomic policy improvement in African countries except through general discussion and persuasion in a consultative group and other meetings and through training of top staff at the Economic Development Institute of the Bank.

With administratively stronger governments in Asia, more could be attempted. In the second half of the 1960s, during George Woods's presidency, the Bank, through the Bell mission, tried to persuade India to carry out a number of macro- and sector-policy reforms—liberalizing import policy, encouraging exports, freeing industry from internal controls, encouraging agriculture by raising domestic prices, etc. The attempt was only partially successful. The sector-policy changes in agriculture were most successful. A strong minister of agriculture was in full agreement with the Bank on the changes needed, while President Lyndon Johnson gave strong support to reform by putting India "on a short tether," allowing only just enough PL480 food to be shipped monthly to meet current needs. The shift from an India dependent on grain imports with a failed monsoon threatening famine, to an India that can feed itself year in and year out, dates from this Bank initiative.

The Bank failed to get the Indian government to free up the industrial sector, to free up prices and allow market incentives to work. The Indian government has still only partially carried out the reforms the Bank recommended on industrial policy—and they are still badly needed.

In Indonesia, at the end of the 1960s, a new government took the initiative in asking the Bank to help it formulate its macropolicies and investment program. Bank staff, working in a permanent field mission, made a major contribution in this regard, working closely with their Indonesian counterparts. This successful cooperative effort was realized through actions taken by the government rather than through "conditions" laid down in loan agreements.

In Latin America, in the late 1960s, the Bank's Latin American Department was headed by an economist, Gerald Alter, who gave great weight to economic policy. Macropolicy elements were largely integrated into country lending programs. Bank economists worked with countries to help prepare public investment programs and financing plans within a comprehensive economic framework. Discussions were held with governments on specific measures to mobilize more resources for financing their public-sector expenditures. The requirement of servicing external debt resulted in discussions, in cooperation with the IMF, on balance-of-payment problems and on measures to encourage increased exports of goods and services.

Economic work in the Bank's member countries at this time always included as an objective the improvement of the microeconomic management through the leverage of the projects being financed. With close collaboration between Bank staff and a borrower during a succession of loans, the Bank's economic analysis of different sectors helped shape the composition of the Bank's lending program and the country's investment program. Priority could be given to loans in sectors where changes in price, interest rates, foreign exchange policies, and management and training of staff were desirable. The Bank professionals thus could work together with the government in planning sectorwide investments, institution-building, and policy improvements. The Bank staff often identified the key personnel in their sector and sponsored them for any needed training at the Bank's Economic Development Institute. In countries where the Bank was an important lender, Bank interest and help in securing improvement in overall economic policies followed naturally.

The sanctions behind these policies were immediate, subtle, and effective. The Bank would refuse to lend in a sector if the policy dialogue indicated that desirable changes would not be forthcoming. If a government failed to implement an agreement, Bank disbursements were officially suspended or the government tactfully would not submit disbursement requests.

The evolution of the Bank's self-image from "investment bank" into "development institution" began under Black. During the early years the Bank had to establish itself as a "sound," worthy borrower in the capital markets. Sometime in 1960, I remember Black commenting that originally every loan not only had to be good but also had to *look* good to the capital markets. But in 1960, the Bank's reputation was now solid; a loan was good because it was the Bank that had made it. It was during Black's term of office that the Bank established the Economic Development Institute, began lending for education, and established the International Development Association (IDA) as a soft-lending-terms affiliate. Building on all this, Woods concluded from the beginning of his presidency that he wanted the Bank to consider itself a development agency.

After the reorganization of 1952, Bank economists were mainly integral parts of the lending departments with their work all oriented to concrete problems in the member countries. As the years went by, it became evident that the experience that the Bank possessed had a value beyond that of internal Bank use.

The birth of an excellent economics research facility in the Bank was due to George Woods's decision to have one. In his first address in 1964 to the entire professional staff, he stated that one of his major objectives was to build the economic strength of the Bank. He added in his devastatingly frank manner: "Gene Black is afraid of economists, I am not." In August 1964, he appointed Irving S. Friedman, one of the senior officials of the Fund, as the economic adviser to the president with the mandate to oversee all of the economic work in the Bank, in the area departments, the Project Department, and the Economic Department. He also became chairman of the Economic Committee, through which all the Bank's economic activities were coordinated.

The Economic Department at that time was the renamed Economic Staff and had been without a permanent head for more than three years since the previous director, Leonard Rist, had been named special representative for Africa in April 1961. It consisted of some twenty people collecting external debt data and studying markets of the principal primary commodities that less developed countries exported, and a handful of economists doing general studies. In January 1965, George Woods telephoned me at UCLA, where I was regents professor on leave from the bank, and offered me the position of director of the department with the mandate to build it into an effective research organization with a new central role in the Bank. I accepted the offer. On my return to Washington, Friedman and I decided to change the name of the old department to the *Economics Department*, to emphasize the new and the discontinuity with the past.

Research and publication based on Bank acquired knowledge was one of the main tasks of the new department. The buildup of the central economics organization led to a flowering of economic research and publication. This, in the early years, was directed to help member countries improve development policy and practice from project design and implementation to macroeconomic policy. The emphasis was on applied research, although some work of purely academic interest was included.

After I was appointed director of the Economic Development Institute and Friedman left the Bank for a lucrative job on Wall Street, McNamara instituted the policy in the 1970s of appointing, for a limited term, the head of the central economic staff straight out of the university without any experience in a policy-making job or in a large bureaucracy. It is tempting for a professor in this job to concentrate not on policy or applied economics but on more or less academic research and publication—there is no friction, no bureaucratic resistance, almost unlimited funds and personnel, and two new Bank research journals, established in the 1980s, to fill. There is a strong impression that some of the central economics staff did not resist this temptation strongly. This preoccupation with academic publication helps explains, in part, the failure of the Bank to provide any creative policy leadership in recognizing and coping with the international debt crisis of the 1980s. Nevertheless, the central economics staff has become the most important and most useful center of developmental knowledge and expertise in the world.

The Bank started collecting external debt information from the very beginning of its operations and had a small staff to do it. There were a lot of problems with the data. With a new division chief and additional personnel, the new Economics Department set to work to do a better job on collecting external debt reports and improving their quality: division personnel accompanied country missions to advise governments on setting up better external debt reporting systems (governments very often had no idea of how much external debt their agencies had incurred). A cooperative system with the regional development banks was organized (they required their borrowers to report to the World Bank and it processed the data for them for a small annual fee). A cooperative system was also organized with the Organization for Economic Cooperation and Development (OECD).[9]

On the other statistical data, the new department started from scratch with a new division headed by an energetic and able Israeli, Emanuel Levy, with its objective the preparation and maintenance of a set of world tables. The United Nations Statistical Office collects world statistics, but their quality tends to be poor since the office for political reasons has to accept whatever countries send them. Shortly after this was started, with Woods's encouragement, the department began publishing *The World Bank Atlas*. It turned out to be so useful that the Bank is still publishing it. By this time, there must have been well over a million copies printed.

It became quickly obvious that one reason the data from the less developed countries were so poor was the deplorable state of the country statistical offices. The Economics Department started a program of trying to upgrade these offices by putting statistics personnel on some Bank missions to work with and advise governments on their statistical work. The very fact that the Bank showed that it regarded such work as important helped the prestige and standing of statisticians. Unfortunately, in later years the Bank carried on with the collection of data but not with the work of improving its quality. The criticism, in recent years, of the quality of the data published by the Bank is undoubtedly justified.

Until Woods's term, the Bank, and in fact much of the development community, believed that the ruling constraint on help to the less developed countries was the shortage of good projects indicating a limited capacity to put capital to work effectively. In 1965 a study by the new Economics Department, drawing on the country specialists and area economists, challenged this conventional wisdom. It found that "the developing countries could effectively use, on the average over the next five years, some $3 billion to $4 billion more of external capital each year than has been provided in the recent past."[10] This was a disturbing conclusion to the donor countries and when, as director of the Economics Department, I presented it to the executive directors in the draft of the annual report, it drew considerable resistance. The directors were mollified by prefacing the conclusion by the softening words: "A preliminary Bank inquiry . . . suggests." With Woods's backing it soon became and has remained conventional wisdom that the constraint on the flow of resources to the less developed countries is from the supply side. This was a notable achievement in changing the intellectual climate.

At the end of the first quarter century, the Bank strategy was described as follows:

> The present position, therefore, is that in all of the World Bank Group's lending: (a) the Bank directly attempts to improve the use of resources in those projects or sectors or institutions where Bank finance is directly involved through attaching conditions to the loans; (b) it also always tries to make a basic analysis of the economic problems and prospects of a country in cooperation with the government of a country. (c) The next step is the most difficult one. It varies from country to country depending on (i) ascertaining what it is that is holding up faster growth and that the government, by appropriate action within its capability, could correct, on the one hand, and (ii) what the World Bank Group can reasonably expect to achieve with the government in securing improved performance in this respect, on the other.
>
> At one extreme, there are countries where the role of the World Bank Group is very small. This may be because the country concerned has reached the stage where it needs very little help from abroad, or because the political or governmental situation is such that the government is relatively helpless to accomplish anything much in improving economic performance, or because the bulk of its external capital comes from a source that is not interested in whatever economic conclusions this group may come to in its economic analysis. In such cases, if anything can be done at all, the World Bank Group may have to limit itself to the influence of the basic economic analysis process or the improvements it can secure through financing a particular sector or succession of sectors. At the other extreme, there are countries where the Bank Group is the predominant source of external capital, and there are sufficient elements in the government who are both eager to and capable of taking action to improve economic performance in a number of ways if they are supported by the World Bank Group in getting the government officially to agree to such measures. In these cases, the World Bank Group may agree with the country, in a more or less formal form, on a lending program in a number of sectors together with understanding on the policy actions the government will take to

improve performance in significant fields. Most countries would, of course, lie between these two extremes.[11]

The Second Quarter-Century—Output as Measure of Success

In Robert S. McNamara's first major policy address on becoming president of the Bank, he announced that the Bank would double the amount of its lending over the next five years. Setting up the volume of loans as the measure of success for the Bank, and internally for the loan officers, meant, as Escott Reid's observation demonstrates, that other aspects of Bank activity in helping LDCs became subordinated. Getting loans out gets priority. During Black's presidency, in contrast, it was the *refusal* of the Bank to lend to Spain until major reforms were instituted that contributed to the rapid takeoff of the Spanish economy in the 1960s.

With lending *output* as the goal, easy projects are chosen, large projects over small, quick disbursing over slower, simpler over complex, single beneficiary over many beneficiaries. The effort to use Bank projects as a means to secure improved economic management of the country's resources was weakened and largely disappeared in practice.

A *Foreign Affairs* note in 1982 on McNamara commented:

> Putting the emphasis on the need to achieve lending targets resulted in what some bitter Bank staff called "reversal of roles." The loan officer's career was dependent on the willingness of borrowers to accept loans. The official Bank line . . . was that the quality of Bank projects was as high as ever. But this is not to the point: a power project during the McNamara years was undoubtedly a good project but the real question is whether the Bank negotiators were as successful as they would have been earlier in getting improvements in rate policy, for instance.[12]

It is now clear that this 1982 statement was too sanguine. Not only was the endeavor to improve the economic management undermined, but in the drive to achieve lending targets, even the quality of Bank projects deteriorated in the 1980s. According to an internal Bank study, the Wapenhans Report (1992), 20 percent of active Bank projects had major problems that could cost their failure if not corrected. A quarter of all agriculture and irrigation projects and a third of those meant to fight poverty were in trouble. That is, Bank investments totaling as much as $28 billion could be wasted. It is significant that the report attributed much of the problem to a failure to appreciate the importance of policy and institutional factors.

The May–June 1993 Newsletter of the 1818 Society (the organization of World Bank retirees) had a letter from Robert Whyte, who worked on projects for the Bank for twenty-six years, that says the Wapenhans Report understates the number of bad project investments. In his experience, Whyte said, "Some of the projects were so flawed that they would make good 'how not to' case histories but nearly all contained fundamental misjudgments which could have been avoided if the Bank had not been so determined to lend."

It is not only the project loans that soured. Fourteen years ago the Bank began a new program of structural adjustment loans (SALs), which have made up as much as a fifth of Bank lending in some years. These so-called policy-based loans are fast-disbursing and not related to any project. They support the borrowing country's balance of payments while the government is supposed to carry out structural reforms in policies and institutions. The importance of finding and empowering key officials who agreed on the desired policies was neglected. Structural adjustment loans were made to countries anxious for Bank financing but in no position, administratively or politically, to carry out the policies they agreed to as conditions of the loans. The program was successful in facilitating an increase in the volume of lending. But studies made of the results have had difficulty in finding instances of restructuring successes. As a result, these loans have almost completely failed.

However, even if the program as such had succeeded, its very existence reveals an important Bank failure. The SALs are made to countries that have been Bank clients for years. If a country's policies are so bad that they require major restructuring, why did the Bank not work with the country to improve its economic management over the years? What was also disturbing about these SAL loans is that the Bank reverted to the interwar pattern of lending to governments without any relationship to any concrete investment. Once the loans are disbursed, there is nothing left behind to demonstrate or symbolize the Bank's help to the country.

The current Bank president, Lewis Preston, now concurs that the pressure to lend was a mistake: "Every guy in this bank thought he was going to get promoted based just on the number of loans he could get approved. It was a crazy way to run a railroad."

Organizational Structure

To be effective in attaining its goals, an organization has to be structured accordingly. In the first few years of the Bank's history, the Bank was constantly being reorganized in the attempt to discover the type of organization that would be best fitted to carry out the purposes of this unique new World Bank.

The two main possibilities are the usual bureaucratic organization and the professional model. The bureaucratic organization has a pyramid of supervision and control; management is sharply distinguished from the mass of workers; workers often have a union or staff organization to defend their rights; the structure is highly centralized, and responsibilities for information, coordination, decision making, setting goals, and monitoring are at the top of the pyramid. This kind of organization is suited to an *output*-oriented organization. This model largely describes the Bank as it was reshaped by McNamara, who was president for more than half of the last twenty-five years, and as it is today.

But this is not the model that was established by Black, Garner, and Woods and which was responsible for the Bank's success. Their's was the senior staff model. The senior staff model proved to be a major factor in the Bank's success. In this organizational model, a group of professionals run the organization. The senior staff is involved, individually or collectively, in making major decisions, in strategic planning, in coordination, and in all other major managerial responsibilities.

Modified by George Woods, this model lasted well into the first presidency of Robert McNamara, who finally changed it drastically in the 1972 reorganization into the basic hierarchical model that exists today in one of its various modifications.

Under Black and Woods, the president headed the Bank but he shared managerial responsibilities with the senior staff. Creditworthiness decisions and economic policy recommendations were made in the Economic Committee of senior economists, and the final lending and other policy decisions were made in the Loan Committee. The Loan Committee of senior staff was chaired by the president or the vice president. Discussions on policy were uninhibited; no one was afraid to advocate any position.

The Bank was amazingly pragmatic and flexible. It was quick to change some procedure when no longer relevant and to adopt new policies as required. It was also almost completely free of stifling red tape—in drastic contrast to the bureaucratic rules and procedures that multiplied in the last quarter-century.

The quality of Bank lending and its contribution to economic development was controlled through the organizational process by which loans were made. After much experimentation, in 1952 Black and Garner established a loan process that relied on creative tension between the projects staff and the area loan officers, with conflicts resolved in the Loan Committee. The projects people were responsible for the quality of the project; the area departments, for negotiating the loans and the country economics. Responsibility for judgments about the merits of individual projects was divorced from responsibility for judgments about the desirability of lending to the country in question.

Separating responsibility for the project from responsibility for the relationship with the country drastically reduced the possibility that a bad or ill-prepared project would be pushed through simply because the Bank loan officer wanted to make an impressive record or because the Bank felt that a loan to the country was important for the president or for other internal Bank political considerations. On the other hand, it also guarded against a particular project's being pushed through simply because the projects officer felt it was technically "sweet."

Finally, all the loans had to pass the Loan Committee. This committee, composed of all the senior officials of the Bank, was a formidable group. The area directors, the general counsel, the head of the Economic Staff, and the president or vice president chairing the meeting were quite happy to demonstrate their grasp of Bank issues by pouncing on any weakness that they perceived in the loan proposal.

Woods added a third leg to the triangle of tension—the economists in the new Economics Department. The area departments had to clear all loans through the

Economic Committee before going to the Loan Committee. The Economic Committee, composed of the Bank's senior economists and the Bank and International Monetary Fund area directors concerned, reviewed the country's economic situation, development policies, creditworthiness, IDA justification, if any, and Bank objectives. Thus, the Bank process ensured that technocrats (advocates for project quality), economists (advocates for improvement in economic management), and diplomats (advocates for loans and other means of pleasing the countries they worked with) were all integral parts of the lending process.

The second quarter-century of the Bank has been dominated by the major decisions made during Robert S. McNamara's presidency. After his first major policy address when he announced that the Bank would double the volume of lending during his term, increasing the volume of lending became the major objective of the Bank. The interdepartmental Economic Committee, which was the one professional support group in the Bank devoted to country economic policy and management, disappeared. The projects people were put under control of the regions. Whereas under Black and Woods, the projects officers were told that there was no excuse if a project failed, under McNamara the projects officers, like the loan officers, had to worry about meeting their lending goals.

The change in the basic operational criterion from *outcome* to *output* went along with changes in the overall organizational structure. As mentioned above, McNamara reorganized the Bank on the standard American hierarchical corporate model. The Bank became highly centralized with the responsibility for policy formation and monitoring of performance at the top of the pyramid. McNamara did not like dissent. An English staff member said meetings in McNamara's office reminded him of a medieval royal court.

Vice presidents and red tape multiplied. The administrative staff invented special perks for top management to differentiate it from staff: the Bank paid first class for their wives to accompany them on every trip they took; a select list of hotels around the world was promulgated that only "President's Council" members were allowed to patronize.

The President's Council did not formulate or make policy, nor did any other group in the Bank. McNamara used the staff to collect the basic data on a problem that he was interested in, but he did not believe in securing staff input in making decisions.

The Bank management policy of setting Bank lending targets as the major objective of the Bank was accompanied by changes in key personnel. It was significant that Richard Demuth, who was one of the Bank officials from the beginning of the Bank and had led in creating and launching most of the successful innovative concepts of the Bank, departed the Bank during McNamara's term. J. Burke Knapp, the senior vice president in the last years of Black's and throughout Woods's presidency, retired in early 1978, thus severing the last effective leadership link to the policies of the early Bank.

The head of the Latin American region, Gerald Alter, an economist concerned with using lending to get policy improvement, was replaced by a Latin American politician appointed from outside the Bank—making this the first time a geographical region was headed by a native of the region. The loan officer in charge of India, Greg Votaw, was displaced by Ernest Stern, who quickly won the approval of McNamara for hitting the loan targets and eliminating all unpleasantness about policy disagreements with the Indian government. This also started Stern on a rapid ascent through the Bank hierarchy to his position where, at the retirement of McNamara, he became the de facto operating head of the Bank through the successive presidencies.

In the early Bank, since there was no single quantifiable measure for the success of any Bank staff member, senior management kept close personal contact with the staff and its work. With lending volume output as a quantified measure of success or failure, a system of monthly statistical reports on the progress of the lending program of each division provided objective, impersonal supervision. Staff was managed rather than led. New members of the staff would complain that they had been in the Bank for two or three years and had never seen the president. This also ramified downward with staff members sometime never having met the vice president in charge of their region.

In the transition in the early McNamara years, many Bank staff had to cope with a conflict between their professional consciences and the career need to get loans out. The consulting psychiatrist for Bank staff told William Clark, a senior Bank official, that he had never worked with an organization that had so high a proportion of people with psychological problems. While I have no statistics to confirm this, internal Bank staff publications indicate that this unhappiness of the staff continues to plague the organization. Last June, for example, in the Bank Staff Forum, a Bank officer commented, "I don't think I have seen staff so alienated from their managerial culture as in this institution. . . . The only participation is around PPR [personnel review] time, which is the most traumatic event in the whole Bank's life. Suddenly the manager who has not talked to you for the whole year comes up and says these things are wrong."[13]

While the volume of loans was the benchmark by which success was measured and was the basis of the incentive structure for the Bank staff, McNamara and successive presidents publicly undertook other goals for Bank lending—the alleviation of poverty, achieving more equitable distribution of income, and, in recent years, protecting or improving the environment. This dissonance between the reward structure and the rhetoric continues to put strains on the staff. As another staff member commented last June, "I think whatever vision we have of the future, it must embrace a much clearer identification of the Bank's objectives. From the point of view of being realistically achievable, they are much too broad and therefore make it very difficult for individuals."[14]

When staff are unhappy with the organization it is not surprising that the nongovernmental organizations (NGOs) in the development field, who come into close contact with them in the field, are also disillusioned with the Bank.

Present Reform Efforts and the Future

The Bank notoriously has no institutional memory. Only in 1993 did it appoint a historian and it has had no archivist for most of its life. And, as we know, if one does not know history, one is condemned to repeat it.

The fact that the Bank has a major problem is apparently coming home to the Bank's president, and he is now apparently trying to learn de novo what the Bank discovered more than forty years ago. Last year, 1993, the Bank announced a new policy agenda, "Getting Results," for improving its work. In this, Bank President Lewis T. Preston declared that the Bank's *effectiveness in terms of development impact* is crucial and that improving this will not be easy: "Bringing about the institutional changes required . . . will require sustained leadership from management . . . and strong and continuous support from the board *in attaching as much importance to lending results as to lending volumes.*"[15] (Emphasis added.)

On June 6, 1994, one of the Bank's present managing directors, Sven Sandstrom, said at a Bank staff meeting that, after surveying the progress of the past twenty-five years, there were

> . . . four broad themes that are coming through very strongly from the outside and increasingly from the inside. First, the need to focus on people [i.e., education and health lending, private sector entrepreneurship, how the environment affects the poor]; second, on participation [i.e., with clients]; third, on partnership [i.e., with other agencies] and finally, on results. . . . That's something we somewhat belatedly have started to give more emphasis to. It's very interesting to see how that has had a resonance among staff. And I think it's much more widely accepted in senior management, the Board, shareholders, that we need to give more attention to the actual results and the development impact.[16]

In July 1994, the president announced that the volume of lending of the Bank group should not be expected to increase and that, in fact, the amount had not increased since 1990.

The Bank management is clearly en route to rediscovering that the Black–Woods criterion of *outcomes* is important. But the conversion from the McNamara–Stern *output* measure is not complete. Lending volume, though downgraded from being the sole objective, is still regarded as one of the two major objectives of the Bank and, of course, Ernest Stern is still managing the Bank.

When the emphasis shifts from output to outcome, close engagement with the member country becomes important, in fact, indispensable. In the new implementation plan, "Getting Results," the Bank management announced, "As the core of its action plan, the Bank will introduce a country-by-country approach into the management of its ongoing lending operations."[17] This rediscovery of the need to work on a country-by-country basis boggles the mind but helps explain some of the criticism of the Bank: how can a development agency possibly work effectively with countries other than on a country-by-country basis?

Bank management has also rediscovered that "sometimes a country may need less, rather than more, lending."[18] This remarkable statement, unfortunately, does make sense in showing that the Bank is beginning to realize that there is no firm rational basis for the lending-volume objective it pursued for so long.

In the rest of the implementation plan, there are provisions for adding more reviews, more public access to the lending process, etc. The reforms are reminiscent of the early reaction of American carmakers to Japanese competition. Detroit did not produce good cars as long as it relied on inspecting and repairing the cars as they came off the line. Quality improved not from adding more inspectors at the end but from changing the process by which the cars are built.

A fundamental improvement requires a change in the measure for success, changing the organizational structure from the hierarchical that stifles innovation back to the more flexible early Bank's model, and changing the relevant process of Bank decision making. The present Bank has not yet rediscovered the lessons learned by the successful early Bank.

In the world of today, the Bank faces challenges perhaps as difficult as those of the early Bank. To cope with them, it will have to become as effective and creative as the early Bank was.

The challenge of tropical Africa can be successfully confronted only by the Bank. Only the Bank can marshal the wide spectrum of resources of knowledge and money to master the obstacles of tropical diseases and pests affecting humans, animals and plants, unfriendly environment, scarcity of skills, administrative weaknesses, etc., that have crippled African economic development. Elsewhere in the world, there are countries that are unwelcoming to foreign private investors for political and historical reasons, but where the Bank can function. On the other side of the equation, there are also countries where private investment is reluctant to venture because of political and security risks, but again the Bank can be effective. Finally, even in those developing countries where foreign private investment is both welcome and unafraid, the Bank can still play a most useful role. As the experience of the 1920s and then again in the 1970s illustrated, foreign private investment tends to have too narrow and too short a vision. Lenders were concerned only with what appeared to be favorable creditworthiness and return for their loans with no concern with the effectiveness of the use of the funds. Only the Bank can ensure that invested funds are properly used for the purposes for which they are intended and that the project is economically justified.

Economic development of a country is a multifaceted process. If the Bank again becomes a creative institution, fully engaged with the country it is helping, there are many countries where it can be useful and, in fact, indispensable. It could work, for example, with a country on the whole wide range of needed change across the board. Such a multiyear broad contract could provide as-needed Bank help in institution-building; investment in basic human capital—from elementary education to training of technicians, managers, and policy makers; and, of course, investment in material capital in both public and private sectors. This kind of innovative creative help can come only from the World Bank.

Are "Fifty Years Enough"? The answer is, "No."

Notes

1. I had a minor supporting role in this through my 1971 seminar paper, "Tropics and Economic Development," which, in an expanded form, was later published as a World Bank book, *The Tropics and Economic Development: A Provocative Inquiry into the Poverty of Nations* (Baltimore: The Johns Hopkins University Press for the World Bank, 1976).

2. Henry Owens, "The World Bank: Is 50 Years Enough?" *Foreign Affairs* 73, no. 5 (September/October 1994): pp. 97–108.

3. Northcote C. Parkinson, *Parkinson's Law or the Pursuit of Progress* (London: John Murray, 1958), pp. 83–94.

4. Linda Gray MacKay, "World Bank and IMF Have Failed, and the Poor Pay the Price," *Boston Globe*, July 14, 1994, p. 13.

5. Doug Bandow and Ian Vásquez, eds., *Perpetuating Poverty: The World Bank, the IMF, and the Developing World* (Washington, D.C.: The Cato Institute, 1994).

6. "Thoroughly Modern Sisters," *Economist* (July 23, 1994): pp. 18–20.

7. The other purposes include: " . . . the restoration of economies destroyed or disrupted by war. . . . To promote private foreign investment . . . To promote the long-range balanced growth of international trade and the maintenance of equilibrium in balances of payment . . . To arrange the loans made . . . by it . . . so that the more useful and urgent projects . . . will be dealt with first. To conduct its operations . . . to assist . . . a smooth transition from a wartime to a peacetime economy."

8. Escott Reid, "McNamara's World Bank," *Foreign Affairs* 51, no. 4 (July 1973): pp. 794–810.

9. This is a more complicated task than it appears at first sight, for data need to be secured on four types of lending: private to government (including all the agencies that borrow); official (government and international agencies to government); official to private; and private to private.

10. World Bank, *Annual Report, 1964–65* (Washington, D.C.: World Bank, 1965), p. 62.

11. Andrew M. Kamarck, "The Appraisal of Country Economic Performance," *Economic Development and Cultural Change* 18, no. 2 (January 1982): pp. 163–164.

12. Andrew M. Kamarck, "McNamara's Bank," *Foreign Affairs* 60, no. 2 (spring 1982): p. 952.

13. World Bank, *Staff Week* (Washington, D.C.: World Bank, 1994), p. 7.

14. Ibid.

15. World Bank, *Getting Results: The World Bank's Agenda for Improving Development Effectiveness* (Washington, D.C.: World Bank, 1993), p. 17.

16. World Bank, *Bank's World* (August 1994): p. 6.

17. World Bank, *Getting Results*, p. 1.

18. Ibid., p. 13.

10

Bretton Woods Fifty Years Later: A View from the International Monetary Fund

Margaret Garritsen de Vries

Introduction

Bretton Woods is the most revered name in international monetary history, perhaps in economic history. Five decades later, financial officials, economists, international relations experts, historians, and others still speak in hallowed terms of the conference held July 1–21, 1944—just three weeks after D-Day—in a remote town, Bretton Woods, New Hampshire. They also speak often of the Bretton Woods system agreed to at that conference, of which the newly created International Monetary Fund (IMF) was to be the guardian.

The Bretton Woods System

The Bretton Woods system had three main features—fixed exchange rates ("par values" agreed to with the International Monetary Fund and changed only in consultation with it); currencies that were freely convertible into each other or into gold; and freedom from exchange restrictions, at least on current payments. Controls on capital movements were permitted. The conferees were eager to win the peace by planning an international monetary system to be put in place once World War II was over. They wanted a system that would differ wholly from the international monetary arrangements that had prevailed between World War I and World War II. Those arrangements had, in the 1920s, included a return to the gold standard that had prevailed before World War I. Then with the failure of the attempts to return to a gold standard in the early 1930s, countries had turned to a variety of monetary arrangements, including fluctuating exchange rates, often involving competitive depreciation, the imposition of exchange controls, the suspension of convertibility, and bilateral and even barter agreements. The conferees attributed much of the low levels of world trade and the low income levels of the Great Depression to these international monetary policies and protectionist trade policies. These policies had come to be labeled "beggar-thy-neighbor" policies because they exported unemployment from one country to another. The purpose of the new Bretton Woods system was to foster high levels of international trade and investment which, in turn, were regarded as the principal way to achieve full employment and economic development, the prime objectives of countries' domestic policies.

The purposes of the IMF as stated in its Articles of Agreement were sixfold: to promote international monetary cooperation through a permanent institution which provides the machinery for consultation and collaboration on international monetary problems; to facilitate the expansion and balanced growth of international trade and to contribute thereby to the promotion and maintenance of high levels of employment and real income and to the development of the productive resources of all members as primary objectives of economic policy; to promote exchange stability, to maintain orderly exchange arrangements among members, and to avoid competitive exchange depreciation; to assist in the establishment of a multilateral system of payments and in the elimination of foreign exchange restrictions; to give confidence to members by making general resources temporarily available to them so that they could correct maladjustments in their balance of payments without resorting to measures destructive of national or international prosperity; and, in accordance with the above, to shorten the duration and lessen the degree of disequilibrium in the international balances of payments of members. The Bretton Woods system in effect defined a code of good conduct in international monetary affairs regarded as essential for world prosperity.

These ideas were at the time revolutionary. Countries surrendered sovereignty over their exchange rates, an action commonly regarded as the major historic advance made at Bretton Woods. Not a few influential persons were opposed to such innovations in international monetary matters.

The money that the IMF has available is to help countries "correct maladjustments in their balance of payments without resorting to measures destructive of national or international prosperity." The IMF is to let members "draw" temporarily on its resources, with adequate safeguards, when they have a balance of payments imbalance, so that they can take measures that seem most appropriate, such as changing their exchange rates in consultation with the IMF, or changing their domestic fiscal or monetary policies. In effect, members are provided with an additional source of foreign exchange reserves so that they can avoid the imposition of restrictions, suspension of currency convertibility, or exchange rate measures not in accord with the code of good conduct, which might harm international prosperity.

Experience with the System

From 1945 onward the IMF and its members gradually attained the full tenets of the Bretton Woods system. The industrial members quickly set par values and changed them, relatively infrequently as it worked out, in consultation with the IMF. They lifted their exchange restrictions and controls and established full convertibility for their currencies. The Bretton Woods system was to last until the early 1970s.

The achievements in the world economy during these first twenty-five years of the existence of the IMF and of the Bretton Woods system were nothing short of remarkable. The economies of the countries of Western Europe and of Japan recovered quickly from their war devastation; and all the Western industrial countries—the United States, Canada, and those in Europe—and Japan experienced unparalleled economic growth and unprecedented levels of prosperity and consumption.

The IMF had a vital role in the attainment of the main features of the Bretton Woods system. Its financial assistance helped support the currencies of some of the industrial countries when they were suddenly confronted with unexpected balance-of-payments pressures. This support was especially helpful, for example, to the United Kingdom on a number of occasions. In this way, the IMF was directly involved in helping to preserve exchange rate stability. But the IMF helped to implement the Bretton Woods system in other ways that were equally important. From the outset, the IMF helped financial officials, especially in the industrial countries, understand the need for cautious macroeconomic policies and the uses of monetary policy to help guide macroeconomic developments as a supplement to the uses of fiscal policy which they had begun to learn in the 1930s. The IMF was especially a key force in getting countries to lower their rates of inflation, reduce their balance-of-payments deficits, and accompany their improved payments positions with an appropriate lessening of their restrictions.

The developing countries did well, too. They also gradually eliminated most of their complex multiple exchange rates and exchange restrictions and introduced more stable exchange rates. Thus, they too became fairly much in line with the tenets of the Bretton Woods system. And in the results that count, namely economic development, it is noteworthy that, in the twenty-five years the Bretton Woods system existed, the developing countries made far greater strides in their economic growth than had the industrial countries in comparable stages of their economic development.

The Collapse of the System

These achievements notwithstanding, after being buffeted by a number of events in the late 1960s, the Bretton Woods system, and in particular the par value or fixed exchange-rate system, began its demise. On August 15, 1971, a date often

noted in international monetary history, the United States suspended convertibility of the dollar into gold, thereby breaking the link between the dollar and gold
that had been the linchpin of the system. Then on March 19, 1973, even while
major efforts to reform the system were in process, the system collapsed entirely
as the regime in which the exchange rates for the principal currencies floated
suddenly erupted into existence. Subsequently, while the countries of the European monetary system have tried to keep their exchange rates fixed vis-à-vis
each other, the rate for the U.S. dollar vis-à-vis all the other major currencies
continues to float, as do the Japanese yen, the Canadian dollar, and several other
major currencies. (Developing countries have a variety of exchange-rate arrangements.)

The fixed exchange-rate system collapsed for a number of reasons. Basically,
exchange rates of the major currencies had become not only fixed but rigid. They
virtually could not be changed, with the result that imbalances of balance-of-payments positions could not be corrected through discrete changes of par values or
fixed exchange rates. Rigidity of exchange rates came about in part because of
the success of the Bretton Woods system. Countries had gone much further in
relaxing restrictions than even the Bretton Woods founders had envisaged. Most
industrial countries had removed restrictions not only on current payments but on
capital movements as well. With such freedom, massive speculative capital
movements would flow from one currency to another in anticipation of an exchange-rate change. These massive capital flows made it impossible for financial
authorities to hold fixed exchange rates or to change from one fixed rate to
another because of the pressure on exchange rates from these massive capital
movements. In addition, countries with sizable balance-of-payments surpluses,
such as Germany and Japan, were reluctant to appreciate their currencies to help
reduce their surpluses. Appreciation would be disadvantageous to their export
industries, the prime movers in their rapid economic growth. And, because of the
way the system operated with the U.S. dollar linked to gold, the United States,
with a large balance-of-payments deficit, could not devalue the dollar without
upsetting the whole par value system. In these circumstances, the United States
eventually did break the dollar–gold link and financial officials of the main
industrial countries, including the United States, found it preferable, and inevitable, to let their exchange rates float. The Bretton Woods system was at an end.

Innovations in the 1960s

Meanwhile, the IMF was gradually adapting its activities, policies, and even its
articles to changes in the world economy. In the 1950s, many developing countries, which had been colonies at the time of the Bretton Woods Conference,
obtained their then-primary goal of attaining political independence, and by the
early 1960s, most of them had signaled their entry into the international community by becoming members of the IMF. With an increasing membership of

developing countries, the IMF turned much of its attention to the special needs of these members. In 1963 it introduced what at the time was considered an innovative facility, a compensatory financing facility designed to enable primary producing members that had suffered shortfalls in their export earnings to draw on the Fund's financial resources. The facility was aimed at helping developing members cope with the consequences of what was then considered their biggest trade and balance-of-payments problem—big fluctuations in world market prices for the primary products for which they were the principal exporters. Subsequently, this facility was liberalized and broadened. As fluctuations in commodity prices continued to be a serious problem for developing members, in 1967 the IMF introduced a buffer stock facility to help primary producing members draw on its financial resources to build up buffer stocks of commodities in connection with agreements to help stabilize commodity prices. The IMF also developed further its standby arrangements under which members could draw on the IMF's financial resources, and developing members drew larger amounts and many more developing members began to draw.

In the 1960s the IMF took yet another direction to help meet the urgent needs of its developing members, especially the increasing number of African members, who, like Asian members before them, signaled their newly acquired political independence and entry into the international community by joining the IMF. To help these members establish central banks and banking systems, learn the techniques of monetary and fiscal policy and budget management, and build other institutions necessary to implement modern economic policies, the IMF set up within its own organizational structure three new departments to provide specialized technical assistance and training of members' officials. Technical assistance and training of officials quickly expanded into one of the IMF's major activities.

The big problem of the 1960s, however, was the widespread and growing concern that international liquidity would become inadequate. As world trade had greatly expanded, gold at then-prevailing prices had already become an insufficient source of reserves to the rest of the world, and the United States had long been supplying dollars as reserves to the rest of the world. But as the United States planned to reduce or even eliminate that source of supply by eliminating its balance-of-payments deficit, fears of an acute shortage of official liquidity spread. This potential shortage of liquidity posed a serious threat to the international monetary system.

To augment official sources of reserves, the IMF created the general arrangements to borrow (the GAB), permitting the IMF to borrow from its ten largest industrial country members if any of the ten drew from the IMF. Beyond being an important source of financial resources for the next several decades, the GAB became a forerunner to additional borrowing arrangements that the IMF undertook in the 1970s and 1980s.

But the IMF did much more in the 1960s to ease the liquidity concerns of financial officials. It embarked on five years of negotiations that led to the creation of the SDR (the special drawing rights facility). When the big ten industrial countries sought to agree among themselves on a special arrangement in which they would be exclusive members, the IMF insisted that it alone had responsibility for any new arrangements to supplement the world's supply of official liquidity. IMF officials then came up with, and successfully won support for, an innovative scheme for adding to world liquidity that included all countries, industrial and developing, on an equal basis.

The IMF thereby gained the power to create its own money. This power had been suggested in the original plans for the IMF in the 1940s, particularly in Keynes's Clearing Union. But the time then was not ripe for agreement on such power for the IMF. Hence establishment of the SDR in the IMF in 1968 gave the institution a power denied to it at its birth. Moreover, in handling these difficult, lengthy negotiations, the IMF proved that it clearly was—as stated in its articles as its first purpose—a "permanent institution which provides the machinery for consultation and collaboration on international monetary problems."

Transformation in the 1970s

The most difficult challenge of all came after March 1973 when the par value system collapsed. In the early 1970s a specially created group called the Committee of Twenty held two years of discussions aimed at fashioning a reformed international monetary system. Those discussions failed, however, and it was clear that no reformed system was likely to come into being in the foreseeable future. Instead, the floating rate system would continue indefinitely. In these circumstances, some argued that the IMF, as monitor of exchange rates, had outlived its usefulness. Even IMF officials conceded that the institution's future was uncertain.

Indeed, in retrospect, the year 1973 can be seen as turning point in the history of the International Monetary Fund. Such dramatic changes took place in the world economy that it was as if a trapdoor had opened and everything fostering the growth and stability of the previous twenty-five years suddenly had disappeared. In March, the par value system collapsed. In midyear, commodity prices soared to levels heretofore unknown in peacetime. Then in the second half of 1973, inflation in industrial countries surged to several times the rates prevailing in the 1950s and 1960s, signaling the onset of double-digit inflation. At the same time there was an underutilization of productive capacity in the industrial countries and a marked slowdown of output expansion. An unusual coexistence of inflation and underutilization of resources thus began and the new term "stagflation" was coined. Then at the end of 1973, as prices for other primary commodities surged, oil-producing countries, acting in unison as OPEC, announced prices for oil that were suddenly four times higher than they had been only a few months before.

These higher oil prices were expected to produce unprecedented disequilibria in international payments—huge surpluses for oil-exporting countries and corresponding deficits for oil-importing countries—and to aggravate both inflationary and recessionary trends in the world economy, as both price advances and cutoffs in production were likely.

With the now prevailing regime of floating rates, the new managing director of the IMF, H. Johannes Witteveen, feared unduly and unstabilizing big swings in exchange rates, and even competitive depreciation and a return to trade and payments restrictions on a scale reminiscent of the 1930s. Hence, on January 3, 1974, only eleven days after oil-exporting countries announced higher oil prices of crude oil, he proposed a temporary facility to finance oil deficits in the IMF.

The means to finance the deficits existed in the surplus revenues of the oil-exporting countries. The question was how to get these funds recycled in the optimum way. While it was expected that private markets would have a large role in recycling and while Iran and Saudi Arabia were making official arrangements to help neighboring oil-importing countries, IMF officials were cognizant of the limits of private markets and governmental arrangements. For its special oil facility, the IMF would obtain funds by borrowing from the governments of its oil-exporting members and of its industrial members with payments surpluses and lend those funds to members with enlarged deficits.

The proposed oil facility proved to be the start of a transformation of the IMF into a major lending institution. The proposal for the IMF to borrow from member governments to lend to other members was also unusual and was to make the IMF a major financial intermediary in world markets.

Considerable debate ensued, particularly because monetary officials of industrial countries welcomed recycling through private markets rather than through official channels, but eventually a relatively small oil facility was set up in the IMF in 1974 and another for 1975. The majority of drawings under the 1974 facility were by developing members. However, drawings under both the 1974 and 1975 facilities were smaller than Witteveen had hoped, and as the 1975 facility was about to end and money was still available, the United Kingdom and Italy also drew.

As is well known, only a small proportion of the financing of oil-related balance-of-payments deficits was to come from the IMF. By far the bulk of the recycling came from a substantial expansion of lending by private commercial banks, which, for the first time, began to lend directly to the governments of many developing members. Readily available credit from private commercial banks, at low or even negative real rates of interest, helped induce developing members to borrow. And steadily rising deposits, particularly as oil-exporting countries banked their vastly enlarged oil revenues, induced creditors to lend. Non-oil-developing members opted to accumulate large external debts rather than take measures to reduce their current account deficits since such measures would have reduced their rates of growth.

From 1974 through 1977, two industrial members that were having trouble financing oil deficits, Italy and the United Kingdom, also came to the IMF for financial support not only under the oil facilities but also under traditional standby arrangements. The IMF's support was vital to helping to stabilize their economies. Italy and the United Kingdom in the late 1970s were the last industrial members to be "customers" of the IMF.

In the early 1970s, the IMF made other innovative efforts to enlarge use of its resources. By then, quite apart from the oil-related deficits, it was becoming clear to the staff that for a number of developing members the basic assumption of the usual one-year standby arrangement was proving to be unrealistic. The assumption was that a member could draw under the standby arrangement for up to one year while it adopted policies that would enable the member to eliminate its balance-of-payments deficit and generate a surplus sufficient to repay the Fund within a three-to-five-year period. In practice, however, payments deficits of many developing members lasted for more than a year, and so for many of these members the IMF was frequently approving one standby arrangement after another.

To help meet this problem, in 1974 the IMF introduced yet another innovative new facility, an "extended facility." An extended arrangement can last for three years instead of the one-year duration of the usual standby arrangement. The new facility marked a pivotal change. For the first time, the IMF undertook financing on a medium-term basis to help developing members put into effect programs and policies that would take more than a year to implement so as to help improve their balance-of-payments positions by making structural changes in their economies. Initially, repayment was to take place as soon as the member had overcome its balance-of-payments problems and, in any event, within an outside range of four to eight years. In December 1979, the maximum repayment period was increased from eight to ten years, where it remains.

Use of the IMF's resources by developing members during the 1970s, however, was relatively small. The IMF got requests mainly from countries unable to get credit from private sources.

The IMF also undertook other broad changes in the 1970s. It undertook a comprehensive revision of its Articles of Agreement. With the entry into force of the Second Amendment in 1978, it was ready legally to deal with the wholly changed circumstances, including the new regime of floating exchange rates. In addition, so that the policy recommendations at the highest political levels might be taken more regularly and in a smaller forum than the annual meetings of the board of governors, the IMF introduced new policy-making bodies, notably the Interim Committee of the Board of Governors on the International Monetary System. This interim committee is an advisory body made up of twenty-four IMF governors, that is, financial officials of member governments at the highest political level, representing the same constituencies as in the executive board. The committee meets twice a year, in April, and at the time of the Fund–Bank annual meetings, in September or October.

Because of the troubles that began to plague the world economy and the international monetary system in the 1970s, the IMF also concerned itself more than ever with analyzing and trying to find solutions for world economic problems. Twice a year the IMF undertakes a comprehensive survey of developments in the world economy and makes projections for the near-term. This survey is based on input from virtually the entire IMF staff, is discussed regularly at length in the executive board, is regularly considered by the interim committee, and is quoted on the front pages of the world's leading newspapers. Even more important, the world economic outlook exercise was gradually to become the main vehicle through which the IMF implements multilateral surveillance over the economic policies of its members. Multilateral surveillance consists of examining the consequences of the policies of individual countries for each other and for the world economy as a whole, and of bringing to the forefront the actions needed in the interest of the international community.

New Bold Undertakings in the 1980s

In the 1980s, the IMF again responded innovatively as yet different potential dangers loomed, this time dangers for the international banking and financial system. The problems causing the need for new bold undertakings by the IMF lay in the difficulties arising in 1979. That year brought a fresh surge of inflation in the industrial countries due to higher prices for many primary commodities, high rates of monetary increases in industrial members, expansionary fiscal policies, price rises in the United States as a result of the sharp depreciation of the U.S. dollar from late 1977 to the end of 1978, and continued inflationary expectations in industrial members that pushed up wages in excess of increases in productivity. Then came another very steep runup in the prices for oil.

The monetary authorities of the large industrial members had a different reaction to the resurgence of inflation and the second oil crisis from what they had to the first oil crisis of 1973–74. Beginning in 1979, they undertook sharply anti-inflationary policies, and these tight anti-inflationary policies continued through 1981 and the first half of 1982 even as world recession continued and persisted. These policies resulted in a steep increase in interest rates, including those rates paid by developing countries on the debts they had been incurring as a result of their borrowing heavily from commercial banks, and in a weakness of demand in industrial countries for exports from developing countries. Weak demand in industrial countries from 1979 on—in combination with inappropriate policies of the borrowing countries and their failure to adjust to the worsened circumstances after 1979—induced a sharp slowdown in the growth rates of debtor countries and in their export earnings, capital flight, and excessive borrowing. At the same time, higher interest rates increased servicing on their indebtedness.

Private creditors became alarmed, and in 1982 abruptly and severely cut back on their lending. Suddenly not only did the balance-of-payments positions of many developing countries become impossibly difficult, but also the inability of some major borrowers to "roll over" maturing loans threatened a massive crisis of confidence in the world's banking system and a possible collapse of worldwide financial arrangements. Mexico was the first to declare that it could not pay interest on its debts, but many other major developing countries were also in danger of default, including Argentina, Bolivia, Brazil, Chile, Colombia, Cote d'Ivoire, Ecuador, Morocco, Nigeria, Peru, the Philippines, Uruguay, Venezuela, and Yugoslavia. Virtual panic shook private bankers and monetary and financial officials. They feared the total collapse of the international financial payments mechanism. This was the "crisis" to which the IMF was asked to respond.

IMF officials, under then-Managing Director Jacques de Larosiere, developed a debt strategy. That strategy reflected several key assumptions. One assumption was that the debt problem of the developing members was temporary. These members had a liquidity problem, not a solvency problem. Most of them, especially those in Latin America, had been growing rapidly for years and had been creditworthy to private lenders and would grow again, and commercial banks would lend again once the immediate crisis was over. In the meantime, commercial banks could not afford forgiveness of debt and could actually fail, bringing on a worldwide bank crisis not unlike the savings and loan crisis in the United States. In any event, equity among developing countries was important, and debt forgiveness for those countries that had run up huge debts was unfair to those developing countries that had not borrowed heavily.

A second key assumption was that the world recession of 1982–83 would be temporary once inflation had been wrung out of the economies of the industrial countries. And industrial countries were taking the appropriate measures to rid themselves of inflation. In fact, by 1984, inflation slowed considerably and growth in the world economy resumed at impressive rates. A third basic assumption was that fiscal and monetary policies of the borrowing developing countries had been excessive. Budgetary deficits had mushroomed because of easy access to foreign borrowing, and monetary policies had been lax as central banks had been giving easy credit to domestic borrowers, especially state enterprises, many of which were operating inefficiently and in need of subsidies. The indebted countries had also followed bad exchange-rate policies, and the resulting overvaluation had discouraged exports and encouraged massive capital flight. In light of these circumstances, the indebted developing members needed to go through some substantial readjustment of their policies in order to obtain more sustainable balance-of-payments positions.

The IMF thereupon developed a debt strategy that was a country-by-country approach in collaboration with all the interested parties—the indebted countries, the industrial countries, official creditors, and private creditors. The strategy had two elements—adjustment and financing. Assisting members to design and implement adjustment programs was a central responsibility of the IMF. The objective was to achieve a viable balance-of-payments position in the medium term. On the financing side, the IMF would not only lend substantial amounts to a member undertaking adjustment measures but would also help put together "financing packages" in which the commercial bank creditors would be asked to continue some of their financing. Taking the view that the private bankers bore part of the responsibility for the debt crisis inasmuch as they had lent so freely to developing members without determining the repayment ability of the borrowers, IMF officials, in an innovative and unusual move, played a central part in the debtor members' negotiations with private bankers. In a sharp departure from the IMF's past practice, they insisted that commercial banks and official creditors commit themselves to providing financing over and above what the IMF itself was financing before the IMF approved the country's adjustment program and the associated use of the IMF's resources. Much of the lending done by commercial banks in these circumstances was involuntary. In addition the IMF helped debtor members and commercial banks put together an unprecedented number of debt restructurings, thereby lengthening maturity schedules and reducing the amounts of current payments required.

Within a year, the strategy seemed to be working. The threat of a crippling cessation of international credit flows had been averted and a considerable easing of tensions in international financial markets had taken place. Nonetheless, the debt problem was by no means solved. Most indebted members were still having trouble meeting their interest payments, without even beginning to amortize their debts. It was becoming clearer that some of the key assumptions on which the IMF had based its strategy were not materializing. Economic growth in the industrial countries was not increasing, and commercial banks were reluctant to lend even involuntarily and were cutting back still more on their lending. Consequently, the magnitude of adjustment required by the indebted members was proving to be much larger than expected and lasting much longer. No one had expected the debt crisis to last so long.

New efforts to deal with the debt crisis were initiated, in 1985 under the Baker plan, named for James A. Baker III, then secretary of the U.S. Treasury, and in 1989 under the Brady plan, named for Nicolas Brady, then secretary of the U.S. Treasury. The Baker plan called for growth so that indebted countries might "grow out of debt" and for more commercial bank lending. Increased bank lending did not, however, come about.

The Brady plan, calling for several forms of debt reduction and menus of options for converting debt into other forms, was much more successful. By 1990 and 1991 commercial banks had built up reserves and "loan loss" funds so that they were able to scale back the amounts owed. A number of heavily indebted countries, especially in Latin America but also some countries in other regions, have since agreed to debt-restructuring, debt-conversion, and debt-reduction arrangements with commercial banks, alleviating their debt-service obligations. And much official debt was reduced. Hence, although the debt problems of many individual members remained far from resolution, by the early 1990s the debt crisis as a systemic problem was over. And several indebted members that had undertaken broad reforms in their economic policies and structural adjustments in their economies, usually with the financial support of the IMF, were experiencing remarkable turnarounds. Economic growth in many indebted countries was resuming at above-average rates, capital was returning in huge amounts, and foreign investment was increasing. The success of economic reforms has been particularly apparent in the Western Hemisphere. Other countries, however, especially in sub-Saharan Africa, continue to face very difficult debt problems. In addition, some Eastern European countries and states of the former Soviet Union continue to have serious debt problems.

From 1982 to 1989, the IMF had lent over $53 billion, over half in the three years 1982–84, the height of the debt crisis. Much of this lending was under an enlarged access policy, which allowed countries to draw larger amounts, and which the IMF introduced in 1981 as a temporary measure. That policy was terminated in 1992.

Thus, during the 1970s and 1980s the IMF had transformed itself into a major lending institution. Indeed, many observers came to regard lending to developing members as the IMF's principal function.

The 1990s

Vastly changed circumstances in the world economy in the 1990s have found the IMF again making still further adaptations. In 1991, at the Houston economic summit of the heads of state of the Group of Seven (G–7), the large industrial nations gave the IMF the principal responsibility for assisting the states of the former Soviet Union on far-reaching economic reforms and on measures for economic stabilization. The IMF was also to be a main conduit for channeling significant amounts of financial aid to these countries.

The IMF has assumed this new responsibility with vigor. The IMF's technical assistance to these countries and the training of their officials has expanded considerably. The IMF works with these countries, for example, to improve their macroeconomic management through training government officials, enhancing the quality of statistical data, helping to reform the tax system and government expenditure management, designing social safety nets, and developing and improving the operations of the central banking and financial systems. To help train government officials closer to their home base, the IMF, in conjunction with other international organizations, has set up a new institute in Vienna. In addition, the IMF has established a new temporary systemic transformation facility (STF) primarily to help Russia and other states of the former Soviet Union and other Eastern European countries which are facing severe balance-of-payments difficulties as they make the transition from centrally planned economies to economies based on market principles. Drawings on this facility have already occurred.

The IMF has had still another challenge in the 1990s. As the IMF became an important source of financing for developing countries and for countries making the transition from command to market economies, attention focused increasingly on the IMF's conditionality, that is, the conditions that the institution attaches to its financial support. These conditions have been subject to criticism from the late 1960s on, but they came under intensive attack in connection with the debt crisis, and the image of the institution became tarnished.

The IMF was said to come into indebted countries with harsh austerity programs, programs that set unreasonable targets for balance-of-payments adjustment, that were excessively biased toward demand restraint, that increased unemployment and the number of persons below the poverty line, that brought about declines in the consumption of essentials and cuts in social spending, which was particularly harmful to the poorest and most vulnerable segments of developing countries. The IMF was accused of aggravating already unequal distributions of income and worsening poverty. These criticisms became emotional as the debt crisis became prolonged and as there was a sizable net flow of funds from developing members to industrial members, that is, from poor countries to private bankers, a total reversal of what had for years been regarded as the acceptable normal balance-of-payments relation between developing members and industrial members. The IMF was criticized for serving as a tool of the commercial banks, helping banks get their money out of the indebted members and at the cost of the poor people in these members. As economic growth in developing countries fell and as per-capita incomes in some members even declined, the IMF came in for the most caustic criticisms in its history.

IMF officials replied to these criticisms with a number of arguments. Primarily they stressed that the debt strategy in which the IMF was participating had necessarily been a pragmatic one, geared to the realities of the situation. Had the IMF not intervened, the very real possibility existed of creditors ceasing to lend to the problem countries altogether. Such a development would have made defaults inevitable and cash-starved debtors would have had no option but to retreat behind a wall of restrictions and controls, with serious consequences for the entire world economy. IMF officials also pointed out that, because they had insisted that commercial banks continue to join in with financial packages, even involuntarily, the IMF was not "bailing banks out," but "bailing them in." IMF officials also repeatedly noted that, as they had warned in earlier years, the postponement of adjustment makes eventual adjustment much more difficult.

By the early 1990s, a sea change had taken place in the attitudes of many developing countries, particularly in Latin America, toward the IMF's conditionality. Many of these countries had come to accept the need for cautious macroeconomic policies, realistic exchange rates, correction of distorted price relationships, and efficiently run enterprises. In addition, under Managing Director Michel Camdessus, the IMF has begun to make changes in the objectives of its lending activities, changes that are so profound as to be considered fundamental. For instance, the IMF has moved in the direction of elevating economic growth to one of its explicit purposes rather than having balance-of-payments adjustment as its sole objective. It puts less emphasis on controlling inflation and on monetary targets and more on price stability. It now puts less emphasis on exchange depreciation and more on exchange-rate stability.

The IMF has also developed a series of secondary objectives for its conditionality—the alleviation of poverty, attention to the environment, containment of military expenditures, and political considerations, such as good governance. These secondary objectives are reflected in its policy dialogue and advice, and in the measures incorporated in programs, as well as in the technical assistance it provides for helping members formulate and implement social safety nets. The managing director puts emphasis on high-quality growth, meaning equitable growth for all segments of society.

The IMF has established some new special facilities, especially for the low-income developing countries facing protracted balance-of-payments problems. A structural adjustment facility (SAF) was established in 1986 and an enhanced structural adjustment facility (ESAF) in 1988, which was renewed in December 1993. Under these facilities, the IMF provides financial support on highly concessional terms to support medium-term macroeconomic adjustment programs. These programs are explicitly directed toward the elimination of structural imbalances and rigidities in the economies of poorer countries.

If these tasks were not daunting enough, the IMF continues to have its unique responsibility as overseer of the international monetary system and as monitor of the world economy. In 1994 this responsibility began to loom larger than it had for some years. Volatility of exchange rates in the short run, and longer-run exchange-rate misalignments—that is, swings in exchange rates that have little to do with changes in economic fundamentals—were increasingly seen as causing serious disturbances to international trade and investment. Big movements took place between the rates for the U.S. dollar and the Japanese yen and between the U.S. dollar and some of the European currencies. In addition, traumas had occurred in 1992 and 1993 in the European Monetary System (EMS).

Many officials and economists were advocating schemes for greater fixity or at least stability of exchange rates. But achieving such stability involved tremendous difficulties. Much of the volatility of exchange rates was due to voluminous and agile movements of private short-term capital over which the IMF had little control. Moreover, as demonstrated by the experience in the collapse of the par value system and by the disarray in the early 1990s in the EMS, exchange-rate stability requires that the economic performance of the participating countries not diverge very much. Indeed, deliberate policies may need to be shaped to effect convergence. Such policy coordination is hard to achieve, particularly since countries want to have considerable independence in their monetary policies, such as interest rates, so as to influence their own domestic economies.

As of the end of 1994, the IMF was increasingly cognizant of its mandate to exercise firm surveillance over its members' exchange rates, which involves surveillance over all the domestic policies impinging on exchange rates. It was seeking ways to intensify its surveillance over countries' exchange rates. It was also seeking ways to have a bigger role in global liquidity. In particular, the managing director was advocating a further allocation of SDRs.

In sum, by being flexible within the framework of its basic purposes, the IMF has been an effective force in international monetary affairs, despite vastly altered circumstances in the world economy and the international monetary system.

11

Bretton Woods and European Reconstruction

Jacob J. Kaplan

At Bretton Woods

A member of the Academie Française, Guillaume Guindey, wrote in 1977: "The men who prepared and brought to fruition the Bretton Woods Conference—in the middle of a war—worked under the influence of their experience and their memories. . . . Deeply conscious of the errors committed between the two wars, they sought to avoid a repetition."[1] Exchange-rate instability, competitive devaluation, trade and payments restrictions, bilateralism, and unilateral economic policy behavior preoccupied them as they sought to devise a new international economic system. If such errors could be avoided, they felt confident that economic expansion on a global scale, high levels of employment, and a vigorous and balanced growth of international trade would ensue.

Recognizing that Europe's economies had been damaged, dislocated, and tightly controlled during the war, they felt that a three-to-five-year transition period should suffice to permit the return to prewar production levels and the inauguration of the Bretton Woods system. In the interim, the World Bank would provide reconstruction financing. Actually, the transition lasted fifteen years, by which time production levels in Western Europe were twice the prewar level.

Meeting within weeks of the successful landing in Normandy, the Bretton Woods founders concluded their agreement at a moment when a more orderly and peaceful world seemed to be on the horizon. Visionary and idealistic as well as extraordinarily technically competent, they felt themselves charged with building the economic foundation of a better global society.

143

Little more than a year later, after the end of the war, the realities in Europe seemed much grimmer. Stalin's intransigence about Poland and the rest of Eastern Europe foreshadowed the descent of the iron curtain and the cold war. Moreover, the economic condition of Europe was much worse than anticipated. It would have required extraordinary prescience indeed to foresee what had occurred.

War damage and the loss of shipping and investment income had been expected. But how could anyone have predicted the westward movement of German and Polish borders, the flood of refugees and displaced persons, the loss of both markets and supplies of food and raw materials from the territory occupied by Soviet troops, civil war in Greece, and a divided Germany, Berlin, and Austria? It came as no surprise that Great Britain and France were determined to continue their role as great powers and would undertake to maintain close ties with the Commonwealth and the overseas French territories. However, the cost of doing so soon proved to be unexpectedly burdensome.

Nor was it readily apparent that the peoples of the Allied countries would expect prompt satisfaction of yearnings for a much better life than the prewar period had provided—not only a higher standard of living, but also greater economic opportunity and more ample social justice. Any political leader who doubted the force of such yearnings received a rude shock when the British electorate deposed their beloved wartime hero, Winston Churchill, only months after the surrender of Japan.

The First Two Postwar Years

Striving to meet popular aspirations, newly installed democratic governments greatly depleted their foreign assets and foreign exchange reserves during the first two postwar years. They rewrote constitutions, reorganized old political parties, and formed many new ones. They nationalized banks and industries, inaugurated substantial public investment programs, and drafted educational, health care, and other social reforms. While each government moved in its own way, a large array of wartime economic controls remained firmly in place everywhere—price and rent controls, rationing, raw material and credit allocations.[2] Only Belgium introduced an early anti-inflation program, using fiscal and monetary policy. Foreign exchange controls, import quotas, and bilateral agreements characterized international economic relations in all of Western Europe.

Responding to U.S. Treasury pressure and the terms of the Anglo-American loan, Great Britain sought, as early as mid-1946, to inaugurate the Bretton Woods system of convertibility and nondiscriminatory multilateral trade, supported by $5 billion in loans from the United States and Canada. Within five weeks, most of the dollars were gone and the experiment was suspended. A poor harvest and a hard winter in 1947 exacerbated economic distress and popular frustrations.

By the time of Secretary George C. Marshall's speech at Harvard in June 1947, the United States had contributed over $15 billion for relief and reconstruction.[3] Although inaugurated in March 1946, the Bretton Woods institutions made funds available to Europe for the first time only a few weeks before the speech. The Bank then lent France $250 million;[4] the Fund allowed France to draw $25 million and the Netherlands about $18 million in dollars and sterling.[5] Both institutions had been preoccupied with organizational difficulties.

Weighted voting made it possible for the U.S. Treasury to control the decisions of the Bretton Woods institutions. Adhering strictly to the letter of the IMF agreement, the Treasury insisted that drawings on the Fund be limited to countries taking appropriate domestic policy measures to correct their balance-of-payments deficits and thus to offer good prospects for repayment. Meanwhile the Fund lectured Europeans about reducing budget deficits and tightening monetary policies. It contended that anti-inflationary policies, combined with devaluation, could bring a country's international payments into balance, eliminate its needs for U.S. aid, and make it possible to accept the post-transitional obligations of the IMF agreement. To European governments, the Fund's advice seemed incompatible with the demands and frustrations of electorates. Unsure of continued popular support, they heeded their voters.

The postwar realities that could not have been foreseen at Bretton Woods were essentially political in origin, and the Bretton Woods institutions were created to be nonpolitical. By adhering rigidly to the letter of their mandates, those in control of these institutions effectively excluded them from playing an active role in the reconstruction of Western Europe, though that was the role uppermost in the minds of the founders. Veteran IMF staff members have described their first decade as a gloomy period. It had to be so for those who had joined with high hopes of helping to manage the inauguration of a new international economic order.

The Marshall Plan

Within the U.S. Department of State, the urgent need for a more realistic approach to the political situation was soon identified and translated into what has become popularly known as the Marshall Plan, though it was officially called the European Recovery Program. Marshall's speech in June 1947 came at a moment when European foreign exchange reserves were near exhaustion and continued increases in European production were threatened by a depleting pipeline of imported food, energy, and raw materials.

The Marshall Plan ranks high among the most applauded and most misunderstood initiatives in international relations. It has become a synonym for a large and successful aid program. Let a major problem be identified, an op ed article is sure to follow, proposing a Marshall Plan to remedy it. The article typically identifies a large, multiyear sum of money as its principal component.

The $13.5 billion (1950 dollars)[6] spent for the Marshall Plan was indeed an indispensable catalyst for the reconstruction of Europe's economies. Every bit as important, however, was its unique organization and management, its extensive institution building, and the unprecedented cooperative efforts of the Europeans.

Two prosperous decades that have been termed the Golden Age[7] ensued, as did the progressive integration of Europe, now under the aegis of European union.

Rather than a detailed plan or a large sum, Marshall offered a compelling idea in his speech, a strategy that captured the imagination of leaders and electorates in Europe and the United States. "There must be some agreement among the countries of Europe as to the *requirements* of the situation and the part those countries themselves will take. . . . The initiative, I think, must come from Europe. The program should be a *joint one*, agreed to by a number, if not all, European nations."[8] (Emphasis added.)

A flurry of activity followed. After a Soviet refusal to join in a cooperative program and a Soviet veto of Eastern European participation, the Western Europeans formed a committee that collected, scrutinized, and consolidated the aid needed by each country and reviewed the results with U.S. officials. Mutual assistance policies among the Europeans were also considered, including a possible customs union and the transferability of European currencies into one another. It required only six months for the State Department to submit a European Recovery Program to the Congress, based mainly on European proposals. Only a few months later, in April 1948, appropriations were available and the first procurement authorization was issued.

The authorizations permitted recipients to make purchases and submit the bills to the United States for payment. The imported goods were sold on the recipient's market for local currency, called counterpart funds. This counterpart could be used by the European government for its own economic purposes, in agreement with the U.S. aid mission.

The United States created a new agency in Washington to administer the program, sent missions to each country to supervise the aid and to advise recipients concerning reconstruction programs and policies, and established a field command in Paris to oversee the work of the missions and to cooperate with European multilateral efforts. The Europeans transformed their intergovernmental committee into a full-fledged international organization, the Organization for European Economic Cooperation (OEEC). It consisted of a secretariat and permanent delegations resident in Paris to organize the cooperative effort. The U.S. field command participated in all aspects of OEEC work.

The European Recovery Program

The overriding purpose of the European Recovery Program was to erect a solid economic foundation for political and social stability in Western Europe. Accordingly, the first priority was increased production, with a view to eliminating the need for further extraordinary aid within four years. The economic policy changes that would have been required to inaugurate the Bretton Woods system were initially pushed into the background, though they were never absent from the documentation and the discussions.

Both the four-year Marshall Plan and the work of the OEEC during its life can be divided into two distinct stages.[9] The first two years were focused on filling the pipeline with imported goods—determining how much aid was needed and how it should be divided among the recipient countries. The second two years focused on freeing and increasing intra-European trade, under the aegis of the European Payments Union (EPU) and its closely associated Code of Trade Liberalization.[10] In those second two years, the emphasis also shifted to financing rearmament after the Korean War broke out in June 1950. Rearmament carried double-digit inflation in its wake. At that time, tighter fiscal and monetary policies came to the fore as governments tried to combat rising prices while simultaneously complying with their commitment to liberalize trade.

An unprecedented era of intensive economic policy coordination was thus inaugurated. By the end of the European Recovery Program, almost every OEEC country had compiled and reported its national income accounts on a consistent basis. Moreover, national income analysis had become a recognized tool of policy making. For the first time, governments debated their fiscal, credit, and trade policies with other governments in a multilateral forum. As a result, a common understanding of the role and effects of such policies began to develop.

The founding fathers of the International Monetary Fund felt that economic distress could be avoided only by international economic cooperation on a scale never previously achieved. In fact, it was first achieved within the OEEC and most intensively under the European Payments Union. The EPU system required each country to keep its payments with all other members in balance over time, while sharply reducing quantitative restrictions on imports. An expert EPU managing board closely monitored imbalances and advised countries concerning internal and external economic policies needed to correct them.

The European Payments Union was a regional monetary system, designed to nurture and supervise the transition to convertibility by applying Bretton Woods principles in a more flexible fashion. Although those who were impatient for the early inauguration of the Bretton Woods system feared that such a regional arrangement would be a formidable obstacle to global convertibility, it proved otherwise. By establishing convertibility among its member currencies, used for at least two-thirds of world trade, the EPU produced an immediate suspension of the bilateral agreements among Western European countries. By offering multilateral monthly clearing of accounts, combined with automatic credit, the EPU also induced members to accelerate the dismantling of their quantitative restrictions on trade with one another.

Germany exhausted its automatic credit within the first few months of the union's operation, whereupon it was offered an additional credit subject to strict fiscal and monetary policy conditions. The EPU thus inaugurated the practice of conditionality, which later became a key tool in developing the IMF's constructive relationship with developing countries. This system of regional convertibility succeeded both in removing trade barriers and in greatly expanding trade within the region. That success encouraged the subsequent progressive lifting of such restrictions on imports from the dollar area as well, and thus to the convertibility of European currencies on a global scale.

Was the ERP Necessary?

Though few have contested the success of the European Recovery Program, inevitably questions have been raised by revisionist historians.[11] Was it really essential? After all, U.S. aid was equivalent to less than 3 percent of the combined GDP of the OEEC countries and less than a fifth of their gross investment. Could not Europe have dispensed with such small percentage additions to its resources? Industrial production in OEEC countries exceeded the 1938 level by mid-1948 when ERP aid began to flow.[12] Were not Europe's economic difficulties the temporary result of very high rates of production increase and investment? Could not anti-inflationary policies, currency devaluation, or import restrictions on capital equipment have eliminated the dollar gap without aid? The United Kingdom exported to the rest of the sterling area as much capital as it received under the ERP.[13] Without such capital exports, would the United Kingdom have needed U.S. aid?

Such statistical evidence is valuable and provocative, but it needs to be interpreted in context and with caution.[14] Agricultural production was well below prewar levels in 1948 and the population was 10 percent greater. More cogent was the fact that prewar levels of production met neither the needs nor the aspirations of the postwar electorates. Memories of the Great Depression were deeply embedded in European consciousness. A significant proportion of the electorates was attracted by the promise of Marxist economic solutions, and Communist parties found strong support, especially in Greece, France, and Italy. Democratic leaders in Europe felt that they had to address popular expectations about employment and higher living standards. Belgium apart, other European governments doubted that their populations would tolerate anti-inflationary medicine soon after the end of the war. They, as well as U.S. officials who closely followed events in Europe, thought that the fragile political stability of 1947–48 might not survive the absence of large-scale U.S. aid. At the time, authorities on both sides of the Atlantic thought that the additional resources provided by the ERP represented a critical margin. Since their prescriptions provided a cure, can the judgment of these statesmen be challenged with any confidence?

Others have followed the early opponents of the EPU in questioning whether convertibility could not have been introduced as early as 1950, thus eliminating the need for an EPU.[15] In 1949, Great Britain sharply devalued the pound sterling by 30 percent and most other OEEC countries followed suit, some by a smaller percentage. A devaluation only slightly larger might have sufficed to bring Europe's current account into balance. The dollar gap fell to $1 billion in 1950, and OEEC foreign exchange reserves in that year were almost as large relative to exports and to GNP as in the 1926–29 period. Germany and Austria might have needed to supplement their 1950 reserves by drawing on the IMF (they were not then members) or a floating rate might have been introduced, negating the importance of reserves.

These are rather strained arguments. The Europeans at the time calculated that the current account of the OEEC metropolitan area with the dollar area had dropped to $1.77 billion in 1950 after the devaluations, but increased again to $3.19 billion in 1951.[16] The post–Korean War inflation negated much of the benefit of a lower exchange rate against the dollar. Adopting a floating rate in 1950 would have violated the IMF agreement. It might also have led to extreme exchange rate volatility during the Korean War, the Algerian and Suez crises, and the demise of the French Fourth Republic—all of which followed within a few years. Europeans were understandably risk-averse in the 1950s and slow to regard their economic recovery as robust and firmly rooted.

Between 1952 and 1955, a British initiative led to careful and prolonged consideration at the highest levels of the OEEC of a limited form of convertibility. A floating rate was proposed but soon abandoned. A decision to take an early leap was finally rejected in favor of a slower process of progressively removing quantitative restrictions on imports from the dollar area. The move to partial convertibility in 1958 and the acceptance of the Bretton Woods obligations in 1961 were both solidly based. The convertibility of European currencies has remained a permanent feature of the international monetary system. Here again, can we confidently challenge the judgment of successful decision makers?

Reconstructing Eastern Europe

Current concern about reconstructing the economies of Eastern Europe and integrating them into the global economy suggests a parallel with postwar Western Europe. Analogies can, of course, mislead; the two situations differ in some important respects. The different approaches then and now to reconstruction and integration are even more striking and significant.

Western Europe was provided with gifts of imported goods and services needed to promote production increases. Shortages of demand for whatever was produced were rare. At the outset, imports and foreign exchange payments were totally controlled and were limited to necessities. Restraints on capital flight were effective for the most part. Controls on both internal and external transactions were lifted progressively, but cautiously, and exchange rates were kept fixed, with few exceptions, for more than a decade after the autumn of 1949. There was no Big Bang, yet significant progress toward the common goals—greater production and use of market forces—was persistent, though sometimes sporadic.

The U.S. government was the sole supplier of foreign aid. Once the ERP began to operate, the resources of the IMF and the World Bank ceased to be available to OEEC members for the duration. Nor was private U.S. capital forthcoming; its flow to Europe did not reach significant sums for another decade.

Apart from technical assistance, the U.S. role in making European investment decisions was very limited.[17] It offered advice to Italy on public investment and used its control over counterpart expenditures to influence some other public investment decisions. However, on the whole, investment decisions remained the province of national governments for public investment and of the private market for other enterprises. Nor did the OEEC attempt to coordinate national investment programs beyond the exchange of information and mutual scrutiny to improve the basis for national decisions.[18]

The primary focus on greater output was expected to lay the basis for subsequent movement away from tight controls and toward freer markets. Nevertheless, hardly anyone expected the market mechanism to be the sole coordinator of economic activity. The Great Depression had firmly implanted the concept of a mixed economy,[19] though the preferred proportions of the mixture varied considerably from government to government and from time to time.

Although both the bilateral agreements and the OEEC Convention called for sound fiscal and monetary policies, as well as the removal of trade barriers and other controls, they established no timetables or priorities for doing so. These matters were discussed intensively with individual governments both by U.S. aid missions and by the OEEC Economic Committee and the EPU managing board. Countries were urged to move toward these goals as expeditiously as possible, but only the managing board withheld credits from countries whose policies failed to satisfy its criteria.

Despite its predominant economic power, the United States did not arrogantly impose its views on needy governments that considered such views to be contrary to their own interests.[20] Conditionality was absent from the U.S. aid program, though U.S. views were presented, openly and sometimes vigorously. The arrogance of power was not manifested; democratic governments were allowed to judge the tolerance of their people for deflationary measures and for the degree and type of state intervention in economic activity.

Finally, the concept of European integration had taken root in Europe and was promoted by U.S. aid administrators. Little resistance was encountered to the idea that full and detailed cooperation was essential, though the form and intensity of that cooperation occasioned considerable debate. Nevertheless, it has continued to evolve over more than four decades.

None of the foregoing is apparent in the effort to reconstruct the economies of Eastern Europe. Neither in the East nor in the West do current policy makers seem more than superficially aware of how the economy of Western Europe was rebuilt. Some of that experience is not applicable, given different conditions and aspirations. But the bottom line is that, for Western Europe, it worked.

Notes

1. Guillaume Guindey, *The International Monetary Tangle* (Oxford: Blackwell, 1977), p. 5.

2. See OEEC, *Interim Report on the European Recovery Program* II (December 1948).

3. Harry S. Truman, *Years of Trial and Hope, 1946–1953* (New York: Doubleday, 1956), p. 116.

4. Edward S. Mason and Robert E. Asher, *The World Bank since Bretton Woods* (Washington, D.C.: The Brookings Institution, 1973), p. 52.

5. J. K. Horsefield, ed., *The International Monetary Fund, 1945–1965* (Washington, D.C.: International Monetary Fund, 1969), p. 190.

6. Equivalent to 1.3 percent of U.S. GNP over the life of the ERP and over 2 percent during its first two years. In current dollars, the cost would be on the order of $75 billion.

7. A. Maddison, *Phases of Capital Development* (Oxford: Oxford University Press, 1982), p. 126.

8. Quoted in Dean Acheson, *Present at the Creation* (New York: Norton, 1969), p. 312.

9. Jacob J. Kaplan and Gunther Schleiminger, *The European Payments Union: Financial Diplomacy in the 1950s* (New York: Oxford University Press, 1989).

10. Lincoln Gordon, "Recollections of a Marshall Planner," *Journal of International Affairs* (1988), pp. 237–239 and 243–244.

11. See, for example, A. Milward, *Reconstruction of Western Europe* (Berkeley: University of California Press, 1984), pp. 1–55, 90–113, and 465–466; and Charles Maier, "The Two Post War Eras and the Conditions for Stability in Twentieth Century Western Europe," *American Historical Review* (1981): pp. 327–52.

12. OEEC, *Interim Report on the European Recovery Program* I (December 1948).

13. Bank for International Settlements, *Twentieth Annual Report* (1950), p. 28; and *Twenty-Second Annual Report* (1952), p. 52.

14. Charles P. Kindleberger, *Marshall Plan Days* (Boston: Allen and Unwin, 1987). Chapter 14 carefully reviews and responds to the literature that questions the necessity or the advisability of the Marshall Plan.

15. Milton Friedman, *Essays in Positive Economics* (Chicago: University of Chicago Press, 1953); A. Berg and Jeff Sachs, "Stabilizing a Previously Planned Economy," *Economic Policy* 14 (spring 1992): pp. 117–173; H. Giersch, K. H. Paque, and H. Schmieding, *The Fading Miracle* (New York: Cambridge University Press, 1992); Barry Eichengreen, *Reconstructing Europe's Trade and Payments* (Manchester: Manchester University Press, 1993).

16. OEEC, "Europe: The Way Ahead," *Fourth Annual Report of the OEEC* (December 1992): p. 4b.

17. Lincoln Gordon, "Recollections," p. 238.

18. OEEC, *Ninth Annual Report* (1959), p. 36.

19. J. B. deLong and Barry Eichengreen, "The Marshall Plan," NBER Working Paper No. 3899 (1991); S. Lieberman, *The Growth of European Mixed Economies* (Cambridge, Mass.: Schenkman Publishing Co., 1977).

20. R. Marjolin, *Architect of European Unity: Memoirs* (London: Weidenfeld and Nicolson, 1989), p. 211. "I have never seen the Americans try to impose on Europe forms of action which the latter considered contrary to its fundamental interests." And Michael Hogan, *The Marshall Plan* (New York: Cambridge University Press, 1987), p. 450. "American initiatives generally succeeded only to the extent that they accorded with the interests and aspirations of key participating countries."

12

From the ITO to GATT—And Back?

William Diebold, Jr.

Introduction

This paper is primarily a reexamination of the past. But it says next to nothing about the combination of ideas, analyses, and hope that led many people to conclude during the Second World War that, to build a satisfactory postwar world economy, they would have to find ways of reducing trade barriers that were quite a bit better than those that had been provided by the modicum of international cooperation achieved in the past. Nor does the paper trace the process by which this conviction took the shape of the proposed Charter for an International Trade Organization (ITO), which is largely a story of negotiation, internal politics in various countries, differences in national priorities, and above all compromise (although something will have to be said about the short and unhappy life of the ITO charter that emerged from the Havana conference in 1948). Rather, most of the paper is taken up with a somewhat selective discussion of the way the ITO's successor, GATT, fared as it was translated from paper into action in the postwar world. Because the division of labor of this book leaves the present and future to others, this paper ends with a few key questions that rise directly from what has been said about the past.

Since it is not a history of the events with which it deals, this paper has to recite bits of history. Most of the paper is analysis and interpretation, but the limits of space prevent the laying out of evidence and reasoning for the views it presents. The result is that there will be many analytical statements that are condensed and flat, lacking the qualification and demonstrations they ought to have. For the same reason the judgments that follow will sometimes seem a bit arbitrary. Perhaps, then, this paper is best thought of as a commentary, and a rather opinionated one.[1]

The International Trade Organization

Once upon a time, in the days when the world economy was being remade purposefully and not accidentally, we all said that the financial and monetary machinery that had been put in place at the original Bretton Woods Conference could not do all the work cut out for it unless trade, too, was dealt with by an international organization embedded in a multilateral intergovernmental agreement containing rules and procedures. Insofar as that meant the ITO, or something close to it, we were obviously wrong—but perhaps not altogether.

It was also clear that to conclude an effective agreement, governments would have to undertake concrete obligations, not just broad commitments. That was one of the "lessons of last time" that did so much to shape the ideas of the people who had been thinking about the postwar world economy. Over and over in negotiations sponsored by the League of Nations, governments had made broad commitments that rarely produced significant results or survived the impact of domestic political and economic pressures responding to conventional concepts of national interest. In terms of the 1940s, that meant going beyond the general language of the Atlantic Charter, Article VII of the Lend-Lease agreements, and the somewhat more precise language of the British loan agreement. Britain was the key partner without whom the Americans thought it would be impossible to build an international economic system that would conform to the Bretton Woods aspirations of liberalization, reciprocity, multilateralism, and equal treatment. The two countries expected to be in rather different positions at the end of the war and the governments disagreed on some important issues, so it was obvious that it would be very difficult to work out concrete commitments that met both their needs and the Bretton Woods principles and were at the same time acceptable to many other countries as well.

Another lesson of the past—probably not as widely understood but in my view the key to the special character of the ITO charter—was that if general and genuine trade liberalization was to be achieved, negotiations would have to cover more than the traditional range of international trade agreements. The primary objective would still be the reduction of tariffs and setting limits on the use of quotas and other border restrictions, but in addition something had to be done to deal with other measures that damaged international trading relations. For example, it would be futile to eliminate governmental trade barriers if they were replaced with private trade barriers imposed by monopolies or cartels. So the charter had a chapter on restrictive business practices, but it was rather weak and in some respects ambiguous. That was not surprising considering the diversity of national laws about these matters and the discrepancies among the attitudes behind them, notably between European practices and the American antitrust tradition.

"Private cartels are bad . . . government cartels are worse," said the National Association of Manufacturers.[2] Though many of the authors of the charter agreed, they thought there should be provisions permitting the use of international commodity agreements in certain circumstances. Basically, there were two quite different lines of reasoning to support this view. One concerned stability: many economists agreed with a committee set up by the Twentieth Century Fund that the great swings in prices and production to which minerals and crops were often subjected showed that ". . . competitive market forces will not do their job in the case of a number of raw materials except after a long period and at very great human and social cost. To avoid that cost and to reduce the risks of unstable production and trade in raw materials intergovernmental commodity agreements with proper safeguards are justified in the interests of the world economy."[3] The other argument was that it was far better to establish standards for commodity agreements than to try to rule them out altogether since, as Clair Wilcox, one of the principal American negotiators, said in what is still the best book about the ITO: "It would be futile to propose that nations agree to abandon all efforts to assist producers of primary commodities. There is not the remotest possibility that any nation would accept such a commitment. Even in the United States it would run counter to established policy."[4] This last remark was a reminder that while Americans might think of the raw-materials issue in terms of tin and rubber, many of them also believed in production controls and price supports for farm products. When I was in the State Department the saying was that "an international commodity agreement is a cartel approved by the Department of Agriculture."

The chapter that emerged pointed a direction by trying to define the circumstances in which commodity agreements could be used and the purposes they might serve. More concrete provisions established procedures for working out agreements and gave countries whose interests were affected, as well as consumers and producers, the right to participate in the governing of the agreements. All in all, the chapter was a good deal stronger than that concerning private restrictive practices but, as Wilcox emphasized, there could be no certainty as to the results or assurance that governments would live up to their obligations. He quoted the report of the Twentieth Century Fund: "The chapter will be what the members of the ITO make it."[5]

That simple truth applied across the board and never more so than in the short second chapter of the charter, entitled "Employment and Economic Activity." The key issue here was not one of working out new international agreements of the sort required for cartels, commodity agreements, and traditional trading arrangements. It was the problem of linking a country's foreign trade policy with its domestic economic programs. The effort combined high aspiration with the utmost realism. Few people quarreled with the statement in a report based on the work of the League of Nations secretariat (then in Princeton) that "the direct association of commercial policies" with national policies to expand production, raise living standards, and achieve full employment was "an essential prerequisite to progress towards international economic cooperation."[6] The aspiration in the Havana charter lay in trying to do something about the connection. The realism lay in Clair Wilcox's defense of the chapter: "There is no hope that a multilateral trading system can be maintained in the face of widespread and protracted unemployment. Where the objectives of domestic stability and international freedom come into conflict, the former will be given priority. . . . It would be futile to insist that stability must always give way to freedom. The best that can be hoped for is a workable compromise."[7] Unfortunately, it was hard to find among the chapter's compromises anything that looked very "workable." Many critics of the charter saw this chapter as a massive escape clause: the risk that it might be used that way could not be denied. Nevertheless, no matter how far short of its aspirations it fell, something like chapter 2 was inescapable. Most of the governments of the world saw it as a safeguard—perhaps a rather weak one—against the impact on them of the instability they all expected from the large American economy.

Another troublesome part of the charter concerned investment. Although the liberalization of trade was supposed to contribute to economic recovery and growth, the American and British authors of the charter did not think that fostering economic development was a central function of the ITO, so the original drafts of the charter mentioned reconstruction and economic development only in quite general terms. But as the negotiations proceeded, successive drafts became more positive on the subject, and a bit more substantive, largely in response to the demands of developing countries. As development in the rest of the world would require a flow of capital from the United States which would, in part, take the form of private investment, difficulties soon appeared in trying to reconcile the assurances investors wanted with the freedom many governments wanted to treat foreign capital as they thought best. Not surprisingly, the resulting wording of proposed articles was not very satisfactory to anyone: a number of European countries lined up with the developing countries; and at a late stage American business groups demanded that the American negotiators insist on much stronger provisions to protect the rights of investors.

It was apparent to informed observers that this was unwise; the United States was nearly isolated on the matter and had used up most of its bargaining power on trade provisions. The State Department argued, quite sensibly, that there was a much better chance to get favorable terms for American investors by separate negotiations with individual countries that wanted American capital. However, the government gave in and the negotiation of language about investment became one of the most contentious issues during the final negotiations at Havana. Predictably, the results fell far short of what the business groups wanted, and even strong supporters of the charter were unhappy with the outcome.

Forty-odd years ago, I concluded that the unsatisfactory provisions on investment had been the decisive factor in leading the major American business groups to come out against the charter and that opposition had, in the end, been the decisive consideration in leading the Truman administration to conclude that it could not get the ITO through Congress. Yet other factors contributed as well, first to delaying and then to giving up the objective. They included the priority that had to be given to new urgent matters such as the Marshall Plan and NATO; the problems of renewing the Trade Agreements Act when for the first time it came before a Republican Congress in 1948; elections in 1948 and 1950; another renewal of the Trade Agreements Act in 1949; the Korean War; domestic economic pressures; the disappearance from government of the charter's main champions. Insofar as people wanted to do something about trade barriers, GATT was already at work and, in the short run at least, provided most of what could be expected from the charter.

Protectionists, in Congress and the country, opposed the charter. In the business community, however, they were outweighed by those who supported the idea of breaking down international barriers. These people had, by and large, backed the Trade Agreements Program. There were features of the charter that many businessmen liked and others that most disliked, especially in the newer fields and in the rights given to countries in balance-of-payments difficulties to control imports. Opinions were divided in business circles as to where the balance of the pros and cons lay. No one can be sure, but it seems likely that, had it not been for the investment provisions, most of the major business organizations would have gone along with the administration as they had on most other international economic matters (although most bankers had opposed the International Monetary Fund). However, once they had flatly rejected the investment provisions, most business groups and many individuals dropped all efforts to make careful assessments, put all their emphasis on the most negative version of each argument, spoke as if complicated matters were to be judged in black and white, and made their case in extreme language.

There is no need to enlarge on the subject here or to trace the demise of the ITO in any detail.[8] We should, though, focus on one central issue. The ITO's place in history was marked by the efforts to find a way to combine the reduction of traditional trade barriers with novel measures dealing with several related and complicated aspects of international trade. The document embodying all these arrangements—or proposals—had to be acceptable to a number of governments, some more important than others. Within each of these countries there was a division of views about most of the matters under negotiation and whether adherence to the agreement as a whole was in the national interest or not. The economic and political systems of these countries varied and so did their positions in the world. The charter had to cope with conditions that were expected to be temporary while establishing processes whose effects could only be judged in the long run. The inevitable result was a lengthy, complicated document full of compromises, novelties, and uncertainties. Anything very much different would have been unrealistic and impossible for many countries to adhere to. But these strengths also carried with them the weaknesses that in the end destroyed the charter.

Comprehensiveness and compromise gained the support of some but generated the opposition of others. Every expansion of negotiations beyond their traditional scope brought additional interests into play; some saw advantages and others losses or hazards. One's final judgment on the charter depended on an algebraic summing of the pluses and minuses and an estimate of what would happen if the charter were not approved. Even among the strongest supporters of the charter in the United States, I cannot recall anyone who did not have some reservations or who believed it would completely settle any of the major issues with which it dealt. Who could be enthusiastic about such a document? In order not to rely entirely on memory for the tone of these views, I have turned to something Percy Bidwell and I wrote at the time:

> A start, some principles, machinery, agreement on some concrete problems and certain standards of conduct—these are the main assets of the ITO Charter. They are not negligible. . . .
> . . . [J]oining the ITO, with our eyes open to its weaknesses and the determination to make it work well . . . will open doors and increase the chances of progress.[9]

That view did not prevail. Still, although what he said was what all negotiators say, Clair Wilcox was probably right when he wrote that, no matter what its faults and inadequacies, the document he brought home from Havana was the best that could be produced in the circumstances: "the only charter that can be considered or adopted by the nations of the world."[10]

In terms of the theme of this paper, the effort by the authors of the charter to adapt the principles and spirit of Bretton Woods to the real world of trade was on the right track intellectually but suffered from the weaknesses of its virtues of complexity and comprehensiveness and then foundered on specific circumstances in the United States. And without the United States it held no meaning for the rest of the world. But before the ITO reached its end, another attempt at adaptation was under way.

The General Agreement on Tariffs and Trade

Before the drafting of the charter was finished, the United States, Britain, and a number of other countries were busy reducing tariffs and other trade barriers. Their aim was to reap some immediate benefits from the general commitments to reduce trade barriers, to maintain some momentum even though the ITO negotiations were dragging, to take advantage of the president's negotiating powers before the Trade Agreements Act had to be renewed in 1948, and perhaps above all to start liberalizing trade before too many producers in Europe and the developing countries became established and called for protection. Will Clayton was supposed to have summed up the situation by saying that it was necessary to act before the vested interests got their vests on.

However, more was needed than just commitments to reduce certain tariff rates. People wanted assurances that the reductions would last and that they would not be offset by new barriers; and ways had to be found to embody the results of more or less traditional bilateral negotiations in an unprecedented multilateral agreement. What was done, in effect, was to write an agreement that would become a chapter of the ITO charter when that document came into effect.[11]

How that supposedly temporary arrangement lasted and became the whole book instead of a chapter is a well-known story. Many formal and informal changes in GATT took place during the next forty-five years and were often important parts of the process by which the Bretton Woods approach was adapted to the real world of trade. They cannot be chronicled here; instead, this section presents a brutally oversimplified interpretation of the major strengths and weaknesses of GATT, from which can be derived a sketch of what its adaptation has amounted to. "Strengths and weaknesses" must, of course, be judged in terms of GATT's primary purpose of bringing about what its preamble calls "reciprocal and mutually advantageous arrangements directed to the substantial reduction of tariffs and other barriers to trade and to the elimination of discriminatory treatment in international commerce."

The great and unquestioned achievement of GATT—which means its members[12] working through GATT procedures and rules—was that by the end of the 1960s it had brought about a major reduction of trade barriers and helped countries settle many disagreements and avoid others. After the end of the Kennedy round in the late 1960s, it was for the first time possible to think realistically of the eventual removal of practically all tariffs on trade in manufactured goods among industrial nations. This was a much greater freeing of trade than anyone had expected when GATT began. Not all the settlement and avoidance of disputes led to the liberalization of trade, but even so a reduction of friction in these matters was thought to help bring about international economic cooperation.

A number of factors contributed to this success. It was a time of recovery, development, and growth in the world economy. Trade grew faster than production. That was partly a result of trade liberalization but it also made people more willing to go further in the same direction. Taking part in GATT bargaining forced governments to decide what barriers they could reduce in return for what they wanted from others. Negotiations were selective: governments could push for what they wanted most from others and avoid reducing the barriers that were politically most delicate at home. No one was committed to "free trade"; no one expected anything like it; the term does not appear in the GATT, which simply calls for a process of liberalization with no stated objective. If every step had been seen as a move toward free trade, it is likely that many steps would not have been taken. At the same time, the most-favored-nation rule (MFN) spread the benefits of each bilateral bargain.

Much of the early history of GATT can be written in terms of the application of its balance-of-payments provisions. There it had the help of the International Monetary Fund. Raymond Vernon called their "close working relations . . . a model for coordinated efforts among related international agencies."[13] GATT's rather elaborate balance-of-payments provisions were used to lay the basis for later opening of European markets by permitting countries with balance-of-payments difficulties to reduce tariffs while at the same time controlling the level of imports (and to a degree determining where they should come from). Meanwhile, the United States was willing to let its nominally reciprocal tariff reductions take effect immediately, both to help European recovery and to keep the trade liberalization process going.

After 1958 when most European currencies became convertible, these rather lopsided bargains were mostly righted without further ado. The balance-of-payments provisions declined in importance, but as time passed, other features of GATT negotiations developed that represent adaptation though they may not always have contributed directly to liberalization. For example, the concentration of negotiations in "rounds" of bargaining undoubtedly delayed some reductions not only because countries rarely made reductions between rounds but also because foot-dragging by any important country could slow everyone's negotiations. However, to put together the large, complex packages that emerged from the rounds, countries accepted compromises and overcame disagreements on specific points. In fact, some rounds were ended because, with so much at stake, heads of government gave their attention to these mundane matters for fear that all the work would be lost if the law giving the American president the authority to reduce duties expired. There is probably also some truth to the much repeated statement that having negotiations under way helped governments resist domestic protectionist pressures for several years.

Although a large and increasing number of countries took part in the negotiations, the final resolution of both the Kennedy and the Tokyo Rounds depended on a bargain between the United States and the principal trading countries of Western Europe (in spite of the great importance of Japan in trade).[14] GATT is a one country–one vote body that is supposed to make decisions by a majority of its many members, but the obvious difficulties of that process were avoided because, as two highly qualified witnesses put it, "the practice developed early whereby the [contracting parties] do not proceed to a formal vote in reaching decisions" except in a few cases.[15] Naturally it was the major trading countries whose views were crucial to the kind of "consensus" this process required.

One could carry this analysis one step further and focus on the essential part the United States played in starting GATT and keeping it going. Although GATT and the ITO reflected the same thinking and came out of the same negotiating process, none of the differences between them was more significant than that the ITO would have to go to Congress while the president could commit the United States to GATT through the power delegated to him by the Trade Agreements Act. After the ITO was no more, important aspects of the history of GATT continued to depend on what the United States could do or not do under that act. But to explain those matters requires one to go into broader issues about what shapes American foreign trade policy with its idiosyncratic structure, how it has changed over time, and, indeed, why the United States started the whole process we are discussing in the first place. And those are matters which go far beyond what can be done in this paper.

An aspect of GATT that may have played a part in its success by enhancing flexibility, or may have reduced or undermined the value of the agreement, is the odd fact that for a long time there has been no complete agreement among the principal trading countries as to just how GATT is supposed to work. The question, as phrased by Raymond Mikesell, is should it "be primarily a legal document with provisions for judicial determination and penalties for violations, or a set of guidelines for realizing mutually agreed objectives and procedures for achieving the objectives through consultation and mediation?"[16] Most of the time the United States has leaned toward the former view—and been accused of undue "legalism"—while Western European countries have often quite explicitly championed the second interpretation—and been seen by Americans as not living up to commitments. Distinguishing what he calls the "adjudicatory" view and the "diplomatic" aim of "lowering tensions, defusing conflicts, and promoting compromise," Andreas Lowenfeld finds, "Over the forty years of GATT dispute settlement, there has been an ebb and flow between the . . . models."[17] An objective observer might suppose that sometimes one and sometimes the other way of dealing with a problem would make the most sense, but that it was not likely the right choice would always be made.

After the Kennedy Round the GATT perspective changed. There was still work to be done on the reduction of tariffs and other more or less traditional matters that had been the main targets of the first twenty years, but the very success of that work had brought into sharp profile the importance of nontariff barriers (NTBs).[18] Some work had been done on these matters but no one doubted that the next GATT round would have to be primarily concerned with them. There would be new difficulties. The broad principles that governed tariff negotiations and the methods for applying them would not suffice to deal with a large number of NTBs: they varied greatly in type; their purposes and effects differed according to circumstances; and some were directed primarily at foreign trade, while for others the impact on trade was incidental to domestic aims. Often NTBs were closely linked to the pursuit of laudable purposes in the national economy; frequently they were embedded in national industrial policies. There would clearly be political complications in trying to reach international agreements about matters that were usually thought of as domestic.

All this was predicted and has proved correct. The results of the Tokyo Round were mixed. There was a major step forward in creating codes concerning the use of some important NTBs. They differed a good bit from one another in scope. Most fell well short of the provisions advocated by many people and some governments. Robert Strauss, who got the Tokyo Round package through Congress, spoke of "that pitiful little subsidy code . . . a feeble first start. . . . It wasn't even very clear because we never really got agreement, if you want to know the truth."[19] As the codes applied only to the countries that adhered to them, they sometimes ran afoul of GATT's basic principle of equal treatment. As time passed it became clear that governments were not willing to make as much use of the NTB codes as would have been needed to produce anything like the degree of liberalization earlier GATT action had brought on tariffs and quantitative restrictions.

The Tokyo Round took place in worse economic circumstances than previous GATT rounds. One major disturbance was OPEC's increase of energy prices: the diverse national responses of the importing countries left them in considerable disarray and produced a good bit of bilateralism. In 1971 the United States gave quite a jolt to the cooperative system by its unilateral action on the dollar. The stagflation of the 1970s stimulated protectionism, which inhibited trade liberalization and led to new barriers. Out of the recycling of petrodollars came debt burdens that had a significant impact on trade. The breakdown of the quasi-fixed exchange rate system, the freeing of the dollar from gold (and some other) responsibilities, and the subsequent volatility of exchange rates upset many past assumptions of trade measures and often overshadowed the significance of commercial policies. Many of these effects were prolonged through the 1980s and 1990s. Although there were ups as well as downs, and international trade increased over the period, GATT—and trade liberalization more generally—was no longer buoyed by the expansion that had helped so much in the first twenty years.

Thus GATT showed some strengths as it was adapted to a changing world, but to assess that adaptation we must also look at GATT's deficiencies. As the list is long and the facts mostly familiar, a key sentence or two will have to do for each. Some of the deficiencies were written into the GATT, some are failures to make the most of its provisions and possibilities, and others are means by which governments pushed GATT aside and acted against the principles they had endorsed when they signed the agreement in the first place. (The list that follows takes no account of changes provided for in the Uruguay Round.)

- GATT grandfathers nonconforming practices.
- The disputes-settlement rules are weak and the procedure slow. They sometimes lead to bilateral agreements that reflect the power of the parties rather than the principles of GATT.
- The codes dealing with NTBs fall far short of what might have been expected both in scope and use.
- The secretariat, at least since the days of Eric Wyndham-White, has been weak. It has not been given a number of functions that could improve procedures and strengthen GATT, and has not always exercised those it would be free to or taken many initiatives to improve its position.

- Escape clauses permitting the temporary restriction of imports are necessary, but the members of GATT have failed to make a serious effort to ensure that these provisions are used to make adjustments that would permit the removal of restrictions in a reasonable length of time. GATT has never developed procedures for trying to work out international programs that would both aid countries and press them to make adjustments under international surveillance that might permit temporary suspension of some rules.
- So-called voluntary export restraints (VERs), which are usually not truly voluntary, have been used extensively and completely escape GATT rules.
- Japan, with its great importance in international trade, does not yet fit fully into GATT. The responsibility is shared between Japan and the other countries.
- The state trading provisions have been neglected instead of efforts being made to give concrete content to their somewhat experimental character and to define the "commercial considerations" that are their dominant note.[20]
- The arrangements for fitting customs unions and free trade areas into the MFN and other multilateral arrangements of GATT are inadequate for dealing with the complexity of the issues raised by these entities (and their relations to one another).
- Among the greatest deficiencies of GATT is the exclusion of major segments of world trade from its provisions—even when they have remained nominally under them. The result has been a hollowing out of GATT that has made it a far less comprehensive agreement than it was supposed to be.

Agriculture was the first to be excluded, though never totally. It was apparent from the beginning that, so long as major countries followed the kinds of farm policies established in the United States and most of Western Europe, there could be only limited liberalization of controls and tariffs imposed at borders; to be useful, agreements would have to deal with measures affecting production, prices, and sales. An opportunity to start this process was missed in the Kennedy Round, but by the Uruguay Round a few steps were being taken.

Textiles came next, with the irony that from the start the arrangements were put under the aegis of GATT so that exporting countries would be more fairly treated than if the original plan had been followed by reaching an agreement in the Organization for Economic Cooperation and Development (OECD) and presenting it to the producers. Over time the scope of the arrangements has spread and the dominant form has been not multilateral and liberalizing but bilateral and restrictive. There is, however, another irony. The first cotton textile agreement was initiated by the United States as a byproduct of the election of John F. Kennedy and supposedly as a necessary condition for the passage of the Trade Expansion Act of

1962. That law was the basis for American participation in the Kennedy Round, which was the high point of GATT's success.

Later such important products as steel and automobiles were subjected to a combination of international agreements and national measures—especially by the United States—that usually paid no attention to GATT or its rules. At one time or another, and in varying degrees, at least some of the trade in oil, gas, chemicals, ships, aircraft, and other products was similarly treated.

Perhaps the biggest default of GATT—that is to say of the governments of the industrial countries that dominated it for most of its life—was in relation to the developing countries. The subject did not loom large in the preparatory thinking. Then decolonization came much sooner than anyone expected. One could no longer treat rubber and tin as the output of British and Dutch cartels; they were major assets of developing countries whose markets were unstable and vulnerable.

The classic argument for infant industry protection was written into the GATT agreement; and the balance-of-payments rules provided further leeway for the policies of import substitution favored by countries for whom development meant industrialization. As time passed, more steps were taken, in law and practice, that were supposed to foster development, such as exempting LDCs from the obligation to make reciprocal concessions when they gained tariff reductions from industrial countries. One result was to reduce the interest of the main trading countries in negotiating with the LDCs, who thus lost opportunities to improve their access to richer markets. It was also a doubtful benefit for the developing countries to escape the external pressure on their trade regimes which had done so much to reduce barriers among the industrial countries. When developing countries asked for, and got, the promise of preferential treatment for their exports to industrial countries, it was predictable that these privileges would be hedged round by exceptions and limitations. Although there was no doubt that LDCs gained better access to the markets of industrial countries than they would have had without GATT, a good case could be made for the view that in toto they were less well treated than industrial countries that had exchanged mutually beneficial concessions as the result of vigorous bargaining with one another. For some years from 1964 on, the United Nations Conference on Trade and Development (UNCTAD) looked attractive to the developing countries but did not produce major results.

In effect, the developing countries were left out of the mainstream of the GATT system and no serious effort was made to try to build up a special system of rules appropriate to their needs and changing circumstances. The lack was underlined when a number of these countries, led by South Korea and Taiwan, became important exporters of industrial products. The arguments that justified special treatment for developing countries hardly applied to them any longer, but there was no altogether acceptable way of bringing them fully into the general system or even into some sort of halfway house. Later a number of developing countries, on their own initiative, moved away from general import substitution to policies of selective import liberalization. Whether this means they can quickly be drawn fully into the GATT system as it has developed largely among the industrial countries remains to be seen. There will continue to be countries for whom some different treatment would be preferable, so the old issue of neglect will not disappear.

• Not all of GATT's deficiencies lay within itself. After close cooperation with the International Monetary Fund in dealing with balance-of-payments difficulties, there seem to have been few occasions when GATT acted as if it were part of the Bretton Woods system. Wherever the responsibility lay—and part of it was certainly due to the exiguous character of the GATT secretariat—the World Bank made loans to support major shifts in the structure of production of some countries, with little or no attention being given to the consequences for trade or to where markets were to be found. When the International Monetary Fund masterminded the reduction and rearrangement of heavy debts, GATT had no part in weighing the consequences for trade.

This is a long and formidable list of deficiencies. There is no good way to set it against the successes described earlier. But perhaps one can get some idea of the results by appraising the status of some of the basic Bretton Woods principles in the world trading system of the early 1990s. It is, to be sure, rather artificial to do this without taking account of the results of the Uruguay Round, but that is no easy matter and in this book is assigned to others.

Reciprocity—meaning that each country receives benefits roughly matching the contributions it makes to the system—is one of the basic principles of the Bretton Woods system. So long as a country stays in the system, that is prima facie evidence that its powers-that-be find the results at least acceptable. It seems futile to press the inquiry much further. These are matters on which opinions differ within each country. Methods of comparing the results among countries have little to be said for them. There is some danger to the system in the disposition (which has grown) to think in terms of reciprocal treatment in specific matters by certain other countries—often Japan—rather than overall benefits.

Multilateralism provides one of the acid tests of the Bretton Woods principles. It has three major meanings: wide participation; accommodation of diversity; and equal treatment.

On the first count, GATT gets high marks; the number of signatories has grown to include most countries. Participation does not give all countries equal weight in shaping GATT's activities, but that is in the nature of things.

GATT's record on the second meaning of multilateralism is less good, as what was said above about developing countries and also state trading make clear. On the latter score, the challenge would have been greater if the USSR had taken part in the negotiations and the balance-of-payments rules had not blunted initial concerns about nationalization and economic planning in Britain and France. Many of the issues are difficult in principle; how well they might have been dealt with in practice is moot. More important, though less clearly defined, problems concerning the accommodation of diversity are reflected in the prolonged inability to find satisfactory ways of fitting Japan into the system of rules on the same basis as most industrial countries. Even though market-oriented private capitalism, to which GATT-like arrangements fit best, has become more popular than it used to be, diversity in developing countries plus the entry into the trading arrangements of former Communist countries and China seem likely to make this aspect of multilateralism of continuing importance.[21]

Perhaps the idea of equal treatment as a third meaning of multilateralism is only implicit in the concept of a "many-sided" agreement, but it was certainly on people's minds when a major objective was getting rid of bilateralism. Here GATT has achieved a good deal, especially through the application of the most-favored-nation principle. Still, a good deal of discrimination remains. Some comes from the use of voluntary export restraints (VERs), the singling out of specific countries against whom to apply safeguards, and a number of other rather common practices. Some comes through fair trade rules and is generally not called discrimination—though it is. The most complex issues of discrimination arise, however, when a few countries — perhaps just two — form a customs union or free trade area. Discrimination against the outside world is inherent in these arrangements: how is one to set the outsiders' losses against the gains of the participants? There are usually good reasons why the membership in the new entity should be limited, but there is also an exchange of privileges which give countries an incentive to keep others out for less acceptable reasons. Moreover, internal liberalization is almost never complete. Each agreement is tailored to circumstances that differ from the others. The usual formulas suggested for such relatively simple matters as tariffs do not work too well; they hardly touch NTBs, government procurement, and complex but increasingly important matters as rules of origin and a range of other practices. Somewhat comparable questions arise from a number of other arrangements, such as the NTB codes and bilateral negotiations on specific issues, including those between the United States and Japan about high technology industries (even if they do not formally violate MFN). There seem to be fairly strong prospects that the formation of customs unions and free trade areas will spread; each will be tailored to specific circumstances and pose some special problems for GATT principles.

It would be wrong to stress only the limited extent to which GATT has lived up to the principles of Bretton Woods. In these matters one must always ask about alternatives. In 1971 I wrote that, in spite of the many justified complaints about the way GATT had been working, it was hard to believe that "the kind of agreements that could be negotiated today would be at all as liberal as those on which the Fund and GATT rest."[22] Today that statement would have to be repeated—and probably underlined. I suppose this means that the survival of GATT, even with all its deficiencies, has to be put on the positive side of a balance sheet of the successful adaptation of the Bretton Woods principles to the real world. Parts of the system continue to work, often quite well, especially compared with what would happen if they did not exist. There are also paradoxical interrelations such as the question of whether the cotton textile agreement made possible the success of the Kennedy Round. (And what did the later textile agreements make possible?) I was reminded of a passage in Thomas Love Peacock's *Misfortunes of Elphin*. Seitheijin rejects the criticism that there are weak spots in his seawall, saying:

> That is the beauty of it. Some parts of it are rotten and some parts of it are sound. . . . The parts that are rotten give elasticity to those that are sound. . . . If it were all sound it would break by its own obstinate stiffness: the soundness is checked by the rottenness, and the stiffness is balanced by the elasticity.

If the question were just one of the adaptation of GATT to the real world, such reasoning would stand up well. But survival is not the whole story; neither are failures to enforce the rules the only deficiencies. It is not hard to think of agreements on textiles, steel, and automobiles that would come closer to applying the Bretton Woods principles than the measures that have led to the hollowing out of GATT. Most of the deficiencies that have developed in GATT were foreseen, but next to no preventive steps were taken or defensive measures worked out in advance. Dependence on rounds instead of some kind of process permitting a wider range of continuous negotiation has slowed GATT's dealing effectively with a number of issues. Governments have been slow to enlarge the scope of GATT to keep up with changes in the world economy.

The liberalization of trade that has been accomplished through GATT processes has increased competition in the world economy. Technological change, the speed of communication, and economic development have led to major structural changes and adjustment. Thanks at least in part to what has been accomplished by GATT and other measures of international economic cooperation, the world is not threatened with anything like the conditions of the 1930s. Nevertheless, one can hardly argue that the Bretton Woods principles are at all fully carried out by the trading system we have. For at least twenty years that system has deteriorated and GATT has been eroded.[23] Governments are less interested in trade liberalization than they once were and are less willing to adjust policies to reach agreement with others. Inevitably the question has arisen, "Has the time come to revive the ITO?"

And Back?

No one would think of simply going back to the old document. The idea would be to return to the basic principle of the ITO by bringing together under one organization agreements for the liberalization of the principal segments of international trade and the handling of disputes about them. One could equally well think of it as strengthening GATT, broadening its scope, and offsetting its deficiencies.[24]

When the ITO has been mentioned in recent years—more than at any time for decades—it has usually been with the idea that it would have provided a stronger core than GATT, with a larger and more authoritative secretariat, and better means of settling disputes, enforcing rules, and avoiding being blocked by one or a few countries. Perhaps so, but one should not be too sure. The charter certainly gave the ITO more strength and power than was ever acquired by GATT. But it was the member governments, and largely the United States, that prevented GATT from becoming a true international organization like the International Monetary Fund and the World Bank with which it was supposed to line up. So one must assume quite different behavior on the part of the governments in the hypothetical ITO, which was also an intergovernmental body. In any case, the move from paper to practice is not always linear, as is shown by GATT's evasion of majority rule and other experiences of international organizations. What is needed is not so much a comparison of texts as the experience of the charter plus forty-five years to know how strong a present-day ITO would be.

That is not to deny that even without much greater power—or the willingness of countries to accept majority rule—a stronger secretariat could have had an influence on the handling of many issues. Simply an increase in the amount of international surveillance of national (and private) practices could have helped. A stronger staff could have helped work out difficult issues, such as the liberalization-discrimination tradeoffs, or the broaching of new issues. There are other possibilities, but it is also true that an ITO might have developed some of the same deficiencies that weakened GATT. One does not get very far trying to imagine how a strong ITO might have altered the international economy.[25] It is more useful to think a bit about the present status of subjects included in the charter but omitted from GATT and then to look at new subjects that might be included in a modern-day ITO.

International commodity agreements may no longer seem important enough to need a special chapter, as in the charter. But that might be changed when international efforts concerning conservation, "sustainable growth," and some environmental issues touch the production of raw materials or if efforts to deal realistically with international trade in agricultural products lead to understandings about national farm policies.

Although private business practices proved less troublesome than the authors of the charter expected, they will certainly deserve attention in the future. It would be easier now than in the 1940s to find areas of agreement in the antitrust policies of most industrial countries, but a "cartel chapter" would have to go well beyond that. It would have to make sense in a world where direct investment, joint ventures, international production, increased size of units, high-cost R&D, global banking, and other factors have expanded the international interconnections of business. Discussions of "competition policy" have become something of the order of the day in a number of countries. An international agreement on discriminatory pricing would help reduce the widespread abuse of antidumping laws. Other issues would range from the informal coordination of the settlements the United States and the European Community make with a company like Microsoft through cartel-like market-sharing agreements to specters of global oligopoly by private enterprises so strong and nimble that they escape any serious attempt at regulation. Patents, once a major weapon of private trade policy, are intellectual property, but it remains to be seen how effectively GATT will be able to rule this new province.

Investment, the Achilles heel of the charter, is a bigger subject than ever and more important to international trade than it was. After the charter failed, there were repeated efforts, usually by investors, to obtain multilateral agreements about investment, but the results were not very impressive. Meanwhile, investments in all forms have grown enormously, and investors and governments have found ways of protecting their interests (or justifying their risks) in one way or another. The field is quite different from what it was when the charter was being written. It is no longer the United States on one side and the rest of the world on the other; most countries appear on both sides of the ledger. Connections with trade are extensive and complex, as to both the purposes of investment and its results. Transactions among affiliated enterprises make up a substantial portion of international trade; they often have a relation to trade policy measures that is different from old-fashioned arm's-length transactions. There are many links between investment issues and the questions about business practices touched on above. More than one businessman would probably prefer to conduct his own investment diplomacy than have to tangle with international rules and government policies which may be influenced by other issues. Whether multilateral agreements about investment are desirable or feasible, and what kinds, are matters that go beyond this paper. So is speculation as to whether the Uruguay Round's provisions concerning trade-related investment practices will turn out to be the nose of the camel in the WTO.

The potential conflict between trade rules and national measures to maintain employment or stability or pursue growth or some other objective remains as existential a matter as it was thought to be in the 1940s. And the difficulty of writing a meaningful provision in a multilateral agreement that would be both effective and widely acceptable is just as great. Efforts to coordinate macroeconomic policies—via summits or, after some early promise, the OECD or otherwise—have not been very encouraging. No one is likely to propose that ECOSOC (the United Nations Economic and Social Council) take on the functions it was thought of as having when Bretton Woods was new. But the problem is inescapable and affects the whole range of international cooperative measures, not just trade, which has usually been left out of past efforts.

There are many other issues that could be considered for inclusion in an expanded GATT or new ITO. Many are old ideas that are being resuscitated to some degree such as the realization that security is more than a military matter; human rights; emigration; labor costs and the treatment of workers; international sanctions; and embargoes and other trade measures undertaken for foreign policy reasons.

Of the truly new issues, by far the most important is the environment. If there had been anything like the present concern at the time the charter was drafted, it would surely have had a chapter on the subject, as Raymond Mikesell has remarked.[26] Without that, environmental questions have taken center stage in trade discussions and will remain there for the foreseeable future. Apart from the question of what kinds of provisions should be made to deal with these issues, there is the question of where they should be. Should one write provisions imposing greater responsibility for environmental issues on GATT or a new ITO?[27] Or would it be better to follow the recommendation of Ford Runge in the best book I have seen on the subject and create something like a World Environmental Organization (WEO), which, with environmental issues as its primary concern, would "work alongside, but separately from, those institutions concerned with trade policy?"[28]

These questions can obviously be asked about the other topics as well. Separate agreements on, say, investment or cartels may make better sense than chapters in a new charter or adding provisions to GATT. What then becomes of the idea that the charter's strength lay in the understanding that, to liberalize trade in the modern world, one needs to deal with more than traditional trade barriers? The effort to do this in a single agreement appeared to be the great virtue of the ITO, but it also proved to be its undoing because comprehensiveness and novelty required many compromises and the inescapable tradeoff between gaining support and creating opposition worked out badly. The same logic and the same risk will apply to any effort to make a new GATT or charter capable of dealing with the problems of international trade fifty years later. Is that the "lesson of last time" for the present day? Or was the demise of the ITO just an accident, or simply the result of a pair of errors by American business and the U.S. government, and not the built-in consequence of comprehensiveness and complexity? Did the problem lie in multilateralism? Would the most realistic approach be to leave progress in each field to whatever handful of countries were able to agree on new measures—which might often be different for different issues—and hope to bring in more countries later on? Might bilateral agreements that could deal concretely with circumstances and cases be better than looser, vaguer multilateral arrangements?[29]

Put this way, these issues seem to have less to do with the fundamental rationale of the most ambitious international trade agreement ever seriously proposed by a major government and look more like questions of tactics, circumstances, and political acceptability. There is certainly no harm in reminding ourselves of the impossibility of escaping from calculations of feasibility and probability. It makes no sense to suppose that they are somehow inferior to prescriptions that are intellectually more elegant. There is something to be said for the credo of all negotiators that what they bring home from a long series of conferences is "the best agreement that could be negotiated."

But there is also no escaping the fact that, as Miriam Camps once wrote, "not only are economies interdependent but . . . issues, too, are interdependent."[30] Whether issues are dealt with together or separately, agreements—and disagreements—will affect one another. And no matter what, the form of the basic problems touched on earlier will persist: judging the pros and cons of liberalizing arrangements among small groups; the many forms of discrimination; hollowing out; and the increased unwillingness of governments to accept international commitments. There is yet another set of difficulties, probably the most important of all.

The Bretton Woods system aimed to set principles and rules for a limited range of relations among interdependent countries, which, so long as they honored those commitments, could pretty well run their economies as they pleased—and had the ability to do so. Fifty years later these inarticulate major premises of that system no longer apply. Interdependence has increased to the point that the management of each national economy depends heavily on what is done in the rest of the world. Familiar facts come into play: the speed of change makes adjustment harder; businesses move into many countries and are swayed by many sovereigns—or none; ownership and control become intricate and perhaps uncertain; the ease with which capital moves and the dependence of production on both exports and imports reduce the ability of governments to control what they still think of as their own affairs. One needs to regard the world economy as interpenetrated as well as interdependent. But thinking about policy has not kept up with the blurring of lines between national economies and the changing and diverse interests of groups within each country—conflicts that are always at the core of foreign economic policy. Governments, responsible to national electorates, try to pursue what they define as national interests in the old-fashioned ways. As these contradictory forces play against one another, trouble ensues that undermines past methods of cooperation without providing new ones.

The question arises whether adaptation of the Bretton Woods approach is sufficient or whether replacements can be found and adopted before a new turbulence and chaos comparable to, but different from, that of the 1920s and 1930s brings about a new willingness to accept an unprecedented degree of international cooperation through unprecedented forms.

Notes

1. My debts to people who over many years have written about these matters or discussed them with me cannot be acknowledged here in any realistic way; a bibliography

would probably be longer than the paper. Worse, I have skimped on footnotes to save space. I apologize to all, but I am grateful.

2. Quoted in Percy W. Bidwell and William Diebold Jr., "The United States and the International Trade Organization," *International Conciliation* (March 1949): p. 219, fn. 20.

3. "A Cartel Policy for the United States," a report published as chapter 12 in G. W. Stocking and M. W. Watkins, eds., *Cartels or Competition?* (New York: Twentieth Century Fund, 1948), p. 442.

4. Clair Wilcox, *A Charter for World Trade* (New York: Macmillan, 1949), p. 115.

5. Ibid., p. 125.

6. League of Nations, *Commercial Policy in the Post-War World: Report of the Economic and Financial Committees* (Geneva: League of Nations, 1945), p. 64. In spite of the Geneva imprint the report was produced in Princeton and was one of a series of analyses that provide some of the best statements of the received liberal opinions of the time about the interwar experience and its implications for postwar policy.

7. Clair Wilcox, *A Charter for World Trade*, p. 131. The discussion of these issues, and the drafting of the article, were muddied by a rather useless and quite ideological dispute in the United States about the term "full employment" in connection with the passage of the Employment Act of 1946.

8. All these points, including the business criticisms, the way the passage of time changed matters, and alternative possibilities are discussed more fully in William Diebold Jr., "The End of the ITO," *Essays in International Finance*, no. 16, October 1952 (Princeton: Princeton University International Finance Section, 1952). Further comments and some reconsiderations appear in a talk I gave, "Reflections on the International Trade Organization," *Northern Illinois University Law Review* 14, no. 2 (spring 1994). Susan Aaronson has thrown light on a number of these issues by a study of public and private archives and, while supporting much of my interpretation, emphasizes some other points as well. Her analysis is summarized in "Policymakers, the Public, and the Abandonment of the ITO," *Diplomatic History*, forthcoming.

9. Percy Bidwell and William Diebold Jr., "The United States and the International Trade Organization," p. 237.

10. Clair Wilcox, *A Charter for World Trade*, p. 199.

11. The matter was a good deal more complicated than this sounds, as is explained at length in William Adams Brown Jr., *The United States and the Restoration of World Trade* (Washington, D.C.: The Brookings Institution, 1950).

12. They are not, strictly speaking, members but will be so called here, at least part of the time. At other times they are called "signatories" or "contracting parties" or something of the sort.

13. Raymond Vernon, "America's Foreign Trade Policy and the GATT," *Essays in International Finance*, no. 21, October 1954 (Princeton: Princeton University International Finance Section, 1954), p. 12.

14. Ernest Preeg, *Traders and Diplomats* (Washington, D.C.: The Brookings Institution, 1970); Gilbert R. Winham, *International Trade and the Tokyo Round Negotiations* (Princeton: Princeton University Press, 1986).

15. Gardner Patterson and Eliza Patterson, "The Road from GATT to MTO," *Minnesota Journal of Global Trade* 3, no. 1 (spring 1994): p. 37.

16. Raymond F. Mikesell, "Antecedents of the ITO Charter and Their Relevance for the Uruguay Round," *Northern Illinois University Law Review* 14, no. 2 (spring 1994): pp. 328–329.

17. Andreas F. Lowenfeld, "Remedies along with Rights: Institutional Reform in the New GATT," *The American Journal of International Law* 88, no. 3 (July 1994): p. 479.

18. The term is a misnomer, as it is usually taken to include fair trade rules concerning

dumping and subsidies and other measures; some raise tariffs, some influence competition by means other than trade barriers. "Trade-distorting practices"—which I think was invented by Robert Baldwin—is somewhat better but I will stick to the shorter and more familiar form.

19. U.S. Congress, Joint Economic Committee, Subcommittee on Trade, Productivity, and Economic Growth hearing, *How to Save the International Trading System*, 98th Cong., 2nd Sess.; June 12, 1984, p. 15.

20. The chief negotiator of Hungary's entry into GATT once told me that he had no trouble in accepting this guidance for his country but worried sometimes about the companies of capitalist countries that were rich enough to let political considerations overrule commercial considerations.

21. Contrary to much folklore, the authors of the ITO charter and the GATT did not think the system applied only to capitalism though it was obvious that rules dealing with traditional trading arrangements could be clearer and more precise than more experimental efforts to bridge systems. The thought—or hope—that a liberal and competitive trading system might encourage the spread of market capitalism is another matter.

22. William Diebold Jr., *The United States and the Industrial World* (New York: Praeger for the Council on Foreign Relations, 1972), p. 347. I hedged a bit by invoking "many experienced people" but I meant to include me. This whole section of the book lists complaints about GATT and suggests improvements.

23. This argument was developed more fully a decade ago in Miriam Camps and William Diebold Jr., *The New Multilateralism: Can the World Trading System be Saved?* (New York: Council on Foreign Relations, 1983; reprint 1986). The same work discusses the question of cooperation on difficult issues that do not lend themselves simply to the enforcement of GATT rules.

24. One of the most fully developed ideas is Miriam Camps's proposal for a Production and Trade Organization which she calls "a modern version of the ITO" in chapter 5 of Miriam Camps with the collaboration of Catherine Gwin, *Collective Management: The Reform of Global Economic Organizations* (New York: McGraw Hill for the Council on Foreign Relations, 1981), p. 190. The chapter was separately published earlier as *The Case for a New Global Trade Organization* (New York: Council on Foreign Relations, 1980). Its introduction gives some account of the earlier discussion of the idea. Other proposals include: John Leddy et al., *GATT Plus: A Proposal for Trade Reform* (New York: Praeger for the Atlantic Council of the United States, 1976); American Society of International Law, *Re-Making the System of World Trade: A Proposal for Institutional Reform*, Studies in Transnational Legal Policy, no. 12 (Washington, D.C.: American Society of International Law, 1976); F. Leutwiler et al., *Trade Policies for a Better Future: Proposal for Action* (Geneva: GATT, 1985). There are also proposals in several publications by John Jackson and some suggestions in Miriam Camps and William Diebold Jr., *The New Multilateralism*.

25. I speculated a bit on these matters in "Reflections on the International Trade Organization," *Northern Illinois University Law Review*.

26. Raymond F. Mikesell, "Antecedents of the ITO Charter."

27. Steve Charnovitz argues that parts of the existing GATT can be read in environmental terms. See "Exploring the Environmental Exceptions in GATT Article XX," *Journal of World Trade* (October 1991): pp. 37–55; and "GATT and the Environment: Examining the Issues," *International Environmental Affairs* (summer 1992): pp. 203–233. These views are challenged by John Jackson, "World Trade Rules and Environmental Policies: Congruence or Conflict?" *Washington and Lee Law Review* (fall 1992): pp. 1227–1278.

28. C. Ford Runge, *Freer Trade, Protected Environment* (New York: Council on Foreign Relations Press, 1994), p. 100.

29. The Hull trade agreements program showed that bilateral agreements could be used in ways that expanded equal treatment and multilateral trade. But at least one government has to want to do that and have enough bargaining power to get its way. An alternative approach—the idea of open-ended agreements that can be joined by others when they are ready to accept the terms—is far more complex and uncertain than it sounds. See Miriam Camps and William Diebold Jr., *The New Multilateralism*, p. 65 of the 1986 edition.

30. Miriam Camps, *Collective Management*, p. 190. In this and other works Mrs. Camps over a number of years has analyzed many basic issues of international cooperation and its organization and management that could not be pursued in this paper or, often, even noted, but her work has had an important influence on my thinking about these matters. In addition to the publications cited, see especially *The Management of Interdependence: A Preliminary View* (New York: Council on Foreign Relations, 1974).

13

An Impressionistic Tour of International Investment Codes, 1948–1994

Walter A. Chudson

The issue of international trade policy, while not on the table at Bretton Woods, was distinctly in the background. The urgency of averting a renewal of the ruinous trade and currency wars of the 1930s must have been high in the thinking of the Bretton Woods negotiators and was reflected in the memoranda of planners in Washington and London. Vows of "never again" and exhortations to avoid the perils of "beggar-thy-neighbor" action were strong.

There was no corresponding call, however, to avoid or moderate what later came to be dubbed "investment wars." In the preparations for the International Trade Organization (ITO) conference, initially a separate chapter on private foreign investment was not included. Over many years, even decades, the balance between protecting the rights and "freedoms" of private investors and the interests of host countries or colonies was the subject of study and ideological and political conflict. Some international action, particularly in the form of bilateral treaties avowing mutual interests, was concluded, but the notion of avoiding mutually destructive action received only passing notice. In this sense, the inclusion of principles concerning the rights and obligations of foreign investors (implicitly in the form of foreign direct investment [FDI] or multinational enterprises [MNEs]) in the Havana Charter for an International Trade Organization can be said to be a watershed in the development of this aspect of economic relations.

It is as well to indicate that this paper is mainly concerned with the developing host countries and their reactions to the growing process of international production organized by MNEs. After several decades of friction, stalemate, and reversals of policy toward FDI, a significant degree of convergence is occurring in these policies. This is expressed in unilateral actions, regional action, of which NAFTA is the outstanding example, and an increasing number of calls, largely from private scholarly sources, to revive the idea of a "GATT for investment," now in the form of an agreement under the WTO or as a separate institution.

The phrase "foreign investment wars," with its context of a no-man's land between overlapping jurisdictions of home and host governments, has a scholarly appeal as a constitutional model; but in the early postwar period this issue (for example, as a problem in international taxation) was less prominent than preoccupation by MNEs and their home governments with host country policies concerning expropriation, symbolized by the assertion of the so-called Calvo doctrine, and a range of restrictive policies by many host countries regulating entry and operation of foreign firms, covered by the word "screening." With varying scope and procedural features for dispute settlement (referring largely but not exclusively to relations between MNEs and a host government), the NAFTA foreign investment provisions, increasingly cited as a model, provide: (1) nondiscriminatory right of establishment (in principle an antiscreening device, with some sectoral exclusions), (2) national treatment; and (3) a dispute settlement mechanism to which firms have independent access. For good measure, the NAFTA agreement contains provisions regarding expropriation and compensation that in effect abandon the right of the host country to assert the Calvo doctrine of host country sovereign jurisdiction.[1]

The GATT–WTO includes related provisions on service firms; intellectual property protection; and control of so-called trade-related investment measures (TRIM), which in effect are a form of screening.

In judging the recent shifting balance of developing countries' willingness to accept obligations of the NAFTA type, it is interesting to recall the text of Article 12 of the Havana charter. It does contain recognition of the positive contribution of foreign direct investment, though with more weight on capital flow than on technology, export links, and other aspects of industrial structure. Concern with rent-sharing and attitudes toward project selection was the assertion of the right of screening, unbundling the components of the direct investment package and an element of retroactivity concerning the status of "existing and future" investments. There was no yielding by the host countries on the issue of compensation in the event of expropriation.

It is now a well-known irony that the initial draft of the Havana charter prepared by the staff of the U.S. State Department did not contain any provisions on private international investment as such. As a condition of support for the charter on trade and other matters, several organized business lobbies pressed for the inclusion of provisions on investment. I have not seen the text of what they proposed, if any exists, but it can be assumed that the issue of compensation for expropriation was high on, if not at the top of, the agenda. The record indicates that the career State Department officials foresaw trouble in negotiating this with the developing countries. William Diebold attributes the withdrawal of the ITO agreement in 1950, and thus the demise of the ITO, largely to the unbending opposition of these groups based on the investment provisions.[2] He points out, however, that there were other features of the many chapters of the charter, for example, on international commodity agreements and full employment commitments, that were also opposed, and that the investment provisions were perhaps the straw that broke the camel's back. In any case, by the standards of the NAFTA provisions or even by the nondiscriminatory provisions of bilateral investment treaties at the time, it is clear that, despite the appearance of adjectives like "reasonable" and "appropriate," no industrial country today would approve the agreement. What is more interesting, fewer host countries are prepared to insist on the screening and similar rights that were in the Havana charter.

Following the demise of the ITO charter and its foreign investment provisions, there ensued a long period of wandering in the wilderness for international investment codes. The exceptions are of limited significance as far as developing countries are concerned. I refer to the OECD principles of 1976 and the arbitration forums of the World Bank and the United Nations.

The lack of interest on the part of the developing countries reflected deep-seated ideological views, but probably more important views on development policy and their development outlook suggested little if any development advantage in nondiscrimination and deregulation. Reinforcing this lack of conviction for a reward for "good behavior" was the predominance in many cases of large-scale, inherently monopolistic investments in mining, natural resources generally, and public utilities. The uncertainty about the profitability of many such projects, coupled with host governments' actual or perceived lack of information on the prospects, generated tension. Some effort was made to reduce friction by devices such as production-sharing and special agreements on taxation of profits. Nevertheless the element of uncertainty is evidenced by a substantial professional literature examining the conflict of interest that might arise between the host country and foreign mining enterprise.[3]

The United Nations Centre on Transnational Corporations, established in 1973, responded to this situation by fostering a technical advisory service to assist host countries in conducting negotiations with foreign firms. Part of this activity was aimed at providing information on alternative forms of foreign participation, notably joint ventures and contracts for the transfer of technology, a program of "workshops" with simulated exercises in the calculation of discounted cash flow, joint venture contracts, and taxation, including even an examination of intrafirm transfer pricing. It seems fair to say that such activities were benign in the sense of accepting or even promoting the contribution of direct investments to development, but they were viewed with some suspicion by some representatives of the business community.

Renegotiation of large-scale projects, particularly in mining, was recognized in the coining of the phrase "obsolescing bargain," implying a shift in the balance in bargaining power, reflecting particularly the sunk capital in large-scale mining projects.

Another factor causing concern about the division of rents arose from profitable foreign investments in manufacturing for the domestic market fostered during the period of import-substituting industrialization from the 1950s onward, particularly in Latin America. While hardly a major factor in the aggregate economy, such projects, stimulated by the existence of a sheltered market in which high costs were matched by high profits, tended to foster government pressure for joint ventures or so-called unbundling to obtain technology and managerial services with little or no foreign equity. Widespread restrictions on remittances of profits and possibly capital for balance-of-payments reasons created pressure on firms to bypass the controls. This tended to stimulate the manipulation of transfer pricing by overinvoicing imports and understating exports.

A short-lived move toward strengthening the bargaining power of host countries was the Andean Pact, Article 24, involving Chile and several other countries. This effort to establish a united front for acquisition of technology, among other things, is a bit reminiscent of recent ideas in the United States of organizing buyers' coalitions to negotiate with health care providers.

In the late 1970s the United Nations Centre on Transnational Corporations began what turned out to be a protracted negotiation or, rather, exercise to formulate a code of conduct. This moved toward a closer balance of rights and obligations, but fell short of the nondiscriminatory rules and dispute settlement mechanisms insisted on by the industrial countries. It is an indication of the trend of the times that as the UN efforts at codification were winding down, the research and reporting activities of the Centre on Transnational Corporations were intensified and expanded. The positive tone of this published material presumably reflected the growth of market-oriented policies in the developing countries, the end of centralized economies dismantled with the end of the cold war, and the growth of export-oriented industrialization in many developing countries.

From the early 1980s, the attitude of many developing countries toward direct investment has obviously been changed by a shift toward export-oriented industrialization. This was mutually reinforced by expanding patterns of international production by MNEs and by the growth of world trade. With this emerging acceptance of direct foreign investment as a key to a "win-win" game, issues of host country screening, compulsory joint ventures, and "unbundling" faded. Problems of exchange control also diminished. A new issue emerged, namely, competing investment incentives offered by host countries in a zero-sum game.

The East Asian "tigers" (Hong Kong, South Korea, Singapore, and Taiwan) moved early in this direction, followed by a second generation of East Asian "cubs" (Indonesia, Malaysia, and Thailand). In addition to direct investment, injections of foreign inputs included technology licensing, capital goods imports, and training programs. Following on closely has been industrial development in Mexico with a major change in regulation of direct investment and codification of the foreign investment regime in the NAFTA treaty.

More or less coinciding with these developments in "real-ekonomik" have been proposals for a new version of "GATT for investment." This was already reflected in the inclusion in the revised GATT agreement of provisions for regulating trade-related investment measures (TRIMs) and international services and intellectual property.

The variations among the proposals for doing so are relatively minor. For example, Graham[4] includes "transparency" of government regulations as a specific provision. Julius[5] specifies "free choice of means" (direct investment, licensing, or other forms of direct investing; e.g., "strategic licensing") as part of national industrial policy. Frank[6] specifies freedom of remittances, hardly a major issue in countries now receptive for direct investment. None of the proposals imposes specific obligations on MNEs. Access to international arbitration for firms as well as governments is contained in all these proposals, with slight differences in procedure.

While not identifying competition policy as an investment issue, Graham and Frank both identify restrictive business practices as a relevant issue to the regime for international investment. It is perhaps significant that neither goes beyond this. Frank proposes that "agreed principles should be negotiated internationally . . . for more convergent national competition laws and enforcement mechanisms."

The subject of transfer pricing is mentioned by several writers as a matter for special treatment in an "ancillary" agreement, rather than in a code of broad principles. It is this thorny problem that comes closest to imposing an obligation on individual firms, although in the last analysis it is an issue between governments.

In recent years there has been action by tax authorities, particularly in the United States, to reduce uncertainties arising from transfer-pricing practices by administrative action, involving consent by advance consultation with the tax authorities. This does not necessarily provide the answer to the quest for an equivalent of an arm's-length price. Nor does it solve the growing problem of allocating headquarters' overhead expense, technology transfer payments, and centralized research-and-development costs. The alternative approach of international apportionment of worldwide income based on a set of criteria is far from acceptable on practical and political grounds. Nevertheless, tax authorities, notably in the United States, do consider estimates of global income in judging the acceptability of income statement based on transfer prices.

In the 1992 presidential campaign, alleged transfer pricing abuse surfaced as an issue when the campaign platform of the Democrats proposed in effect an alternate minimum tax on United States subsidiaries, particularly of Japanese firms, which had recorded little or no net income in several recent years. This was advanced as offering substantial revenue for the federal budget. The idea originated earlier in discussions and draft legislation in the House Ways and Means Committee. In the end, the idea quietly disappeared from the proposed budget of the new administration, but not before some diplomatic representations were made by a few European governments on the grounds of arbitrary unilateral action on an international tax matter.

Apart from more "sophisticated" advance consultation, including consultation between governmental tax authorities, the frequent mention of the transfer-pricing problem by proponents of investment codes does not suggest any major progress on this front. The subject continues to spawn a substantial amount of business for accountants and lawyers. Perhaps a reflection of this is the suggestion by Peter Kenen to turn over the taxation of corporate (multinational) income to an international institution, the proceeds to be used for developmental, environmental, and other international projects.[7]

The extent of transfer-price manipulation is among the unknowns of multinational business. It is possible that the effective tax rates on corporate income in major industrial countries have reduced the incentive to repatriate profits for tax reasons. Also, the shrinking of exchange controls on remittances by developing host countries presumably reduces the incentive to overinvoice imports by local subsidiaries.

Frank states that "the time has clearly arrived for a new global accord on foreign investment." The convergence of developing host country policies toward market openness and deliberate attraction for direct investment provides political support for this view. This obviously refers less to the concern about conflicts between one home government and another than between the issue of discrimination and control by host governments, particularly developing countries. Since they are opening their doors unilaterally, some may question the need for an external political push to reinforce their pragmatic pull. Competition for direct investment by host countries, using various taxes and their incentives, is obviously one concern of those who aim at more efficient international allocation of production by leveling the playing field at least with regard to overt incentives. Industrial policy is a complex affair; one cannot expect a formal nondiscriminatory code to prevent various forms of incentive for locating international production.

Notes

1. Convergence in proposals along these lines can be seen in the following: C. Fred Bergsten and Edward M. Graham, "Needed: New International Rules for Foreign Direct Investment," *International Trade Journal* 7, no. 1 (1992): pp. 15–44; John M. Kline, "International Regulation of Transnational Business: Providing the Missing Leg of Global Investment Standards," *Transnational Corporations* 2, no. 1 (February 1993); De Anne Julius, "International Direct Investment: Strengthening the Policy Regime," in Peter B.

Kenen, ed., *Managing the World Economy* (Washington, D.C.: Institute for International Economics, 1994), chapter 6; Edward M. Graham, "Towards an Asia Pacific Investment Code," *Transnational Corporations* 3, no. 2 (summer 1994); and Isaiah Frank, "Post–Uruguay Round Trade Policy for a Global Economy," this volume.

2. William Diebold Jr., "The End of the ITO," no. 16, October 1952 (Princeton: Princeton University International Finance Section, 1952).

3. See, for example, Raymond Mikesell, *Foreign Investment in the Petroleum and Mineral Industries* (Baltimore: Johns Hopkins University Press, 1971), chapter 2.

4. Edward M. Graham, "Towards an Asia Pacific Investment Code."

5. De Anne Julius, "International Direct Investment."

6. Isaiah Frank, "Post–Uruguay Round Trade Policy."

7. Peter B. Kenen, ed., *Managing the World Economy*, p. 402.

14

The Bretton Woods–GATT System after Fifty Years: A Balance Sheet of Success and Failure

Richard N. Gardner

> *In Washington Lord Halifax*
> *Once whispered to Lord Keynes:*
> *It's true they have the money bags*
> *But we have all the brains.*

Introduction

This mischievous little verse, written on a yellowing piece of paper left over from the first Anglo-American discussions on the postwar monetary system, stirs memories of one of the great adventures of economic diplomacy in our time. It recalls an effort of creative statesmanship that has seldom been equaled—an effort to construct an international economic order capable of serving the two overriding goals of world peace and the general welfare of nations.

A great gulf of years now separates us from this scrap of paper and from the American and British negotiators, half of whom, at least, it presumably delighted. As these lines are written, it is half a century since the charters of the International Monetary Fund (IMF) and the International Bank for Reconstruction and Development (IBRD) were completed at Bretton Woods, New Hampshire. Nearly the same time has passed since the first discussions leading to the General Agreement on Tariffs and Trade (GATT).

In this half-century, the international setting has radically changed. The United States and Great Britain—the two main protagonists in this history—no longer hold a virtual monopoly on international economic policy making. Continental European countries that at the time of Bretton Woods were occupied, enemy, or neutral countries—France, Germany, Italy, and Spain—have emerged as major participants in economic diplomacy, either through the developing European Union or in their own right.

Japan has become an economic powerhouse and an essential participant in trade, monetary, and aid negotiations. The nations of Asia, the most dynamic part of the world economy, are now major economic actors, including a China whose trade and income are growing at unprecedented rates. Latin America, after years of uneven and inward-looking development, is now embarked on rapid growth and hemispheric integration. And with the end of the cold war, Russia and the countries of its former empire are rejoining a world economic system from which they deliberately excluded themselves at the end of the Second World War. Today the "moneybags," the "brains," the economic weight, and the political influence are all better distributed than they were a half-century ago.

Yet the old and difficult issues that confronted the "founding fathers" of the Bretton Woods–GATT system are still with us—how to reconcile the freedom of international trade and payments with high levels of domestic employment and growth, how to balance the need for effective international economic institutions with still-powerful demands for national economic sovereignty, and how to relate regional and bilateral economic arrangements to a global economic order.[1]

A "Political Miracle"

The work of the postwar planners in designing the Bretton Woods institutions and GATT may fairly be described as a "political miracle," because these institutions had to be created against powerful political and intellectual currents on both sides of the Atlantic. Today, when political realities impose severe constraints on new efforts of constructive internationalism, it is worth recalling for a moment how great the obstacles were for the "founding fathers" fifty years ago.

On the British side, there was profound skepticism throughout the establishment that a system based on open multilateral trade would be in Britain's interests. The Federation of British Industries and the London Chamber of Commerce were hostile. Many felt that the tide of the future was barter trade, managed markets, discriminatory arrangements, currency controls. Many believed that the United States was destined to go into a deep depression after the war, dragging Britain into the abyss and destroying Britain's postwar commitments to the welfare state and full employment. To these people it seemed folly to lie down with the United States in an international system based on liberal economic principles. There were also doubts whether Britain's postwar balance of payments would be strong enough to permit it to operate successfully without exchange and trade controls. And, of course, there were those on the right who wanted to make imperial preference and the sterling area the basis for a postwar order.

Those two pillars of establishment opinion in Britain, the *Economist* and the *Times*, looked at the postwar planning with deep misgiving. As the *Times* put it:

> We must . . . reconcile ourselves once and for all to the view that the days of laissez-faire and the unlimited division of labor are over; that every country—including Great Britain—plans and organizes its production in the light of social and military needs, and that the regulation of this production by such "trade barriers" as tariffs, quotas, and subsidies is a necessary and integral part of this policy.[2]

One member of Parliament warned that acceptance of the American postwar monetary proposals "will be the end. The end of all our hopes of an expansionist policy, and of social advance. It will be the end of the Beveridge Plan, of improved education, of housing reconstruction, the end of the new Britain we are fighting to rebuild. It will lead again to world depression, to chaos, and, ultimately, to war."

The U.S. ambassador to Britain, John Winant, cabled Washington in 1944 that "a majority of the directors of the Bank of England are opposed to the Bretton Woods program. . . . It is argued by those in opposition that if the plan is adopted financial control will leave London and sterling exchange will be replaced by dollar exchange."

A leading financial journalist said that, in the view of many members of Parliament he had talked to, "it would be preferable to have two international systems, a dollar bloc and a sterling bloc. It is argued that conditions, interests, and mentality within the two groups differ fundamentally, and that for this reason any attempt to lump them together is foredoomed to failure."

One of the things that inflamed British opinion was the American emphasis on nondiscrimination, the insistence that imperial preferences would have to be eliminated. Lord Croft described this demand as "the Boston Tea Party in reverse," and an "interference with the freedom of our own country to manage its affairs that I regard as unparalleled in the history of the world." On the other end of the political spectrum, Lord Lindsay of Birker was no less incensed: "When I heard Americans making snooty remarks about that poor little preference of ours, I thought it was the limit, and I still think so." One MP rose in the House of Commons and solemnly declared: "If the Government tries to eliminate Empire Preference a number of us will conduct such a nationwide campaign in this country as will light the very beacons on the hills. We will attack them in the marketplace, in the towns and the cities, we will rouse this whole country against them in such a crusade as will overcome this Government, because we will not have it."

The postwar economic plans had no smoother reception on the American side. The *Wall Street Journal* called the Keynes plan "a machine for the regimentation of the world." The *New York Times* considered the Bretton Woods proposals unnecessary—it favored going back to the gold standard, "the most satisfactory international standard that has ever been devised." The American Bankers Association said, "a system of quotas or shares in a pool which gives debtor countries the impression that they have a right to credits up to some amount is unsound in principle, and raises hopes that cannot be realized." The Guaranty Trust Company, progenitor of Morgan Guaranty, called both the British and American plans for Bretton Woods "dangerous" on the grounds that they would "enable nations to buy merchandise without being able to pay for it." Senator Robert Taft, leader of the right wing of the Republican party, denounced the Bretton Woods agreements, charging that the United States was "putting all the valuable money into the Fund," and would be "pouring money down a rat hole." A senator from Utah rose in indignation on the floor of the Senate, brandished a fistful of foreign currencies, and defied any one of his colleagues to "go downtown in Washington and get his shoes shined with this whole bunch of bills." And, again, the American Bankers Association objected to the founding of the International Monetary Fund because "we should be handing over to an international body the power to determine the destination, time, and use of our money"—abandoning, without receiving anything in return, a vital part of American bargaining power.

The postwar trade arrangements were also bitterly opposed by many in the United States. In their final form, free traders found them too protectionist and protectionists found them too liberal. When the International Trade Organization (ITO) was completed in 1948, the U.S. Congress wanted no part of it. The National Foreign Trade Council, the National Association of Manufacturers, and the U.S. Chamber of Commerce were strongly against it. Even the General Agreement on Tariffs and Trade, which survived the demise of the ITO as a multilateral trade agreement, lived for years in a kind of political limbo. Congress was so skeptical of being restrained in the use of its tariff and other foreign commerce powers that in successive renewals of the trade agreements program it inserted a clause stating that renewal of the legislation "shall constitute neither approval nor disapproval" of the GATT.

It is in the light of such attitudes in the two countries that the creation of the postwar institutions deserves to be called a "political miracle." The "miracle" was only possible because it was accomplished at the end of a war, when public opinion could be mobilized in the hopeful enterprise of building a better world, and because both countries were led by men of great vision, surrounded by dedicated internationalists of outstanding ability. The great leaders were Franklin D. Roosevelt and Winston Churchill, who saw the need to provide firm economic underpinnings for the postwar world even though, preoccupied with the problem of winning the war, they left the details to others. The job of constructing the postwar international organizations was overseen by Cabinet- and sub-Cabinet-level officials such as Secretary of State Cordell Hull, Secretary of the

Treasury Henry Morgenthau Jr., and Undersecretary of State Will Clayton on the American side, and Sir Kingsley Wood, Sir John Anderson, and Richard Law on the British side. But the critical choices in the complex and technical negotiations were made by career civil servants together with professional economists and lawyers on temporary leave from their universities and law firms. The key figures in the Bretton Woods negotiations, of course, were John Maynard Keynes of the United Kingdom and Harry Dexter White of the United States. Among the most important trade architects were British negotiators Sir Percivale Liesching, James Meade, and Lionel Robbins and American negotiators Myron Taylor, Dean Acheson, and Harry Hawkins.

These "founding fathers," a relatively small group of men, were united by a common commitment to practical and constructive internationalism. They conceived of a postwar economic system ruled by law. They wanted it to be a universal system, if possible, including the Soviet Union and Communist countries, but, failing that, at least a single multilateral system including everyone else, rather than a collection of trading blocs. They wanted permanent international institutions to promote cooperation on monetary, trade, and development problems. And they wanted somehow to reconcile the concept of maximum possible freedom in trade and payments at the international level with the domestic pursuit by governments of progressive economic and social policies.

How well did the founding fathers succeed in their bold vision? How should we judge their efforts today?

The Achievements of Cooperation

To begin with, I would argue that the most important achievement of the founding fathers was in creating durable structures for cooperative international problem solving. Their handiwork represented a victory over the economic nationalism and "beggar-thy-neighbor" policies of the interwar period.

Perhaps most important, the founding fathers averted the very real danger that after victory in the war the United States would revert to isolationism as it did after the First World War. They managed to establish a framework for U.S. cooperation in the solution of the international economic problems of the future. They thus laid the foundations for the Marshall Plan and a host of other cooperative enterprises that have supplemented and reinforced the postwar institutions right down to the present day.

We can also judge the work of the founding fathers by some hard economic facts. The half-century since Bretton Woods has been a period of prosperity and growth unprecedented in history. In very round numbers, world production has soared from $300 billion a year at the end of World War II to nearly $30,000 billion a year today. World trade has grown from $30 billion a year to well over $3,000 billion a year. Even allowing for inflation and population growth, these hundredfold increases represent an extraordinary increase in the welfare of the common man. The past five decades have seen more progress in improving living standards than any previous time in recorded history. Life expectancy has increased by 50 percent. Infant mortality has been halved. Average per-capita incomes worldwide have doubled. In the industrialized democracies and in some of the more successful Pacific Rim nations, per-capita income has grown considerably more than that—by three to ten times in some cases.

Western Europe survived the challenges of fascism and communism and enjoyed the benefits of political and economic freedom. Japan rose from the ashes of defeat to become a prosperous democracy. Asian countries such as Korea, Taiwan, Hong Kong, and Singapore achieved income levels approaching those of established developed countries like Australia and the United Kingdom. Latin America, led by Mexico, Chile, and Argentina, finally began to take off in economic growth after years of stagnation. Only Africa and a few diehard Communist countries such as Cuba and North Korea remain exceptions to this economic success story.

While it would be an oversimplification to give all the credit for this economic success to the international economic institutions established during and after World War II, it is clear that the postwar planners must have done *something* right. The institutions they created—the International Monetary Fund, the World Bank, the General Agreement on Tariffs and Trade—have demonstrated an extraordinary ability to adapt themselves to the changing needs of the world economy. This is particularly remarkable when one considers the handicaps under which each of them was founded.

To be sure, the balance sheet of international economic cooperation contains its full measure of debits as well as credits. For the United States and Western Europe, the rapid growth of income registered in the first quarter-century after Bretton Woods was not matched in the most recent quarter-century. For reasons we shall explore in a moment, the Bretton Woods system of fixed parities collapsed in the early 1970s, and since then the world has experienced both volatile exchange rates and currency misalignments. The interrelated energy and debt crises raised further questions about the adequacy of international economic arrangements, as have recent years of sluggish growth and rising unemployment. Successive GATT rounds of tariff reduction have been accompanied by the growth of nontariff barriers. And despite the multiplication of international aid institutions, more than a billion people in developing countries still live in abject poverty.

But if the recent record is less than satisfactory, the fault may lie more with the policies of governments than with the deficiencies of the international agencies. Moreover, it is hard to imagine how the world today could deal with its many challenges without the help of the institutions we have inherited from the early postwar years.

To form a balanced judgment on the Bretton Woods–GATT system, it is necessary to look in more detail at the record of the international institutions in accomplishing their objectives in the three areas for which they were originally established—monetary, trade, and development cooperation.

The International Monetary Challenge

As this historical account makes clear, the founding fathers saw the creation of a new international monetary system as an essential foundation for a just and stable postwar political and economic order. It was therefore no accident that the Bretton Woods Conference of 1944 was held even before the San Francisco Conference of 1945, which created the United Nations—as well as before the conferences of 1947–48 that created the GATT and the ill-fated International Trade Organization. Monetary questions had to be dealt with before trade questions, in the founding fathers' view, because countries would not be willing to commit themselves to tariff reductions if the conditions of competition could be completely altered by large and unforeseen changes in exchange rates.

In their early thinking about the postwar monetary order, the British and American governments had a supranational design. The postwar planners saw fluctuating and misaligned exchange rates, completely free capital movements, and completely autonomous national monetary and fiscal policies as incompatible with an open trading system and the achievement of high levels of employment and growth. They wanted collective intergovernmental management of the quantum of international liquidity, of international capital flows, and of exchange rates and national adjustment policies. The following statement by the Chancellor of the Exchequer eloquently summarized the original concept shared by both John Maynard Keynes and Harry White:

> We want an orderly and agreed method of determining the value of national currency units, to eliminate unilateral action and the danger which it involves that each nation will seek to restore its competitive position by exchange depreciation. Above all, we want to free the international monetary system from those arbitrary, unpredictable and undesirable influences which have operated in the past as a result of large-scale speculative movements of capital. We want to secure an economic policy agreed to between the nations and an international monetary system which will be the instrument of that policy. This means that if any one Government were tempted to move too far either in an inflationary or deflationary direction, it would be subject to the check of consultations with the other Governments, and it would be part of the agreed policy to take measures for correcting tendencies to disequilibirum in the balance of payments of each separate country.

The collective intergovernmental management of money envisaged in the early postwar planning proved impossible to realize. The ambitious Keynes plan for overdraft facilities in *bancor* in a Clearing Union was set aside in favor of White's more modest conception of a system based on gold and IMF drawing rights. But in the postwar world of rapidly growing trade and inflation, neither gold nor IMF quotas could provide sufficient international reserves. The world thus ended up on a dollar standard, in which the quantum of international reserves was determined mainly by the balance-of-payments deficits of the United States—which is certainly not what Keynes or White or the other postwar planners had in mind.

The creation of special drawing rights (SDRs) in the First Amendment of the Fund articles at the end of the 1960s was meant to signal a return to a truly international reserve system. Yet this has not worked out either. SDRs represent only a tiny fraction of world liquidity today, and although some developing countries continue to press for SDR issues as a form of development aid or as a means of improving the distribution of world liquidity, neither Britain nor the United States, nor any major developed country, now favors moving toward an international reserve system based on SDRs. The idea of a limited form of reserve consolidation, with national holdings of dollars being placed in the Fund in exchange for SDRs, proved nonnegotiable during the Carter administration and has been set aside indefinitely. Today, interest in London, Washington, and other financial capitals is no longer in the collective management of liquidity but in a more modest and achievable objective—the gradual movement toward a multicurrency reserve system in which the yen and the mark (and perhaps eventually a European currency unit) can join the dollar as international reserve assets. Whether such a multicurrency reserve system can be managed so as to assure the international monetary stability sought at Bretton Woods is an open question.

The original ideas of the founding fathers for collective international monetary management proved no more feasible for capital movements than for liquidity creation. The IMF articles approved at Bretton Woods provided for freedom from exchange controls only on current transactions; significantly, the postwar planners envisaged that countries would need the latitude (and, in extreme cases, should be required) to control disequilibrating movements of short-term capital. In those days there was a strong belief in both London and Washington that governments would have to protect the system against the uncontrolled activities of private bankers. Secretary of the Treasury Henry Morgenthau Jr. went so far as to describe the purpose of the Bretton Woods Conference as "to drive the usurious money lenders from the temple of international finance."

It is precisely here, of course, that the world of today contrasts most dramatically with the world envisaged at Bretton Woods. The "money lenders" are very much with us. We have developed a highly sophisticated, twenty-four-hour-a-day global capital market, which facilitates instantaneous transfers of funds on a scale that the founding fathers could not have imagined. We are now in a world in which capital flows have displaced trade flows as the principal determinant of currency relations; some $1 trillion of exchange transactions take place every day, only about 2 percent of which are linked to transactions in goods and services. As the postwar world evolved, both the British and the American governments, like the governments of most countries, came to attach a high priority to freedom from controls on capital as well as current transactions. Moreover, few people have much confidence that international capital movements could be effectively limited, even if we were to want to do so.

All of this brings us to the last respect in which the original design for international monetary management proved inoperable—the international adjustment process. The postwar monetary order was to be based on fixed exchange rates which could be adjusted only to correct a "fundamental disequilibrium" through a process of international consultation and agreement. In their original versions, the American and British currency plans envisaged that such a regime would be made possible by far-reaching international control over the economic policies of deficit and surplus countries.

Under the first (unpublished) draft of the White plan, members were obliged "not to adopt any monetary banking measure promoting either serious inflation or serious deflation without the consent of a majority of member votes of the Fund." The published version omitted this far-reaching (and politically unrealistic) provision, but authorized the Fund to make recommendations for changes in the economic policy of countries going too far toward deficit or surplus. Moreover, recommendations could be reinforced by sanctions—the denial of the use of Fund resources beyond a certain point for a deficit country, the rationing of the "scarce currency" of a surplus country by means of exchange restrictions employed against it. Under the Keynes plan, the Clearing Union could require a deficit country that drew more than half of its overdraft facilities to deposit collateral, depreciate its currency, control outward capital movements, or surrender liquid reserves in reduction of its debit balance. It could recommend to that country internal economic measures needed to restore equilibrium. It could require a surplus country whose credit balance exceeded half its quota to carry out such measures as the stimulation of domestic demand, the appreciation of its currency, the reduction of import barriers, and the making of international development loans.

With the notable exception of the "scarce-currency" clause, most of these references to international supervision of the economic policy of deficit and surplus countries were eliminated during negotiation of the Fund articles. In the course of the negotiations leading to Bretton Woods, it proved impossible for the British and the American negotiators to agree on the appropriate balance between deficit- and surplus-country responsibilities; references to international oversight of domestic economic policies were watered down to facilitate approval of the IMF by Parliament and Congress. By the time of the Bretton Woods Conference and its aftermath, national autonomy was being emphasized instead of supranationality. Keynes went so far as to assure the House of Lords that, under the IMF, the external value of sterling "would be altered if necessary so as to conform to whatever de facto internal value results from domestic policies, which themselves shall be immune from criticism from the Fund."

Thus the Bretton woods compromise left a good deal of ambiguity about the responsibilities for adjustment of surplus and deficit countries. It ruled out adjustment through freely fluctuating exchange rates or by controls on payments for current transactions—since exchange stability and multilateral trade were two primary Bretton Woods objectives. But it said very little about how adjustment was to be achieved. The architects at Bretton Woods apparently hoped that, with the aid of Fund resources, deficit and surplus countries could be relied on to restore a balance within a relatively short time by reasonable domestic policies and by occasional changes in exchange rates to correct a "fundamental disequilibrium." Unfortunately, however, this system just didn't work out.

The inadequacies of the Bretton Woods adjustment mechanism were camouflaged in the early postwar years when the United States was in surplus and the rest of the world was in deficit. Nobody paid much attention to the problem of how the Fund would police surplus and deficit nations to assure their good behavior. In effect, during these years the United States policed the economic policies of deficit countries unilaterally, using the leverage of postwar aid to encourage the adoption of internal and external policies it regarded as appropriate. It also, in a sense, policed itself—adopting liberal aid and trade policies appropriate to a surplus nation because it quickly recognized that, if it were to fail to do so, the rest of the world would go broke. This was not so much a question of American altruism as of enlightened self-interest.

The United States was the economic giant among nations; there was no one with whom to share responsibility; it alone had the power to save the wartime multilateral dream and assure the survival of freedom in the West. The political costs of failure were unacceptable to it and, consequently, it was willing to pay the price in the Marshall Plan, in other measures of postwar aid, and in non-reciprocated trade concessions providing liberal access to the U.S. market. Nobody had to invoke the principal IMF sanction envisaged for policing the creditor—the "scarce-currency" clause considered so important by Keynes. It was unavailable, in any case, since the Fund was inactive during the period of U.S. reconstruction aid and dollars in the Fund were not technically "scarce." But for the reasons mentioned above, it was not needed.

When the "dollar shortage" gave way to "dollar glut" and a U.S.-centered system was replaced by a more balanced distribution of economic power, the shortcomings in the Bretton Woods design became apparent. The countries of Continental Europe and Japan did not police themselves in the direction of creditor-country responsibility following the earlier American model. It was not that they were more "wicked" than the United States; but because none of them was big enough to be decisive, they did not assume the same responsibility the United States had for "saving the system." The scarce currency clause was now a dead letter; nobody, least of all the United States, wanted to use exchange controls on current transactions as a sanction against surplus countries. It was becoming uncomfortably clear that a system of fixed exchange rates, in which gold and the dollar (supplemented by the possibility of international credits) were the main components, was rather asymmetrical in its pressures for adjustment. The deficit countries were under pressure to adjust when they ran out of reserves and had to go to the Fund or to the central bankers for aid; but there was no similar pressure on the creditors to reduce their surpluses.

The deficiencies of the system were also evident on the deficit side, particularly where the United States was concerned. To begin with, there were some difficulties in applying conventional balance-of-payments accounting concepts to the United States in its role as central banker to the world. There was very little agreement as to the relevance of the concept of payments equilibrium for a country such as the United States, which in its role as world central banker had to supply a large part of world liquidity needs. When dollars are the principal instrument available to increase world reserves, are U.S. deficits benign or malignant? Given the desire of the Europeans to run surpluses in the early postwar years and the slow growth of the stock of monetary gold, how would it have been possible for the United States—at least before 1967 when its record of price stability compared favorably with that of Western Europe—to have achieved equilibrium without taking measures destructive of its own and the general welfare and inconsistent with the IMF and GATT rules?

Was there also some measure of truth in the view that a modest U.S. payments deficit was an appropriate reflection of the "financial intermediation" performed by the United States as central banker to the world and the world's most highly developed capital market? Or were those Europeans right who claimed this was but a sophisticated rationale by which the United States was trying to spend beyond its means at Europe's expense—refusing to accept the discipline it urged upon Europe when the situation was reversed? Perhaps all we can say here on this difficult conceptual problem is that, while U.S. payment deficits were in the general interest in the 1940s and 1950s given the responsibilities of the United States in the international monetary system, its deficits were too large for most of the 1970s and 1980s to be acceptable to U.S. allies in Europe and Japan.

In practice, therefore, the postwar international monetary system, so far as developed countries were concerned, permitted a large degree of national autonomy. Despite the original concept of international oversight of domestic policy, there was no adjustment process worthy of the name. Yet the system still provided for fixed (though adjustable) exchange rates. The system might have functioned if countries could have been relied on to manage their affairs voluntarily with due regard for the requirements of international adjustment in a regime of stable currency relationships. This was to prove an impossible dream. The two great English-speaking democracies themselves set no good example. In the first postwar decade, Britain tried at one and the same time to run a welfare state, maintain a world currency, and continue a world military role. This led to sterling devaluations and to sluggish domestic growth. More serious for the international system, the United States began in the 1960s to overreach its resources just as Britain had done, refusing to trim the Great Society in the face of the Vietnam War; it thus inaugurated an era of high inflation and large U.S. balance-of-payments deficits, leading to the suspension of dollar convertibility into gold in 1971 and the final collapse of fixed currency relations in 1973.

The world of the 1980s and 1990s has been characterized by a high degree of exchange rate volatility and by periods of substantial overvaluation and undervaluation of the dollar in relation to the yen and the mark, currencies that replaced the pound sterling as other major international currencies. Recent years have also been marked by large and chronic U.S. current account deficits and by large and chronic Japanese current account surpluses that have proved both difficult to reduce and a continuing source of international friction. These imbalances have been a reflection of the U.S. inability to control its domestic budget deficits and of the Japanese propensity to oversaving and underimporting. In the last year, progress has been made on the U.S. side toward greater fiscal responsibility; but whether Japan is willing or able to discharge its economic responsibilities to the rest of the world is still an open question.

With the increased interdependence which exists today, including the high degree of capital mobility between nations which was unforeseen at Bretton Woods, it is essential that countries adjust their domestic economic policies with a view to maintaining a mutually beneficial world economic system. It is simply impossible to have complete national policy autonomy and maintain an open international system of trade and capital flows. If we wish to preserve the latter, we shall have to accept some limitation on the former.

It was in recognition of this fact that the 1978 amendment to the IMF Articles of Agreement legitimizing floating rates also provided for "firm surveillance" by the Fund over the exchange-rate policies (and by implication the domestic monetary and fiscal policies) of member countries. This surveillance is exercised through the so-called Article IV consultations between the Fund and its members. But so far these consultations have had little influence on the policies of the United States, Japan, Germany, and other major industrialized countries. Unlike most developing countries, these countries can finance their deficits by borrowing from the international capital market; therefore, they have no need for IMF assistance and its accompanying conditionality. In fact, no major industrialized country has borrowed from the IMF since 1977, the year when the United Kingdom and Italy both entered into standby arrangements.

During recent years the search by industrialized countries for a more structured international monetary system with greater exchange-rate stability and a more effective adjustment process has taken place outside the IMF through meetings of the Group of Seven (the United States, the United Kingdom, Germany, France, Italy, Canada, and Japan). The G–7 process involves not just annual summits at the head-of-government level, but also periodic meetings of treasury ministers and central bank governors. Beginning with the Plaza agreement in 1985 and the Louvre agreement in 1987, efforts have been made toward greater international management of the floating rate system. The G–7 has gone so far as to experiment with a set of economic indicators designed to provide a framework within which countries could coordinate their monetary and fiscal policies. So far the practical results of these efforts have been limited because of an obvious fact of international economic life: the governments of the major economic powers are not prepared to subordinate their domestic policy objectives to the goal of keeping their currency in some agreed international alignment. As long as this continues to be the case, world leaders will continue to call for a new international monetary system while refusing to adopt the concrete measures to bring it about. Probably the best we can achieve in the foreseeable future is a deepening of the G–7 consultative process, so that peer pressure is exercised on the major countries to take greater account of the international consequences of their domestic economic actions.

Given the difficulty of achieving more stable currencies and more effective adjustment on a worldwide basis, it was only natural that hopes for greater monetary stability should focus on limited regional arrangements. The European monetary system and its Exchange Rate Mechanism (ERM) did for many years provide a zone of relative monetary stability. Yet the ambitious plan for a European Monetary Union (EMU) provided for in the Maastricht Treaty suffered a major setback in the fall of 1992 when the pound sterling and the lira abandoned the fixed-exchange-rate parities of the ERM in favor of unilaterally managed floating. For Britain and Italy, the high German interest rates triggered by the massive fiscal requirements of German unification were transmitting through the ERM an unacceptably depressing effect on their economies. Forced to choose between domestic growth and employment on one hand, and international monetary stability on the other, the two countries understandably chose to give priority to their internal economic requirements. When Germany digests the costs of unification, progress toward an EMU may well be resumed. But the lack of convergence in inflation rates and budget deficits between EMR members, as well as unforeseen future cyclical developments, make it unlikely that the EMU will be realized within anything like its original timetable for more than a core group of European countries.

If the Fund's original purpose as supplier of liquidity and monitor of sound adjustment policies has been largely frustrated with regard to the industrialized countries, it has nevertheless found a compensating role in relation to the developing countries that the founding fathers could not have imagined. For many of the developing countries the Fund has become the international arbiter of those sound domestic policies that qualify a country for external aid. Its financial assistance to these countries has tended to certify the creditworthiness of the borrower and has thus made it easier to obtain credit from private lenders as well as governments. The Fund's capacity to mobilize not just its own resources but also those of central banks and commercial banks was of critical importance in enabling the international community to cope with the debt crisis of the 1980s.

The Fund's usefulness to developing countries has grown significantly with the growth of its resources and with the creative devices developed over the years in the way these resources could be made available. At the outset the Fund's quotas totaled less than $8 billion. Successive increases have brought these resources to about $182 billion today (SDR 130 billion). Equally important have been innovations like the standby arrangements developed during the Fund's early years that assured countries that they could make drawings on the Fund up to a certain amount provided they carry out economic programs agreed to in consultation with the Fund. More recently the Fund established the structural adjustment and enhanced structural adjustment facilities to provide loans on concessional terms to low-income developing countries. In these and other ways, the Fund transformed itself from a rather tightfisted short-term lender at near market-interest rates to finance temporary balance-of-payments difficulties to a more generous and policy-based lender financing structural adjustments over longer periods at nominal interest rates. For this evolution of the Fund a large share of the credit should go to successive farsighted managing directors—Johannes Witteveen, Jacques de Larosiere, and Michel Camdessus.

The Fund has been criticized in many parts of the world for the harsh economic medicine it forces upon borrowing countries, sometimes with explosive political consequences. It has been said—only half in jest—that the Fund has "toppled more governments than Marx and Lenin combined." The Fund itself has admitted that it needs to pay more attention to the impact of its adjustment programs on social spending and on the welfare of the poorest segments of the population.

Still, much criticism of the Fund in its policy-based lending has been misplaced. The Fund cannot be faulted when a developing country is obliged to make sacrifices in order to live within its means after years of overborrowing and overspending. The reforms it asks of borrowing countries, on the whole, have been sound: minimization of unproductive expenditures, particularly military spending and overgenerous subsidies; a firm anti-inflation policy and a realistic exchange rate; opening up the economy to international trade and investment; price liberalization and the reform of public enterprises; the improvement of labor markets and the creation of social safety nets; and better governance, meaning participatory forms of government, a transparent legal framework, and the elimination of corruption. While progress in those directions still leaves much to be desired in the developing world as a whole, it has certainly been greater than it would have been without the Fund.

Perhaps the greatest challenge to the Fund has come since the end of the cold war in its help to former Communist countries in transition to market economies. The Fund has created a systemic transformation facility which permits disbursement of aid to deal with the special problems of these countries once it is satisfied that a satisfactory program of reform is in place. The experience with this new function of the Fund is still too brief for us to enter an unambiguous judgment on its success or failure. In Central Europe, where progress is being made in controlling inflation and restarting economic growth, one can perhaps say that Fund resources combined with its useful policy oversight are making a positive contribution. For Russia, on the other hand, where economic prospects are uncertain as of this writing, the Fund is blamed by some for failing to do more to help the economic reforms in Boris Yeltsin's critical first two years. Yet a good case can be made for the proposition that Russia's poor economic management in those same years, due mainly to the inflationary policies of its central bank, would have wasted Fund assistance and undermined the credibility of its lending standards. It remains to be seen whether the Fund can find a useful role to play in Russia and in other republics of the former Soviet Union where so little exists in the way of effective institutions or policy consensus.

According to the very first purpose laid down in its Articles of Agreement, the IMF was "to promote international monetary cooperation through a permanent institution which provides the machinery for consultation and collaboration on international monetary problems." Keynes hoped the Fund might be the embryonic economic government of the world. He feared that the decisions taken when the Fund was inaugurated at Savannah meant the destruction of this ambitious aim. Certainly the Fund is an international, not a supranational, organization. In accordance with the Savannah decisions, its directors serve full-time rather than part-time at the headquarters of the Fund and act as representatives of the governments that choose them. Yet over the years they have also developed the "world, objective outlook" for which Keynes had argued. The board of the Fund, like the board of the Bank, has developed a large measure of solidarity and "team spirit." The directors can bring this common approach to bear on their respective treasuries, thus assisting accommodations in national policies.

No less important is the fact that senior government officials both in treasuries and central banks are to an increasing extent alumni of the Fund board or Fund staff. Even where this is not true, they are in frequent contact at the annual meetings and periodic consultations. They all know one another better because of the Fund and have a degree of shared experience and outlook that would have been hard to achieve without the Fund. Add to this the fact of seventeen hundred officials a year from member countries in IMF training institutes and hundreds of Fund experts working in the banking systems and treasury ministries of those countries. In the long run, the Fund's influence on a rising generation of policy makers from developing countries and former Communist countries in transition may prove to be one of the institution's most lasting contributions to a better world economic order.

The International Trade Challenge

The postwar Anglo-American design for a reasonably free and nondiscriminatory world trading system has fared somewhat better than the original design for
a postwar monetary system. The refusal of the U.S. Congress to approve the
International Trade Organization was an initial setback, but substantial progress
in reducing trade barriers has been achieved through the General Agreement on
Tariffs and Trade. Successive rounds of trade negotiations have brought the
average height of tariffs in industrial countries down to a level of about 4 percent. GATT has also managed to deal with many of the nontariff barriers that
emerged as the most significant obstacles to trade with the reduction of tariffs to
modest levels. And with the conclusion of the Uruguay Round in 1993, the world
has finally established a comprehensive set of rules covering virtually all trade
barriers and a World Trade Organization to assist in their enforcement. In addition, a half-century of trade negotiations has produced two huge areas of free
trade that were not remotely foreseen by the founding fathers—the single market
of the European Union and the North American Free Trade Area.

This record of achievement is surprising when one considers the uncertain
prospects for international trade cooperation in the early postwar years. Unlike
the Bretton Woods institutions, which had the advantage of being negotiated by
a relatively small number of countries in the midst of the wartime idealism, the
ITO had to be negotiated by a larger and more diverse group of governments
who were struggling with the hard postwar realities of reconstruction and development. Its charter attempted to cover too many controversial areas on which
consensus did not exist—trade and employment, commodity agreements, foreign
investment, and restrictive business practices. The U.S. Congress recoiled from
the complex provisions designed to deal with these subjects. More fundamentally, Congress was not yet ready to approve a full-fledged international organization that seemed to impinge upon its constitutional powers to regulate U.S.
foreign trade.

Drawn up as a trade agreement pending the creation of the International Trade
Organization, GATT had to live on as an organization when the ITO was with-
drawn from Congress. Its legal basis as an organization was insecure. It had no
adequate secretariat or budget. For nearly a decade visitors to GATT headquarters were greeted with a sign reading "Interim Commission for the International
Trade Organization."

That GATT was obliged to live for years in a state of legal obscurity and
institutional undernourishment was due mainly to the facts of political life in the
United States. It was bad enough that the Congress was unwilling to approve the
ITO; to add insult to injury, it disclaimed approval or disapproval of GATT in
successive renewals of U.S. trade agreements legislation. The Eisenhower
administration's attempt to give GATT a firm legal and institutional underpin-
ning with the Organization for Trade Cooperation negotiated in 1955 suffered

the same fate as the ITO charter: refusal of the Congress to act. U.S. contributions for the support of the GATT secretariat had to be smuggled through the Congress each year under a category in the State Department budget entitled "international conferences and contingencies." Some members of the Congress deeply resented the restraints that GATT seemed to place on American freedom of action in the trade field, particularly since U.S. participation in GATT had never received congressional approval. Not until 1968 did an administration dare to ask the Congress for permanent authorization for contributions to the GATT secretariat—an acknowledgment of legitimacy enjoyed by every other major international agency. United States coolness to GATT was a major limitation on its effectiveness, since in the absence of American leadership not much could be done by others to strengthen GATT as an instrument of liberal trade.

In light of these handicaps, GATT's accomplishments have been rather extraordinary. Much of the credit for this must go to the United States, since in spite of its allergy to a world trade organization, it was willing to open its domestic market to the products of Europe and Japan during the early postwar years when these countries were still severely restricting their imports of U.S. goods. This one-way act of trade liberalization had at least as much to do with the remarkable postwar recovery of Europe and Japan as did the Marshall Plan and other measures of U.S. aid. One must also be impressed at how, under the skillful leadership of Eric Wyndham-White, GATT's chief executive for its first twenty-one years, the institution survived its initial difficulties and became a vital instrument for trade expansion for countries accounting for more than 80 percent of world trade. Despite the absence of a formal organizational structure, the contracting parties established a permanent council to operate between their meetings, a network of specialized committees, and a small permanent secretariat. Quietly but perceptibly, GATT developed authority in a threefold role—as a forum for trade negotiations, as a body of principles governing trade policy, and as a center for the settlement of trade disputes.

As a forum for trade negotiations, GATT has promoted an unprecedented amount of tariff disarmament in eight major bargaining rounds—Geneva, 1947; Annecy, 1949; Torquay, 1951; Geneva, 1956; Geneva, 1960–61 (the "Dillon Round"); Geneva, 1964–67 (the "Kennedy Round"); Geneva, 1975–79 (the "Tokyo Round"); and Geneva 1986–93 (the "Uruguay Round"). In the Kennedy, Tokyo, and Uruguay Rounds, which dwarfed all the others in importance, the average height of tariffs in industrial countries was brought down to about 4 percent. The United States has reduced its average tariff to this level from the 60 percent that prevailed before the Trade Agreements Program began in 1934.

These achievements, to be sure, were the result of commitments undertaken by national governments, but they would not have been possible without GATT. In each of the difficult bargaining rounds, GATT—or more precisely its chief executive—was an indispensable element in laying the groundwork for the negotiations and guiding them to a successful conclusion. This function was reinforced in the Dillon and Kennedy Rounds, when Eric Wyndham-White became chairman of the negotiating group. Indeed, when differences between the United States and the European Economic Community seemed irreconcilable, it was his last-minute intervention that saved the Kennedy Round from collapse and provided the basis for the final settlement. More recently, GATT Directors General Arthur Dunkel and Peter Sutherland have played equally decisive roles in bridging national differences that threatened to derail the Uruguay Round. From the standpoint of both results achieved and GATT's role in producing them, the wartime goals for the bargaining down of tariff restrictions have enjoyed a considerable measure of realization.

The role of GATT in dealing with nontariff barriers has been much more difficult, but since its failures in this field have been so widely publicized, it may be useful to recall some successes that are often forgotten. We need only recall, for example, the bitter differences over quantitative restrictions (QRs) in the postwar negotiations of 1945–48. The compromises reached in the negotiation of GATT worked out much better than the skeptics believed possible. To some American critics, the exception permitting QRs to protect the balance of payments and a country's domestic employment policy constituted an "economic Munich." Yet by the 1960s QRs had been largely eliminated among developed countries on trade in industrial goods (with the notable exception of textiles). To some British critics, the limitations on the use of QRs threatened to frustrate full employment policies and postwar recovery. Yet in not a single instance did they actually do so. As to that other explosive issue in the GATT negotiations—imperial preference—it has gradually faded from sight. Successive rounds of tariff reductions together with inflation have reduced the preference margins to insignificance.

The really difficult nontariff barrier issues have turned out to be quite different from the ones that preoccupied the British and American negotiators at the time of GATT's creation. Substantial nontariff trade barriers arose in the form of "gray area" restrictions—voluntary export restraints and bilateral orderly marketing arrangements whose existence was not foreseen when GATT was negotiated. The proliferation of antidumping actions forced trade negotiators to seek new rules in this area. Government procurement practices and domestic subsidy programs emerged as major trade-distorting measures that were not adequately dealt with in the original GATT rules. And the GATT rules turned out to be totally inadequate to deal with agricultural protectionism. Ironically, this was mainly due to the desire of the United States to assure the maintenance of its agricultural import restrictions in pursuance of New Deal price support programs on behalf of American farmers. When the United States began to suffer from the impact of Europe's Common Agricultural Policy in the 1960s, it had occasion to regret its earlier success in carving out such a generous agricultural exemption in the GATT rules.

Decades of postwar experience also revealed the necessity of broadening the scope of GATT regulation to cover three other areas whose importance was not anticipated by the founding fathers. One was trade in services—banking, insurance, securities, construction, and the like—which grew dramatically in relative importance to merchandise trade. A second was the protection of intellectual property—copyrights, patents, and trademarks—where the lack of universal rules and their enforcement has proved increasingly costly to business in advanced industrial countries. The third area was that of trade-distorting requirements placed by governments on foreign investors, including domestic content requirements and minimum export requirements.

By the middle 1980s, a widespread conviction had developed that GATT had to "grow or die"—it needed to extend its regulation to cover all these areas or slip into increasing irrelevance. It was this conviction that led to the Uruguay Round, certainly the most ambitious trade negotiation in world history. After seven years of arduous negotiations which stalled repeatedly and at times seemed close to collapse, the United States, Europe, Japan, and their trading partners were able to come up with new or improved rules in all the trade areas mentioned above. These rules, to be sure, are replete with exceptions and ambiguities in deference to divergent economic interests, but they provide a framework on which GATT can build and become stronger in the years ahead.

To be really useful, any set of principles requires effective procedures for interpretation and enforcement. In its early years, GATT made a courageous beginning at developing such procedures. Its panels of experts, drawn from member countries with no direct interest in the subject matter, managed to resolve a number of dangerous trade disputes that could have unraveled painstaking accomplishments in trade liberalization. In 1963–64, for example, a GATT panel helped to bring a truce in the famous "chicken war" between the United States and the Common Market resulting from the latter's system of variable levies. Unhappily, this early record of success in dispute settlement was not matched in GATT's later years. Too often, a country found in violation of its obligations by a GATT panel availed itself of GATT's unanimity rule to prevent the contracting parties from confirming the decision. The whole dispute settlement process was too slow and became fragmented after the Tokyo Round with different procedures for the different nontariff barriers dealt with in the various Tokyo Round codes.

Fortunately, the Uruguay Round has produced a historic breakthrough in the system for the interpretation and enforcement of the international trade rules. The process is now subject to strict timetables. In place of a variety of dispute settlement procedures under different GATT codes, there is now an integrated system for the settlement of all trade disputes, with only minor exceptions. A country that loses a case before a GATT panel will no longer be able to block the decision. If it does not bring its laws into conformity with its GATT obligations within a set period of time, it must compensate the affected countries with equivalent trade concessions, or trade retaliation will be authorized against it.

The creation of a new World Trade Organization (WTO) to supplement the GATT is another historic achievement that belatedly fills the vacuum left by the failure of the ITO. By bringing together under one constitutional umbrella the rules and disciplines on government practices affecting trade in goods and services and the protection of intellectual property, the WTO facilitates cross-retaliation in an integrated dispute settlement mechanism. Thus a country that violates its obligations to respect intellectual property rights, for example, can be subject to WTO-authorized retaliation in the form of higher tariffs on its exports of manufactured or agricultural goods by countries that are injured by its action.

In addition, the WTO will help resolve one of the serious weaknesses of GATT—the "free rider" problem. In the past, a GATT member could claim the benefits of most-favored-nation treatment from GATT codes or GATT-sponsored tariff reductions without taking comprehensive commitments itself. Now the benefits of the WTO will be available only to countries that are contracting parties to the GATT, agree to adhere to all of the Uruguay Round agreements, and submit schedules of market access commitments for industrial goods and agricultural goods and services.

The world has thus taken a major step toward an enforceable system of international trade law. But it remains to be seen how the system will actually work in practice. It is already apparent that the United States and some of its trading partners disagree on whether WTO members will be free to employ their trade remedy laws in unilateral fashion. The United States has asserted that it will continue to apply Section 301 of its trade legislation. For matters covered by the Uruguay Round agreement, this congressional authorization to retaliate against foreign trade practices considered unfair will be exercised in conformity with the new dispute settlement procedures. For matters not covered by the Uruguay Round agreement, the United States will continue to reserve the right of unilateral action. Even if this U.S. claim is not challenged by other countries as a matter of principle, disputes are likely to arise over what matters are covered or not covered by the Uruguay Round agreement.

The conclusion of the Uruguay Round and the creation of a World Trade Organization have certainly remedied some of the major weaknesses of the international trading system, but there are more than enough new challenges remaining to keep the fraternity of international trade experts busy for the foreseeable future. One of the major challenges is posed by the worldwide trend toward regional arrangements. Customs unions and free trade areas are specifically authorized by Article XXIV of GATT, provided they meet certain conditions of openness to assure that they will be more trade-creating than trade-diverting. Unquestionably, the European Union and NAFTA meet these tests, but other regional trade arrangements developing in parts of Latin America and Asia will require careful scrutiny from the new WTO. And the likely evolution of the European Union and NAFTA into much larger trading areas in their respective regions during the decade ahead will introduce a new level of complexity in the continuing effort to reconcile global and regional trading rules. Another unresolved issue occupying the trade experts will be the special problem of Japan. Despite years of negotiations aimed at opening up the Japanese market, Japan continues to run a trade surplus with the rest of the world that has averaged about $100 billion a year. Japan's imports of manufactured goods remain at the low level of 3 percent of its GDP compared with 7 percent in the United States and 8 percent in Europe.

The difficulty of penetrating the Japanese market is the result of many factors—Japanese industrial policy, the discriminatory policies of its Keiretsu industrial groups, restrictions on inward foreign investment, and impediments in distribution channels for imported products. Even the new WTO and the expanded GATT rules are not likely to provide answers to the special kinds of barriers that Japan presents to the world. This has led the United States to its controversial demand that Japan accept objective criteria, either quantitative or qualitative, to assess progress in opening its market. Some denounce this as "managed trade," but could this not be regarded as a result-oriented set of benchmarks to open up a market where trade is already managed? Some compromise in this controversy must be found if disputes between the world's two most powerful trading nations are not to disrupt the entire trading system.

One last challenge that requires special mention derives from the growth of the GATT to near universality. In one sense, this represents a triumph for the goals of the founding fathers, since Third World and former Communist countries that used to denounce the GATT as a nefarious capitalist club are now clamoring to get in. But this victory for trade openness is also a new challenge, since it takes place at a time when the worldwide spread of capital and technology has created a true global marketplace. In 1970 the poor countries of the world sold just $3 billion worth of manufactured goods to their wealthy counterparts; today that figure is in excess of $150 billion.

The opening up to world trade of formerly closed economies in Asia, in Latin America, and in countries of the former Soviet Empire has brought well over two billion new people into the global marketplace. They are potential new consumers, but they are also producers, many of whom are prepared to work at one-fifth or one-tenth of wage rates in the United States, Western Europe, and Japan. Even as the Uruguay Round was being concluded, we began to hear second thoughts from leaders of the industrialized democracies about the dangers that low-wage foreign competition might pose for the jobs and living standards of their people. Is it possible that, with the achievement of near universality for the GATT system, we have planted the seeds of its eventual destruction?

The International Development Challenge

The effort to promote the economic development of the less developed countries is another major challenge of our time. The most important international financial institution engaged in this effort in terms of the size of its resources and the weight of its influence is the International Bank for Reconstruction and Development. We take this for granted now, but in the early planning for the postwar economy the Bank came almost as an afterthought. Virtually all the attention of the British and American governments was focused on the International Monetary Fund. When, on the eve of Bretton Woods, the negotiators finally focused on the Bank, they were in a conservative mood—the British did not expect to be beneficiaries, the Americans were afraid of the Congress. The Bank's lending capacity was limited almost entirely to what it could raise by bonds issued on the private capital market. There was simply no conception of the vast needs of the less developed countries and of the role the Bank should play in meeting them. Indeed, the Bank was conceived mainly as an institution for reconstruction. Incredible as it seems today, the word "development" did not even appear in Harry White's first draft circulated within the U.S. Treasury Department.

As it turned out, the Bank played only a marginal role in the accomplishment of its primary purpose—the reconstruction of a war-devastated Europe. The financial requirements of reconstruction were far beyond the Bank's comparatively modest resources. In 1946–47 two great Americans—Dean Acheson and Will Clayton—persuaded President Harry Truman that a special effort of enlightened U.S. statesmanship was required. The result was Secretary of State George C. Marshall's famous address at Harvard University in June 1947.

In the light of history, there are three aspects of the Marshall Plan that deserve particularly to be remembered. First, the United States pumped $16 billion (the equivalent of about $100 billion in today's dollars) into the European economies over a four-year period—half of it on a grant basis—thus laying the essential foundation for the "economic miracle" of the Continent in the 1950s and 1960s.

Second, the Marshall Plan was not conceived as a cold war instrument; on the contrary, the Soviet Union and its Eastern European satellites were invited to join. As Secretary of State Marshall declared in his Harvard address: "Our policy is not directed against any country or doctrine, but against hunger, poverty, desperation, and chaos." The postwar division of Europe was sealed when Stalin refused to participate in a Europe-wide recovery effort and prevented the participation of other Eastern European countries as well.

But it is the third aspect of the Marshall Plan that is most relevant to this history: the entire program was conditioned on a cooperative recovery effort by the European countries themselves. Indeed, in the Marshall Plan legislation, the U.S. Congress made steps toward European unity a requirement of American aid. The Organization for European Economic Cooperation (OEEC), established to manage American assistance, worked effectively to increase trade and financial cooperation among the aid recipients. The dismantling of intra-European trade barriers, the European Payments Union, the Treaty of Rome itself, all can be traced back to the Marshall Plan initiative. After years during which the United States has been denounced for "imperialist" and "hegemonical" designs on Europe, this is worth special emphasis. It is, after all, a strange kind of "imperialism" that urges weak and divided countries to unite so that they may become strong political and economic rivals.

No doubt the Marshall Plan was motivated not only by U.S. altruism and enlightened economic interest but also by the fact that Europe's free institutions could be engulfed by Soviet-led Communist movements unless economic conditions improved. And no doubt in later years a resurgent and self-confident European Community came into conflict with the United States on many trade and financial questions. But neither of these facts can obscure the objective benefits of European recovery and European integration that are now enjoyed not only by the Europeans themselves but also by the United States and the rest of the world. And it is a source of satisfaction that successive U.S. administrations have continued to support the great historic movement toward European unity, even while wishing to be sure that it proceeds as far as possible in harmony with the global institutions that emerged as liberalizing forces after World War II. As these lines are written, the United States is giving its full encouragement to the process of political and economic unity in Europe in the belief that this process serves the enlightened interest of the United States in greater global stability and welfare.

The Bank, like its Bretton Woods twin, took some years to overcome its initial handicaps. As a reconstruction agency it was inevitably overshadowed by the Marshall Plan. In the 1950s, when it began to focus at last on the less developed countries, its dependence on the private capital market kept it in a rather conservative banker's role. It financed only specific projects that promised profits sufficient to repay the initial investment, covered only foreign exchange (not local currency) costs, and concentrated on traditional "public utility" investments in power and transportation. Equally important, it lent only on commercial terms—with market interest rates and repayment schedules of ten to twenty years.

Yet even in these early years, the Bank's contribution was by no means unimportant. After the disastrous experience of defaults in international bond issues during the interwar period, it is doubtful that the capital market of the United States could have once again been tapped on such a large scale, particularly for the less developed countries, without the International Bank as intermediary. World Bank bonds, representing a diversified package of investments undertaken by an experienced and prudent management and backed by guarantees of borrowing governments as well as by the U.S. capital subscription, were soon regarded in Wall Street as a first-class investment. Gradually, the Bank diversified its borrowing operations as Europe recovered and the United States slipped into balance-of-payments deficit. By the middle and late 1960s, European capital markets were providing substantially more of the Bank's new money than the capital market of the United States.

Moreover, the Bank's role in stimulating the flow of private capital was enlarged with the creation of two Bank affiliates. The first—the International

Finance Corporation—put government money to work in equity investments in private enterprises in less developed countries. The second—the International Center for the Settlement of Investment Disputes—created a center of arbitration for the resolution of disputes between foreign investors and governments.

These achievements in mobilizing and stimulating the flow of private capital for development can be credited in large part to two experienced figures from the U.S. financial community, Eugene Black and George Woods. But the Bank's evolution under their presidencies was not limited to the area of "bankable" investment. The really big breakthrough was the launching of the International Development Association as the Bank's "soft-loan" affiliate for the making of very long-term loans at nominal rates of interest. It was with the creation of IDA in 1960 that the member governments, responding to U.S. leadership, finally recognized the inadequacy of the original Bretton Woods conception which made the Bank almost entirely dependent on the private capital market. Today Bank lending of more than $20 billion a year on near-commercial terms is supplemented by some $5 billion annually in interest-free IDA loans repayable over fifty years with ten-year grace periods.

By the middle and late 1960s the Bank and IDA were making program as well as project loans, were financing local as well as foreign exchange costs, and were moving into new fields such as agriculture and education. Later the Bank enlarged its activities to embrace projects in health and family planning. To carry out projects in these fields, the Bank began to work closely with such agencies of the United Nations as UNESCO, the Food and Agriculture Organization, the World Health Organization, the UN Development Program, and the UN Population Fund. In these and other ways the Bank altered its original attitude of splendid isolation from the United Nations system.

During the presidency of Robert S. McNamara in the 1970s, the character of the Bank changed even further. Its focus became not just economic development but also poverty reduction and basic human needs and the access of the poor to education, health care, and family planning services. More recently, under Tom Clausen, Barber Conable, and Lewis Preston, the Bank has financed projects to protect the human environment in such areas as forestry, water resources management, and energy efficiency. It now manages a Global Environmental Facility (GEF) in cooperation with the UN Development Program and the UN Environment Program. The GEF, replenished recently with $2 billion to be spent over four years, is serving as the centerpiece of global efforts in support of the international conventions on climate change, biodiversity, and the protection of the ozone layer, as well as of efforts to combat marine pollution.

The Bank's historic contribution—like that of the Fund—cannot be measured by its financial operations alone. It has served as an inspiration and model for the establishment and growth of regional development banks in Latin America, Africa, and Asia, and, more recently, in Europe. Its consortia and consultative groups have brought donor countries together and coordinated their aid in support of internationally approved development plans. This "multilateral-bilateralism," or multilateral coordination of bilateral aid programs, is now an important element in international financial cooperation—a vital supplement to the discussions of bilateral aid policy among donor countries in the Development Assistance Committee of the Organization for Economic Cooperation and Development, the successor of the original OEEC.

When all of this is taken into account, it is clear that multilateral cooperation in development lending has come a long way. At the present time the United States is doing much of its development lending through the multilateral development banks. All in all, about half of total development assistance is being disbursed by multilateral agencies, and most of the rest is being transferred pursuant to arrangements worked out by consortia and consultative groups. The multilateral banks, like the IBRD, now have hard loan windows lending on near market terms to the most advanced developing countries, and soft loan windows lending on concessional terms to the poorest and least creditworthy developing countries. The hard loans are financed by borrowing on the world's capital markets, the soft loans mainly by donor contributions. The total annual lending commitments of the banks have reached $45 billion a year.

The World Bank's ability to mobilize increasing amounts of capital, together with its prestige and experience, has given it a growing influence on the aid policies of the rich and the development policies of the poor. Its presidency is becoming one of the world's most influential platforms for improving the aid efforts of the developed countries. Its role in training, advice, and technical assistance enables it to shape profoundly the development efforts of the poor countries. Its Economic Development Institute, the visiting Bank missions, the Bank's assistance in project preparation and execution—all of these help encourage those sound internal policies without which no amount of external assistance can possibly bear fruit. It should also be added that, in response to criticism, the Bank has become a more open institution, willing to provide information and engage in a dialogue with nongovernmental organizations. No doubt, as we will suggest in a moment, aid is still insufficiently large and the economic performance of many developing countries continues to be disappointing. But the Bank's achievements since Bretton Woods represent a quite spectacular advance in international collaboration for development over anything that came before.

Perhaps the most eloquent measure of the success of the development efforts of the last fifty years has been the growth of private capital flows to the developing world. In 1993, of $177 billion in total capital flows to these countries, $113 billion, or about two-thirds, came from the private sector. Some $56 billion of this amount was in the form of foreign direct investment, $13 billion in the form of portfolio investment, and $43 billion in lending from commercial banks and other sources. It is clear that Henry Morganthau's "usurious money lenders"— far from being "driven from the temple of international finance"—are providing an indispensable and rapidly growing source of finance for world economic development.

Yet we cannot end this survey of fifty years of efforts in international development on an entirely sanguine note. Two debit entries must be entered on this balance sheet, concerning the development policies of the poor and the aid policies of the rich.

What used to be called the "Third World" now comprises a highly differentiated development universe. China, Hong Kong, Taiwan, Singapore, Korea, and a number of Asian countries have registered phenomenal growth. Mexico, Chile, and Argentina and a few other countries of Latin America have begun to take off after years of disappointment. In contrast, Africa south of the Sahara, with the exception of South Africa and one or two other countries, is a continent in agony. Per-capita income has been declining, on the average, for over a decade. The World Bank has estimated that if present trends continue, it will take Africa forty years to recover the income levels it had in the 1970s. These examples of development success and development failure serve to remind us that no amount of help from the international financial institutions can solve the development problem without the right set of conditions in recipient countries.

Paul Hoffman, the U.S. administrator of the Marshall Plan, remarked at the beginning of the plan that "only the Europeans can save Europe." In the final analysis, the developing countries' progress will depend on their own efforts. Only their own commitment to putting their houses in order, to wealth-creating strategies, to realistic foreign exchange and interest rates, to providing incentives to domestic and foreign investors, to family planning and environmental protection, and to less corrupt and more responsive government can assure them a better future. How to help the poorest of the developing countries to do these things remains a major challenge for the international community.

The other major source of concern lies in the growing "aid fatigue" of the rich countries. After years of impressive growth, the total amount of "official development assistance"—aid supplied by the developed countries on concessional terms—has begun to stagnate. It is now at 0.35 percent of GDP as compared with the target of 0.7 percent approved some years ago by the UN General Assembly. Whatever one thinks of the UN target, it is clear that current aid levels will not be sufficient to achieve the goals of "sustainable development"— assisting economic growth in developing countries while preserving the human environment—that were agreed to in Rio in 1992 at the UN Conference on Environment and Development.

The United States, which demonstrated such exceptional leadership in world development efforts for most of the last fifty years, is now a major part of the problem. Its aid level as a proportion of GDP is 0.15 percent, at the bottom of the OECD ranking of developed countries. Its funding for the multilateral development banks has fallen by 40 percent since 1978, and its arrears in contributions to those banks now exceed $800 million. This falling off of U.S. commitment results mainly from congressional and public demands that the government cut back on foreign spending and devote more resources to neglected domestic needs. These demands are understandable, but if sustainable development fails on a global scale, U.S. economic and environmental goals will be undermined as well.

It would seem that the challenge to political leadership in the United States may be just as great today as it was when the founding fathers laid the groundwork for the postwar economic order a half-century ago: to make a convincing case to Congress and the public on behalf of policies of enlightened internationalism.

Economism, Universalism, and Legalism Revisited

In assessing the work of the founding fathers some years ago I identified three "errors" in wartime and postwar economic diplomacy—economism, universalism, and legalism. But in the light of fifty years of history, my original judgment about these "errors" clearly needs to be revised.

It was my judgment that the postwar planners were guilty of *economism* in building a set of postwar economic institutions before the political setting could be more clearly foreseen. But they had to start somewhere. If the British and American governments had not used the period of their wartime collaboration to establish the Bretton Woods institutions and chart the main outlines of what became the GATT, these institutions might never have been created. From the perspective of half a century, we can be grateful that the economic foundations of a decent world order were laid while the fighting was still going on, even if those foundations might have been better shaped to postwar political realities. It would have been difficult to have held a successful Bretton Woods conference after the war. Not only would the wartime spirit of idealism and solidarity have been dissipated, but also it would have been necessary to contemplate closing the exchange markets until the conference reached a successful conclusion.

It was also my judgment that the postwar planners were guilty of *universalism* in sometimes considering universal institutions as a substitute for cooperation on a bilateral or regional basis. It is certainly true that they failed to supplement these institutions soon enough with measures to deal with the special problems of the pound sterling and of European reconstruction. To say that they were guilty of *universalism*, however, does not mean they made a mistake in founding universal institutions in the financial and trade field. Quite the contrary. Precisely because of their universal character, the Bretton Woods institutions and GATT have been indispensable vehicles not only for cooperation between North America, Europe, and Japan, but also for assistance to the nations of the less developed world and to the former Communist countries. Indeed, the role of these institutions in promoting economic reforms ·in China and in the countries of Central and Eastern Europe may one day be judged as one of their most important achievements. None of these possibilities could have been realized had the

British and American governments sidetracked the International Monetary Fund in favor of a bilateral financial agreement, as was urged by the opponents of Bretton Woods in the "key currency" proposal.

It was my judgment, finally, that the postwar planners were guilty of *legalism* in exalting agreement in form over agreement in substance. Certainly some agreements were negotiated in excessive detail, without any real meeting of minds and without adequate procedures for adjustment in the light of changing circumstances. The notorious example was the Anglo-American Financial Agreement, with its inflexible timetable for sterling convertibility and its camouflaging of divergent intentions with respect to the funding and writing off of the wartime sterling balances. A second example was the ITO charter, so weighted down with rules and exceptions that it collapsed of its own weight even before it could take effect.

Yet the Bretton Woods institutions and GATT are also legal instruments and, as history reveals in abundant detail, they certainly were the subject of very different interpretations on the two sides of the Atlantic. But most of the differences that seemed so important half a century ago have disappeared, removed by changes in American and British policy or simply overtaken by events. Perhaps these institutions have succeeded where the Anglo-American Financial Agreement failed because they have provided a framework for continuing consultation and adjustment of policy. Thus history suggests that the self-serving statements negotiators made to please domestic opinion may have been a price worth paying given the common interest in enabling the institutions to work in practice. Whether they do, in fact, work depends not only on this measure of common interest but also on the leadership of the international staff, the evolution of national policies, and the procedures by which original ambiguities can be clarified in changing circumstances.

"There is," Keynes warned at Savannah, "scarcely any enduringly successful experience yet of an international body which has fulfilled the hopes of its progenitors. Either an institution has become diverted to be the instrument of a limited group, or it has been a puppet of sawdust through which the breath of life does not blow." One cannot escape the conclusion that Keynes, perfectionist though he was, would have been the first to acknowledge the service to the general interest as well as the continuing vitality of the institutions in whose conception he played such a leading part.

Conclusion

In his book *Present at the Creation*, one of the founding fathers of the postwar system, Dean Acheson, wrote that the early postwar period "was one of great obscurity to those who lived through it. Not only was the future clouded, a common enough situation, but the present was equally clouded. . . . The significance of events was shrouded in ambiguity. We groped after interpretations of them, sometimes reversed lines of action based on earlier views, and hesitated long before grasping what now seems obvious."

The end of the cold war has thrust us into another period of uncertainty. But in contrast to the situation fifty years ago, we do not need to establish a whole new set of international institutions to cope with our longstanding challenges or with the new ones we have just examined. Our need is rather to use the institutions we have inherited with the same spirit of constructive internationalism that was demonstrated by the architects of the postwar economic order. For despite all the changes the world has experienced, the basic objectives that inspired the work of the founding fathers are as valid today as they were at the time of Bretton Woods fifty years ago.

Notes

1. This essay is adapted from the new Spanish edition of *Sterling-Dollar Diplomacy: The Origin and the Future of the Bretton Woods–GATT System* (La Diplomacia del dolar y la esterlina, origenes y futuro del sistema de Bretton Woods–GATT) (Barcelona: Circulo de Lectores, 1994).

2. References for the quotations contained in this chapter may be found in various chapters of *La Diplomacia del dolar y la esterlina*, where the quotations appear in their historical context.

Section III

Future

15

Bretton Woods, Prosperity
and Security

Paul H. Nitze and J. H. McCall

As we stumble into a new era of international relations, and feel our way through now unfamiliar territory, it is fitting that we reflect upon the purpose, impact, and lessons of the institutions we commemorate upon the fiftieth anniversary of Bretton Woods. Such reflection is not only necessary, it is also timely. While the world's economic health in 1994 contrasts favorably with that in 1944, our goals today are not so different and perhaps no less urgent than they were then: to seek a better international economic environment and to promote lasting international prosperity and stability. For now, as in 1944, failure to plan for international economic stability and prosperity could undermine the peace we have at last achieved.

We need little remind ourselves of the international economic situation at the end of the Second World War, nor of the preoccupations and concerns of the participants at Bretton Woods. The economists and government officials at Bretton Woods had witnessed the failure of the old international economic system and the ensuing two decades of economic and political turmoil and suffering. They were determined to prevent such evil from repeating itself. As Franklin Roosevelt told the delegates in his welcoming message in 1944, they were about to discuss part of the arrangements necessary to "ensure an orderly, harmonious world. But it is a vital phase, affecting ordinary men and women everywhere. For it concerns the basis upon which they will be able to exchange with one another the natural riches of the earth and the products of their own industry and ingenuity." Roosevelt, and those present at the conference, understood the importance of international economic prosperity for lasting political stability and ultimately for international peace and security. Theirs was a daunting task, one by no means certain to succeed either in design or practice. However, they were successful both in creating the appropriate arrangements and in managing them for nearly twenty-five years. That success owed much to a very deliberate approach to the economic problems before them and to the practical means to implement working solutions. It is an approach to which we should pay close attention as we look to the prosperity of our own era.

As we look back at the Bretton Woods of 1944, we tend to think mainly of the conference itself. However, Bretton Woods was the culmination of two years of careful negotiations. In practice, these negotiations translated into extended consultations among the leading economic powers of the day, what one might call the "economic great powers." These few countries arrived at a consensus of views about the reasons underlying past instability and then hammered out the economic institutions they saw as necessary to restore confidence and stability to the international economy of the day. It was also understood that these powers would ultimately manage whatever arrangements were made. After all, they would form the practical substance of the economy itself. In short, the Bretton Woods process ensured that all the economic voices that must be heard were heard, and were given due influence both in creating the institutions and in managing them.

Whether and how well the international economic institutions launched at Bretton Woods worked up until the collapse of the system in the 1970s are still favored topics of debate. Some argue that their success in meeting unexpected challenges for the first twenty-five years derived from the flexibility and adaptability of the institutions and their rules. Others point to the coincidence of American national and strategic interests, U.S. global economic dominance, and international need (as the importance of the Marshall Plan to European recovery and security might suggest). It is probably a great deal of both, and perhaps a bit more.

The Bretton Woods institutions and the Marshall Plan did indeed lend themselves well to the practical requirements of the era: heavy, directed capital investment well spent to rebuild productive economies coupled with a stable but ultimately flexible monetary system that facilitated the trade engendered by those economies. Furthermore, the Marshall Plan had built-in requirements that disciplined how these economies were rebuilt, with specific strings attached to aid to ensure that the vulnerable war-torn economies were built along free-market—not socialist or centrally planned—lines. While one cannot claim the architects of Bretton Woods or the Marshall Plan sagely anticipated the full range of the future requirements of the international economy, they did grasp well the common need to facilitate prosperity and stability and implemented practical measures necessary to achieve them. They recognized the underlying practical needs of the system and acted upon them, not managing but tending.

It is also true that part of the practical recipe for success in establishing the

Bretton Woods institutions and in their early work lay in the strong postwar leadership of the United States, both as the preponderant economic power and as leader of the Western Alliance. But there was more. The Bretton Woods system was organized and implemented by a relatively small number of countries which could, and for a time did, reach consensus and decisions fairly easily. They had a common understanding of the importance of creating and adhering to the institutional rules of the system they created. It was a streamlined decision-making process, a system that included all the essential, influential economic powers.

Some have criticized the Bretton Woods arrangements for the very same reasons we may point to for its success: limited membership and the economic domination of the European states and the United States. In particular, there was justifiable complaint about its lack of inclusiveness as the international economy evolved and new economic players gained influence in the practical affairs of the international economy but not a weighted voice in its institutions. But the Bretton Woods system was not about the developing world, nor was it really about development. It was about creating the basis for stability and prosperity. In fact, its lasting legacy is the prosperity it offered that part of the world willing to accept it for the last fifty years.

The end of the cold war in 1990–91 was the end of an epoch, not simply a benchmark in geopolitics. That it closed as it did, in peaceful political and economic revolution, reflected the extent of the evolution of international politics and of the international economy. Nothing underscores that evolution better than the experience of the Soviet Union and its allies. The growth, sophistication, and penetration of an international market economy and its prosperity played a major role in the collapse of the Soviet bloc, just as much as the inherent flaws of their centrally planned economies had for decades progressively undermined the economic health of those states. The Soviets not only fell behind the First World; the Third World had begun to overtake them as well. The international economy had evolved beyond the ability of a socialist state saddled with a self-destructive economy to cope with it. The question we must now ask is whether that evolution has also moved beyond our own collective ability to instill the stability in the system necessary to ensure continued prosperity for all.

The international economy of 1994 is healthier than that of 1944. Quantitatively, it is a far larger economy, yet it is qualitatively different as well, far more complicated and resistant to meddling for good or ill. The most important changes are the growth in influence of the developing world in the international economy, reflected in the rise of new economic powers among their ranks, and fundamental changes in the structures of the international economy itself. Each poses new challenges.

The developing world now accounts for nearly half of the world's production and in many cases enjoys sizable growth rates. The economic performance of some of these countries now rivals or surpasses older economic powers. Yet the economic growth of the past half-century has been uneven, and the very success of Bretton Woods and of the developing world has deepened international divisions over debt, wealth, pollution, migration, resource exploitation, and economic weight. There are challenges to the existing economic order and calls for a new one. As the players in the international economy become more heterogeneous and the stakes higher, a more pronounced lack of consensus will grow and make it harder to reach essential decisions. Uneven development may also lead to new regional tensions, and greater potential for domestic and international political instability, especially among vulnerable economies experimenting with market principles for the first time. Once again, the link between global prosperity and security should merit the attention of policy makers, along with the still poorly comprehended truth that long-term prosperity for one nation relies more than ever on the prosperity of all.

The structural changes in the international economy reinforce the importance of grappling with economic interconnectedness. There is no longer a single dominant economy, and even the top economies no longer can exert the influence they once could. We have witnessed the evolution of the international economy into a more global economy, one less bound by nations and by the controls of states. This is more than a difference of semantics. Politically, states still exist, with governments that can enter into agreements on their behalf, but the influence of those governments over their own economies has become more limited and uncertain. A gap has arisen between an international economy and national trade and monetary policy. Economic developments move faster than an individual government's ability to react, and market forces quickly outrun their policy decisions. Governments must now struggle just to catch up with international private finance and the rapid shifts of world capital, the influence of which is felt but only poorly understood or counterbalanced. Even the terminology of international trade is misleading. States do not trade, companies do, and now those companies often "trade" within themselves, subsidiary to subsidiary, their national allegiance one of convenience, blurring notions of import and export.

Some would say that this growing importance of market forces in pushing the global economy should rightly mean the withering away of international regimes aimed at managing them, but never has there been greater need to watch over the economy. The fragility of new market economies, of new, elaborate financial structures, and the deprivation and poverty an economic breakdown would entail are too important, too explosive, to be left simply to market forces. We need to look for greater stability and predictability to ensure wider, deeper, and long-lasting prosperity. We cannot return to Bretton Woods for stability as a system, but we can take a cue from its objectives and methods as we search for new approaches.

As in the 1940s, we must identify what we really must accomplish, not simply what we wish to accomplish. We should concentrate on the essential requirements for anchoring and fostering prosperity. Again, our predecessors were on the right track. Franklin Roosevelt's message to the delegates to the Bretton Woods Conference underscored that a stable monetary regime is the central tenet of economic prosperity: it provides the predictability that commerce requires. It also offers the control that central banks and their governments need to manage policy. But is a regime possible that can bridge the gap between a dozen or so influential national economic policies and an international economy far greater than their sum? How can we hope to construct new institutions if we cannot address all the variables with which they must grapple?

Our experience with the League of Nations taught us that for an international institution to work, the players that matter in the world must be part of it. For any revised monetary system or economic arrangement we devise to function, it must include all the influential economic players; this may now mean broadening our notion of how we fashion our international institutions beyond simply governments. What are the real economic powers at work and how can we bring them into better harmony of purpose and influence? If the private sector now exerts such influence, can we develop international institutions to include them?

Although we are not economists, we might offer some general ideas on the direction we might take. We clearly need some kind of monetary system with flexible target zones, working with an institutionalized coordination of domestic economic policies among the major economic powers, in consultation with rising powers. Presently, the Group of Seven (G–7) attempts to address monetary misalignments, but theirs is at best an improvised approach. Instead we should institutionalize a sort of concert of great economic powers, a body with defined membership requirements which, unlike the Security Council, would necessarily alter as long-term national economic influences rise or fall. We could also use a substantial deliberative and consultative body, comprising both senior state or government representatives as well as senior outside, private-sector advisers from finance and industry. Their purpose would be to function as an economic "cabinet," to consult, cooperate, coordinate, and advise but not to attempt to manage or regulate what they cannot and should not.

A great deal of what must be done relies on collective action, itself based upon cooperation and above all a sense of common purpose. These are intangibles which require skilled and informed diplomacy, consensus building, and strong and able leadership. We cannot negotiate goodwill; it must be inspired and instilled in a common sense of necessity. We are not yet at the point that we might hope for the inclusive universal institutions we need. We lack the international political will, a common agreement between developing and developed economies upon the rules and structures, and the expertise to bring nongovernmental institutions and players into a truly universal system. However, we do have the essentials for less ambitious and truly useful interim institutions.

For the short term, we should improve the instruments we have and use them well. For the most practical reasons, our international economic institutions should become better representative of the economic powers that be. We might also combine their activities under a more central authority to expedite and streamline their interfunctional coordination. Presently the International Monetary Fund (IMF), the General Agreement on Tariffs and Trade (GATT), and the G–7 operate only marginally cooperatively. In addition, future international negotiations should focus less on tariffs and quotas and begin to coordinate domestic economic policies and laws. We should also reinforce regional and other free-trade arrangements to encourage true nondiversionary practices. These arrangements perform an overlooked service, that of experimentation with new structures and policies. They are therefore laboratories, or works in progress. Furthermore, regional arrangements such as the European Union allow the possibility of regional central banks, with greater influence or control over monetary issues in concert. Taken together, these all are steps toward practical, more universal economic arrangements.

We must also keep in mind the underlying problem which our planning for stability and prosperity is meant to address, one etched in the minds of those at the 1944 conference: the international security which economic stability and prosperity affords. Past discussion of strategic security planning has been couched largely in terms of the preservation of the political and territorial independence of individual states. Political and territorial independence is, of course, closely tied to economic independence, and the economic independence we still too often take for granted has often eroded as many states find themselves closely tied to neighbors and even distant partners. While many point to the idea of economic interdependence as part of the foundation for international peace and stability, we should remember that it is no guarantee of peace. According to the wisdom of the era, economic interdependence should have prevented World War I; it did not. In an era of increasing interconnectedness, economic disaster for a few means catastrophe for all, and with it the threat of war. We must include more consciously in our security plans the economic security of nations, and begin to think in terms of economic strategies designed to preserve the long-term economic well-being of the people whom economies serve—not merely the machinery of economies themselves.

In the end, however, we should be wary of an attempt to engineer and manage in detail the form and substance of any international economic order. Just as the numerous attempts at social engineering have failed—in the Soviet Union as well as in the West—detailed economic engineering cannot hope to succeed. Our objective should be first and foremost to facilitate, not regulate; we should assume something more like the functions of a watchman, not a policeman. Economics is a social science, inexact and at best a mix of educated guessing and weather predictions. Above all, we should avoid making the most common mistake, losing sight of our purpose: to strengthen the basis for truly international prosperity and the hope for lasting peace.

16

Challenges and Opportunities
for the World Bank

Barend A. de Vries

Introduction

As it approaches the twenty-first century, the World Bank can look back on decades of often rapid change and a process of steady adaptation to new problems. It now faces many challenges at present and ahead. Three of the most important challenges for the Bank are:

1) **Widespread poverty**. More than fifty countries have poverty rates ranging from 25 to 50 percent, and more than one billion people subsist in deepest poverty with per-capita incomes of less than a dollar per day.
2) **The environment**. The environment opens up an entirely new range of opportunities. There is widespread clamor, particularly from nongovernmental organizations (NGOs), that the Bank pay more attention to environmental degradation. Traditional Bank projects such as electric power generation, dams, and roads have direct consequences for the environment and require special review for their impact. Fortunately, the Bank is well suited to deal with many environmental phenomena that reach across national boundaries.
3) **The transition from socialism to democratic and free-market economies**. The transition from socialism to democratic and free-market economies going on in Eastern Europe (EE) and the former Soviet Union (FSU) has opened up an entirely new area for applying the kind of policy advice and investment lending that the Bank has been extending elsewhere, for

example, the reform and establishment of market-related financial institutions, infrastructure investment, and the rehabilitation and restructuring of large manufacturing enterprises.

These three areas are linked in many ways. Poverty reaches well beyond the borders of the poorest countries into many that have made progress in policy reform and attract substantial new private capital and now experience strong economic growth. At the same time poverty is a major cause of environmental degradation, which itself impinges most on the poorest groups in society. Poverty is an issue in many regions of the EE–FSU countries, and in the absence of effective safety nets is aggravated by the ongoing transition to a market economy. In the rehabilitation of these countries, improvement in environmental conditions must be an essential component of policy reform.

In addition to the demands from these three areas, the World Bank must meet a number of other claims on its resources: the reconstruction and recovery of the many countries that have been hit by revolution, ethnic strife, and destruction, especially in Africa; the reconstruction of the formerly Israeli-occupied territories of Palestine; the building of a new postapartheid economy in South Africa; and, of course, the many ongoing demands from programs in Brazil, China, India, and elsewhere.

Fighting Poverty

The World Bank faces an increasing urgency in stepping up antipoverty lending, including loans for improving basic conditions through strengthening primary education, sanitation, health, and nutrition, and lowering population growth. After almost fifty years of Bank operations, the number of people living in deep poverty, with per-capita incomes of less than a dollar per day, continues to be more than one billion. Many countries suffer poverty rates between 25 and 50 percent of their populations. Deep poverty has continued in part because of high population-growth rates, especially in Africa and some parts of the Middle East. Poverty rates increased in the decade of the 1980s under the adverse impact of the debt crisis and of adjustment in some countries, especially in Africa. Poverty conditions have persisted even though there have been important improvements in critical social indicators such as life expectancy, infant mortality, access to safe water, primary school enrollment, and immunization. Even where poverty rates have remained constant, infant mortality has gone down because of greater access to health services, while more children are attending primary school because of the spread of free public education.[1]

The Bank's structural adjustment lending in the 1980s was designed to help middle-income countries reform their policies to overcome adverse conditions in the world economy and instability at home. In many of the poorest countries, especially in Africa, structural adjustment programs did not work as well because these countries lacked the institutional capacity for policy reform and did not have sufficient supply response. Moreover, in most countries the poor, especially in urban areas, suffered from cutbacks in social expenditures and from increases in prices of food and of imports as subsidies were removed and exchange rates set at more realistic levels.

With structural adjustment lending pointing to an aggravation of poverty conditions in some recipient countries, the Bank sharpened its attention to poverty issues. The 1990 *World Development Report*[2] was entirely dedicated to a new poverty reduction effort that became the focus of operations. Staff started to undertake country-by-country poverty assessments to ascertain the who, where, and why of poverty; to identify the need for strengthening the database; and to lay the groundwork for policy discussions with governments. An increasing proportion of lending is now dedicated to fighting poverty directly. At the same time, structural adjustment loans were redesigned to make sure they would not affect the poor adversely, and some loans were made to improve the delivery of social services to the poorest population groups (e.g., the 1994 loan to Zambia). In the two years ending June 1993, half of adjustment operations paid explicit attention in one way or another to poverty issues.[3]

The Bank's poverty assessments assemble data that are essential to a dialogue on poverty issues confronting the countries concerned. They identify, from the vantage point of their impact on the poor, shortcomings in policy, planning, sector priorities, investments, and the delivery of social services. They consider the impact of long-term economic management on the ability of the poor to build up assets as well as the effects of short-term economic measures, inflation, and cuts in public expenditures.

The Bank's new poverty initiative was associated with more intense attention to women in development under the guidance of President Barber Conable (1986–91). Women suffer the brunt of poverty. Development policies have to explicitly address the need for improving the condition of women. The Bank has given greater attention to the education of women, a crucial element in reducing population growth, and a higher proportion of loans for human resource development address women's issues.[4]

The Bank's lending operations were guided in part by a program of targeted interventions, loans with the primary objective of poverty reduction through basic education, productivity of small farmers, basic health conditions, sanitation, and water supply, especially for women and children, and basic infrastructure in regions of concentrated poverty. Loans in this category amounted to one-fourth of total investment lending in 1992 and 1993. Moreover, the Bank's lending for human resource development—education, health, family planning, and nutrition—has tripled since the early 1980s and is now 15 percent of the total.

It is clear, moreover, that the sharpened focus on poverty issues is an integral part of the Bank's advice on overall development policies. In his keynote address to the Bank's 1994 Annual Conference on Development Economics, Michael Bruno tied together three critical elements in basic development policy:

1) Attainment of sustained average per capita growth is a necessary condition for sustained reduction in poverty.
2) Implementation of an adjustment package of policy reform is a necessary condition for sustained per capita growth.
3) Fiscal and monetary restraint is a necessary condition for adjustment.

But these necessary conditions are not sufficient. Growth must be combined with direct policies targeted on improving conditions of the poor. At the same time, antipoverty policies require an increase in public resources for the financing of various measures.

The Bottom Line Is People

The World Bank can intensify and broaden the fight against poverty and provide global leadership in this endeavor. To do so will require policy change in at least two areas: it must give its staff more opportunity to concentrate on situations in individual countries so it can be more in tune with the social and cultural diversity of these countries; and it must formulate a coherent overall *strategy for poverty eradication*. In addition, the Bank will need to mobilize adequate resources for an expanded antipoverty program which must necessarily compete with claims from other important programs such as those discussed below.[5]

Dedicate Staff Resources to Fighting Poverty

To be effective in assisting individual countries in their fight against poverty, Bank staff must have intimate knowledge of these countries' culture, institutions, politics, and social fabric as well as the economic and technical ramifications of an antipoverty program. Staff may have to spend considerable time, even years, working on individual countries or regions to attain an adequate level of knowledge and experience.

But present Bank personnel management is de facto opposed to staff gaining adequate familiarity with a country. After three years staff is encouraged to rotate and "move on" if it is to move "up the ladder." Movement is in the interest of managerial efficiency.

If the Bank is to be serious about fighting poverty in many diverse country situations (or even diverse regions within individual countries), it will have to change its personnel management policy. It must encourage interested staff to stay put and to attain the familiarity that is needed for fighting poverty in ways suitable to the social and economic circumstances and conditions of individual countries. More generally, this is also an essential condition for obtaining local participation in project and program preparation and execution.

At present the Bank's poverty assessments are technically competent reports. But they are highly standardized and do not allow for countries' cultural and social characteristics. In fact, the reports read as if the subject matter were a faraway community; it could be on a distant planet, where one must approximate reality in an abstract manner. That must change if the Bank is to put flesh on its skeleton models and reach genuine undertakings with the countries concerned and see them make the social, political, economic, and financial commitments necessary for effective action.

Toward an Antipoverty Strategy

The World Bank has undertaken a competent and professional job, starting with the 1990 *World Development Report*, of studying the dimensions of poverty, indicating basic measures to overcome it, mapping out different policy options, instructing staff how to proceed, and laying the base for dialogue with member countries. But all this does not add up to an overall strategy. So far the Bank has refrained from formulating such a strategy.

The Bank has the tools to formulate an overall strategy which can give the world a new vision of what can and cannot be accomplished and enable the Bank to provide badly needed leadership in this area. An overall strategy would as a minimum have the following elements:

1) Set forth the objective of eradicating poverty in different types of developing countries as well as those now in transition in Eastern Europe and the states of the former Soviet Union.

2) Specify the policies needed to reach this objective: (a) by the countries themselves; (b) by the international community, including financial assistance for country programs and investments for overcoming poverty, and associated operations in related areas such as environmental programs of particular interest to the poor; and (c) by the industrial countries, particularly in areas of trade of special interest to poverty eradication.

3) Clarify the time frame in which the Bank expects the recipient countries, the industrial countries, and the international community to work.

4) Indicate the resources and sacrifices required to reach the objective, on the part of the countries taking action, and in capital, financial, and technical resources on the part of the World Bank, other lenders, and bilateral donors.

5) Present regular *performance progress reports* on what lenders, industrial countries, and the international community are doing, and on what progress is being achieved in poverty eradication. These reports would assess the performance of Bank and non-Bank programs. They would do for the poverty eradication program what the Wapenhans report expects the Bank to do on the impact of projects that have been completed, and what the Bank is currently planning to do on performance-underadjustment lending.

Given the comprehensive nature of continuous performance stock taking in poverty eradication, the Bank also may want to obtain cooperation from other institutions, but it is important that it provide the essential leadership in this effort which so clearly falls in its domain.

An effective antipoverty strategy brings into play both macroeconomic and microeconomic policies, savings and investment priorities and design, and pricing and incentive policies. Moreover, the effort must extend to a wide variety of sectors.

Environmental Policies

Closely related to a global antipoverty effort is the increased attention now given to environmental issues. Parallel with its poverty reduction program, since 1988 the World Bank has organized itself for a more responsible role on environmental questions. It has sought to become in tune with a growing worldwide gain in ecological awareness, which in the view of many must be supported by specific programs and initiatives (see Annex 2). Its 1992 *World Development Report* was devoted to the environment, and served as background material for the Rio Earth Summit.

Explicit attention to environmental issues opens a new window on antipoverty action. The poor suffer most from environmental degradation, unclean water, and indoor air pollution. Environmental degradation depresses the poor's income by diverting more time to routine tasks (e.g., collecting firewood) and lowering productivity of natural resources. The poor cannot afford to make investments in natural resources (e.g., soil conservation) that produce long-term results. To the contrary, they will tend to overuse resources, as for example the overgrazing of lands in Africa. In Bangladesh, the poor have deforested the land, which in turn has become more prone to flooding.

The Bank came late to helping improve environmental policies and integrating its operations with pro-environment activities. It still has a long way to go. Although many environmental economists and some more general economists (like Kenneth Boulding and Herman Daly) have been aware for decades of the shortcomings of conventional economics, until recently they had little impact on the economic analysis used in the World Bank or in other lending institutions. Likewise the 1987 edition of the widely used text *Economics of Development,* by Malcolm Gillis et al., makes no mention of environmental factors.[6]

Once environmental considerations are given explicit recognition, no strand of conventional economic reasoning is left untouched. For example, exports from Indonesia or Côte d'Ivoire of tropical hardwood logs that take centuries to grow must make allowance for depreciation of natural resources. The foreign exchange earned from such exports is not the net gain assumed in conventional economics. Similarly if higher economic growth causes a deterioration of health conditions, the cost of the latter must be deducted from the benefits of the former. Capacity to produce goods depends not only on manmade capital, as conventionally assumed, but on natural and human capital as well. Net capital accumulation must therefore reflect the change in stocks of both manmade and other capital. More generally the greening of the national accounts means they must be adjusted downward. They must allow for resource depletion and for the monetary cost of degradation; these two adjustments alone add up to 13 percent of net domestic product in Mexico.[7]

In addition to making explicit allowance for the causes and consequences of environmental degradation, environmental policies can be linked directly with antipoverty measures. For example, distribution of food during periods of drought can help avoid the overuse of natural resources.

The Bank has now begun to introduce the concept of sustainable development into its operations (although few environmentalists will be fully satisfied with the work of an institution as complex, diverse, and large as the World Bank). The Bank's environmental activities cut across many sectors, including electric power generation and distribution and agriculture. As a global institution it is well suited to deal with problems of a cross-border nature. It is administering a global environmental facility and is managing several environmental programs (e.g., for the Mediterranean Sea, the Black Sea, the Baltic Sea, and the Danube River basin). For individual borrowing countries it is formulating environmental action plans that lay the basis for discussions about countries' environmental policies. And in the year ending June 1993 it lent $2 billion for twenty-four projects with a primarily environmental objective (i.e., projects with over 50 percent environmental costs or benefits).

Looking Ahead

On the road ahead the World Bank will have to meet many challenges, some of which it has already begun to tackle, including:

1) rewriting the economics of development with explicit allowance for environmental effects, and testing it out in project and policy analysis, country and trade analysis, etc.;
2) building environmental considerations into poverty assessments and dialogue;
3) reaching agreements with governments on environmental policies and investments, and building these into the lending process;
4) reviewing all lending (project as well as sector) for its environmental impact;
5) redesigning the present lending program with an expanded environmental component;
6) expanding lending with the explicit purpose of environmental protection (e.g., the reduction of indoor and outdoor air pollution, the treatment of industrial waste, and the application of new industrial designs);

7) giving special emphasis to environmental projects with an international character and those that are justified on the basis of cross-border effects (e.g., the salvation of the Amazonian rain forest);

8) pursuing with persistence, and seeking to implement (where appropriate with new lending), programs that require action over periods of several years, the completion of various large-scale projects (e.g., the Baltic Sea, the Mediterranean Sea, the Black Sea, and the Danube River basin projects), and the restoration of a sane environment in Eastern Europe and the former Soviet Union.

The Transition from Socialism to Free-Market Economies

The countries of Eastern Europe (EE) and the former Soviet Union (FSU) are in various stages of transition from socialist command to more market-oriented economies. The different degrees of progress they have made so far depend in large part on the nature of the initial disequilibrium in which they found themselves at the start of the transition; the power of various entities in the system, especially the labor unions; and the forthrightness of the new policies, in particular the extent to which they used the opportunity offered by the first flush of political freedom. All these countries are bound to experience severe setbacks as they proceed and learn that each stage of the process brings painful change.

The transition entails stabilization and liberalization combined with restructuring. Stabilization of the balance of payments, the finances of the dominant state sector, and the price level has followed, in practice, different courses. In some countries it has been more orthodox in that all variables are initially set free, while in more heterodox situations some variables like wages or the exchange rate are initially pegged. Pegging wages gives state enterprises some breathing space in becoming profitable. Private-sector development has in many countries become part of the stabilization package of policies. Liberalization consists of freeing prices and abolishing controls: prices are moved to new, more rational relationships in tune with levels prevailing in world markets. Stabilization and liberalization usually go hand in hand, although in the past some Western countries have been able to proceed with liberalization without having reached even a reasonable degree of stabilization. All economies face the problem of shrinking the public sector and increasing the role of private enterprise. State budgets are swollen by massive state intervention and subsidies of all kinds. Societies must learn new rules and behavioral attitudes compatible with the free market and private ownership.

At the core of restructuring is the overhaul of the often monstrous state enterprise. The level and composition of its production were set by the master plan, not by the market. Its production mix, quality, and size may be totally out of tune with the realities of the marketplace. Yet it is a major provider of employment and a critical element in countries' safety nets. Many of them have educational facilities for their employees and their families, hospitals, and child care centers, etc. Many of the state enterprises operate at a loss, which, financed by the state budget, is at the root of the government deficit.[8] Because enterprise restructuring is a time-consuming process, stabilization that hinges on the financial viability of state enterprises is bound to stretch over a period of years.

In brief the major tasks are:

1) stabilization, a process that involves painful steps, especially in budget and balance-of-payments finance, a process which must be supported by external assistance;

2) liberalization, a process of freeing prices from controls that most countries have initiated in one drastic step—the "Big Bang";

3) restructuring, especially of state enterprises, a complex process of establishing financial autonomy without reliance on government support, accommodating to market prices of inputs and outputs, modernizing technology, and increasing the productivity of workers (many Western advisers urge that state enterprises be privatized all at once or at least as rapidly as possible, another element of the "Big Bang");

4) introduction of private ownership in agriculture, manufacturing, and trade, a process that entails a wide range of legal measures as well as fundamental change in personal attitude and behavior;

5) establishment of a market-oriented financial system with commercial and investment banks that can mobilize capital and provide various forms of credit and equity for large and small enterprises. (The socialist system did not have a financial sector with different types of banks and a supporting and supervising central bank as is known in the West, and in particular it did not give a governing role to a market-related interest rate. One hopes that the emerging banking system will be able to provide resources to manufacturing enterprises. In practice so far, the banks in most EE countries are draining resources from the enterprise sector, quite contrary to the positive assistance they are giving in China. In practice, reform of the financial sector is difficult in the absence of progress of reform of the enterprise sector.)

There is wide agreement among outside advisers that the best way to proceed is by the "Big Bang," to take all steps at once and especially to do as much as possible at the start of the process. They also argue in favor of all-out privatization. That does not mean that all economists, particular some who are familiar with local conditions, agree on the efficacy of this method. Some countries, like China, have gone forward in a more gradual manner (see Annex 3). The argument in favor of the all-out approach, especially to privatization, is that the state enterprise sector is so dominant that it can simply not be tackled in a step-by-step manner. Nevertheless, one has to face up to the questions: who will be the new owners and managers, what financial and technical assistance is available, and what is the experience of countries that have followed a more gradualist approach?

In assisting the transition in EE and the FSU the World Bank may best concentrate on areas where it has built up expertise over the years and that need urgent attention. For example:

1) Reconstruction of infrastructure (e.g., transportation, electric power, and water supply), which in many countries has become rundown and fallen behind modern standards.

2) Restructuring of state enterprises. This requires the combination of engineering, economic, and financial skills the Bank has used in its operations elsewhere. Restructuring is at the heart of the stabilization process. Stabilization cannot prevail without putting state enterprises on a financially autonomous footing. Both stabilization and restructuring are preconditions for the start of foreign private investment. Restructuring of state enterprises is also crucial for improvement in labor productivity.

3) Financial sector reform, including the establishment of new banking institutions capable of operating in a free-market environment and assisting both large and small enterprises in agriculture and manufacturing, and technical assistance to existing financial institutions that must adapt themselves to the new environment. In this endeavor the World Bank would draw on its experience of helping to organize, over four decades, hundreds of development finance companies that mobilize long-term credit and equity capital for both small and medium-sized enterprises, as well as on in-depth studies of the financial sector of numerous countries.

4) Technical assistance to improve productivity and introduce up-to-date technology in agriculture and industry, and to improve the allocation of investment resources in the public sector.

5) Coordination and mobilization of medium- and long-term finance, mostly from official sources, based on economic, financial, and technical studies prepared by the Bank. (In June 1994 alone, the World Bank hosted coordinating meetings for four EE and FSU countries [Turkmenistan, Kyrkys Republic, Romania, and Bulgaria]; these meetings followed many others for countries in this region.)

In parallel with the World Bank the affiliated International Finance Corporation can provide assistance to private companies and private financial institutions.

One would hope that the technical and financial assistance of the kind described will not be displaced by a claim on World Bank resources for substantial amounts of balance-of-payments assistance. In any case, the World Bank is normally able to provide only limited amounts of balance-of-payments assistance. As described earlier, this kind of assistance has been linked with structural and sector-adjustment lending, and in the case of EE/FSU countries it has been associated with the modernization of the agricultural sector and the institution of a social safety net. Lending of this kind usually does not exceed 25 percent of the total. Some have argued the case for much larger stabilization assistance to the Russian Federation and other countries than they have been able to obtain. In this line of reasoning the "Big Bang" must be fed by Big Bucks.[9] Whatever its merits and prospects, the provision of such stabilization aid has not been a central function of the World Bank, and is unlikely to be in the EE/FSU countries.

The Bank's assistance to China's transition to a free-market economy teaches some lessons as to what it may be able to do for the EE/FSU countries. China has followed a more gradualist and partial approach to the transition and has not embraced political freedom. Yet it has provided a base for substantial World Bank assistance, a total of $9.2 billion until June 1993, of which $3.2 billion was in 1993 alone. The composition of lending in 1993 shows the many areas in which the World Bank has been able to assist China: water supply; agriculture (infrastructure, flood control, improvement of productivity in poor regions, institutions); development banking; education (equipment for middle schools); transportation (highways, railroads, ports); electric power generation; industry (water pollution control); and technical assistance (for the Ministry of Finance, central bank, and other institutions engaged in reform and some in environmental protection).

Mobilizing Adequate Financial Resources

As the three major programs discussed—poverty eradication, environmental protection, and transition to a market economy in Eastern Europe and the former Soviet Union—build up, the World Bank may need to increase lending by both the International Bank for Reconstruction and Development (IBRD) and the International Development Association (IDA). If the Bank is to give essential leadership in these three areas, it must be able to provide substantial resources, both financial and technical.

From the viewpoint of poverty eradication, this program will have to compete for resources with other important programs such as the reconstruction and rehabilitation of states in transition from socialism; environmental and infrastructure lending; continued major programs in China, India, Latin America, and the Middle East; special new programs in the former Israeli-occupied territories, South Africa, and hopefully soon the republics of the former Yugoslavia Federation; and the salvation of the Amazonian rain forest. Moreover, poverty eradication will become more ambitious; for example, it will have to extend to countries which, though they have successfully followed policies of stabilization and adjustment, still have regions with deep-seated poverty. These countries have a greatly strengthened economic and financial base for fighting remaining poverty and, moreover, attract substantial amounts of private capital. But private capital does not deal with Chiapas in Mexico and regions of concentrated poverty in Thailand and Venezuela, not to speak of countries like Brazil that until recently lagged in adjustment. The Bank will have to extend its poverty lending to countries like these if it is to lead a truly comprehensive antipoverty effort. In this respect, the antipoverty program should extend well beyond assistance to the poorest countries.[10]

It is reasonable to assume that the Bank will be able to mobilize the resources necessary to undertake a more ambitious antipoverty program, and that it will get cooperation from other lenders, both multilateral and bilateral, for this and other programs. Many countries that are creditworthy for IBRD loans are also candidates for antipoverty assistance, both technical and financial. Most lending to countries in EE and the FSU will be on the terms of IBRD loans. And in countries where poverty rates are in the upper ranges, continued IDA financing will be necessary. In the end, many parties will have to collaborate if the global community is to create a realistic poverty eradication program, stem the tide of environmental destruction, and promote a successful transition for the EE/FSU countries.

Summing Up: The Major Challenges

The World Bank has equipped itself, financially and technically, to contribute to economic remedies needed by the countries in development or transition. They themselves must provide political, social, and cultural cohesion. For its part, the Bank must maintain its financial strength so it can be flexible and respond to continuously changing circumstances.

In carrying out its job, the Bank faces many—sometimes opposing—pressures. For example, some argue that the Bank must retrench and leave more room for private capital.[11] Two comments can be made with respect to this view. First, the Bank has always regarded the promotion of private capital flows and the private sector as one of its major functions. To further this objective, it has set up many new institutions, starting with the International Finance Corporation (IFC) in 1956, the International Center for the Settlement of Investment Disputes (ICSID), and the Multilateral Investment Guarantee Agency (MIGA). It has devised special forms of lending to accommodate and promote private investment, stimulated the establishment of locally organized development banks, and cofinanced with private credit. In addition, it has helped reform or rehabilitate the financial sector and organized local capital markets. The Bank's assistance to essential domestic infrastructure also has been a means of supporting private activities.

Second, even though private capital flows have greatly increased, they still must be supplemented by public capital. For example, Mexico benefited greatly from the boom in private foreign direct investment, but that did not prevent the outbreak of hostile discontent in Chiapas. Private capital does not deal with the deepest pockets of poverty; it barely finances essential education and health; and it skimps on critical environmental investments and essential highways and feeder roads. Further, where private capital does enter into high-priority investments, such as restructuring state enterprises, private investors often welcome the World Bank or IFC as a partner.

On another front, some nongovernmental organizations (NGOs) have criticized the Bank for harming or ignoring the environment; shunning participation from local populations; ignoring outside complaints; etc. NGOs are the new players in the field, and some have become positively harmful: they do not hesitate to obstruct the mobilization of funds for the neediest countries through the IDA. In fact, some NGO representatives proudly admit that they are paid to obstruct the Bank.

For its part, the Bank has made an impressive number of policy or organizational changes in the last seven or eight years. As a result it has become a very different institution from what it was before. A few of these changes include:

1) an in-depth look at the effectiveness of its own operations and a renewed realization that quality of lending is more important than quantity;
2) the start-up of environmental work under a new vice presidency of sustainable development;
3) a new focus on fighting poverty and special attention to women in development;
4) a requirement that all projects actively seek local participation;
5) the institution of an inspection panel, and further widening of its policy of informing the public by opening public information centers and publication of project documents.

Moreover, human resource development, including population policy, is now the fastest-growing category of loans.

Some of the most compelling challenges facing the Bank today may be summarized as follows:

1) Developing strong and imaginative leadership. The complex nature of World Bank operations calls for strong presidential leadership, supported by capable senior staff. In the past, the Bank has always had the benefit of highly experienced presidents. This is even more necessary today as the Bank faces major challenges in a rapidly changing external environment.
2) Sustaining the marked shift in lending to address essential issues of population, poverty, and environment (Bank operations have undergone a major shift in emphasis, and this trend is bound to accelerate and continue to be reflected in a continued shift in lending toward human resource development and environmental protection); yet at the same time continuing infrastructure and other conventional lending, especially to countries in transition and Africa, and continuing to supplement the development efforts of major countries such as Brazil, China, India, and Indonesia.

3) Continuing to build the private sector, and the role of foreign private capital, without weakening its own ability to respond to critical demands.

4) Maintaining its financial strength as a basis for new initiatives.

5) Providing leadership by focusing its research and its external positions on well-articulated issues as they arise; among others, helping define the issues now confronting countries as they are integrating into the global economy, and with considerable export success are now in a position to contribute to global leadership.

6) Continuing to act as a coordinator of external assistance where this proves useful and constructive; continuing its long-standing policy of assisting in the coordination of the activities of numerous other multilateral and bilateral aid agencies, which is now especially relevant in Africa and the countries in transition.

7) Actively supporting the process of trade liberalization by helping countries get ready for more liberal trade regimes, contributing to the analysis of the consequences of global trade liberalization, and designing and financing projects of special interest to the liberalization process.

8) Encouraging technological development and assisting countries to move up the ladder of product complexity in export development.

9) Working creatively with other agencies in the United Nations family and the regional development banks, and building on their respective strength.

10) In line with global change, restructuring internally and retrenching staff without weakening its ability to respond to critical demands.

11) Being proactive rather than reactive in dealing with its critics.[12]

In responding to these challenges the Bank will have to build on its strengths and achievements of the past, while continuing to build its capacity for innovation. There is no reason to assume that it cannot do that. In fact, taking a longer perspective, it is evident that over the years there has been a marked trend of continuity in Bank policies and approaches. This may, for example, be illustrated by the Bank's relations with Colombia. In the 1950s the Bank initiated a series of general survey missions which, staffed by various technicians able to review both economy-wide and sector-specific issues, identified development priorities and recommended actions and policies to address them, both with new investments and with essential administrative measures. The first of these missions was to Colombia, and under the able leadership of Laughlin Currie, led to the establishment of a national planning office, which has often been able to make an effective contribution to development policy. Without such planned attention to economy-wide issues, it would not have been possible to undertake a systematic review of public investment priorities in the early 1960s (when Colombia returned to democratic constitutional government), which in 1963 led to the establishment of the Bank's first consultative group for the coordination of external assistance.

After 1968 Bank President McNamara was able to build on and make more general the Bank's overall approach to the economy developed in the earlier years. He had the staff prepare and keep up to date country program papers. These papers specified for individual countries a broad range of social and economic problems and the Bank's plans for responding to these problems by various activities such as the nature and content of a continuing policy dialogue with the country, lending, technical assistance, and economic and sector studies. By this means McNamara set the stage not only for an increase in various Bank activities, but also for managing an increasingly complex set of operations in a global environment of greater diversity.[13]

Yet while there is ample evidence of the Bank's rising to new challenges and building on past initiatives and achievements, it cannot rest on its laurels. One must be keenly aware that the Bank has not always come through with appropriate action. This is clear for the minuscule role it played in the external debt crisis that dominated the development scene of the 1980s. In the 1960s Bank staff formulated new ways of analyzing the economics of external debt management. It also developed the essential quantitative techniques to dissect and project countries' debt problems. By 1980 the Bank had in hand a comprehensive set of country-by-country debt analyses, and it was aware of the possibilities of major problems ahead in the servicing of external debt. Yet when the crisis burst on the scene, the Bank did little to contribute to solutions and instead stood on the sidelines without providing the kind of assistance to debtor countries which it would have been eminently qualified and able to deliver. One can only hope that in the years ahead the Bank will be proactive in tackling emerging development issues for which it has been well prepared during many years of experience.

Annex 1
A Brief History of the World Bank's Attention to Poverty Conditions

As background for the Bank's current ability to fight poverty, it is useful to review briefly how it has dealt with poverty issues in the past, and in particular what effect its structural adjustment lending had on poverty in the 1980s.

In its early years the World Bank had an almost overwhelming concern with efficiency and sound investment and business practices. Its primary interest was to ensure that projects were well conceived, economically and financially viable, and operating on a businesslike basis. The Bank sought to establish itself as a financial institution recognized in the financial markets that had to absorb the Bank's bonds at a reasonable price.

But it is good to remember that the people who conceived of the Bank and wrote its initial charter were concerned with the welfare of individuals, their development and full employment. It is therefore no surprise that once it was well established as a financial institution in the 1960s, the Bank began to sharpen its focus on poverty conditions. Under the leadership of George Woods (1963–68) it initiated lending for education and sanitation and began the long journey of professionalizing the Bank's economic work. It continued during McNamara's management (1968–81), especially after his 1973 Nairobi speech which signaled the start of the Bank's involvement in battling rural poverty by helping small-scale agriculture. This was followed later by assistance for urban development, including housing, sewerage, and sanitation, combined with more intensive attention to urban employment. In these "new style" projects the Bank was prepared to take considerable risks. Subsequent evaluation has shown that these projects had often much smaller rates of return than more traditional projects in electric power generation and distribution and road transport. During this time the Bank also began broadening its analysis of projects by paying attention to the social value of inputs and outputs, thus allowing for poverty effects rather than efficiency alone. Under this method the labor cost of projects designed to provide jobs and absorb abundant low-skilled labor could be set at zero. The low social cost of such projects would make it easier for the Bank to justify less conventional lending.

In the 1980s the Bank once again put efficiency on the front burner while attention to poverty receded to the background. The debt crisis which dominated the development scene in the past decade brought a setback in growth and social development and worsened poverty conditions, particularly in Latin America. In the late 1970s the Bank began to increase nonproject lending to assist countries in adjusting their economies to the changes in the world economy brought about by the second oil price increase and the consequences of adverse terms of trade, high interest rates, and recession in the industrial countries. Structural adjustment loans are of special interest here because in many countries they were associated with an increase in poverty conditions.

Structural adjustment loans were designed to help countries overcome adverse conditions by providing quickly disbursed aid that helped smooth cuts in consumption and imports; promoting essential policy change to adjust to worsening external conditions; and overcoming domestic inflation and fiscal imbalance. The more important of the policies encouraged under adjustment loans were changes in real foreign exchange rates, introduction of more rational pricing and incentives for productive investment and labor-intensive manufacturing, and improved allocation of government resources, especially in public investment and state enterprises (by putting them on a self-financing footing so they would no longer be a drain on the government budget). These policies were to increase export earnings, to improve the internal terms of trade in favor of agriculture where most labor was employed, to free financial resources for private investment by reducing the government budget deficit, and to enhance the growth and efficiency of the economy.

In general, structural adjustment lending was most effective in countries that had an institutional framework for policy reform and a high degree of supply response. To allow for essential institutional changes, a much longer-term perspective was required in low-income countries, and in particular in sub-Saharan Africa, where growth declined, investment went down in relation to gross output, and inflation got worse regardless of whether the countries adopted adjustment policies. Social indicators (calorie intake, infant mortality, life expectancy, primary grade enrollment, etc.) in sub-Sahara showed no improvement in the 1980s.

Poverty eradication or even alleviation was not an initial objective of adjustment lending. But it turned out that the poor, especially in urban areas, suffered from the cutback in social expenditures and from the increase in prices of food and imports as subsidies were removed and exchange rates adjusted. Reduction in primary education outlays would have long-lasting effects. With contraction in the public sector, many civil servants were laid off and joined the ranks of the poor (e.g., in Senegal). The rural poor benefited from higher agricultural incomes and especially exports where small farmers are involved in export agriculture (e.g., Ghana) as against producing for the home market. But in many African countries, small and poor peasants are outside the export economy and the organized economy to which structural adjustment lending is addressed. By the late 1980s, and especially with the publication of the 1987 UNESCO report, "The Human Face of Adjustment," it became clear that structural adjustment entails a setback for the poor, not poverty eradication.

In view of the poverty issues identified in the course of implementing certain adjustment programs, the World Bank started to modify the design of these programs in the late 1980s. For example, subsidies can be reduced and producer prices raised in a more gradual manner. The consequences for budget expenditures may be compensated by selective increases in taxation, especially on the well-to-do. Social expenditures can be maintained when they have a disproportionate benefit for the poor (e.g., medical programs in Korea), or these expenditures are targeted on the poor where this is possible administratively (e.g., in Chile). Finally, some countries have undertaken compensatory programs, like small public works in Ghana, Bolivia, and Mexico, often with the help of external financing and NGOs. In Senegal retrenched civil servants have been retrained and relocated.

Annex 2
Toward Greater Ecological Awareness

The indiscriminate application of advances in science and technology has produced harmful long-term effects in industry and agriculture. This has led to the painful realization that we cannot interfere in one area of the ecosystem without paying due attention to the consequences of such interference in other areas and to the well-being of future generations.

The depletion of the ozone layer and the related "greenhouse effect" has now reached, in the view of many, crisis proportions as a consequence of industrial growth, massive urban concentrations, and vastly increased energy needs. Industrial waste, the burning of fossil fuels, unrestricted deforestation, the use of certain types of herbicides, coolants, and propellants—all of these are known to harm the atmosphere and environment. The resulting meteorological and atmospheric changes range from damage to health to the possible submersion of low-lying lands.

While in some cases the damage already done may well be irreversible, in many others it can still be halted. It is necessary that the entire human community—individuals, states, and international bodies like the World Bank—take seriously the responsibility that is theirs.

Delicate ecological balances are upset by the uncontrolled destruction of animal and plant life or by reckless exploitation of natural resources. All of this, even if carried out in the name of progress and well-being, is ultimately to mankind's disadvantage.

From the vantage point of the World Bank, it is noteworthy that in many cases the effects of ecological problems transcend national borders and their solution cannot be found solely at the national level. Existing international instruments will need to be adapted to the new tasks at hand. At the same time, the need for joint international action does not lessen the responsibility of individual countries. Within their own territories they must prevent the destruction of the atmosphere and biosphere and monitor, among other things, the impact of new technological and scientific advances.

The ecological crisis reveals the urgent moral need for a new solidarity in the relations between developing and industrial countries. Both groups of countries share responsibility for the promotion of a natural and social environment that is both peaceful and healthy. The newly industrializing countries cannot be asked to apply restrictive environmental standards that the industrial countries have not adopted within their own borders. At the same time, countries in the process of industrialization are not free to repeat the errors made in the past by others, and recklessly continue to damage the environment through industrial pollutants, radical deforestation, or unlimited exploitation of nonrenewable resources. In this context there is urgent need to find a solution to the treatment and disposal of toxic wastes.[14]

No plan or organization, however, will be able to effect the necessary changes unless world leaders are truly convinced of the absolute need of this new solidarity, which is demanded of them by the ecological crisis and which is essential for peace. This need presents new opportunities for strengthening cooperative and peaceful relations among countries.

Proper ecological balance will not be found without addressing the structural forms of poverty that exist throughout the world. Rural poverty and unjust land distribution in many countries have led to subsistence farming and to the exhaustion of the soil. Once their lands yield no more, many farmers move on to clear new land, thus accelerating uncontrolled deforestation, or they settle in urban centers which lack the infrastructure to receive them. Likewise, in some heavily indebted countries, the push for expanded export earnings has caused environmental degradation and aggravated existing ecological imbalances. In the face of such situations, it would be wrong to assign responsibility to the poor alone for the negative environmental consequences of their actions. Rather the poor, to whom the earth is entrusted no less than to others, must be enabled to find a way out of their poverty. And where their action is primarily justified by international effects, they should be compensated with special external help. (This is envisaged under the Global Environment Facility [GEF] set up under the auspices of the World Bank, the United Nations Development Program [UNDP], and the United Nations Environment Program [UNEP].)

In this spirit Vice President Al Gore has proposed broad international action to support both LDCs and the industrial countries in a global environmental endeavor.[15] He advocates a coordinated international effort aimed at realizing a number of strategic objectives:

1) stabilize world population;
2) create and develop environmentally appropriate technologies;
3) introduce and apply new global "eco-nomics," for example, economic measurements and criteria which allow for the environmental effect of economic activities and decisions;
4) negotiate and approve a new generation of international agreements that will embody institutional agreements for implementing a global environmental plan;
5) establish a cooperative plan for educating citizens about our global environment.

Annex 3
World Bank Assistance to the Transition in China

For over a decade the World Bank has assisted China in its transition to a market economy. The Bank's performance and experience in China provide some guide to what the Bank can do in EE/FSU countries. China has, of course, pursued a reform pattern that is quite different from the one currently advocated for Russia. In the case of manufacturing industries and state enterprises, Russia is following a top-down forced privatization. China has sought partial reform of state-owned enterprises; improved incentives in all sectors, including the state-owned; and encouraged institutional reform required for a more market-oriented economy. Private industry has grown, but still produces less than 10 percent of total output. Industries owned collectively by cities and regions have shown the most spectacular growth; they now account for 12 percent of total output. Output by state-owned enterprises has shrunk, but still accounts today for almost half of total industrial output. There has been no wholesale privatization like that currently practiced in Russia. Yet after fifteen years of partial reform, the Chinese economy is on the brink of a market system.[16]

As is well known, China has put in a spectacular economic performance, with average annual growth of 9 percent and export growth at 17 percent since 1978. Foreign direct investment is now increasing rapidly and reached $11 billion in 1992. However, in the next phase of reform, further restructuring of state-owned enterprises will have to shed much redundant labor and is critical to improving productivity. There are severe imbalances among regions and income groups, rapid changes in relative welfare, increasing environmental destruction, and periodic high inflation. The high growth rates have resulted primarily from high investment, not from rising productivity. In sum, China will have to address five key needs: macroeconomic stability, reform of inefficient state enterprises, improving basic infrastructure, environmental sustainability, and continued efforts to reduce poverty.[17]

China's broad effort to modernize production methods, to adapt existing enterprises to internationally more competitive standards, and to reform existing institutions so they can provide leadership in a market economy has laid the basis for substantial World Bank assistance. By June 1993 lending reached a total of $9.2 billion, of which $3.2 billion was in 1993 alone. The composition of lending in 1993 shows the many areas in which the World Bank has been able to assist China: water supply; agriculture (infrastructure, flood control, improvement of productivity in poor regions, institutions); development banking; education (equipment for middle schools); transportation (highways, railroads, ports); electric power generation; industry (water pollution control); and technical assistance (for the Ministry of Finance, central bank, and other institutions engaged in reform and some in environmental protection).

Notes

1. This said, there is considerable disparity among regions, with Africa lagging behind and the Pacific countries making rapid progress. The latter have had the benefit of strong economic growth associated with effective adjustment policies, slower population growth, and early and steady attention to basic education. See World Bank, *World Development Report 1992* (Washington, D.C.: World Bank, 1994).

2. *World Development Report 1990* (Washington, D.C.: World Bank, 1992).

3. *World Development Report 1992.*

4. See, for example, *World Bank Annual Report* (Washington, D.C.: World Bank, 1993), p. 44.

5. Barend A. de Vries, *Remaking the World Bank* (Washington, D.C.: The Seven Locks Press, 1987).

6. Malcolm Gillis, Dwight H. Perkins, Michael Roemer, and Donald R. Snoddgrass, *Economics of Development*, 2nd ed. (New York: W.W. Norton and Co., 1987).

7. Andrew Steer and Ernst Lutz, "Measuring Environmentally Sustainable Development," *Finance and Development* 30, no. 4 (December 1993).

8. See, for example, Leszek Balcerowicz and Alan Gelb, *Macropolicies in Transition to a Market Economy: A Three-Year Perspective* (Washington, D.C.: World Bank, 1994).

9. Jeffrey D. Sachs, *Russia's Struggle with Stabilization: Conceptual Issues and Evidence* (Washington, D.C.: World Bank, 1994).

10. Barend de Vries, *Remaking the World Bank*, chapter 5.

11. See, for example, Bretton Woods Commission, *Bretton Woods: Looking to the Future* (Washington, D.C.: Bretton Woods Committee, 1994), p. A-9.

12. See, for example, Katrina Brandon, "Environment and Development at the Bretton Woods Institutions," in *Bretton Woods: Looking to the Future*, pp. C-135–137.

13. See, for example, Barend de Vries, *Remaking the World Bank*, chapters 6 and 7.

14. John Paul II, "Peace with God the Creator, Peace with All of Creation" (1992).

15. Al Gore, *Earth in the Balance: Ecology and Human Spirit* (Boston: Houghton Mifflin, 1992), chapter 15.

16. Gary H. Jefferson and Thomas G. Rawski, *How Industrial Reform Worked in China: The Role of Innovation, Competition and Property Rights* (Washington, D.C.: World Bank, 1994), p. 35.

17. *World Bank News* (May 19, 1994).

17

Post–Uruguay Round Trade Policy for a Global Economy

Isaiah Frank

Introduction

The purpose of this chapter is to look beyond the Uruguay Round, to define key emerging issues of high priority for future U.S. trade policy, and to suggest courses of action on each.[1]

U.S. trade policy makers in the Clinton administration, preoccupied with the daunting problems of obtaining congressional approval of NAFTA and the Uruguay Round and dealing with the "Japan problem," have had little opportunity to consider the longer-term future of U.S. trade policy beyond the Uruguay Round. Yet, it is essential to begin public discussion of the new issues that have to be addressed globally as the world trading system approaches the end of the twentieth century.

These issues will have to be faced because the world does not stand still. More than a decade has passed since 1982 when the United States took the initiative to propose the agenda for an eighth round of GATT trade negotiations as a followup to the Tokyo Round that concluded in 1979. During that period, the pace of change in the nature and composition of international trade has accelerated. International trade no longer conforms to the textbook model of an exchange of British cloth for Portuguese wine. The specialization of national firms in particular products is being increasingly replaced by the globalization of production, in which different processes required for the production of individual goods and services are performed in different countries. An American automobile may be designed in Japan, assembled in Canada or Mexico, and consist of parts manufactured in Taiwan, Brazil, or just about anywhere.

Globalization, therefore, means increased trade in parts, components, and semi-finished goods. It also implies an increase in intrafirm trade as single global companies move components and partially finished goods from their facilities in one country to those in another. In short, the traditional horizontal pattern of trade in final products is being overtaken by a form of vertical trade in which countries specialize in different parts or stages of the production chain for individual products.

This globalization of production is made possible by two developments: the rapid advances in transportation and communications technology, which have enabled managers to coordinate widely dispersed activities; and the steady reduction of trade barriers under the aegis of GATT, which has made possible the movement of components and semifinished goods across national frontiers with a minimum of penalties in the form of tariffs or other restrictions.

Another major development in international trade is the rapid rise in the importance of trade in services. In addition to travel and transportation, it includes a wide range of other services such as advertising, accounting, finance, insurance, architecture, construction and engineering, education, medical, and many others. Between 1986 and 1992, U.S. exports of services more than doubled to $179 billion, or 41 percent of the value of U.S. merchandise exports in 1992. In contrast to trade in goods, the service sector has been generating sizable trade surpluses. The U.S. surplus in service trade in 1992 amounted to $56 billion, offsetting 58 percent of our merchandise trade deficit of $96 billion.[2] Many types of service exports cannot be provided effectively through cross-border exports but only through the establishment of a local presence in the foreign countries in which the service is provided. In the service sector, trade policy and investment policy converge.

What globalization implies, therefore, is the need to extend the horizon of international negotiations from the liberalization of strictly border measures, such as tariffs and quotas, to the coordination of various areas of domestic policy that substantially affect the ability of firms to conduct their operations worldwide. For example, it is difficult to conceive of a company producing parts of a complex product in different countries if each country were to accord widely different treatment to intellectual property rights or mandate sharply divergent technical standards. Nor is it conceivable that international trade in a wide variety of specialized services could flourish if firms were to encounter exclusionary business practices abroad or if they were to be subject to limitations on their right of establishment or discriminatory treatment as compared with domestic firms once they are established.

The sections that follow focus on several areas where the intersection of trade and domestic policies affects the ability of firms to compete effectively in the global market. Specifically highlighted are the main trade-related issues in competition policy, environment policy, and investment policy. Finally, the question is addressed of the extent to which future trade negotiations should proceed on a multilateral, regional, or other basis.

Trade and Competition Policy

The relationship between trade and competition policies has long been recognized both in principle and in the competition policies of the European Union and recent initiatives of the Organization for Economic Cooperation and Development (OECD). Trade policy regulates competition among firms across national boundaries; competition policy regulates competition among domestic firms. Since domestic anticompetitive practices of firms or governments can undermine trade policy agreements to foster fair competition, an open world-trading system may require international accords that harmonize competition policy among nations.

The most noteworthy bilateral consideration of competition policy in a trade-oriented context has been the talks between the United States and Japan under the structural impediments initiative (SII), begun in response to the difficulties American firms have faced in entering Japanese markets. The discussions on competition policy have focused on collusive behavior among Japanese firms affecting the ability of foreign firms to penetrate the Japanese market. Of particular concern have been the networks of affiliated firms known as "keiretsu," which engage in discriminatory and exclusionary practices. The SII talks have also included the adequacy of Japanese enforcement of antimonopoly laws; access of foreign firms to existing distribution channels and the right to establish new channels; and impediments to foreign investment.

The issues discussed in the SII talks illustrate types of domestic restrictive practices and regulations that affect foreign trade. But the reverse effect also exists—that is, widely practiced international trade policies can, in turn, foster noncompetitive behavior among domestic firms. One example is the gray-area practice of so-called voluntary export restraints (VERs). They force the foreign country to limit its exports of particular products and to allocate its national export quota among competing firms in the industry. To the extent that the allocative function is assigned to a private industry organization, it can encourage cartel-like practices of market-sharing and price-fixing. Fortunately, under the terms of the Uruguay Round agreement, VERs are required to be phased out over the next four to six years.

Another example of possible conflict between trade and competition policies is the rules applying to dumping. Dumping often reflects the ability of a firm to charge high prices and enjoy excessive profits at home, which in turn enables it to sell at lower prices abroad. This pricing power in the home market is generally due to protection from imports, cartel-like practices among domestic firms, or both. Getting rid of these conditions would make a major contribution toward undermining a company's ability to dump in foreign markets.

Both GATT and U.S. trade law permit an importing country to apply anti-dumping duties when material injury to domestic producers can be demonstrated as a result of a foreign company's exporting a product at prices lower than those charged in its home market. However, unlike the rules applying to foreign trade, U.S. law does not regard price discrimination between different domestic markets as constituting unfair competition per se. Rather, the test is whether the pricing policy is predatory—that is, intended to put competitors out of business. Under the Robinson-Patman antitrust law, "meeting competition" is a justification available to a defendant in a domestic price-discrimination suit. As anti-dumping actions have become the principal modern instrument of trade protection, this inconsistency in the treatment of price discrimination between foreign and domestic commerce urgently needs to be resolved.

All the major OECD countries have antitrust laws and policies reflecting each country's individual history and distinctive social and economic institutions and attitudes. However, there are basic elements that they share in common—e.g., the prohibition of cartels and cartel-like practices, such as the fixing of prices and the allocation of markets; and the surveillance of mergers and acquisitions. Where the countries differ is in the transparency of the systems of law and regulation and in matters such as principles of application—i.e., whether certain practices are illegal per se or are subject to a rule of reason. Differences also exist with respect to remedies and penalties as well as the scope of jurisdiction. Some countries apply their antitrust laws only to conduct occurring within their national territories, whereas others extend their jurisdiction to conduct abroad.

As a first order of business, agreed principles should be negotiated internationally as a basis for the adoption of more effective and convergent national competition laws and enforcement mechanisms. At a later stage, existing international trade rules would need to be examined, and modified if necessary, to remove inconsistencies with the agreed competition principles.

Because the industrial countries have the most advanced competition and trade regimes, the ongoing research and groundwork on competition policies have been carried on in the OECD. However, with the conclusion of the Uruguay Round and the reform and strengthening of GATT's institutional structure, the entire exercise should be transferred to GATT, where the developing countries and other nonmembers of the OECD would have an opportunity to participate in the preparation and negotiation of international principles on trade-related competition issues.

Another area of competition policy that has increasingly been the source of trade disputes is domestic subsidies. Recent examples include the struggle in the Uruguay Round over the European Union's subsidization of agriculture and U.S. objections to the subsidization of Airbus. These issues are difficult to address because, unlike export subsidies, domestic subsidies are recognized in GATT to be legitimate "instruments for the promotion of social and economic policy objectives." However, GATT also acknowledges that they may cause "serious prejudice to the interests of another signatory" and may therefore warrant countermeasures.

The domestic-subsidies issue is becoming more important in such areas as the development of high-technology industries that have significant domestic "spillover" benefits in terms of productivity growth and high-paid jobs. It has been suggested, therefore, that the United States should itself adopt preferential treatment, subsidies, and/or trade restrictions to promote the development of these industries.

An effort to resolve the subsidy issue was made in the Uruguay Round. The result is a definition of "traffic light" categories: red (prohibited subsidies); yellow (permissible subsidies which are actionable multilaterally and countervailable unilaterally if they cause adverse trade effects); and green (nonactionable and noncountervailable subsidies provided they are structured according to criteria intended to limit their potential for trade distortion).

Subsidies for industrial research are included in the permissible or nonactionable category if they are limited to 75 percent for basic research and 50 percent for applied research. Rather than restricting the use of subsidies, this provision opens it up and, given the latitude for interpretation, is potentially a source of increased conflict. Fortunately, there is a sunset clause in the Uruguay Round agreement which calls for the automatic expiration of the provisions on industrial research subsidies after five years unless it is decided to continue them in current or modified form.

Included in the prohibited subsidies category are export subsidies. However, nothing was done in the Uruguay Round to alter the exclusion of concessional export financing from GATT's jurisdiction. At present, subsidization by export financing agencies falls within the purview of the OECD, where repeated, but only partially effective, efforts have been made to constrain their use through agreed limitations on interest rates and other financing terms. The time has come to bring export financing subsidies within the jurisdiction of GATT and to tighten the discipline on their use.

One subsidy issue on which progress was made in the Uruguay Round is that of offsets. Offsets are government requirements for local subcontracting as a condition for the granting of a contract to a foreign firm. This practice has been quite common in the aircraft industry. Under the government procurement provisions of the Uruguay Round agreement, the use of offsets is prohibited as a condition for the award of a contract unless a derogation is specified in a country's schedule of commitments. This is a welcome improvement over the existing government procurement code that authorizes offsets.

Trade and Environment Policy

The subject of the relation between trade and environment policy has burst to the fore in recent years as environmental groups have increasingly expressed strong opposition to new trade liberalization agreements (NAFTA and the Uruguay Round) on the grounds that they would impede progress toward national and global environmental goals. The opposition became especially strident in the atmosphere created by the 1992 Earth Summit in Rio.[3] Moreover, trade restrictions have become a major tool favored by the environmental community to enforce environmental standards.

Several broad concerns have been expressed by some environmental groups about the effects of trade liberalization on the environment. One is that the removal of trade barriers would lead to increased income and production that could result in environmental degradation and unsustainable development. Another is that a successful Uruguay Round and the proliferation of free-trade agreements will tighten existing constraints on the use of trade measures to protect the environment. And the final concern is that the relaxation of controls on international trade and investment will encourage industrial flight from the rich countries to pollution havens in the Third World.

Improvement of the environment is a vital objective that properly commands wide support. However, the implication that trade and development are fundamentally in conflict with environmental objectives is open to serious question. Recent research has shown that only after reaching a certain threshold in development do countries tend to adopt policies that significantly improve a wide variety of environmental indicators.[4] In short, not only are economic growth and an improved environment compatible, but also the former may be an essential condition for significant progress in accomplishing the latter.

Although the link between trade and the environment has acquired special salience since the 1992 Rio conference, the subject was given formal GATT recognition as early as 1972 when, in the aftermath of the Stockholm conference, a GATT working group was established to study the subject. After a long period of dormancy, the working group has been revived and is considering the compatibility of existing international environmental agreements with the trade provisions of GATT. Moreover, the Uruguay Round agreement establishing a World Trade Organization (WTO) recognizes in its preamble the importance of environmental concerns and calls for a work program to ensure the responsiveness of the multilateral trading system to environmental concerns.

Twenty years ago the OECD released a set of recommendations on some of the key issues involving trade and the environment. They were entitled "Guiding Principles Concerning the International Economic Aspects of Environmental Policies." The three main principles, which are directly relevant to today's debate, deal with the allocation of pollution abatement costs, the harmonization of environmentally related product standards, and the desirability of using trade measures to offset differences in environmental control costs.[5]

On the issue of pollution abatement costs, the guidelines enunciate the "polluter pays principle" (PPP) as a way of avoiding trade distortions that might arise from differences among countries in the financing of pollution abatement. The principle means that the producer, rather than the taxpayer, should pay the cost of pollution abatement in the private sector. In practice, the producer can, of course, shift part of the cost forward to the user of the product to the extent that market conditions permit.

The economic rationale for PPP is twofold: by internalizing pollution abatement costs, it ensures that product prices reflect the full environmental cost of production; and by harmonizing internationally the way in which abatement is financed, it avoids a distortion of trade. Internalizing costs results in a more efficient allocation of resources. And harmonizing financing promotes the adoption of environmental protection measures by assuring firms that their competitors in other countries will not benefit from environmental subsidies.

What if a country does not follow PPP but instead pays for pollution abatement in the private sector out of public revenues? The implication of PPP is that exports benefiting from environmental subsidies should be subject to countervailing duties in the importing country on the same basis as any other subsidized export under Article VI of the GATT.

However, some environmentalists have argued against the countervailing of domestic environmental subsidies, on the grounds that it would discourage financial support by governments for environmental cleanup activities. In partial deference to this view, the Uruguay Round agreement declares government assistance to meet environmental requirements to be a nonactionable subsidy to the extent that it is limited to a one-time measure equivalent to 20 percent of the costs of adapting existing facilities to new standards. However, because such subsidies can distort international trade, a five-year automatic phaseout provision is applicable to environmental subsidies.

The second guiding principle requires countries to avoid applying environmentally related product standards as covert barriers to trade. It also seeks to minimize the economic costs of differences in standards through harmonization. Harmonization of product standards (e.g., food purity) will be difficult to achieve, however, in the absence of scientific consensus as to what the international standards should be.

Where differences in product standards do exist, a country should accord national treatment to like imported products—that is, treatment identical to that accorded to domestic products. This principle is consistent with the general GATT obligation of national treatment for imports with respect to internal taxes, standards, and regulations (Article III). Applying this principle, Thailand, for example, was barred from restricting imports of U.S. cigarettes on health grounds since Thailand imposed no comparable restriction on domestically produced cigarettes. However, the principle would permit a country to impose on imports the same labeling requirement, for example, that it applies domestically regardless of whether such a requirement exists in the exporting country.

The third major component of the OECD guiding principles deals with the potential competitive consequence of national differences in environmental policies relating to production processes rather than to products. Should a country with stringent standards be permitted to adopt border-adjustment measures (import tariffs, export rebates) to offset the trade advantage of the lower costs of complying with less stringent standards in another country? This question differs from the PPP issue in that it addresses differences in the environmental standards themselves rather than differences in the way the enforcement of standards is financed.

On this issue I concur in the OECD opposition to compensatory border adjustments, which is based on both economic and practical grounds. On economic grounds, it acknowledges the legitimacy of a diversity of environmental standards based on differences in countries' economic structure, income levels, and capacity to assimilate pollutants. On practical grounds, the OECD believed that it was not possible to distinguish such legitimate differences in standards and costs from nonlegitimate differences resulting in artificial competitive advantage and trade distortion. To attempt to do so and to sanction border adjustments as an implementing mechanism would encourage protectionist pressures and endless trade disputes.

The assumption underlying the OECD guidelines is that environmental damage is local. Increasingly, however, the focus of interest has shifted to the appropriateness of trade measures to deal with the adverse international environmental consequences of domestic economic activity—for example, transborder pollution, or damaging effects on global resources such as the ozone layer or endangered species.

Perhaps the most prominent recent example of a dispute over this issue is the U.S. embargo on tuna caught by Mexico with drift nets that injure dolphins. A similar international dispute arose over the European Union's embargo on furs of animals caught with leghold traps. The underlying question in these and similar cases is whether a government should have a unilateral right to require foreign as well as domestic producers to make changes in their methods of production in order to minimize a perceived or actual adverse impact on environmental resources.

On this issue, GATT rules are clear and eminently reasonable. They prohibit a country from making access to its market dependent on changes in the domestic production processes of the exporting country. The rationale is that to do otherwise would invite unending restrictions on imports as countries attempt to impose their own domestic environmental standards (or social policies) on other countries or use such attempts as a pretext for outright protection. Low-income countries especially would be vulnerable to standards on minimum wages, health, and safety.

The fact that GATT rules bar the unilateral use of trade measures to dictate changes in the environmental policies of other nations does not imply that governments are powerless to advance international environmental goals. After all, GATT rules can be waived or amended by negotiation. The best option, however, is to negotiate specific multilateral solutions such as the Convention on International Trade in Endangered Species (CITES) or the Montreal Protocol on Substances that Deplete the Ozone Layer. Both of these international agreements sanction trade measures as enforcement mechanisms.

Although the GATT articles came into force forty-five years ago, they are not oblivious to the need to safeguard the environment. Article XX on general exceptions explicitly states that nothing in the agreement should be construed to prevent the adoption or enforcement of measures "necessary to protect human, animal or plant life or health" (XX-b) or "relating to the conservation of exhaustible natural resources if such measures are made effective in conjunction with restrictions on domestic production or consumption" (XX-g). In the light of the intense recent concerns about the trade-environment nexus, a review of the GATT articles should be undertaken for the purpose of determining whether changes are desirable that would advance the goal of mutually supportive liberal trade and environmental policies and whether such changes should be incorporated in a separate code.

Trade and Investment Policy

Foreign trade and international investment are inextricably linked. Today, they can no longer be regarded simply as alternative means by which a producer seeks to penetrate a foreign market. As a result of the globalization of production, trade and foreign investment have increasingly become integral elements in a firm's unified strategy for optimizing the deployment of its resources worldwide. Firms operating in global markets are under strong competitive pressure to specialize, not only in final products but also vertically—that is, to carry out each separable operation in a production chain in the most advantageous worldwide location, whether in its own facilities or in facilities owned by subcontractors or independent suppliers.

The symbiotic relationship between trade and investment is reflected in the increasing proportion of foreign trade that takes place within individual multinational firms. A recent study showed that in 1986, 55 percent of U.S. exports consisted of intrafirm trade. Of this total, 32 percent was made up of U.S. exports by American multinationals to their foreign affiliates, and 23 percent consisted of exports by foreign-owned firms in the United States to their parent companies abroad or to other affiliates.[6]

Another perspective on the trade-investment relationship is provided by a comparison of U.S. exports to the European Union (EU) with sales to the EU by the European affiliates of U.S. multinationals. While U.S. exporters shipped $75 billion of American goods to the EU in 1988, European affiliates of U.S. firms sold some $620 billion worth, or eight times as much, principally but not exclusively to European customers.[7]

The role of multinational corporations as organizers of economic activity in an increasingly integrated world economy has expanded rapidly. Worldwide flows of foreign direct investment (FDI) rose at unprecedented rates in recent years. Their annual average growth of 34 percent between 1985 and 1990 far exceeded that of exports (13 percent) and nominal GDP (12 percent).[8]

FDI accounts for an increasing share of total investment in most countries, and for many developing countries it has become the primary source of foreign capital. With the decline of commercial bank lending to developing countries in the 1980s, the share of FDI in total long-term private capital inflows increased from 30 percent in 1981–85 to 74 percent in 1986–90.[9]

Data on flows of FDI understate the impact of multinational corporations in host countries. Associated with FDI are technology transfers from parent firms in home countries to foreign affiliates in conjunction with both equity investments and non-equity arrangements. International transfers of technology are reflected in the payment of licensing and other fees, most of which are made on an intrafirm basis. Since technological change provides a primary impetus to economic growth, the multinational corporation plays a crucial role in expanding the world economy.

The foregoing trends have profound implications for international economic governance in the future. Traditionally, trade was considered the "engine of growth" in the world economy, and a comprehensive international framework was established in GATT to reflect that perspective. Today, however, with many foreign markets served more by sales of foreign affiliates than by exports, with much of foreign trade occurring as intrafirm transactions, and with technology flows heavily associated with FDI, foreign direct investment is increasingly the driving force of international economic transactions.

Yet, no global institution comparable to GATT exists that would provide a framework of norms and a mechanism for resolving conflicts and removing obstacles to international investment. Given the continuing widespread restrictions on the free flow of foreign investment, it is essential to rectify this asymmetry by negotiating a comprehensive international accord on foreign direct investment that would include a binding set of rules, a dispute settlement facility, and a mechanism for liberalizing national policies and regulations regarding foreign enterprise.

The absence of a global GATT-like accord on investment should not be taken to imply that no international investment agreements exist. Indeed, the United States is party to a number of bilateral investment treaties as well as earlier bilateral treaties of friendship, commerce, and navigation that include investment provisions. In addition, the United States subscribes to a 1976 OECD "soft law" arrangement in the form of nonmandatory guidelines for multinational enterprises.

The two most recent trade negotiations involving the United States—the GATT Uruguay Round and the North American Free Trade Agreement (NAFTA)—recognize the close link between trade and investment by including important provisions on investment. In the Uruguay Round agreement, trade-related investment measures imposed on foreign enterprises are prohibited when they take the form of domestic-content or export requirements. The framework agreement on services also enunciates the principles of national treatment and the right of establishment for trade in services in acknowledgment of the necessity for a foreign presence in order for many service industries to sell their services abroad.

More comprehensive provisions safeguarding the rights of foreign investors are contained in NAFTA. They apply, of course, to investment in any one of the three member countries—Canada, Mexico, the United States—by investors from either of the other two. NAFTA provides nondiscriminatory treatment; eliminates the need for government approval of investments in most sectors; ensures freedom to remit profits and royalties and to repatriate capital; prohibits performance requirements in the form of local content or export mandates; protects against unjust or uncompensated expropriations; and grants access to international arbitration to enforce investor rights.

The most novel of NAFTA's provisions on investment relates to the protection of the environment. The treaty prohibits the lowering of environmental standards as a means of attracting investment, and permits the parties to require environmental impact statements on new investments.

In sum, what we have today is a patchwork of intergovernmental arrangements on FDI. Some are bilateral, others are regional, still others are multilateral; and they vary widely in scope and degree of binding force. Taken together, existing arrangements hardly qualify as a comprehensive and coordinated global regime for international investment.

The time has clearly arrived for a new global accord on foreign investment. The two pillars of an agreement would be the right of establishment and national treatment. The right of establishment would ensure that national markets are open to foreign firms through direct investment in both new and existing enterprises. National treatment would ensure that, once established, foreign investors would be treated no less favorably than domestic enterprises with respect to national laws, regulations, and administrative practices.

The most difficult issue related to these basic principles is how to define permitted exceptions. For example, the United States and many other countries restrict the right of foreign establishment in certain sectors, such as telecommunications, shipping, and nuclear power. And national treatment is circumscribed in a number of countries on security or other grounds—for example, foreign-controlled enterprises may be barred from bidding on defense contracts or from joining government-subsidized research consortia. Because of the difficulty of negotiating a consensus on exceptions, consideration might be given to a limited reciprocity test for certain sensitive sectors under which national treatment would be accorded only to firms whose home governments also accord national treatment to foreign enterprises.

Other provisions of an international investment accord would proscribe performance requirements; discourage special government incentives or disincentives that distort international capital flows; bar limitations on the remittance of profits and royalties and on the repatriation of capital; require appropriate compensation for expropriation; and provide for dispute-settlement facilities, including international arbitration.

An acrimonious issue that keeps recurring is that of conflicting assertions of jurisdiction over foreign enterprises by the governments of host and home countries. The problem has arisen mainly in the areas of antitrust, trade controls, and banking and securities regulation. Here the basic principle, which has been endorsed by the OECD, is that affiliates of multinational enterprises located in various countries should normally be subject to the laws and regulations of those countries. Although there may be exceptional cases, host-country jurisdiction should as a rule take precedence over that of the home country.[10]

Two other vexing issues have a special resonance among the concerns of developing countries about foreign direct investment. One is intracorporate transfer pricing; the other is the question of tax holidays and other specific incentives to attract foreign investors. The pricing of transactions among affiliates of individual multinational enterprises can affect the location of profits and consequent tax liabilities as among different national jurisdictions. An international investment accord should confront this issue and seek common principles to guide transfer pricing.

Special incentives to attract foreign investment are another subject for inclusion in a "GATT for Investment." Especially when offered by developing countries, incentives, such as tax holidays, are often regarded by multinational enterprises as too transitory to induce location in a particular country, but the incentives result in a reallocation of the benefits of the investment to the detriment of the host. More generally, incentive schemes can result in mutually disadvantageous competition among developing countries to attract foreign investment and simply raise the returns to foreign firms that would invest anyway.[11] Just as GATT limits the use of subsidies that distort international trade, a "GATT for Investment" should attempt to constrain the use of incentives intended to distort the flow of foreign investment.

As global production in today's economy implies a close link between international trade and investment, the new World Trade Organization (WTO) established in the Uruguay Round is the logical negotiating forum for an international investment accord. Additionally, it has the advantage of universality of membership at a time when the developing countries are playing an expanding role as both host and home country for direct foreign investment.

Multilateral vs. Alternative Approaches

Since the end of the Second World War, the United States has been the staunchest supporter of an international trading system based on multilateralism and nondiscrimination, as epitomized by GATT. The policy was a reaction to the prewar experience of bilateralism, Commonwealth and other preferences, and various spheres of economic influence that fragmented world trade and impeded recovery from the Great Depression. Under the new postwar regime of multilateral trade liberalization, the world economy has expanded and prospered at an unprecedented rate.

Why, then, did the United States turn in the 1980s toward regional[12] free trade agreements (FTAs), first with Israel, then with Canada, and now with both Canada and Mexico in the North American Free Trade Agreement (NAFTA), which may ultimately be expanded to include other countries in the Western Hemisphere? All of these arrangements are inherently discriminatory against nonmembers and represent sharp departures from the multilateral approach traditionally espoused by the United States.

Several factors have been at work in bringing about the shift in the U.S. position. As successive rounds of GATT trade negotiations took place, the number of participants grew from the original twenty-three to more than a hundred in the Uruguay Round. The task of forging a consensus among so many diverse participants became ever more difficult, so that each round took longer than the previous one.

Moreover, the negotiating dynamics of the GATT system have tended to slow the liberalization process. Countries have been inclined to withhold concessions in the hope of benefiting from the generalization of others' concessions without making their own. The only way to prevent such "free riders" is for all participants to make concessions at the same time. As a result, the pace of progress in negotiations is determined by the most reluctant major participant, just as a convoy's speed is determined by that of its slowest ship.

As the relative economic position of the United States declined in recent years, it became less able to exert the decisive driving force needed to strengthen the international trade rules and step up the pace of liberalization. This was dramatically demonstrated at the 1982 GATT ministerial meeting which, despite the strong urging by the United States and some other countries, failed to reach agreement on an agenda for a new round of multilateral trade negotiations. It was not until four years later that the eighth round was launched at Punta del Este, Uruguay. The failure of the 1982 meeting marked a watershed in U.S. attitudes toward multilateral negotiations as the sole route to trade liberalization.

Other considerations also encouraged the U.S. willingness to consider alternative approaches. The increasing globalization of national economies exposed the need to address in negotiations not only border restrictions on trade, such as tariffs and import quotas, but also a host of other domestic policies that have an impact on economic activity. To some extent, this realization was reflected in the Tokyo Round and in the agenda ultimately adopted for the Uruguay Round, which included the protection of intellectual property and certain trade-related aspects of investment. But it has proved far more difficult to reach a consensus on sensitive areas of domestic policy in a global as compared with a more limited regional context. For example, NAFTA goes far beyond the Uruguay Round in including comprehensive rules on the treatment of foreign investment as well as provisions on the protection of the environment.

Finally, the U.S. turn to regional trade arrangements was bolstered by developments in Europe: the European Community's original reluctance to sign onto the agenda proposed by the United States for an eighth round of multilateral trade negotiations; the deepening of European economic integration foreshadowed by the signing of the Single European Act in 1986 with the goal of establishing a single market by the end of 1992; and the prospective widening of the community by the inclusion of the EFTA countries and ultimately a number of Eastern European countries as well.

As the United States simultaneously pursues both the multilateral and regional approaches to the liberalization of trade and investment, the question naturally arises as to whether free trade areas further the cause of globalization or hinder it. On the one hand, FTAs may be *trade-creating*, as when the reduction of internal barriers results in a member country's importing from another member what it previously produced itself. This effect brings about a reallocation of resources among the members that improves efficiency and raises incomes.

On the other hand, such arrangements may also be *trade-diverting* when, because of the discriminatory treatment of outsiders, a member country simply shifts the source of its imports from a traditional foreign supplier to a new, higher-cost FTA partner. In this case, trade flows are rearranged in a way that reduces overall efficiency and incomes.

Typically, a free trade area has both trade-creating and trade-diverting effects so that an evaluation of the arrangement depends on which effect is dominant. If trade creation exceeds trade diversion, free trade areas are generally deemed to be beneficial. But beneficial for whom? The answer is that they are beneficial for their members collectively. However, the outside world cannot gain in the short run regardless of whether trade creation or trade diversion is dominant. The reason is that nonmember countries experience only trade diversion in the short run.

The inherently negative effect of FTAs on outsiders is related to the static nature of the trade creation–trade diversion framework. It focuses on the consequences of once-and-for-all changes in the allocation of existing resources resulting from the formation of the FTA. However, the more important dynamic results flow from the growth induced by economies of scale and the stimulus to competition, investment, and technological progress provided by the enlargement of the market.

When these dynamic effects are taken into account, they may not only overshadow the static results for the members, but also have positive spillovers for outside countries. In short, whereas in purely static terms nonmembers cannot benefit from the formation of an FTA, in dynamic terms, they are likely to gain in the longer run from a secondary form of trade creation induced by a more rapid growth of the FTA as a market for their exports.

Although nondiscrimination and multilateralism are basic pillars of GATT, the agreement recognizes the potential contribution of FTAs to world trade and therefore sanctions their formation (Article XXIV). However, the article lays down conditions designed to minimize the discriminatory effect of FTAs on nonmembers. One condition is that trade barriers against outsiders may not be raised. This provision is intended to ensure that the preferences inherent in an FTA are a consequence of the removal of restrictions on trade among members rather than the imposition of new barriers against outsiders. The other GATT condition requires that restrictions be removed on "substantially all the trade" between the parties to an agreement. The logic here is that, if countries were allowed to pick and choose among products, they would inevitably choose those that maximize trade diversion and minimize the painful domestic adjustments implied by trade creation.

U.S. initiatives to form FTAs consistent with GATT, such as NAFTA, promote more rapid liberalization of trade and investment and deeper economic integration among their members than can be achieved in global negotiations. Regional and other FTAs among limited groups of countries should therefore be encouraged as stepping-stones to broader integration on a world scale.

Despite the safeguards in GATT to ensure that FTAs will be outward-looking, there are legitimate concerns about the consequences for the international trading system of a proliferation of FTAs. Countries left out of FTAs understandably feel disadvantaged. Even the United States reflected this feeling when it objected strongly to the proposal by President Mahatir of Malaysia for a regional free trade zone in Asia that would have excluded the United States.[13] The concerns of excluded nations are bound to be exacerbated as the two principal existing regional arrangements, the EU and NAFTA, are extended to new members in Europe and the Western Hemisphere. Moreover, as demonstrated by certain provisions of NAFTA, rules of origin for free trade areas can be highly restrictive of trade with outsiders.

Two steps can be envisaged that would make regional approaches to free trade more compatible with an open world-trading system. The first pertains to rules of origin. Instead of tailoring rules of origin to particular industries, only one rule should be allowed. That rule should be that the origin of a product is where substantial transformation occurs. A change in the customs category would be prima facie, but not conclusive, evidence of substantial transformation. Second, countries negotiating regional agreements should be encouraged to include liberal terms of accession that would in effect leave the arrangement open to membership by any country willing to abide by its rules.

However, the most important way to ensure that regional arrangements become building blocks to an open global system of trade and investment would be to promptly initiate post–Uruguay Round negotiations that include, in addition to the unfinished business of the round, new issues of regulatory harmonization that are becoming increasingly important for efficient global production. To the extent that multilateral negotiations reduce trade barriers and regulatory distortions globally, they decrease the margins of preference enjoyed by members of FTAs, so that the two strands of liberalization—global and regional—will tend to converge. After all, the best free trade area is one that encompasses all trading nations.

Institutional Reform

With the conclusion of the Uruguay Round, the time is ripe to reform the institutional framework of GATT to make it a more effective instrument for implementing the results of the round to facilitate the negotiation of new accords required by the global economy at the end of the twentieth century.

In thinking about structural reform, it is useful to recall how GATT came into being. In the late 1940s the United States rallied the main trading nations to negotiate a comprehensive charter for world trade, to be administered by an International Trade Organization (ITO). The ITO was conceived as one of the three pillars of a new liberal world economic order, along with the International Monetary Fund and the World Bank. However, when Congress failed to ratify the ITO, it was replaced by an interim accord known as the General Agreement on Tariffs and Trade (GATT), consisting essentially of the commercial policy chapter of the ITO.

In the strict legal sense, therefore, GATT has not been an organization but an agreement among governments, which are consequently referred to in the text as "contracting parties" rather than as "members." Although, de facto, GATT has possessed the attributes of an organization, including a permanent secretariat, its lack of a definitive legal basis has adversely affected its status in the domestic law of a number of member countries and its relationship to the other international economic institutions.

However, the need for a strengthened institutional framework for GATT derives from more than the inadequacy and impermanence of its historical legal foundation. Despite the creative institutional improvisation of its leaders, GATT's modus operandi needs to be reformed to accommodate the vast expansion of its agenda and the explosion of its membership, from 23 countries at its inception to the present 111, with many others waiting in the wings.

Traditionally focused on border restrictions to trade, such as tariffs and quotas, GATT began in the Tokyo and Uruguay Rounds to deal with a number of sensitive aspects of internal policies that substantially affect international trade, such as government procurement, technical standards, domestic subsidies, and intellectual property rights. As explained in this paper, future GATT negotiations will undoubtedly address the need to harmonize a range of additional domestic regulatory policies, including those pertaining to competition, environment and foreign investment.

I do not presume to recommend how GATT and the new WTO should be cast to enable the institution to cope more effectively with its expanded agenda and membership. Rather, I propose that the organization move immediately to establish a group of independent "wise persons," broadly representative of the GATT membership, to study this question and come forth with a report and recommendations.

Among the issues that should be included in the agenda of the "wise persons" are the following: the composition of the WTO management body; the system of voting; the functions of the secretariat; whether trade negotiations should continue to be conducted in "rounds" as in the past; how the continuing negotiations agreed in the Uruguay round can fit into the new areas for negotiation; the utility of subagreements in the form of codes on specific topics; the dispute settlement mechanism; and the desirability of a closer link between the new WTO and the IMF and World Bank. On each of those issues a brief elucidation follows that is intended to identify considerations to be taken into account rather than to offer solutions.

Management Body

The day-to-day business of the WTO is to be carried on by a general council consisting of all members of the organization. The question is whether a body of more than a hundred members can be run by what amounts to a committee of the whole. One alternative arrangement would be the model adopted by the Bretton Woods institutions. For example, the IMF, with a membership of 178 countries, is run by an executive board consisting of twenty people. Five are appointed by the five major economic powers (the United States, the United Kingdom, Germany, France, and Japan), and fifteen are elected by groups of the remaining members. Many other formulae are conceivable that would provide for both universal representation of the views of the membership and a management body small enough to enable the organization to operate efficiently.

Voting System

GATT provides de jure for joint action on the basis of one vote for each contracting party (Article XXV). In practice, however, a consensus "rule" has been followed, which in effect recognizes that decisions not supported by the principal members cannot be carried out. Is there any reason to change the present de jure voting system based on one vote per member, in which legally the United States and Mauritius (population one million), for example, have an equal voice in decision making? Should other systems such as weighted voting or some form of formal veto power for the major trading nations be considered?

The Secretariat

Though generally recognized to be of high quality, the GATT secretariat has functioned essentially as a servicing body that carries out the decisions of the signatory governments. The question is whether the scope of the secretariat's responsibilities should be enlarged to include the power to initiate proposals that would have to be considered by member governments. Such a role would be similar to that of the commission of the European Union, which has the right to put proposals before the European Council (consisting of member governments) for its decision. As a body not answerable to individual governments, the GATT secretariat's proposals might be regarded as more reflective of the common interest than initiatives taken by individual members, which, of course, would not be precluded.

Rounds

In the past, GATT negotiations have been carried out in discrete "rounds," of which the Uruguay Round is the eighth. In principle, there are two advantages to this modus operandi. First, by scheduling a limited period for a round, pressure builds up to complete the negotiations by the agreed terminal date. Second, by including multiple issues and all GATT members as participants in negotiating rounds, the scope for tradeoffs is enhanced.

In practice, however, neither of these theoretical advantages has always materialized. The "round" approach would appear most appropriate when tariff bargaining constitutes the prime agenda of GATT negotiations. As the agenda widens into the realm of harmonizing domestic regulatory regimes, the tradeoffs become less transparent and less quantifiable. Moreover, inevitable long hiatuses between rounds have provided enhanced opportunities for protectionist pressures. A pattern of more continuous negotiations might achieve more rapid progress.

Continuing Negotiations

At the conclusion of the Uruguay Round a series of "ministerial decisions and declarations" were adopted. They state the views of the participants on a number of issues relating to the operation of the global trading system and also mandate carry-over negotiations in certain fields. In the service sector particularly, continuing negotiations are called for in financial, basic telecommunications, maritime, and other services. Besides the specifically mandated subjects, any agenda for future negotiations should include areas such as tariffs, subsidies, and agriculture, where further progress should be sought beyond what was accomplished in the Uruguay Round. How should these categories of negotiations be organized in relation to the new areas proposed in this statement?

Codes

A departure from the traditional method of negotiation occurred in the Tokyo Round, where a number of subagreements or "codes" were negotiated among more limited groups of countries than the membership of GATT as a whole. All the major OECD countries and a number of the more important newly industrializing countries have subscribed to the codes.

Some of the codes address the need to harmonize domestic regulatory policies—for example, the codes on government procurement, domestic subsidies, and technical standards. As regulatory harmonization in additional sensitive areas of domestic policy will be a prime subject for future GATT negotiations, the question arises as to whether the code approach of negotiating among limited groups of like-minded countries should be an optional or even a preferred method of negotiation on selected issues. Of course, the codes would be open to subsequent signature by all GATT members.

To the extent that the code approach is adopted, a major issue is how the codes would be applied. Although only signatories are bound by the Tokyo Round codes, their benefits have generally been extended to all GATT members on an MFN basis. The major exception is the United States, which unilaterally decided to apply several of the codes on a conditional basis. Should conditional MFN become a multilaterally acceptable optional standard for future codes as a way of denying their benefits to "free riders" and inducing nonsignatories to join?

An example of where this approach might be useful is financial services. Not much progress was made in the Uruguay Round in achieving market access and national treatment commitments in this area except among the industrial countries. By and large, the newly emerging countries did not come up with significant offers. Would the code approach and conditional MFN provide an appropriate framework for future negotiations that would induce these members to make meaningful commitments in order to avoid discriminatory treatment?

Dispute Settlement

An effective dispute-settlement procedure is essential to achieving a strong and stable multilateral trading system. However, a widely recognized weakness of the past GATT procedure has been the requirement for consensus. If a dispute settlement panel ruled against a country, that country could block adoption of the ruling by the GATT council. Such blockages occurred in a significant number of recent cases, especially in those involving complaints about subsidies. Since 1983 all panel reports under the subsidies code have been blocked by one or more GATT signatories.

A substantial strengthening of the dispute-settlement process was accomplished in the Uruguay Round by eliminating the offending country's ability to block GATT action. Instead, it establishes an appellate body to hear appeals of panel cases, with its membership comprised of persons of recognized authority in law, international trade, and GATT. An appellate report is adopted by the council and unconditionally accepted by the parties to the dispute unless the council decides by consensus not to adopt the report.

Other improvements include strict time limits for each step in the process as well as for when a member must bring its laws into conformity with panel rulings and recommendations; and authorization of retaliation in the event that a member has not brought its laws into conformity with its obligations within the set period. In the case of the United States, restrictive action under Section 301 of the Trade Act of 1974 will be legitimized if another member fails to comply with its obligations at the end of the dispute settlement process.

The "wise persons" group should assess the new procedures and consider whether further improvements are desirable to strengthen the dispute-settlement process.

Link with the IMF and World Bank

One of the anomalies of the present structure of global institutions responsible for improving the world trade and financial system is the relatively minor role played by GATT in the reform and liberalization of trade and regulatory policies in the developing countries. In these areas the major responsibility is exercised by the IMF in conjunction with its stabilization programs and by the World Bank in the context of its structural adjustment lending.

It would seem only sensible that the GATT secretariat be accorded a more active role in collaborating with the IMF and World Bank in the design of trade policy reforms. A modest beginning would be the inclusion of GATT staff representatives on IMF and World Bank country missions when the reform of trade policy is on the agenda. In addition, regular consultations could be scheduled among the heads of the three institutions or their designated deputies.

Conclusion

The time has come for the United States to assert its unique role as rallier of nations in support of a more open and integrated global economy based on market principles. The conclusion of the Uruguay Round is a landmark on the road to that objective, but we must not stop there. Important unfinished business remains, such as the liberalization of financial and audio-visual services. Moreover, in the decade since the Uruguay agenda was set, basic changes in the world economy have given rise to new issues that must be addressed as we approach the end of the twentieth century. In addition, many new countries have joined or are ready to join GATT.

History has demonstrated that, in the absence of an ongoing multilateral liberalization process, the forces of protection take over because they are "the only game in town." As with riding a bicycle, the vehicle topples over without forward motion.

Beyond the Uruguay Round, we should therefore promptly launch new multilateral negotiations with an agenda that includes both the unfinished business of the round and new domestic regulatory issues with important international trade implications. In this chapter, I have focused on three such areas—competition, the environment, and investment—and propose a course of action to achieve greater harmonization of national policies on the basis of mutually supportive domestic and international goals. Progress in reducing domestic regulatory distortions to international trade and investment would constitute a major step in building a more integrated and efficient global economy from which all nations would benefit.

With the consolidation of the single European market and the signing of NAFTA, it has become clear that regional and other less-than-global free trade and investment arrangements constitute valuable practical steps toward the ultimate goal of an open world system of trade and investment. Suggestions are offered to help reinforce the consistency of the multilateral and regional approaches. But the principal contribution to that objective would be the continuation of successful multilateral negotiations, because they would automatically bring about a reduction in the margins of preference enjoyed by members of regional free trade areas. To the extent that we continue to reduce barriers and harmonize regulations multilaterally in the post–Uruguay era, the two approaches will tend to converge. Finally, it is essential to make GATT a more effective instrument for preserving and strengthening a liberal international system for trade and investment by strengthening its institutional structure. In addition to welcoming the more definitive legal status for GATT by creating a World Trade Organization (WTO), I propose the appointment of a "wise persons" group to recommend ways of enabling the new WTO to deal more effectively with its expanded agenda and membership. A number of issues that such a group should address are highlighted in this chapter.

Notes

1. This chapter is adapted from a paper prepared by the author for the Committee for Economic Development.

2. U.S. Department of Commerce, "Summary of U.S. International Transactions" (Washington, D.C.: GPO, June 15, 1993).

3. The following is a quotation from a full-page advertisement in the *New York Times*, April 20, 1992, sponsored by fifteen environmental groups:

> President Bush has been pushing for new international trade rules that give a secretive foreign bureaucracy vast new powers to threaten American laws that protect your food, your health, your wilderness and wildlife, and your job. It's part of the hidden agenda in the new GATT agreement in Geneva.

4. World Bank, *World Development Report 1992* (Washington, D.C.: World Bank, 1994).

5. Currently the OECD is in the process of expanding the principles, especially to address the question of how trade measures should be used to advance international environmental objectives. See Charles Pearson, "Trade and Environment: Seeking Harmony," OECD Economic Directorate, Version II, January 1992.

6. De Anne Julius, *Global Companies and Public Policy: The Growing Challenge of Direct Investment* (London: The Royal Institute of International Affairs, 1990), p. 74.

7. Gary C. Hufbauer, ed., *Europe 1992: An American Perspective* (Washington, D.C.: The Brookings Institution, 1990). Of course, the economic significance of the two types

of sales is not the same. Most of the $75 billion in U.S. exports represented income for U.S. workers and profits for U.S. firms, whereas most of the $620 billion in sales by U.S. affiliates consisted of revenue paid to European factors of production.

8. United Nations, *World Investment Report 1992* (New York: United Nations, 1993), p. 1.

9. Ibid.

10. OECD, "Guidelines for Multinational Enterprises," *International Investment and Multinational Enterprises*, rev. ed. 1984, introduction, paragraph 7.

11. Isaiah Frank, *Foreign Enterprise in Developing Countries* (Baltimore: The Johns Hopkins University Press, 1980), chapter 9.

12. "Regional" as contrasted to "multilateral" is used here as a convenient generic term to refer to arrangements more limited in terms of participants than those pursued through global institutions such as GATT, whether or not the participants are located in the same region of the world. Some have suggested "plurilateral," but that term is unfamiliar and not found in most dictionaries.

13. In "A Pacific Perspective for the President," *International Economic Insights* (January/February 1993), Takatashi Ito declared, "The strong objection issued by the U.S. left people in Asia puzzled: how could the U.S., an architect of NAFTA, object to movement toward an Asian free trade zone?"

18

Agriculture and Multilateralism

Fred H. Sanderson

Almost from the inception of GATT, agriculture has been its problem child. It presented the greatest difficulties in the Uruguay Round and came close to causing it to fail.

Agriculture had been left behind in the successful liberalization of trade that earlier GATT rounds had accomplished for industrial products. The basic reason is the pervasive nature of government intervention in the domestic agricultural markets of most industrialized countries, which dates back to the 1930s. As early as 1958, a panel of four wise men, chaired by Gottfried von Haberler, was asked by the contracting parties to address the problem. Their report was well ahead of its time.[1] It pinpointed the complicated system of agricultural support schemes as the principal culprit. It analyzed the wide variety of methods of protection and recommended the development of a comprehensive measure of the degree of protection, on the basis of a comparison of the total return received by farmers and the return that would correspond to the world price. It made specific recommendations: (1) to separate protection from stabilization; and (2) to refrain from using trade policy to achieve domestic stabilization.

The recommendation of the von Haberler report to focus on domestic policies as the ultimate source of trade distortions in agriculture was taken up in the Kennedy Round and again in the Uruguay Round. During the Kennedy Round, the European Community's offer to negotiate a measure of total support and protection of grains it called the *montant de soutien* (support margin) went nowhere because, in the end, the community proved unable to accept any reduction in its high level of protection. An alternative approach, aimed at reducing its degree of self-sufficiency, failed for the same reason. In 1982, the OECD (following up on

work by Tim Josling for the Food and Agriculture Organization and by Rodney
Tyers and Kym Anderson for the World Bank) launched a study aimed at quanti-
fying the extent of direct and indirect support of agricultural producers and its
effects on agricultural production, consumption, and trade. In 1987—just in time
for the Uruguay Round—it came up with a report highlighting the "producer
subsidy equivalent" (PSE)—the kind of index the von Haberler report had called
for a quarter-century earlier.[2] Estimates of PSEs and of the cost of agricultural
support to consumers and taxpayers have since been published annually for an
expanding list of commodities and countries.[3]

There seemed to be a growing consensus, early on in the Uruguay Round, that
domestic policies are at the root of the problem and that border measures are the
external manifestation of these policies. Even the European Community, which
considered U.S. deficiency payments to be trade-distorting, seemed amenable to
a "concerted, significant reduction in domestic support."

Study groups were convened to examine the suitability of the PSE for use in
the GATT negotiations. It offered some obvious advantages. But skeptics were
quick to point out problems. The aggregate does not distinguish between subsidies with very different effects on production and trade. It does not take account
of supply controls or of the adverse effects of market price supports on consumption, as distinct from a system of deficiency payments. Moreover, it is sensitive
to fluctuations in world prices and exchange rates that are largely beyond the
control of agricultural policy makers.

At first, these problems tended to be dismissed as "transitional." Some problems were taken care of by modifying the PSE into the AMS (aggregate measure
of support), which was intended to exclude subsidies that have negligible effects
on trade. Fixed base-period reference prices, expressed in national currencies (or
ECUs in the case of the European Community) were substituted for current
world prices at current exchange rates. The use of the total (rather than per unit)
AMS was intended to take account of supply controls or limits on quantities
eligible for support.

The tricky problem of defining what constitutes a "trade distorting" subsidy
was not specifically addressed until late in the Uruguay Round. The consensus
was that subsidies were to be grouped into green, red, and amber categories. The
"green box" was to be exempted from GATT disciplines but was to be strictly
limited to programs such as research and extension, or domestic and international food aid, which were considered to be innocuous or even helpful in a trade
context. The "red box," containing prohibited subsidies, soon dropped out of
sight. The vast majority of producer subsidies, including U.S. deficiency payments and similar payments elsewhere, were to go into the "amber box," and
would be subject to reductions.

When it became apparent that nothing even approaching the total elimination
of internal subsidies was in the cards, the United States joined the other traditional exporting countries in supplementing the AMS approach by parallel com-

mitments on market access and export subsidies, as well as commitments on sanitary and phytosanitary measures. This four-pronged approach became the negotiating framework for agriculture set forth in the Mid-Term Agreement (Geneva, April 1989). At that time, the declared U.S. objective was a 75 percent reduction in internal support and a 90 percent reduction in export subsidies.

Subsequent developments led to a further shift of emphasis away from disciplines on internal support and toward increased reliance on border disciplines. The most important development was the Mac Sharry proposal in December 1990, leading to the European Community's decision in 1992 to move from a support system relying on high internal market-price supports and export subsidies, to a system of lower internal supports supplemented by direct payments and acreage set-asides (as in the United States).

What prompted the Common Agricultural Policy (CAP) reform is still a matter of debate. Few people had anticipated that the European Community would so readily jettison the heretofore sacrosanct "mechanisms" of the CAP, but it is clear in retrospect that it was a smart move for the community to trade in some of its *methods* of protection if it could thereby salvage its *high level* of protection. CAP reform made it easier for the European Community to go along with the reduction in external protection sought by the exporting countries: lower internal market prices would reduce the need for high import duties as well as export subsidies. The European Community also proved amenable to replacing its variable levies by equivalent fixed tariffs and to negotiate reductions in these tariffs.[4]

To make CAP reform palatable, the community committed itself to compensating its farmers for any price cuts by direct payments. This caused it to reverse its position on the treatment of direct payments in the GATT: while it had previously been adamant that such payments be subject to reduction, it now insisted that they be exempted as non-trade-distorting.

The United States proved to be receptive to this argument. Its largest farm organization, the American Farm Bureau Federation (AFBF), which in the past had been critical of deficiency payments, became attached to them. The United States also could take comfort from its success in persuading Japan to replace its import quotas on beef and citrus by tariffs, which, in the case of beef, are now less than half the tariff equivalent of the previous level of protection. The subsequent growth of beef imports seemed to prove that the "tariffication" approach could be effective in opening agricultural markets.

As the differences in the positions of the major contenders seemed to be narrowing, the director general of GATT, Arthur Dunkel, undertook to draft a compromise agreement which was released in December 1991. With few exceptions, this draft rather accurately forecast the terms on which the negotiations were concluded two years later.

The final stages of the negotiations are known chiefly for the interminable haggling over the degree of reduction in export subsidies. In the end, agreement was reached on a 21 percent cut in the volume, and a 36 percent cut in the value of subsidized exports from the 1986–90 base. Another prominent feature of the agreement is the minimum market access provision (equal to 3 percent of consumption, rising to 5 percent by the end of the century). Where current access opportunities exceed these minimum levels, they must be maintained at least at those higher levels. These measures are to be implemented by reduced-tariff quotas. Regrettably, these modest quantitative measures are likely to be the only ones that will have any significant practical effects on trade.

What is too often overlooked is the fatal slippage that occurred, beginning with the Dunkel report, in the crucial areas of total support and corresponding import protection. What we hear about is the "20 percent reduction" in the aggregate measure of support, the conversion of NTBs (including variable levies) into tariffs, and the "36 percent reduction" in tariffs. These cuts in protection would be modest achievements if they were real but, unfortunately, they are not what they seem to be.

The 20 percent cut in the aggregate measure of support is required only on an agricultural sectorwide basis, and leaves considerable flexibility in its application to individual commodities. For example, U.S. sugar, though heavily protected at an AMS of about 70 percent, remains untouched, as cuts from the 1986–88 level already in place (e.g., for milk) are sufficient to result in a 20 percent cut in the total AMS. Because the base period was one of unusually low world prices (and hence, high-price support levels), neither the European Community (now the European Union) nor the United States will have any difficulty in complying with the 20 percent average cut in the AMS.

The more serious erosion of the AMS concept was the enlargement of the "green box" to exempt the most important subsidies (U.S. deficiency payments and European Union compensation payments) from any reduction requirement. The only "discipline" here is the provision that leaves any increase in total support over "levels decided in 1992" open to a possible nullification and impairment challenge. Given the dismal experience with such challenges in the past, it is difficult to believe that this provision will impose an effective ceiling on commodity support.[5]

The agreement to convert all existing trade barriers into tariffs and to cut these tariffs by an average of 36 percent will not result in any significant expansion of trade. There are several reasons for this.

1) "Dirty tariffication": The agreement provides no guidelines for the calculation of the tariff equivalents of previous nontariff barriers; as a result, most tariff equivalents are inflated.
2) The tariff equivalents are based on a period in which world prices were lower and levels of border protection were higher than normal.
3) As a result of (1) and (2), most initial tariffs from which the cuts are to be made are even higher than the already prohibitive existing levels of border

protection,[6] and new "bound" tariffs exceeding 100 percent ad valorem are quite common in the country schedules.[7]

4) Countries are permitted to change their methods of protection from market price support, requiring high levels of external protection, to internal supports that meet the requirements for exemption from cuts in those supports. In the European Union this shift will allow internal market prices to fall by as much as one-third for grains. As a result, the bound tariffs are becoming ever more redundant. Although market price supports for livestock products have not been lowered as much as those for grains, the new regime, with its lower internal feed prices, will allow the European Union to comply with the mandated tariff cuts without any loss in effective protection.

5) The "36 percent cut" is an unweighted average of tariff line items, regardless of their importance in trade. Thus, all countries can avail themselves of the possibility of making minimum permissible cuts of only 15 percent on major "sensitive" products so long as they meet the required unweighted average cut for all agricultural products.[8]

6) The potential stabilizing effect of tariffication on world markets has been reduced by the "special safeguard" provisions that enable importers during the implementation period to partly offset temporary declines in world market prices, or "import surges," by additional duties.[9] Moreover, import duties may remain variable where bound tariff equivalents are highly redundant or where minimum import prices are in effect (grains, fruits, and vegetables in the European Union; pork in Japan). "As a result the European Union probably will be able to continue to apply a border regime which in practice may resemble its old system of variable levies."[10]

For all these reasons, analysts have concluded that the practical effects of tariffication and of the agreed tariff cuts will be extremely limited. Most of the trade benefits of the Uruguay Round agreement—such as they are—will come from the quantitative commitments providing for current and minimum access and the partial rollback of export subsidies. These are in the nature of quotas and can hardly be characterized as "liberalization" as economists understand it. In fact, these provisions correspond to the old GATT rules which provided that any quantitative restrictions were to be applied proportionally to both domestic and traditional foreign suppliers, and that any export subsidies should not result in more than a "fair share" in export markets—fair share being defined as the share in a recent representative period. The old rules, which were susceptible to varying interpretations, have now been replaced by explicit quantitative floors and ceilings, detailed in the country schedules, which should be more difficult to evade.

Any assessment of the Uruguay Round agreement obviously depends on the standards one applies. Given modest expectations,[11] the agreement is a small improvement over the status-quo-ante. Its most important achievements are the partial disarmament in the export subsidy war and the partial opening of the Japanese and Korean rice markets. Analysts agree that most of the benefits for agricultural trade will come, not from the GATT agreement on agriculture, but from the effects of the Uruguay Round as a whole on world economic growth.[12]

There are those who contend that this analysis of the practical results of the negotiations misses the real significance of the agreement. For the first time, it is said, agriculture has been brought into the GATT mainstream. At least in principle, all major government policies affecting agricultural trade have been brought under some degree of international discipline. This, in turn, should facilitate progressive liberalization in future GATT rounds.

The principal basis for this claim is the agreement to convert all NTBs—including not only quantitative restrictions but also so-called voluntary export restraint agreements, minimum import prices, and variable levies—into bound tariffs. Although many of the resulting tariffs are prohibitive to start with and will remain so even after the agreed reductions, it is argued that at least a framework has been created for meaningful reductions in future negotiations comparable to those that have been so successful in reducing protection in the industrial sector.

What is generally overlooked is that, at the same time, the agreement legitimizes a wide range of domestic agricultural subsidies that would be recognized as protectionist when offered in other economic sectors. Some of the most important (and therefore most trade-distorting) subsidies, including the new European Union compensation payments and the U.S. deficiency payments, have been exempted from reduction requirements, and largely exempted from challenges in the GATT. Other potentially trade-distorting subsidies, such as "structural" assistance, disaster payments, subsidized crop insurance, income insurance, and safety net programs, as well as regional and environmental aids, are also exempted. This is a serious flaw that may come to haunt us in the future, much as the exceptions for agricultural NTBs and export subsidies (insisted upon by the United States in the 1950s) embarrassed us in the 1980s.[13]

The argument that domestic subsidies are not of great concern because they will inevitably run into taxpayer resistance is not convincing. Powerful and well-organized pressure groups will always find suitable pretexts for government assistance. What is more natural than compensating farmers for lower market prices resulting from international agreements? The European Union is already taking full advantage of the exemptions provided by the GATT agreement on agriculture. It is also allowing the new entrants (Austria, Sweden, and Finland) to compensate their high-cost producers for having to compete in the slightly less protected European Union market. The *Economist*, in one of its occasional lapses from free-trade orthodoxy, applauds this approach, and proposes to extend it to compensate European Union farmers for having to compete with low-cost Central European farmers once their countries join the union. And the *Economist* would even go so far as to give each European Union member government more freedom to "top up" farm incomes as it sees fit.[14] It is not difficult to see how domestic subsidies can get out of hand.

These problems are not necessarily confinable to agriculture. While there has been a reassuring trend toward less government intervention in the market, particularly in developing countries, some disturbing countercurrents can be observed in the industrialized world. Adjustment problems caused by competition from emerging industrial countries, and by the end of the cold war, have given rise to calls for industrial policies to support both declining and high-tech industries. The growing burden of environmental regulations provides yet another argument for government assistance. Accession to GATT of the countries of the former Soviet Union and of China, with their legacy of state control, will fuel demands for defensive measures.

So there is a larger reason for concern that what we have done in the agricultural sector may set bad precedents elsewhere. It may well be that when the next GATT round is launched, around the year 2000, agriculture will no longer stand out as a special case. With the proliferation of industrial policies, strict disciplines on domestic subsidies will also be needed in other sectors. Exceptions should be few and well defined. The only major exception should be adjustment assistance, provided it minimizes trade distortions and is subject to international supervision and phased out according to a firm timetable.

Like the nine-headed Hydra of Greek mythology, protectionism tends to grow two new heads whenever one is chopped off. Shut the door to increased border protection and you will get pressures for domestic subsidies. Try to dam the flood of export subsidies and governments will resort to "commercial diplomacy" (Secretary Ron Brown's euphemism for the use of diplomatic muscle in bilateral trade relations). And shall we ever find an effective way to deal with state trading and trade-distorting private agreements? The new World Trade Organization is certain to face challenges that will make our current problems seem like child's play.

Notes

1. GATT, *Trends in International Trade* (Geneva: GATT, October 1958).
2. OECD, *Agricultural Policies, Markets and Trade* (Paris: OECD, 1987).
3. See Fred H. Sanderson, ed., *Agricultural Protectionism in the Industrialized World* (Washington, D.C.: Resources for the Future, 1990).
4. Internal considerations also played a role in the decision. The mounting cost of export subsidies had become an issue within the European Community, with Germany taking the lead in arguing for a shift in the methods of protection. Its Ministry of Agriculture had long been critical of export subsidies as a means of farm support: instead of subsidizing French wheat exports (and third-country importers), it preferred to spend the available funds on direct assistance to German (and other community) farmers. And direct payments could serve to fend off (or cushion the effects of) the alternative option: to cut real support prices.
5. Another problem is the failure to "lock in" the existing levels of supply control.

6. This is true of virtually all major products in the European Community, dairy products and poultry in Canada, and sugar and dairy products in the United States. See Merlinda D. Ingco, "How Much Agricultural Liberalization Was Achieved in the Uruguay Round?" paper presented at the International Agricultural Trade Research Consortium, Washington, D.C., December 15, 1994.

7. For example, the bound tariffs for wheat and feed grains in the European Union are about 150 percent; for rice, sugar, beef, and dairy products about 300 percent. In Canada, the border protection is over 200 percent for poultry and 300 percent for dairy products; in the United States, 200 percent for sugar and about 150 percent for dairy products. Japan, which has reduced protection on some major products since 1986–88 and has refrained from "dirty tariffication," nevertheless retains tariffs of several hundred percent on wheat, feedgrains, and dairy products and about 100 percent on sugar and pork; its tariff on rice, to take effect only in the year 2000 (or later), will probably amount to 500–600 percent. Many developing countries, which were given virtual carte blanche in setting ceiling bindings on products subject to unbound duties, took advantage of this flexibility to table tariffs of 100 percent or more across-the-board. Analyses of the country schedules can be found in the "Summary of Commitments for Selected Country Schedules" (Center for Agricultural and Rural Development [CARD], Ames, IA: Iowa State University, August 1994); and in "The Uruguay Round Agreement on Agriculture: An Evaluation" (Washington, D.C.: IATRC, 1994).

8. One result of this provision is to increase the dispersion of agricultural rates of protection, causing trade to become more distorted.

9. These additional duties do not require proof of injury.

10. "The Uruguay Round Agreement on Agriculture: An Evaluation" (IATRC, 1994).

11. See, for example, the Atlantic Council of the United States, *The Uruguay Round of Multilateral Trade Negotiations under GATT* (Washington, D.C.: Atlantic Council of the United States, 1987).

12. For a more detailed analysis of the probable effects of the agreement, see my discussion paper, "The GATT Agreement on Agriculture," National Center for Food and Agricultural Policy, February 1994. Also, "The Uruguay Round Agreement on Agriculture: An Evaluation" (IATRC, 1994); "The Impacts of the Uruguay Round on U.S. Agriculture" (Center for Agricultural and Rural Development [CARD], Iowa State University, June 1994); "Analysis of the Uruguay Round: Impacts on U.S. Agriculture" (U.S. Department of Agriculture, Economic Research Service, April 1994).

13. Another problem is the failure of the agreement to deal effectively with state trading organizations and private export cartels.

14. "Tilling the Soil in a Wider Europe" (August 20, 1994).

19

Regionalism, Multilateralism, and American Leadership

Joseph A. Greenwald

Introduction

At this stage in the evolution of U.S. international economic policy and American leadership, it is indeed a daunting task to provide an analysis of the future directions of U.S. global trade policy. The world economy is changing rapidly and the Clinton administration is still feeling its way. The U.S. trade negotiator proclaims an absence of ideology. Thus far, he has completed the initiatives of the previous administrations.

The conventional summary of current policy is that the United States is moving from a policy of multilateralism to a multitrack policy which embodies unilateralism, bilateralism, regionalism, and multilateralism. This paper will discuss each of these approaches, how they may or may not fit together, and what the impact will be on the world trading system.

Another short-hand usage that needs some elucidation is the term "trade policy." Over the past fifteen years, this term has grown to cover not only nontariff trade barriers (NTBs), which are primarily linked to trade in goods, but also trade in services, "trade-related" investment measures, measures to enforce intellectual property rights and other domestic policies and regulations that result in trade distortions.

The U.S. agenda for future negotiations expands the term "trade policy" to cover the effect of trade on the environment, trade and competition policy, and trade and labor standards. The substantive extension of trade policy for the future will also be discussed in this chapter.

Historical Pillars of Trade Policy

Before moving into the future directions of U.S. policy, a brief review of the post–World War II international trade principles and structure may provide a useful point of departure.

The General Agreement on Tariffs and Trade (GATT)

After the failure of the United States to ratify the comprehensive Havana charter for an International Trade Organization (ITO)[1], twenty-three countries negotiated GATT,[2] which was based on the commercial policy provisions of Chapter IV of the ITO charter. The United States adhered to GATT as an executive agreement, using the president's authority granted by the Congress to negotiate and implement reciprocal tariff concessions.

GATT thus became the main international trade policy instrument. The fundamental GATT principles were unconditional most-favored-nation treatment (nondiscrimination), removal of quantitative restrictions, national treatment, and reduction of tariffs through negotiated concessions.

The first six rounds of GATT negotiations were concerned primarily with the reduction of tariff duties. During this same period, economic recovery in Europe and Japan led to the removal of import restrictions applied for balance-of-payments reasons. The trade liberalization from these developments led to substantial increases in international trade and economic growth. The GATT system worked well and was generally supported in the United States and most other developed, market-economy countries.

The GATT Questioned

Starting in the mid-1970s, a series of developments raised questions about the efficacy and effectiveness of GATT and its principles. First was the expansion of the European Community (EC)[3] from the original six members to nine and then twelve. This development took place under the GATT exception to the principle of nondiscrimination, which allows the formation of customs unions and free trade areas.[4] Further broadening and deepening of European integration extended the scope and area of discrimination and raised concerns about a "Fortress Europe" adversely affecting outside countries. The Kennedy Round[5] was directed primarily at reducing this discrimination by lowering the European Community's common external tariff. In the mid-1980s, these fears were intensified by the launching of a program to establish a single market in Europe with the free flow of goods, investment, services, and people.[6]

The second development raising questions about GATT was increased competition in world markets from a revived Europe and Japan and from low-cost exports of the newly industrialized countries, particularly the four Asian tigers

(South Korea, Taiwan, Hong Kong, and Singapore). The perception grew in the United States that we were the only truly open market and that only the United States observed GATT rules. In other words, there was not a "level playing field" for U.S. business. This led to the increased use of U.S. unfair trade laws (antidumping and countervailing duties) and voluntary export restraints. GATT permits the application of antidumping and countervailing duties in cases of serious injury.[7] But the "voluntary" restraint technique was a way of dealing with increased imports causing serious injury to a domestic industry circumventing GATT escape clause or safeguard provisions, which allowed—temporarily— a higher level of protection for the domestic industry being injured. The proliferation of such measures was contrary to the spirit (and perhaps the letter) of GATT.

The third development was the structural change in industrialized economies and in the composition of international exchanges. High-technology industries, services, and investment grew in importance. For high tech, the most important subject was the protection of intellectual property rights, which were not effectively dealt with in the existing international agreements under the World Intellectual Property Organization (WIPO) and not substantively covered in GATT. Trade in services was not covered at all. There were few provisions dealing with trade-related investment measures. Thus, GATT was perceived as not addressing the most important current issues and as needing updating.

Finally, GATT was considered weak in the area of dispute settlement,[8] which had become increasingly important. The process took an inordinately long time in many cases and losing defending parties could block action.

In the early 1980s, the United States took the initiative in seeking a comprehensive round of negotiations to promote further liberalization, to update GATT, and to strengthen its operations. This effort led to the ministerial meeting in Punta del Este in September 1986 to launch the Uruguay Round.[9]

The Uruguay Round

The successful conclusion of the Uruguay Round represents the high-water mark of the multilateral track of U.S. trade policy.[10] The Uruguay Round had a very ambitious agenda and the outcome may not have satisfied everyone. But it is a major achievement and points the way to some of the continuing directions of U.S. global trade policy.[11]

The fact that the Clinton administration adopted the two major trade initiatives of the previous administrations—NAFTA (albeit with modifications) and the GATT negotiations—and pushed them through suggests that "liberal" trade policy continues to have bipartisan support. Internationally, the participation of over a hundred countries in the Uruguay Round, plus the desire of other important countries like China and Russia to join, indicates that GATT is alive and well.

Agriculture

The negotiations on agriculture were inordinately, and perhaps unnecessarily, protracted. This was due, at least in part, to a flawed U.S. strategy with respect to agriculture. At the outset, the United States put on the table a proposal that was clearly unacceptable to the other main party involved, the European Community.[12] The United States held this position for a number of years without the negotiations really being engaged.

Considering that agriculture had been effectively taken out of GATT forty years ago when the United States obtained a waiver for certain agricultural import restrictions and removed primary products from the prohibition of export subsidies, it was unrealistic to expect anything but a modest start in the Uruguay Round in applying GATT disciplines to agriculture. The introduction of a highly protectionist and trade-distorting Common Agricultural Policy (CAP) by the European Community compounded the problem of bringing agriculture back into GATT. Not surprisingly, the outcome was an agreement that roughly matches what the European Community had already decided to do in the context of the reform of its own system and what the Congress had done in U.S. legislation. Nevertheless, it is most worthwhile to have agriculture subject to GATT rules.

Until the six-year agreement covering commitments on market access, domestic support, and export subsidies[13] has run out, it is unlikely that either the United States or the European Community will be prepared to negotiate again on agriculture. The future direction may be more in the field of sanitary and phytosanitary regulations, a set of issues being pressed by environmental and consumer interests.

In retrospect, it was probably a mistake to give top billing to agriculture. From the overall U.S. point of view, the priorities should have been market access for goods, intellectual property rights, services, investment, and operation of GATT. An analysis of how these subjects came out will help determine the future directions of U.S. global trade policy.

Market Access for Goods

There was an important breakthrough, with significance for the future, on the market-access issue. With the support of interested industries, the United States proposed the elimination of duties in certain sectors by all major suppliers and users in each sector. This was dubbed the "zero for zero" formula and proved to be surprisingly successful. For the Uruguay Round, it raised the overall level of liberalization achieved (to the 34–36 percent range). But the longer-term importance is that it points the way to what should be a key element in the multilateral track of future U.S. global trade policy.

With the decline in import tariff levels to 5 percent or less for many of the industrial sectors among the industrialized and industrializing countries (except, of course, for sensitive sectors like textiles and apparel), it would be a great boon to commerce to set a target for tariff elimination after the Uruguay Round cuts have been phased in, early in the twenty-first century. Such a move would also help avoid a complex set of tariff schedules. The combination of more free trade areas or customs unions and special duty-free treatment under programs like the generalized system of preferences (assuming it is extended by the United States) means that tariff duties are becoming less significant as trade protection (and they should not, in any event, be used for revenue purposes, especially in developed countries).

Intellectual Property Rights

The agreement on trade-related aspects of intellectual property rights, including trade in counterfeit goods,[14] met most of the U.S. objectives. It includes a very high level of substantive norms and effective enforcement provisions. The lead in this case was taken mainly by a U.S. industry coalition which brought other countries along through a combination of persuasion and threats.

It is likely that the main task for the future will be to monitor the application of the agreement, bring it up to date where necessary, and ensure that the same high standards or better are included in bilateral or regional arrangements.

Trade in Services

Not so successful was the extension of GATT to include trade in services. This disappointment was due not only to the inherent complexity and sensitivity of the services sector, but also to a flawed conceptual strategy.

The negotiators decided to start with a framework agreement and then fill in specific concessions. The obvious model was GATT. The first principle adopted was nondiscrimination or MFN. However, it apparently was not understood that the MFN principle (GATT Article I) cannot stand alone. It must be coupled with GATT Article II (schedule of concessions).

Nondiscrimination can be achieved by keeping everyone out of the market, but this is clearly not the intent or the objective of the agreement. Much time was spent in the negotiations on the nonapplication of MFN to various sectors. It should have been made clear at the outset that the MFN principle had no meaning without an acceptable schedule of concessions.

Negotiations are continuing to improve the concessions offered in the General Agreement on Trade in Services (GATS).[15] These negotiations will continue into the future. In the meantime, however, the United States has adopted a policy of "conditional" MFN; that is, new liberalization measures by the United States will not be extended to other countries unless they provide "reciprocity." This approach carries the risk of getting into the question of what kind of reciprocity is required, a problem which arose in connection with the Second Banking Directive of the European Community. In that case, the community demanded "mirror" reciprocity, which U.S. laws at the time precluded the United States from offering. The community accepted the U.S. market as "open" to European banks (since the target was Japan), but it reveals the problems arising in the application of the reciprocity concept.

Services will undoubtedly continue to be pursued on the multilateral track of future U.S. trade policy, but a question has been raised as to whether the other tracks may not be more profitable in the near future.

Investment

Similarly, relatively little progress was made in expanding the GATT coverage of investment issues.[16] Short-term, the bilateral (e.g., bilateral investment treaties) or regional (NAFTA) tracks may prove to be more effective. Medium-term, there is promise in the effort under way to negotiate a "wider investment instrument" using the OECD forum.

World Trade Organization (WTO) and Dispute Settlement

The final element of the Uruguay Round package which is relevant for the direction of future U.S. global trade policy is the establishment of the World Trade Organization and the strengthening of the dispute-settlement provisions.[17]

The WTO represents the first permanent international trade organization joined by the United States. As Ray Vernon points out in his essay in this volume, up to now the United States has resisted constraints on its freedom of action.

There are two features of the WTO that could affect the direction of U.S. global trade policy. First, the agreement establishing the WTO is designed to deal with the "free rider" problem. Previously in the GATT, contracting parties could pick and choose among the ancillary codes, for example, those on standards or subsidies negotiated in the Tokyo Round.

Under the WTO, membership requires acceptance of all the separate agreements or codes with the exception of four "plurilateral trade agreements," the most important of which is the Government Procurement Code. It remains to be seen how this will affect national decisions on membership in the WTO. Countries which were GATT contracting parties will be able to continue that status, but other parties may break off relations under WTO provisions.

The second feature is the continuity provided by the establishment of a permanent organization. This development could make it easier to shift from a system of discrete negotiating rounds to a continuing negotiation. The main argument in favor of the change is the great time and effort involved in mounting and carrying to a conclusion the separate rounds—the Uruguay Round providing the most recent and horrendous example. On the other hand, experience has indicated that the prospect of a negotiating round or the ongoing negotiations has served to contain pressures for protectionist actions, arguing in some cases that the problem can be dealt with in the negotiations. Another argument in favor of the old system is that it is necessary to have a fairly large agenda to find the tradeoffs required to put together a final package acceptable to the negotiating parties.

The answer to this question will probably depend on the nature of the subjects ripe for negotiation and the pressures for early action. It may also be possible to have a combination of continuing negotiations on some subjects and plurilateral or multilateral negotiations on others.

The new dispute-settlement system may turn out to be a mixed blessing. Under the GATT, one party, including the defendant or party complained against, can veto a request for a panel or the acceptance of a panel report. In other words, unanimity is required. The new dispute-settlement understanding turns this on its head and requires unanimity to reject a request or a panel report. The new system also sets up strict and enforceable time frames which are designed to deal with earlier problems arising from the process's being dragged out for years.

These changes will presumably meet demands for a more certain and speedy adjudication. The new system also is intended to force the losing party to make prompt redress. To the extent that the United States is the winning party, it will please business interests and the Congress. Acceptance of panel recommendations against the United States will depend, in part, on the quality of the report and the economic/political clout of the winning party.

Over the years of operation of GATT, there has been a difference between what was originally the European view and the American view of dispute settlement. The Europeans felt that trade disputes were heavily loaded with political considerations. They argued, therefore, that the GATT should not be applied as a strict legal instrument. In their view, dispute settlement should rely more on negotiation and diplomatic compromise. Rule-of-law-dominated Americans, on the other hand, rejected the pragmatic approach and stressed the adjudicatory function of the GATT dispute-settlement provisions.[18]

My own view is that both functions can and should be taken into account in a dispute settlement system. The ultimate objective in most cases should be for the panel report to provide a basis for resolving the dispute.[19] In other cases, the offending law or regulation must be condemned in order to maintain the integrity of GATT.[20]

To get the European Community member states to accept the new dispute-settlement process in the Uruguay Round (in a sense reversing the former "European" position), the European Community Commission said that it would restrain use of Section 301 of the Trade Act of 1974[21] outside the GATT framework. The community has announced that it will very carefully monitor the U.S. implementing legislation to find out whether any provision will undermine this expectation.

The potential differences over the use of Section 301 lead into the next section on the unilateral track.

Unilateralism

Section 301

Section 301 (and related sections) of the Trade Act of 1974 is the present-day archetype of U.S. unilateralism. Most of our trading partners look upon this legislation as the main instrument of U.S. application of power and pressure.

From the perspective of the U.S. Congress and the business community, Section 301 has been a highly effective tool in the effort to open foreign markets and "level the playing field."

Neutral observers consider that the previous administration used Section 301 with a good degree of care and finesse, recognizing that it is like a doomsday device: the game is usually lost when it has to be used. In most cases, GATT procedures were used when they were clear and effective. But even when GATT did not cover the measure (e.g., adequate protection of intellectual property rights) and the United States felt it had to impose sanctions, if the affected country was a GATT contracting party, the matter was settled out of court.

Section 301 itself is not contrary to the existing GATT. Its status under GATT 1994 is not entirely clear, although the United States insists it is unaffected. Unless the United States changes the law to make it a per se violation of the GATT, the problems arise when a specific action, like increasing bound duties in retaliation for "violation of an agreement" or for an "unjustifiable" measure, is taken by the United States. Regardless of the legalities, the political reality is that Section 301 is here to stay, perhaps until the WTO and the world has changed so that public and congressional perceptions support reliance on international processes. In the meantime, the best hope is that unilateral actions by the United States are carefully crafted to serve the other aspects of future global trade policy.

The danger of less careful application of Section 301 than has been the case in the past is that it could lead to what is generally referred to in the press as a "trade war." This could result if the Section 301 process leads to U.S. retaliation against a trading partner by raising bound duties.

If the country against whose trade the Section 301 action is taken is a GATT contracting party, it can seek redress (under GATT Article XXIII). If the GATT process goes to a dispute panel and the aggrieved party wins, the recommendation will likely be for the United States to restore the bound duties or to offer other tariff reductions to restore the balance of concessions. If the United States does not take either action, the complaining party would presumably be authorized to withdraw equivalent concessions. This "unraveling" process is the feared outcome of extensive and careless use of Section 301. Another risk is that U.S. abuse of the new dispute-settlement mechanism may undermine the credibility of the WTO.

Antidumping and Countervailing Duties

Although the application of antidumping and countervailing duties is permitted under GATT Article VI (paragraph 1 states that dumping "is to be condemned" if it causes or threatens material injury), U.S. laws and procedures[22] are sometimes put in the category of unilateralism. The fact is that, while the United States is among the countries with the largest number of cases, other parties like Australia, Canada, and the European Community resort as often to such "unfair trade" laws.

In the United States, private parties have the right to bring an action so the government does not control the number of cases. Second, the U.S. process is much more open and transparent, so public awareness is greater compared to other countries that deal with such matters behind closed doors. Finally, other countries have other methods of combating "unfair" trade practices.

A more justifiable accusation is that U.S. antidumping and countervailing duty law and practice encourage the filing of cases and make affirmative findings more likely, even in dubious cases. This was one of the factors driving the Canadian interest in a free trade agreement and resulted in the Chapter 19 binational dispute-settlement provisions in the U.S.–Canada Free Trade Agreement.[23]

U.S. law and practice have also been a long-standing issue in GATT. One of the hotly disputed subjects in the Uruguay Round was the revision of the GATT code. A compromise was struck which dealt with some of the complaints that the United States and other main users of antidumping duty laws did not apply their practices consistently with the spirit of GATT Article VI. But U.S. implementing legislation may not conform entirely to the Uruguay Round compromise. The result may be an increased resort to the new unified dispute settlement process, putting more strains on the WTO.

As suggested below, the antidumping problem will probably not be solved until trade barriers are completely removed and it will be possible to "dump back." Only at that point will it be possible to substitute competition policy measures for border trade measures, as in the case within the single markets of the United States and the European Community.

Bilateralism/Regionalism

The mid-1980s also saw a move into bilateralism with the negotiation of a free trade agreement with Israel. But this was taken as more of a political move than a trade policy departure.

The real bilateral/regional track began with the Canadian FTA in 1989 and gathered steam with the successful negotiation of NAFTA. By the GATT standards established in the European Economic Community (EEC) and European Free Trade Area (EFTA) cases, the U.S. agreements are clearly GATT-consistent.[24]

More important from the point of view of maintenance of an open trading system, these agreements did not raise barriers against outside countries and, except for a few overly restrictive rules of origin, they did not establish any trade policy precedents that may undermine our longer-term objectives in the multilateral track.

More serious problems may arise when we face the question of extending NAFTA to other countries in the hemisphere or beyond. The conventional wisdom is that the first candidate for accession to NAFTA will be Chile, which already has made requests and is generally considered economically and politically qualified to take on NAFTA membership.

Beyond Chile, there are questions about countries that are not yet in a position to take on full NAFTA obligations, countries that are in economic groups with free trade area or customs union pretensions and even countries outside the region. The administration is obviously aware of these problems and is taking a cautious approach.

Looking at the problems in terms of not prejudicing U.S. global interests, there are a few points to consider. First, any arrangements should be consistent with GATT, our main multilateral track. Second, agreements that are less than full NAFTA accession should be worked out very carefully. This caution applies not only to the obligations undertaken by the other hemisphere countries, but also to the benefits offered from the U.S. or NAFTA side. Less than fully "GATTable" agreements will become unfortunate precedents. To avoid this development, obligations and benefits should not be sought outside trade measures as defined in GATT 1947. That is, sectoral or partial trade agreements should not be offered. If interim agreements before full accession are necessary, they should be in the form of framework agreements that deal with matters like intellectual property rights or right of establishment not traditionally part of trade agreements until NAFTA.

Another possibility for interim action as a step toward bringing hemisphere countries into NAFTA would be to add a dispute-settlement system along the lines of NAFTA (including the supplementary agreements on labor and the environment) to the framework agreements. These framework agreements have consultation provisions and the United States would presumably be urging potential NAFTA candidates to make unilateral reforms as Mexico did. But they may be seeking something more from the NAFTA parties to make the reforms more palatable at home. The offer of binational dispute settlement might help politically to show the interest and good faith of the NAFTA countries and to further the process of getting candidates used to NAFTA disciplines.

In addition to the narrow trade policy issues, another pitfall to be avoided is accepting lower standards in fields like services, investment, and agriculture, and to avoid a watering down of what has been achieved in NAFTA. One of the values of NAFTA is that it can be held up as a standard for agreements between developed and developing countries. It would be unfortunate to lose this advantage.

Future Agenda for U.S. Global Trade Policy

Beyond NAFTA and the Uruguay Round, what are the substantive issues to be taken up? There is general agreement, and the president endorsed it in Brussels early in January 1994, that the top items for future negotiations, probably on both the multilateral and the bilateral/regional tracks, are trade and the environment, trade and competition policy, trade and labor standards, and investment.

Trade and the environment has been on the agenda for some time, particularly after the GATT panel report in the tuna–dolphin case.[25] Discussions at the governmental level have been under way in the OECD and GATT. An informal exercise between the business sector and government officials indicated that there would be no problem on the U.S. side in taking over the environmental provisions from NAFTA into GATT. But it is doubtful whether the environmental community will now be satisfied with that, particularly in the area of transparency and Nongovernmental Organization (NGO) participation.

The main substantive issue is the use of trade measures for environmental reasons. Most of these problems affecting outside countries (cross-border pollution or global commons issues) should be dealt with by international environmental agreements. In GATT/WTO terms the best solution would be to negotiate a new Article XX exception following the pattern set in paragraph (h) designed for intergovernmental commodity agreements.[26]

Trade and competition appeared on the agenda more recently. It has been discussed at the OECD in Paris, but the cross-education process is still in the early stages. The range of possibilities goes from the multilateralization of the European Community–United States bilateral agreement on enforcement cooperation, through the idea of international antitrust codes (of various kinds), to the notion of using competition policy tools instead of (or with) trade measures to deal with unfair trade practices.

The administration has recently introduced a bill to permit the exchange of confidential information bearing on antitrust violations with other countries. If this legislation can be worked out, a more effective system of antitrust enforcement cooperation may be possible.

The next step of international harmonization of competition policy or a code will be much more difficult to achieve. Equally difficult and far off will be the "ultimate" step of moving to the use of competition policy instruments to replace border measures against dumping and subsidization. A basic prerequisite for this development is the removal of substantially all barriers to trade on a global basis and readiness to accept greater discipline in the use of domestic subsidies. Because of the sensitive political issues involved, much more preparatory work is necessary in the OECD before attempting to reach agreement on firm legal commitments in GATT.

Trade and labor standards are a subject that has been taken up in GATT for over forty years without finding any solutions. We now have the NAFTA supplemental agreement as a possible model.

Political pressures will drive this agenda item, without much hope of success that will satisfy domestic U.S. interests. On both the environment and labor standards, the developing countries are suspicious of hidden protectionism, so progress may be more likely on the bilateral/regional or plurilateral track.

Investment was dealt with effectively in NAFTA as far as a developing country is concerned. But new issues are arising among the OECD countries like participation in governmental research projects and other aspects of industrial policy. The question of "piercing the corporate veil" to look at ownership is likely to become a more important and troublesome issue.

Outside basic bilateral and plurilateral agreements on foreign investment (mostly with developing countries), more complicated and sophisticated issues have arisen among the industrialized countries. Work in the OECD on a "wider investment instrument" will have to get further along before commitments will be possible in GATT or in a separate international agreement.

American Leadership

The basic thesis of this paper is that U.S. interests will be best served by maintaining the open, multilateral trading system as embodied in GATT 1994. This policy will provide the stability of bound concessions and a set of rules under which trade and investment can flourish. In a world characterized by the internationalization of production, services, and investment, sustainable economic growth can be best achieved by the free flow of the factors of production.

The question is whether the United States has the capability and the will to exercise leadership as it has in the past. No single power or group of countries has moved up to take the place of the United States. But there will continue to be a need for leadership in maintaining and expanding an effective global trade and investment regime. Until the next big multilateral push (or series of negotiations) leads to the elimination of substantially all barriers to trade and investment in the next century, unilateral and regional pressures will have to be carefully managed. Perhaps the "Quad" (the United States, Canada, European Union, and Japan) can, for the next decade, fulfill the dual role of organizing new liberalization initiatives and ensuring that national or regional actions do not undermine the system.

An important step that should be taken after 1996 is to propose to the major trading countries that duties on all industrial products (with some sensitive exceptions if necessary) be phased out among the developed countries. This step would not only lift a burden from traders, but also remove a source of friction and complication arising from the likely proliferation of bilateral and regional arrangements as well as existing preferences like the generalized system of preferences (GSP) and the Caribbean systems. This initiative might be a follow-on (after more careful thought and preparation) to the abortive U.S. effort at the recent Group of Seven (G–7) meeting in Naples.

In terms of strengthening the trade and investment pillar of the Bretton Woods structure, special care must be taken to avoid a deterioration of GATT. The expansion of GATT to a membership of over a hundred, the growth of regional and subregional groupings, and the entry into more difficult and sensitive domestic policy areas like environment, competition policy, investment, and labor standards will require careful management and constant attention of the major trading countries. In addition, the move to a tighter legal and adjudicative regime can go badly wrong unless there is a strong WTO director general supported by the key countries. The issues in GATT 1994 and the future "trade and" agenda are politically sensitive. The WTO will flourish only if the traditional consensus system continues to work.

Notes

1. Department of State Publication 3206, Commercial Policy Series 114 (Washington, D.C.: Department of State, released September 1948).
2. GATT/1986-4 (Geneva: GATT, 1986).
3. *Treaties Establishing the European Communities*, abridged ed. (Luxembourg: Office for Official Publications of the European Communities, 1987).
4. GATT Article XXIV.
5. John W. Evans, *The Kennedy Round in American Trade Policy* (Cambridge, Mass.: Harvard University Press, 1971).
6. "The Single European Act," in *Treaties Establishing the European Communities*, pp. 523–577.
7. GATT Article VI.
8. GATT Articles XXII and XXIII.
9. For the text of the Ministerial Resolution see Annex A of Atlantic Council Policy Paper, *The Uruguay Round of Multilateral Trade Negotiations under GATT* (Washington, D.C.: Atlantic Council of the United States, 1987).
10. Testimony of Ambassador Michael Kantor, United States trade representative to the House Ways and Means Committee, January 26, 1994, and to the Senate Finance Committee, February 8, 1994.
11. *Final Act Embodying the Results of the Uruguay Round of Multilateral Trade Negotiations*, version of December 15, 1993 (Washington, D.C.: Office of the U.S. Trade Representative, Executive Office of the President, 1993).
12. *The Uruguay Round of Multilateral Trade Negotiations*, pp. 45–60.
13. *Final Act Embodying the Results of the Uruguay Round*, II Annex 1A3.
14. Ibid., II Annex 1C.
15. Ibid., Annex 1B.
16. Ibid., II Annex 1A7.
17. Ibid., II and II Annex 2.

18. For a good discussion of this issue, see Andreas F. Lowenfeld, "Remedies along with Rights: Institutional Reform in the New GATT," *American Journal of International Law* 88, no. 3 (July 1994): pp. 477–488.

19. For an example, see the "Semiconductor" case, GATT document L/6309 (March 24, 1988) and the actions subsequently taken by the parties, the European Community and Japan.

20. For an example, see the "Screwdriver" case, "EEC Regulation on Imports of Parts and Components," GATT document L/6657 (March 22, 1990).

21. Public Law 93-618, approved January 3, 1975, 19 USC 2411.

22. Title VII of the Tariff Act of 1930 as added by the Trade Agreements Act of 1979 and amended by the Trade and Tariff Act of 1984 and the Omnibus Trade and Competitiveness Act of 1988, USC 1671 and 1673.

23. Communication from the president of the United States transmitting the final legal text, July 26, 1988, 100th Congress, 2nd session, House Document 100-216.

24. GATT Article XXIV.

25. "U.S. Restrictions on Imports of Tuna," Report of the Panel, September 1991 (Geneva: GATT, 1991).

26. For a detailed presentation of this idea, see United States Council for International Business, "International Environmental Agreements and the Use of Trade Measures to Achieve Their Objectives" (New York: United States Council for International Business, 1993).

20

Bretton Woods: Fifty Years After

Tran Van-Thinh

Some History

The agreement reached in Bretton Woods in 1944 was based on the tragic experience of the 1930s. The consensual rules then laid down were designed to permit money to play a double role in the postwar period: as capital in the economic order, and as a stabilizing factor in the political order.

In Jamaica in 1976, these consensual rules were abandoned. There is no longer a monetary order to prevent or to cushion crises that arise and to back up the indispensable transfer of resources.

The International Monetary Fund (IMF) and the International Bank for Reconstruction and Development (World Bank) have continued to operate as best they can without the safety net provided by a multilateral agreement. In the absence of an overall vision and an overall strategy, the action taken has inevitably been limited and has sometimes been an inadequate reaction to the needs of countries in difficulty.

The Group of Seven (G–7) has frequently patched up the situation. The world's seven richest countries and the European Commission have been able to contain the damage done. They have been able (sometimes at the last minute) to avoid catastrophe. But they have, above all, demonstrated their inability to agree on a long-term strategy and their impotence vis-à-vis the financial markets.

Since the fall of the Berlin Wall, obstacles separating different and differing economic systems have also fallen one by one. Since then, markets, their signals and their rules, have in different degrees regulated trade, competition, growth, and economic development. By rules, I mean essentially multilateral rules, contractually negotiated and agreed.

Countries with centrally planned economies have now been converted and are firmly resolved to effect the transition to a market economy, which is today's panacea. Developing countries are also following the credo of the liberalization of trade and an open economy. But at the same time, in the rich industrialized countries, the capitalist heaven has been turned into hell for whole sectors of production, and whole sections of the population have been marginalized.

Explosive Imbalances

In the last decade of the century, movements that are apparently contradictory, and certainly erratic, instantly create excitement, depression, and panic on stock exchanges worldwide. Financial markets practically escape the authority of central banks. The volume of monetary and financial transactions is now fifty times that of transactions related to world trade. During the 1930s these were only twice the volumes of such transactions. A gigantic amount of capital can now readily be moved across national borders. This is already a first indication that a truly global economy is being created with quasi-mechanical interconnections and interactions. Reality is nevertheless complex and is both national and global, as well as international, transnational, and plurinational.

Behind this reality lies another: one of striking imbalances that are structural as well as the result of short-term factors. The American economy, for instance, suffers from profound disequilibria: insufficient savings, chronic public deficits, indebtedness of households, businesses, and governments, and current-account external deficits. In any other country, such deficits would have led to sanctions by the markets and above all by the International Monetary Fund (IMF). It must also be added that in the United States, the marginalization of a great number of those excluded by the rigors of competition, by misery, by illness, by urban violence, and by the absence of an effective social security safety net leads me to fear the worst. However, for the moment, the American economy remains, paradoxically, a source of dynamism which stimulates the world economy, particularly that of Asia and the Far East.

In short, on the threshold of the year 2000, our rapidly evolving world is destabilized and threatened by the multiplication of imbalances and inequalities which are often profound: overpopulation and underdevelopment, growth and ecological degradation, riches and misery, gluttony and famine. All against a background of marginalization, exclusion, and mass unemployment. Unemployment and underemployment are the gangrene of our age and result from many different causes. There are 20 million unemployed in Europe and 270 million without jobs in China. This relationship is illustrative of the explosive imbalance between the world's wealthy regions and its deprived areas. The problems created by this imbalance must be dealt with during the present decade, for national frontiers will not prevent the exodus of those without jobs.

Money, Finance, and Trade: The Three Traditional Pillars of Any Economic Order

It is now fifty years since the world began to rebuild on the ruins left by the Second World War. The initiative came from what we in France call the Anglo-Saxon countries and in particular from visionary and generous American statesmen. Politically, the charter of San Francisco led to the creation of the United Nations. On the economic side, the Bretton Woods agreement provided for the establishment of the International Monetary Fund and the International Bank for Reconstruction and Development. The Havana Charter foresaw the creation of an International Trade Organization (ITO). The Marshall Plan and, to a lesser extent, the Columbo plan, led to an unprecedented expansion in the world economy. But the edifice which was to have been supported by the three pillars of money, finance, and trade remained incomplete because the United States did not ratify the Havana Charter and because the world was split into several antagonistic economic blocs.

Today, the difficulty of coordinating monetary policies and the impossibility of organizing the monetary system around a single supranational reserve currency have forced the G–7 to lower their sights. The richest countries now only aim to do just enough to contain instability within acceptable limits. The financial markets, which are dominated by information technology and the fax, tend to get carried away and need reassurance. Cooperation between governments has reached its limits. Conflicts between international obligations, where these exist, and national interests have become more intense and more frequent. American leadership is less decisive. The relative decline of the United States has made it more reluctant to make economic transfers to its partners and to new countries in order to preserve global stability. The United States is no longer capable of dealing with the many priorities with which it is confronted in the world.

Even though the dollar is no longer the anchor of the world monetary system, it is still used as a reserve currency and as a point of reference regulating rates of exchange in a large part of the world. But how much longer will the leadership of the dollar, if not American leadership, remain convincing? The power of Japan as the world's main creditor, the rise of Asian economic powers, the potential of European unification already suggest an alternative to the leadership of a single great power. This alternative can only be based upon a collective responsibility.

The Bretton Woods institutions have had their failures, caused notably by their most powerful members, even as recently as in Madrid. But they have also proved themselves. They need to be renovated and adapted to the twenty-first century. The creation of the new World Trade Organization (WTO) provides a good opportunity to trim and reinvigorate them.

In Marrakesh, King Hassan II of Morocco was not mistaken when he said: "In giving birth ... to the WTO, we recognize the rule of law in international economic and trade relations by asserting the primacy of universal rules and disciplines over the temptations of unilateralism and the doctrine of might is right."

Currencies are indispensable for the conduct of trade and economic policies. There is therefore a risk that the aim referred to by King Hassan II will not be achieved if erratic fluctuations in the value of currencies and currency manipulation and speculation are not also brought under a greater degree of control. The solution is within our reach. The WTO will come into being in 1995 and will be able to enter into a dialogue with, into consultation with, and even into cooperation with, the IMF and World Bank. The aim of this process should be to draw up and implement a contractual multilateral monetary regime. Governments would, of course, have to cooperate in this process and agree on its results. This regime should ensure the coherence, or at least the convergence, of macroeconomic policies at both the multilateral level (that of the IMF, the World Bank, and the WTO) and at the national level. Only in this way will a sound basis be provided for the rapidly emerging global economy.

The IMF, the World Bank, and the WTO will not be effective in the future unless they are more open. I therefore agree with the ideas set out in the valuable report presented by the Center of Concern and its cosponsors in "Rethinking Bretton Woods,"[1] which pleads for more transparency and more democracy in their operation.

A Necessary Pillar: Economic Development

To the three traditional pillars of the world economic order must be added another: economic development. The development dimension has, up to now, been integrated into other policies dealing with money, finance, and trade. It has been the subject of much solicitude at all levels. It has also given rise to north-south confrontations. The results have been slim. They have thrown into relief new south-south imbalances. And they have engendered a terrific international bureaucracy, especially in the United Nations. The approach adopted in the 1960s was misguided and wrong. It is time to rethink development policies. These must recognize the responsibility of each country for its economic development as well as the responsibility of the multilateral system. The relationship between development policies and all other policies must be reexamined. We must no longer be concerned only with the distribution of wealth between rich and poor countries but also with the reduction of disparities in each and every country, including the United States. It is still astonishing to learn that, even in this country, 38 million people lived below the poverty level in 1992 and that in 1993 this figure rose to 39.3 million, or just over 15 percent of the American population. In addition, this poverty is not egalitarian. Forty percent of those living in poverty are children. African-Americans and Hispanic-Americans are harder hit than Asian- or Caucasian-Americans. The disparity between the incomes of rich and poor is greater in the United States than in any other wealthy country, although this disparity has also grown in the United Kingdom and in France. The situation is hardly better in many developing countries. Such domestic disparities make it more difficult for wealthy countries to help developing countries and explain, at least in part, the poor results achieved in the foreign aid field. One can even understand those in the Congress of the United States and public opinion in Europe who doubt whether financial transfers should be made to the south while problems of poverty, aggravated by unemployment, threaten social and political stability in their own countries.

The Environment: An Essential Pillar

The need to produce and to consume cleanly and to protect the environment is now widely accepted so long as it does not lead to excesses in the opposite direction. The conference in Rio consecrated this realization and its global implications. But practical results are a long while coming and those actually achieved are almost insignificant. The exercise of sovereign national power follows other paths. In any case, the agreements painfully reached will not reduce the disparities between developed and less developed countries. Their preliminary and partial character, and the fact that they are not binding, may even threaten to attenuate these disparities.

Measures and initiatives designed to protect the environment have an impact on the competitiveness of enterprises. Governments therefore find them difficult to apply if others do not do the same. This applies to all countries, however economically powerful they are. Consultations to promote the coordination of trade policies and environmental policies, at the national, regional, and multilateral levels, are therefore indispensable. These consultations should also relate to development, money, finance, and trade, which cannot and must not be treated separately any longer. Such an initiative is essential if our planet is to be saved. Negotiations will be necessary to put in place contractual disciplines which lay down the rights and obligations of states. Any violation would be subject to sanctions. This will be one of the priority tasks of the WTO.

When all the policies to which I have referred are in place and working in harmony together to prevent slippages and speculation, and to reduce disparities between rich and poor zones, ministers of trade and ministers of environment of all countries will no longer be second- or third-class ministers. Governments will then have understood the priorities that they should give to trade, which received its *lettres de noblesse* in Marrakesh, and the environment, which is still awaiting the recognition that is its due.

The time appears favorable. Economic recovery has begun in various parts of the world. It has been estimated that implementation of the Uruguay Round GATT agreement would lead to an increase in world trade of about 500 billion of today's dollars over a period of ten years. This enormous increase will have a beneficial effect on employment and education. It will also help to reduce the economic and social disparities which may be accentuated by the play of market forces both inside and outside national boundaries.

The Social Dimension to Attenuate the Rigor of the Market

Total reliance on the state turns free citizens into dependents. Total reliance on market forces marginalizes and pauperizes them. The social dimension should not be used as a protective shield, nor as the spearhead of unilateralism. It should simply attenuate the rigor of the marketplace. In order to do so, we must rise above the sterile debate on the share of the costs of the social dimension to be borne by companies, or by workers, or by the state. We must set ourselves a higher goal. We must ask ourselves how, at the world level, capitalism can be given a human face. It must be emphasized once again that social problems cannot be solved by actions at the national level only. No individual state, however powerful or however weak, is able, in isolation, to assure the social well-being of its citizens over the long term.

Over the decades, capitalism has demonstrated its ability to adapt and to survive. Mercantile capitalism gave rise to industrial capitalism, with its tangible products, its factories, and its excessive energy consumption. The industrial revolution has been followed by the revolution in communications, which burns less energy. This new capitalism will influence, directly or indirectly, all forms of human activity: industrial, agricultural, tertiary, multimedia, technological, scientific, cultural. New products will result from the interplay of technical and scientific research, investment in both goods and services, the collection and diffusion of knowledge and information, and integrated management. This new capitalism has overcome all the obstacles in its path. Its tentacles are everywhere, but it depends on growth. Its message is seductive because it is simple, direct, and without sophistication: laissez-faire. Let us get on with it and we will let you get on with it. But what of happiness? What of the inability of many people to feel concern for the well-being of others?

The new capitalism has established itself because there is no credible alternative to it. The globalization of the economy will make it easier to take the social dimension into account. We must make a collective effort in this direction.

Some Conclusions

These are avenues to be explored, rather than a detailed blueprint to be followed. Having left my official functions, I can now enjoy the luxury of taking some distance from the bureaucracy and having imagination. As Einstein said, "Imagination is more important than knowledge." Therefore, it is no longer for me, but for others, to deal with the negotiations of these new ideas.

The new capitalism is triumphant and appears invincible. But we must not allow wealth to create poverty. Let us rediscover riches other than purchasing power and the consumption of material goods. We must not allow money to domesticate human nature. We must not allow prosperity to destroy our countryside. We must not allow the economy to cause tension, conflicts, and wars. The economy should be the servant, not the master, and must not be allowed to give rise to a new totalitarianism.

A human face for the new capitalism calls for social solidarity at the world level. It is by education that we shall succeed, notably by reducing the deep-seated nationalistic reflexes of peoples and states.

A Masai proverb says: "The planet that we hand on to our children must be passed on intact to future generations."

Note

1. Center of Concern, "Rethinking Bretton Woods" (Washington, D.C.: Center of Concern, 1994).

21

The "Informatization" of World Affairs

Harlan Cleveland

. . . the ideas of economists and political philosophers, both when they are right and when they are wrong, are more powerful than is commonly understood. Indeed the world is ruled by little else. Practical men, who believe themselves to be quite exempt from any intellectual influences, are usually the slaves of some defunct economist. Madmen in authority, who hear voices in the air, are distilling their frenzy from some academic scribbler of a few years back. I am sure that the power of vested interests is vastly exaggerated compared with the gradual encroachment of ideas.

—John Maynard Keynes (1936)

From "Places" to "Networks"

I'll start with these propositions about the fifty years we have just been through. Most of the star performers in the postwar world economy chose a market path to prosperity. In the Atlantic and Pacific democracies, deregulation has been the story of the 1980s. The brightest meteors—South Korea, Taiwan, Singapore, and a lengthening list of export-led copycats—bet on systems in which, while different from each other, open markets were a priceless ingredient. The wager paid off handsomely.

Meanwhile the world's richest countries began to take full advantage of new information technologies—rapid data processing combined with reliable electronic telecommunications—that spurred their growth and widened their reach.

In France, this was called *l'informatisation de la societé*, the informatization of society. That paid off handsomely too—though the growing numbers of unemployed were not impressed, and the big imbalances of trade and payments were often embarrassingly severe.

At the same time, a flood of information about others' prosperity and opportunities elsewhere flowed steadily into the misnamed "controlled economies." The apostates of central planning in Eastern Europe and the former Soviet Union, and even its apostles in Beijing, then started gingerly to let many perestroikas bloom.

In these dramatic and interconnected scenarios, was there an "invisible hand" traceable to the memorable meeting held in Bretton Woods fifty years ago? Not likely.

Richard Gardner has implied—diplomatically, in the form of a question—that the International Monetary Fund has not even tried to pressure the world's rich countries to balance their payments.[1] The International Bank for Reconstruction and Development (World Bank) made its first loan to Denmark, but never followed through on the "Reconstruction" part of its mandate and was soon elbowed aside by the Marshall Plan. Both these "Bretton Woods institutions" wound up as cautious handmaidens of development in Asia, Africa, and Latin America—which does not seem to be what those who were present at the creation in 1944 thought they were doing.

Moreover, the record of the past few years does not suggest that either the World Bank or the IMF has helped much to make the world money system rational or even workable. Don't look now, but the "invisible hand" seems palsied.

Just when so many nations seemed to be adapting market economics to their domestic advantage, world markets are spinning in unruly, ungovernable, unpredictable gyrations. Watching stocks, bonds, commodity futures, and the U.S. dollar these past few years, even a devoted disciple of Adam Smith would have to conclude that the invisible hand has taken to playing with a yo-yo.

What's going on here? The diagnosis is now plain. The "information revolution" has stormed the ramparts of the nation-state, and most of our favorite economic theories—capitalist as well as Marxist—have been trampled in the rush. Peter Drucker, the oracle of business management, wrote many years ago that information had become "the central capital, the cost center, and the crucial resource of the economy." He was writing then about the United States. His prescient words now apply almost as well to what the French economist Albert Bressand, compressing two words for rhetorical effect, calls the "worldeconomy."

Data networks of extraordinary speed and complexity already link commodity traders, airline ticket agents, air traffic controllers, weather forecasters, public health officials, currency speculators, music lovers, modern librarians, and multinational executives with each other. Criminals and police forces both depend heavily on electronic networking. Grain merchants have an intelligence system that (on subjects in which they share a vital interest, such as the internal politics of Argentina) certainly overmatches the dwindling capacities of the CIA.

Given what Roberto Campos has called "the globalization of financial markets,"[2] it no longer matters so much where *you* are if you are electronically plugged into what the buyers and sellers you care about are doing, wherever *they* are. The notion of a "New York market," a "Tokyo market," a "Zurich market," or a "London market" (which Ray Mikesell tells us the British delegation at Bretton Woods was so anxious to protect)[3] already sounds quaint.

The idea of *markets* as *places* evaporated before our eyes on Black Monday 1987, as information about prices and pessimism ricocheted around the globe. There is no longer much reason, save tradition and personal convenience, for the New York Stock Exchange to be in New York. It could probably work just as well, with much lower overhead, if it were put in South Dakota, alongside Citicorp's credit-card operations, or in Fort Lauderdale, Florida, where American Express conducts a worldwide business by computer-assisted communications. Even time zones seem dated. If you are buying and selling money, precious metals, commodities, bonds, or shares in big companies, you (or your surrogate) had better be awake twenty-four hours a day—or you will be overtaken by those who are.

It is not yet true of culture, but it is certainly true of finance, that modern civilization is built less and less around communities of place, more and more around communities of people. All the really important markets are world markets. Daniel Bell, the premier philosopher of the information society, foresaw long ago "a change in the nature of markets from 'places' to 'networks.' " The change has come.

The Confidence Game

The almost instantaneous transport of data and its rapid processing into usable information have not only blurred the frontiers between nations. They also have blurred the line between investment and speculation, detached both from the slower-moving world of production and from trading goods and services, and torn the exchange of national currencies loose from the moorings of public responsibilities.

What made world business an increasingly "single market" was not primarily trade, aid, or alliances—even the North Atlantic one that was so successful it dissolved its Eastern rival in Europe. What happened was that, with the help of fast computers and reliable telecommunications, capital (because it is a form of information) could flow so much faster and more freely than things.

Money exchange between countries is needed to pay for *things* shipped right now, and for trade "futures" (promises to buy things that are not available yet). Money is also sent across frontiers to buy things that *do not move*, like automobile plants in Europe, forests in Brazil, rubber plantations in Indonesia, golf courses in Hawaii, and Rockefeller Center in New York. Large amounts of money, contributing greatly to bank-created credit inflation, are devoted to the even larger chance to make money by buying money itself, and money futures too.

Money is information. The communities of people who arrange investments and move money around—bankers, credit agencies, foreign exchange markets, futures traders, and all those whose business it is to guess about future financial flows—have been enabled by information technology to create an explosive growth in their own activity, sustained by credit inflation out of all proportion to the trade in things that money flows used to reflect.

In the decade of the 1980s, money used to finance trade expanded by only 63 percent, while all foreign exchange transactions grew by 447 percent. At the end of that decade, money exchanges that buy and sell numbers (once bits of paper, now electronic bytes) amounted in 1989 to thirty-four times the money exchanged for goods and services (what we call "trade"). The world economy does keep knitting itself more tightly together, but within it, the exchange of information about money favors a much tighter weave.

The numbers are numbing and not in themselves very revealing. Let's try thinking with a metaphor.

It is as if a bright light nearby were shining on the "real" world economy, projecting a huge shadow play on a faraway wall. It is a play with a complex plot full of fast breaks and arthritic adjustments as people make sudden judgments about the future values of present realities, compounded by guesswork about the future value of each national currency in its relation to all the others. None of the actors has a clear idea of the script of the next scene. Each lender sells the debt he is owed to another, usually bigger, lender (usually for less than its face value, reflecting an agreed guess about when or whether the debtor will ever pay up).

The whole shadowy pyramid is sustained by confidence, the confidence of the alcoholic who assures his friends that he can handle that next drink, and the one after that. But a confidence game is always vulnerable to a breakdown of trust. Any loss of confidence in the creditworthiness of the debtors can turn the pyramid on its head, as each player scurries to leave the confidence game just before everyone else does.

No one knows just how big the shadow can become; that depends on the lenders of last resort. The ultimate suckers in this shadowy game of musical chairs used to be government, especially the U.S. government. ("Governments aren't like companies, they can't go bankrupt." This tenet of the banker's belief system has been badly frayed by recent experience.)

Just when U.S. banks realized that getting most of their profits from impoverished countries, high-risk junk bonds, and overvalued real estate was not the way to stay in business, the Reagan-era budget and trade deficits and the savings-and-loan crisis removed what everyone else in the confidence game had been secretly counting on—the capacity and willingness of the United States of America to pick up the check when the binge was over.

In consequence, no national government now controls the value of "its own" money. Banks and other governments create dollars as required, lots of them, without so much as a curtsy to Washington, D.C. The international monetary system—already out of national control, not yet under international control—is chronically at risk of a nervous breakdown.

In the first half of the postwar period, the monetary system had a measure of "stability"—that is, companies and countries knew roughly what their money would be worth in other countries because exchange rates were fixed by international agreement (the Bretton Woods agreement, administered by the International Monetary Fund). But as Edward Bernstein lucidly explains in his paper in this volume, once the United States (and promptly everyone else) got off that train in the early 1970s, currencies started to "float" in their comparative values. From then on, what each major country's money was worth (compared to other nations' money) depended on how well it managed its own affairs: nursed its growth rate, avoided too much inflation, recovered handily from recessions.

Meanwhile, *market* does increasingly mean *international*. The earlier, more successful deals (among fewer countries) to dismantle obstacles to commerce, under the General Agreement on Tariffs and Trade (GATT), helped the volume of trade across frontiers to grow by as much as 500 percent between 1950 and 1975, while the increase in global output was growing less than half as fast, by about 220 percent. And that meant "national" economies were increasingly beyond the reach of presidents and prime ministers, parliaments and congresses, or even the formerly powerful central bankers.

Since nobody is in charge of the system, more and more of the policy making has to be done by negotiations among governments. Trade experts at GATT in Geneva hammer out international codes and rules, trying to make national policies compatible with the continued growth of international trade. Central bankers intervene in the money markets to prop up their own and each other's currencies, increasingly with diminishing effect. Finance ministers lecture each other about the dangers of inflation. And the heads of the seven biggest industrial democracies (Britain, Canada, France, Germany, Italy, Japan, and the United States) gather in "summit meetings" to pretend that they are steering the global barge. Meanwhile the barge, loose from its moorings, is drifting in the cross-currents created by millions of buyers and sellers in largely unregulated worldwide markets for things, services, information, and money.

Markets and Democracy

Many people in government and business, feeling that world markets are too unstable and the international business environment too unpredictable, are tempted to blame its openness—and invent complex ways of closing it by erecting Maginot Lines to protect their own national parts of it. But the first rung of the ladder of understanding is that *openness is a technological imperative in the global-knowledge society.*

An impressive passion for "market economics" has nearly everywhere been part of what bubbled up along with aspirations for democracy in politics and government. Both "democracy" and "market" were more metaphor than policy analysis, of course; but the instinct of dissidents and protesters, in one Communist country after another, to glue them together in their rhetoric was sound.

The connection between "market" and "democracy" is basic. Market divides and distributes economic power, as democracy does political power. Markets may lead to concentrations of economic power (producers' or labor monopolies), which can be dangerous or inefficient or both. And democracy, if narrowly defined as majority rule, may also lead to oppressive concentrations of political power.

What is needed are "constitutional" rules that define the limits of power of political majorities and of economic power centers (whether public or private or mixed). Only on the basis of well-understood norms—a "social contract," if you will—can a durable and widely acceptable balance be achieved between *liberty* and *equality*, or *efficiency* and *fairness*, in both political and economic realms. The critical "constitutional" principles are those which *define the frontier between the realm of the state* (deciding by majority rule tempered by minority rights) *and that of civil society*, where decisions are made by countless interactions—not only buy-and-sell agreements, but also other forms of cooperation and competition in relationships that are in their essence neither "political" nor "market" (voluntary agencies, colleges and universities, professional associations, scientific academies, and the like).

This frontier between the state and civil society cannot be defined by cookie-cutter ideologies: for example, that fairness will be assured by having government employees decide just how what is produced will be distributed, or that efficiency will be guaranteed if private entrepreneurs are just left alone. Defining and redefining that frontier, which is the essential task of governance, requires concrete, case-by-case analysis of the tradeoffs involved in assigning a particular decision to a public authority or a private market.

The best economic outcomes seem to be the product of mixed systems. The worst are those that rigidly divide the distributive decisions from decisions about production—such as "social democracy" dogmas designed to bring about a continuous wrestling match between a private sector (responsible for productive efficiency) and a public sector (responsible for deciding who gets how much of what is produced), or "free market" dogmas that depend for fairness on trickle-down assumptions, and for efficiency on leaving concentrations of power alone.

Similarly, the most durable political arrangements try to balance liberty and equality in thousands of concrete instances, without assuming that either should ever "win it all." A French aphorism is apropos: "Entre le fort et le faible, c'est la liberté qui opprime et la loi qui affranchi": Between the strong and the weak, it is liberty that oppresses and law that liberates.

Part of the connection between "democracy" and "market" is that people governed by consent want to do business (shop, invest, work, watch television) across borders that are as open as possible. The other part is that a democracy's economy (the goods and services that are traded, the information that is shared) is necessarily and inevitably more open to the rest of the world—and the rest of the world will be more open to it.

That ensures a growing role for global companies, already the most dynamic actors in international affairs. It also seems bound to accelerate the leakage of economic power from national governments to international regulators and cooperation systems, and to international nongovernments—not only global companies but also influential associations of professionals, such as the international communities of scientists, engineers, lawyers, and economists.

Economic power is leaking also to subnational authorities and enterprises (in the United States, the states and metropolitan cities already are taking the initiative on issues that used to be preempted by the federal government). Again a Daniel Bell dictum is validated: ". . . the nation-state is becoming too small for the big problems of life, and too big for the small problems of life. In short, there is a mismatch of scale."

Geography: No Longer the Way to Organize

During the forty years from 1949 to 1989, those two great and growing stockpiles of unusable nuclear weapons seemed so overwhelmingly important that changing economic power relations did not get the attention they deserved. When that bipolar world so abruptly disappeared, three great centers of economic strength stood out in sharp relief.

Some scholars and analysts, pundits and political leaders—people predisposed to harden their thinking in tidy categories—leapt to the conclusion that the world of the 1990s and beyond would be organized around the three geographic regions dominated by the world's economic locomotives: the European Community's "single market"; a North American "free trade" zone; Japan and the reincarnation of its prewar "coprosperity sphere" in East Asia. In this scenario, pity the poor developing country that would not attach itself to one of the three trading empires.

The three blocs were coming into being because the alternative was working so badly. That alternative was freer trade for all countries at once, by worldwide decisions arrived at in suffocatingly tedious negotiations arranged in Geneva by GATT. The so-called Uruguay Round of GATT negotiations from 1985 to 1992 set a new standard for long delays, stubborn diplomacy, and sluggish "progress" that did not nearly keep pace with technological change, the integration of the "worldeconomy," or the emergence of *information* rather than *things* as the world's dominant resource. However, the failure of GATT requires not a retreat into trade blocs defined by geography, but a better mechanism for achieving freer trade worldwide.

The idea that geography is the key to power, that your potential depends on location and propinquity, dies hard. "Geopolitics" was the idea that a nation's clout depends largely on its geographic setting: how defensible its frontiers, how rich its bedrock mineral deposits, how fertile its soil, how plentiful its fresh water, how extensive its coastline. Cities often developed because they were seaports or on critical inland waterways, or (earlier) on important overland caravan routes, or (later) on important railway lines.

The importance of countries often seemed based on the natural resources they had discovered—or conquered—and developed, on "their" territory. The spices of the Orient, the rubber and tin of Southeast Asia, the coal and iron of Central Europe, the diamonds (and later uranium) of South Africa, the fruits of Central America, the petroleum reserves of Indonesia and Mexico and Venezuela and North Africa and North America and the North Sea and the Persian (or Arabian) Gulf, the soils that produced those "amber waves of grain" in the Ukraine and the North American Great Plains—these crucial resources left an indelible mark on the peoples that found them in their control. But it was the brains of the people who found and exploited them— often, like the explorers and colonists of earlier centuries and corporations in our own time, coming from great distances to do so—that made them "resources" at all.

Nowadays, it's the countries with the biggest flows of information that we call "developed." We know that anybody can extract knowledge from the bath of information that nearly drowns us all. You do not have to find it in your own factories or put it together in your own assembly plants. But you do have to "get it all together" in your own brain, and then combine your insight and imagination with other human brainwork in networks, companies, and alliances.

The passing of remoteness, in a world of speedy computers, responsive space satellites, and global telecommunications, is one of the least heralded and most important consequences of the "information revolution." The dwindling relevance of geographic regionalism, in this extraordinary time of our lives, bears witness.

In the late 1940s and early 1950s, the founding fathers of the postwar system (there was only one founding mother, Eleanor Roosevelt) thought that the one way to avoid global paralysis would be to build strong regional organizations, disaggregating world order by continents. But except for the European Community, geographic nearness turned out to be a precarious principle of international cooperation.

In security matters, courage is quite commonly proportional to the distance from the problem. In merchandise trade the items with the most value added, such as microchips, are bought from low-cost suppliers wherever they happen to be. In the sharing of facts and ideas by modern information technology, geography is almost wholly irrelevant.

Outside of Western Europe, only in Southeast Asia has a geography-based organization (ASEAN, the Association of Southeast Asian Nations) shown a spark of life. Those in Eastern Europe, Latin America, Africa, and South Asia, and the Arab League in the Mideast, never became major players in international affairs. Some are notably overstaffed and underemployed. One, the Communists' COMECON, has disappeared altogether. By contrast, networks that link like-minded people wherever they are located—such as oil cartels, drug traffickers, the international community of scientists, Islamic fundamentalists, and the rich nations' club called OECD—have proved more cohesive, more durable, and more influential in world affairs.

In this perspective, geography-based trading blocs, even very big ones, are revealed as a throwback to the era before the sharing of information began to edge the exchange of things out of the center-stage spotlight. Like the dinosaurs of old, they may last quite a while, requiring brainier but smaller creatures to be nimble enough to avoid being squashed underfoot.

But it seems overwhelmingly probable that a comprehensive international "public sector" regulating both trade and money will now have to be built to match the private markets for commodities, manufactures, capital investment, and money—none of which is much constrained by geography, all of which are global in their reach. That needed "public sector" does not sound much like *either* GATT *or* the Bretton Woods institutions.

This economic probability is reinforced by a political imperative. The main trading economies are, by no coincidence, the world's leading democracies. It is in their mutual interest to enhance the economic environment for expanding political democracy worldwide. In this larger context, for three groups of democracies to circle each other warily like three tomcats in the presence of a desirable pussycat in heat—with the likely result that by fighting each other none will get his heart's desire—simply does not make sense.

Some Advice and a Suggestion

In conclusion, a word to our friends from the "successor generation." For those of you who will be present at the *next* creation, I propose a handful of reminders based on a half-century of trial and error in building international institutions.

1) Take very seriously the idea that, from now on, *the spread of knowledge* will be the dynamo of world affairs—the engine of political change, the road to sustainable economic growth, the condition of human development, the drivewheel of human rights, the key to making the world safe for diversity.

2) Do not start by rewriting the *purposes and principles* of the United Nations charter and the other documents of that yeasty time at the end of World War II. Note that every success in international organization in the past fifty years found those purposes and principles energizing and functional—but most of them, in order to last into the twenty-first century, have had to play fast and loose with *procedures* invented before the middle of the twentieth.

One example, out of hundreds: The UN charter speaks much of votes, but does not require voting. The experience of the postwar years suggests that when governments want to record their disagreements ("divide the house," as Western parliamentarians say), they resort to voting. But when they have to work together to make something different happen, they increasingly decide from the outset to act by consensus. In many cultures accustomed to decision making by consensus, that word "consensus" does not mean "unanimity." It means something more like "acquiescence of those who care (about the particular decision), supported by the apathy of those who do not."

3) Remember that a global free market requires a *global public sector* to keep it more or less free by keeping it reasonably fair. The global *private* market is already there. The needed global *public* sector has yet to be conceived, invented, and agreed—by consensus, of course.

4) Practice thinking about *trade* and *money* as if they were aspects of the same subject (which they are), and build the global public sector accordingly.

5) Do not try to make *geography* the main principle of international organization. In the global information society, remoteness is going out of fashion—and so, in time, will regional trade blocs.

So, all you have to do is keep the peace, make world markets work efficiently *and* fairly, and maintain the soundness of the world's key currencies. It is an ambitious agenda for "postwar planning without having the war first."

But—sorry—it's still not enough. Even a coherent strategy for peaceful change will not "work" if the world's poorer peoples are left out of the worldeconomy, if they challenge world security with more and more powerful weapons, if they help us make the global environment uninhabitable in the twenty-first century. Then all the rich countries' peacekeeping and wealth creation, all the promotion of growth, stability, and environmental protection, would deserve the sour comment of Jean Girardoux: "It is the privilege of the great to watch catastrophe from a terrace."

The antidote to this unpleasant prospect is an unprecedented international venture to achieve growth with fairness in those large parts of Asia, Africa, and Latin America where poverty is still more important to most people than either market economics or political democracy.

Those of us in our seventies or eighties cannot tell you what to *do*, exactly. But I'll make bold at least to suggest the *attitude* with which you in your twenties and thirties might approach this century's final world-scale exercise in policy analysis and policy making.

The suggestion is as simple as it is fundamental. Next time someone says to you, in our civilization's universal cliché greeting, "Have a nice day," try responding this way: "Thanks, but *I* have other plans."

Notes

1. Speech by Ambassador Richard N. Gardner at the "Bretton Woods Revisited" conference, Bretton Woods, New Hampshire, October 15, 1994.

2. See Roberto Campos, "Fifty Years of Bretton Woods," in this volume.

3. Raymond F. Mikesell, "The Bretton Woods Debates: A Memoir," *Essays in International Finance*, No. 192 (Princeton, NJ: Princeton University International Finance Section, 1994).

Index

About the Institute for Agriculture and Trade Policy

The Institute for Agriculture and Trade Policy is a nonprofit, independent research and education organization. We are dedicated to fostering economically, socially, and environmentally sustainable communities and regions and to forging links between rural and urban communities.

Our strategic focus is in the policy-making arena, where we are working to democratize the policy-making process. We help public interest groups and individuals participate in the decision-making process and make local, national, and international institutions more accessible, open, and accountable to their participation.

The institute also develops and promotes innovative policy options and models designed to improve economic, ecological, and social conditions for all people, here and abroad.

To accomplish our goals, we engage in the following activities:

- monitoring policy-making institutions and events;
- researching, analyzing, and reporting on potential impacts of policy options;
- educating citizen groups, opinion leaders, and the public about our findings;
- providing information services, training, and technical assistance;
- forging coalitions and building bridges among diverse groups;
- establishing local, national, and international networks.

For more information, please contact:

Institute for Agriculture and Trade Policy
1313 Fifth Street, S.E., Suite 303
Minneapolis, MN 55414-1546
Phone: (612) 379-5980
Fax: (612) 379-5982
E Mail: iatp@igc.apc.org

About the Contributors

Edward M. Bernstein served as the chief technical adviser and executive secretary for the U.S. delegation to the Bretton Woods Monetary and Financial Conference in 1944 and was the first director of research at the International Monetary Fund (IMF) (1946–58). Since then, Mr. Bernstein has participated in a variety of government projects, including the Treasury Department's Advisory Committee on International Monetary Arrangements (the Dillon Committee) (1965–68) and OMB's Advisory Committee on Presentation of the Balance of Payments (1975–76). From 1974 until 1989 he was the director of the Washington Institute of Foreign Affairs. Mr. Bernstein is a Guest Scholar at the Brookings Institution.

Sir Alexander Cairncross served as an economic adviser to the U.K. Board of Trade from 1946 to 1949. Since then he has been director of the Economics Division of the Organization of European Economic Cooperation (1950); professor of applied economics at the University of Glasgow (1951–61); head of the British Government Economic Service (1964–69); president of the Royal Economic Society (1968–70); and chancellor of the University of Glasgow (since 1972).

Roberto Campos was a member of the Brazilian delegation to the Bretton Woods Monetary and Financial Conference in 1944. Following the war, he served as director, general manager, and president of the National Economic Development Bank of Brazil (1952–59); secretary-general of the National Development Council (1956–59); ambassador for financial negotiations in Western Europe (1961); ambassador to the United States (1961–63); and minister of state for planning and coordination (1964–67). Mr. Campos was a member of the Inter-American Committee for the Alliance for Progress (1964–67), and served as Brazilian ambassador to the United Kingdom (1975–82). He is currently a member of the Brazilian Senate.

Walter A. Chudson attended the Bretton Woods Monetary and Financial Conference in 1944 as an official observer for the United Nations Relief and Rehabilitation Agency (UNRRA). He also was a principal adviser to the United Nations Conference on Trade and Employment (1947–48). From 1946 to 1980 Mr. Chudson was a senior economist with the United Nations Secretariat.

Harlan Cleveland worked with the Board of Economic Warfare and the Foreign Economic Administration during World War II. In the immediate postwar years he was an official with the United Nations Relief and Rehabilitation Agency (UNRRA), serving as the director of UNRRA's China office from 1947 to 1948. Since then, he has held numerous government positions, including assistant secretary of state for international organization affairs (1961–65) and U.S. ambassador to NATO (1965–69). Mr. Cleveland is Professor Emeritus of Public Affairs and Planning at the Hubert H. Humphrey Institute of Public Affairs, University of Minnesota.

William Diebold Jr. was research secretary for the Economic and Financial Group of the Council on Foreign Relations' War and Peace Studies Project from 1939 to 1945. From 1941 to 1943 he also served as a trade policy consultant to the Department of State. Following the war, Mr. Diebold worked in the Department of State's Division of Commercial Policy (1945–47), and served, in succession, as staff economist, director of economic studies, Senior Fellow, and Senior Fellow Emeritus, at the Council on Foreign Relations.

Barend de Vries served as a research associate with the Cowles Commission at the University of Chicago (1946–48), and as an economist with the Research Department and Exchange Restrictions Department at the International Monetary Fund (IMF) (1949–55). From 1950 to 1984 he worked at the World Bank, where he served as economist and division chief in the Latin America Department; chief economist for Latin America and West Africa; deputy director of the Economics Department; director of the Creditworthiness Studies project; and senior adviser for Industrial Policy. He has been a Guest Scholar at the Brookings Institution (1984–86), and a lecturer at Georgetown University (1985–89).

Margaret Garritsen de Vries served with the International Monetary Fund (IMF) as senior economist (1946–53); assistant chief of the Exchange Restrictions Department (1953–57); chief of the Far Eastern Division (1957–58); consultant (1963–73); and official historian (1973–87). She taught at Georgetown University from 1958 to 1963.

Isaiah Frank served in various capacities with the Department of State from 1945 to 1963, including director of the Office of International Trade (1957–59), director of the Office of International Financial and Development Affairs (1961–62); and deputy assistant secretary of state for economic affairs (1962–63). Mr. Frank was the executive director of the President's Commission on International Trade and Investment Policy (Williams Commission) (1970–71). Since 1963, he has been the William L. Clayton Professor of International Economics at the Paul H. Nitze School of Advanced International Studies, The Johns Hopkins University.

Richard N. Gardner was deputy assistant secretary of state for international organizations (1961–65); a member of the President's Commission on International Trade and Investment Policy (Williams Commission) (1970–71); U.S. ambassador to Italy (1977–81); and a consultant to the secretary of the UN Conference on Environment and Development (UNCED) (1992). Mr. Gardner is author of the classic study of the creation of the Bretton Woods–GATT system, *Sterling-Dollar Diplomacy*, and currently is U.S. ambassador to Spain.

Joseph A. Greenwald was with the Department of State from 1947 to 1969, where he served as international economist (1947); chief of the Commercial Policy Branch of the Office of International Trade (1955–58); director of the Office of International Trade (1963–65); and deputy assistant secretary of state for international trade (1965–69). Mr. Greenwald was U.S. ambassador to the Organization of Economic Cooperation and Development (1969–72), and ambassador to the European Communities (1972–76). Since 1976 he has been a private legal consultant on trade and finance issues.

Andrew Kamarck was a senior economist with the Office of International Finance at the Treasury Department (1945–48), and a Treasury Department representative to the Marshall Plan (1948–50). Mr. Kamarck served with the World Bank from 1950 to 1977, where he was chief of the Africa Section (1950–64); director of the Economics Department (1965–70); and director of the Economic Development Institute (1972–77). From 1979 to 1986 he was an associate fellow at the Harvard Institute of International Development.

Jacob J. Kaplan served with the Department of State from 1943 to 1948, where he worked on foreign aid problems. He also served as assistant chief and chief of the European Regional Organizations staff of the Economic Cooperation Administration (ECA) and successor organizations (1951–55), and U.S. representative to the European Payments Union (EPU) managing board (1955–59). Following this, he served as assistant coordinator for the Mutual Security and Foreign Assistance Program, Department of State (1959–61), and director of the International Development Organizations Staff, AID (1962–64). Since 1987 he has been a private consultant on international finance and economics.

Orin Kirshner is a Senior Fellow at the Institute for Agriculture and Trade Policy, where he organized the "Bretton Woods Revisited" conference. At the institute, he directs the Multilateral Democracy Project—a multiyear effort to build U.S. domestic support for multilateralism by enhancing the opportunities for citizen participation in global policy making. He holds a Ph.D. in political science from the New School for Social Research in New York.

James H. McCall is a speech writer and staff assistant for ambassador Paul H. Nitze. He holds an M.A. degree in international relations and economics from the Paul H. Nitze School of Advanced International Studies, The Johns Hopkins University, and an M.A. in modern European history from Georgetown University.

Raymond F. Mikesell was a member of the U.S. delegation to the Bretton Woods Monetary and Financial Conference in 1944. Since then he has been a member of the President's Council of Economic Advisers (1955–57); a senior research associate at the National Bureau of Economic Research (1970–74); and a consultant to the World Bank (1968–69 and 1990–91). Mr. Mikesell is professor of economics at the University of Oregon, Eugene.

Paul H. Nitze worked with the Board of Economic Warfare, the Foreign Economic Administration, and the United States Strategic Bombing Survey during World War II. Since then he has held numerous government positions, including director of policy planning, Department of State (1950–53); assistant secretary of defense (1961–63); secretary of the Navy (1963–67); deputy secretary of defense (1967–69); special adviser to the president and the secretary of state on arms control matters (1985–88); and ambassador-at-large (1986–89). Mr. Nitze is diplomat-in-residence at the Paul H. Nitze School of Advanced International Studies, The Johns Hopkins University.

Simon Reisman was a member of the Canadian delegation to the United Nations Conference on Trade and Employment (1947–48), and was a delegate to all the sessions of the General Agreement on Tariffs and Trade (GATT) from 1948 to 1954. Since then he has served with the Canadian Department of Finance (1954–64); and as deputy minister of finance from 1970 to 1975. Mr. Reisman was the chief negotiator for Canada of the Canada–U.S. Free Trade Agreement.

Fred Sanderson served as an economist with the Department of State from 1946 to 1959. Following this, he was director of the Finance Division, Organization of European Economic Cooperation (1959–62); on the planning and coordinating staff of the Department of State (1971–73); and a Senior Fellow at the Brookings Institution (1974–83). Since 1992 Mr. Sanderson has been a Senior Fellow at the National Center for Food and Agricultural Policy.

Tran Van-Thinh was an official with the Commission of the European Communities from 1961 until his retirement in February 1994. During these years he held a wide variety of positions, including principal administrator responsible for textile negotiations, and head of the Permanent Delegation of the European Communities to the International Organizations in Geneva. Most recently, Mr. Van-Thinh served as the European Union's ambassador and permanent representative to GATT in charge of trade negotiations during the Uruguay Round.

Victor Urquidi was a member of the Mexican delegation to the Bretton Woods Monetary and Financial Conference in 1944. Since then he has been an economist with the World Bank (1947–49); an adviser to the Mexican Ministry of Finance (1949–51); the director of the Mexico Office of the UN Economic Commission for Latin America (1952–58); an adviser to the Ministry of Finance and Bank of Mexico (1958–64); and president of El Colegio de Mexico (1966–85). Currently, Mr. Urquidi is a research professor emeritus at El Colegio de Mexico.

Raymond Vernon served with the Department of State from 1942 to 1954, as assistant director of the Trading and Exchange Division (1942–46); acting director of the Office of Economic Defense and Trade Policy (1954); a U.S. delegate to the GATT Geneva (1950) and Torquay (1951) rounds; vice chairman of the U.S. delegation to GATT Geneva Round (1952); and a special consultant to the undersecretary of state (1962). Since then he has served as the director of the Center for International Affairs at Harvard University (1973–78), and a special consultant to the Department of Treasury (1978–79). He is currently Clarence Dillion Professor of International Affairs Emeritus at the Kennedy School of Government, Harvard University.